Rong Chen
Toward a Motivation Model of Pragmatics

Mouton Series in Pragmatics

Editor
Istvan Kecskes

Editorial Board
Reinhard Blutner (Universiteit van Amsterdam)
N.J. Enfield (Max-Planck-Institute for Psycholinguistics)
Raymond W. Gibbs (University of California, Santa Cruz)
Laurence R. Horn (Yale University)
Boaz Keysar (University of Chicago)
Ferenc Kiefer (Hungarian Academy of Sciences)
Lluís Payrató (University of Barcelona)
François Recanati (Institut Jean-Nicod)
John Searle (University of California, Berkeley)
Deirdre Wilson (University College London)

Volume 27

Rong Chen

Toward a Motivation Model of Pragmatics

DE GRUYTER
MOUTON

ISBN 978-3-11-153612-5
e-ISBN (PDF) 978-3-11-078770-2
e-ISBN (EPUB) 978-3-11-078785-6
ISSN 1864-6409

Library of Congress Control Number: 2022934807

Bibliographic information published by the Deutsche Nationalbibliothek
The Deutsche Nationalbibliothek lists this publication in the Deutsche Nationalbibliografie; detailed bibliographic data are available on the internet at http://dnb.dnb.de.

© 2024 Walter de Gruyter GmbH, Berlin/Boston Typesetting: Integra Software Services Pvt.
This volume is text- and page-identical with the hardback published in 2022.

www.degruyter.com

To Sharon, Takford, Lou, Ethan, Evan, and Aiden

Foreword

This monograph is a proposal of a theoretical model, called "the motivation model of pragmatics" (MMP). The gist of the model is that language use can be adequately and elegantly studied by looking at the motivation behind it. There are two levels in the motivation structure in MMP. At the first level, motivations are categorized into the transactional and the interactional. At the second level, the transactional is divided into clarity and effectiveness and the interactional is divided into the maintaining of the public image of other and the maintaining of the public image of self. The two components of each pair, further, display a gradient relationship on a conflictive vs. assistive cline, i.e., depending on context, they can be in opposition; they can be mutually assistive; and they can be anywhere in between. It is hoped that MMP provides a framework in which connections between things that might otherwise appear unrelated be revealed; reasons for what we find in our empirical studies be sought, and the dynamic context in which communication takes place be coherently accounted for.

The thought of writing this monograph began to percolate about a decade ago. But once it was completed, I realized that the preparation for it had actually (and "secretly") commenced three decades earlier when I was a graduate student at Lancaster University, UK (1981–1983). That stint exposed me to the teachings of the late Geoffrey Leech (who talked about "principles of politeness", the title of his influential 1983 monograph), the bubbling ideas of critical discourse analysis (Norm Fairclough was never shy about what he was working on), the writings of the Oxford ordinary language philosophers: John Austin, John Searle, and H. Paul Grice, and the politeness theory by Penelope Brown and Steven Levinson – not in the better-known iteration (1987, CUP), but as part of a volume edited by Esther Goody (*Questions and Answers*, 1978, also by CUP).

Thus hooked was I to pragmatics. Returning to China, I began to write about pragmatics (Embarrassing to say that many believe I was the person to have brought Grice's theory of conversational implicature and Brown and Levinson's theory of politeness to linguists in China through my earlier publications in Chinese.) I found myself, in the ensuing years and decades, dabbling into quite a few subareas of pragmatics (as verified via a glance at the References), in addition to areas typically viewed as outside pragmatics (e.g., cognitive linguistics).

Being a Rong of more than one trade has enabled me to appreciate the diversity of pragmatics. If pragmatics was thought of as a waste basket by Charles Morris (He did not exactly say so), its practitioners have found treasure aplenty from it. Given the "charge" of pragmatics – studying language use in context – we have claimed (and should continue to claim) territorial rights on all things language. The argument is on our side: language is always used in context; context includes everything; so all things language are our sphere of responsibility. Little wonder that, of the three major divisions in the study of language – semantics, syntax, and pragmatics – carved out by Morris, pragmatics emerged from virtual non-existence before the 1960s to have become the biggest brother of the three, attracting demonstrably more practitioners than its siblings.

When I was doing a particular project, I would feel that I was examining the fallen leaves in a forest with a magnifying glass. You can't find any two leaves falling from the same tree to be the same in every way – size, color, thickness, dryness. Okay, that is complicated. You narrow down your focus, to color. Then you find that every leaf is unique on that front too – you cannot find two leaves of exactly the same color! You then get down one more level to study the color of one leaf and then down again to chroma, putting aside hue and value, as studying all three still seems too general. What you end up doing (and publish on) would be a detailed description of the chroma of Leaf A from Tree J in Forest X. You feel satisfied. Your work has contributed to the understanding of leaves, hence enlarging the reservoir of the knowledge of forestry (and eventually botany).

A sense of unease gradually crept into me as I chugged along, looking at not only leaves of trees but also their trunks and roots. The determination of the value of a particular leaf, the description of the grain patterns in the intercession of a trunk, and the evidence for the depth of the roots are all worthwhile discoveries. Is there a need, though, in figuring out the connections between one leaf and another, between the leaves, trunks, and roots of a particular tree, between the tree I am studying and its neighbor five feet away, and between the forest I am in and another one on the other side of the hill – and then the globe? Granted, these are all different things we are looking at, but does the fact that they all exist on Planet Earth mean something? Is there a deeper reason for all this beyond the reason behind the chroma of Leaf A?

I am sure the readers will answer in the affirmative. But the readers might also agree that, in our "forestry" – pragmatics – looking for deeper connections and reasons is frowned upon. We have taken a "discursive turn"; we value looking at the dynamic, moment-to-moment unfolding of social interaction; we emphasize difference. Theories that aim at abstraction and generalization are viewed as top-down, as introspective, and – in a word – as naïve (or arrogant). Many of these theories are accused of ethnocentricity and are dismissed without carefully examining their usefulness, nor demonstrating their purported weaknesses.

So, I felt, for a decade, that maybe we should not abandon our effort to seek connections and reasons; maybe there is a need for us to look at the forest while looking at the trees in it; maybe . . . well. . . maybe I could give it a try? However, life found a way to keep me from embarking on the project, until 2020 when I, like everyone else in the world, got stuck inside the house, with little more than a computer for entertainment.

This monograph, therefore, represents my attempt to seek connections among and deeper reasons for a host of things that might otherwise appear disconnected and random. The model that will be advanced in the book is anchored with motivation simply because human actions are motivated actions. The reader will find, therefore, that the book has a greater coverage than an average monograph on similar subjects; that it relies more on the product of the research efforts by colleagues in the field; and that it casts Mr. Donald Trump and the coronavirus pandemic as frequent characters in the examples. The reader, too, will find errors, for which I claim exclusive responsibility.

What I shall say in the monograph is the result of learning from scholars in pragmatics – both those who are cited and those who are not, both those whom I have had the privilege of knowing personally and those I have not. They are all hereby acknowledged for inspiring me. Also heartedly thanked are the anonymous reviewers of the proposal and the manuscript, whose comments helped shape the final product; Rueyling Chuang, Dean of the College of Arts and Letters at CSUSB, for her support via the college's Writers' Group grant; and Sunny Hyon, who named the theory I had in mind into MMP ("I like the sound of the acronym", she explained). Itsvan Kecskes, editor of the *Mouton Series in Pragmatics*; Birgit Sievert, de Gruyter's Editorial Director; and Michaela Göbels, the press's Content Editor, were one heck of a team. They played their roles exemplarily. Bomi, Sharon, Takford, Lou, Ethan, Evan, Aiden: there is no way to overstate what your love and support mean to this project and to me.

Rong Chen
Dalian University of Foreign Languages
California State University, San Bernardino
April 2022

Contents

Foreword —— VII

List of figures —— XV

List of tables —— XVII

Chapter 1
Pragmatics then and now —— 1
1.1 From logical positivism to Oxford ordinary language philosophers —— 1
1.2 Expansion of the field —— 12
1.2.1 Expansion in theory —— 12
1.2.2 Expansion in practice —— 17
1.3 Further notes —— 20

Chapter 2
A motivation model of pragmatics (MMP) —— 22
2.1 Definitional properties —— 22
2.2 MMP —— 26
2.2.1 First-level motivations —— 27
2.2.2 Second-level motivations —— 29
2.3 Further notes on MMP —— 38
2.3.1 "Top-down?": A rejoinder to an anticipated critique —— 38
2.3.2 MMP as a unifying framework —— 39

Chapter 3
MMP and (im)politeness —— 42
3.1 Other-politeness —— 42
3.2 Impoliteness —— 46
3.3 Self-politeness —— 48
3.4 (Im)politeness seen in MMP —— 49
3.4.1 Impoliteness motivated by self-politeness —— 53
3.4.2 MMP and moral order, morality —— 58
3.4.3 Institutional impoliteness and entertaining impoliteness —— 62
3.4.4 "Mock impoliteness" —— 65
3.5 A note on evaluation studies —— 68

Chapter 4
MMP and cross-/intercultural variation —— 73
4.1 Compliments and compliment responses —— 73
4.1.1 Survey of research —— 73
4.1.2 MMP and compliments/compliment responses —— 87
4.2 MMP and the East-West Divide —— 92
4.2.1 Setting the scene —— 92
4.2.2 Politeness Japanese and West: Similar or different? —— 93
4.2.3 Politeness Chinese and West: Similar or different? —— 98
4.2.4 MMP and the debate —— 107
4.2.5 Further notes —— 116

Chapter 5
MMP and diachronic pragmatics —— 118
5.1 A sketch of historical and diachronic pragmatics —— 118
5.2 Cross-generational pragmatics —— 120
5.3 Compliment responses —— 123
5.4 End-of-dinner food offering —— 128
5.4.1 Introduction and methodology —— 128
5.4.2 Findings and discussion —— 133
5.5 MMP and diachronic changes —— 143
5.6 Further notes —— 144

Chapter 6
MMP and discourse —— 147
6.1 Setting the scene —— 148
6.2 Transactional motivations —— 153
6.2.1 Information structure —— 153
6.2.2 Genre structures —— 157
6.2.3 Conversational structures —— 161
6.3 Interactional motivations —— 165
6.3.1 Identity construction —— 165
6.3.2 Writer stance —— 171
6.3.3 Critical discourse analysis —— 176
6.3.4 Conversation analysis revisited —— 181
6.4 Discourse markers —— 193
6.4.1 Topic management —— 196
6.4.2 DM *so* and topic management —— 199
6.5 Chapter summary —— 210
6.6 Notes on "the discursive turn" —— 211

Chapter 7
MMP and metaphor —— 215
- 7.1 Setting the scene —— 215
- 7.2 Metaphors for the transactional —— 218
- 7.2.1 Effectiveness through domain mapping —— 219
- 7.2.2 Effectiveness through domain elaboration —— 225
- 7.2.3 Effectiveness through contextual interaction —— 226
- 7.3 Metaphor for the interactional —— 230
- 7.4 Further notes —— 236
- 7.4.1 In comparison with simile and metonymy —— 236
- 7.4.2 Metaphor in specialized genres —— 240

Chapter 8
MMP and the non-literal —— 243
- 8.1 Setting the scene —— 243
- 8.2 NLUs and camaraderie —— 245
- 8.3 NLUs for image —— 250
- 8.4 Irony (and sarcasm) —— 254
- 8.5 Parody (and satire) —— 262
- 8.5.1 Parody for amusement —— 263
- 8.5.2 Parody for satire —— 265
- 8.5.3 Parody for amusement and satire —— 269
- 8.6 Lies —— 274
- 8.7 Further notes —— 281

Afterword —— 283

References —— 287

Appendix —— 317

Subject index —— 321

Author index —— 327

List of figures

Figure 2.1   Maslow's model of needs —— 24
Figure 2.2   Motivation model of pragmatics (MMP) —— 26
Figure 3.1   Kinds of (im)politeness —— 50
Figure 3.2   (Im)politeness and motivations —— 51
Figure 3.3   (Other)-politeness, self-politeness, and impoliteness —— 52
Figure 3.4   Map of Hurricane Dorian —— 55
Figure 3.5   Near-bell curve —— 70
Figure 4.1   Compliment responding strategies and interactional motivations —— 89
Figure 4.2   Motivation, strategy, and language —— 91
Figure 4.3   Matching of expression and people —— 104
Figure 5.1   A three-way comparison —— 142
Figure 6.1   Prince's given-new information —— 150
Figure 7.1   Domain Mapping —— 220
Figure 8.1   Tweet by Steele —— 261
Figure 8.2   Parodies of masking —— 264
Figure 8.3   Lie-likeness —— 278
Figure 8.4   Objectionability —— 279

List of tables

Table 4.1	Chinese compliment acceptance and rejection	82
Table 4.2	Category of people and ratings	104
Table 5.1	Comparison of Chinese compliment responses	125
Table 5.2	A longitudinal comparison	127
Table 5.3	Frequency of occurrence of Adjacency Pairs	130
Table 5.4	Structure of end-of-dinner food offering	130
Table 5.5	Findings: American	133
Table 5.6	Findings: Chinese	137
Table 6.1	Single-author self-reference	174
Table 6.2	Use of *must*	178
Table 6.3	Use of *have to*	178
Table 6.4	Preferred and dispreferred seconds	183
Table 6.5	Distribution of DW *so*	199

Chapter 1
Pragmatics then and now

In this monograph, I propose a theoretical model of pragmatics. The theory is based on the goal-orientedness of human action – that all human actions are motivated actions – and is called "the Motivation Model of Pragmatics", *MMP* for short. By anchoring language use with motivation, MMP is meant to be an umbrella theoretical construct that provides a framework within which the myriad findings in pragmatics can be coherently accounted for and future research can be conducted.

To prepare for the actual proposing of MMP in Chapter 2, I will in this beginning chapter offer a brief sketch of the historical development of the field of pragmatics. Section 1.1 starts from where pragmatics did: logical positivism and the reaction to it, in the middle of the 20th century. Section 1.2 outlines the rapid progression of the field, bringing the reader to its current state of affairs.

1.1 From logical positivism to Oxford ordinary language philosophers

In a seminal essay, philosopher Charles Morris (1938) classifies the study of language (*semiotic*, in his own terms) into three branches: *syntactics*, *semantics*, and *pragmatics*. Syntactics is "the study of the syntactical relations of signs to one another in abstraction from the relations of signs to objects or to interpreters" and "is the best developed of all the branches of semiotic" (1938: 13). "Semantics deals with the relation of signs to their designate and so to the objects which they may or do denote" (1938: 21). In reference to the term "pragmatism" first used by C. S. Peirce, Morris coined the term "pragmatics" to refer to "the science of the relation of signs to their interpreters" (1938: 30). He further writes, "It is a sufficiently accurate characterization of pragmatics to say that it deals with the biotic aspects of semiosis, that is, with all the psychological, biological, and sociological phenomena which occur in the functioning of signs."

Morris' tripartite of linguistics – which he calls "the science of the study of signs" – is considered to be an insightful classification of a diverse field of study. It not only captures the entire field of linguistics at the time but also foretells what was to take pace after him. *Syntactics*, in the first few decades of the 20th century, had been the focus of linguistics in American structuralism spearheaded by Edward Sapir and Benjamin Whorf and formalized by Leonard Bloomfield. It was to be thrust onto the center stage by Chomsky (Chomsky 1957) and colleagues less than two decades later. Semantics grew, from its earlier obscurity in the early 1900s, into an area focusing on the meaning of the lexicon (Leech 1974; Lyons 1977). More recently, semantics is recognized as the most privileged branch of linguistics – far more so than syntax – by cognitive linguists (Lakoff 1987; Langacker 1987, 1991; Talmy 2000).

Of the two disciplines – syntax and semantics – the latter is a closer cousin to pragmatics, due to their shared interest in meaning, a notion that was to morph into different iterations such as intention and implicature (see below). For a greater part of the 20th century, though, the study of meaning was dominated by language philosophers. A cursory look at Frege's ([1892]1990) work on sense and nominatum, Russel's treatises on denotation (1905) and description (1919), Strawson's (1956) and Donnellan's (1966) discussions on reference, and Putnam's (1973) deliberations on meaning and reference, gives a birds'-eye view of the field from the turn of the century to the 1970s.

Lying at the heart of these studies of meaning is truth. The popular view of meaning of the time is logical positivism, which treats sentences, in terms of truth conditions. A sentence can be said to be either true or false if and only if "it is analytical or contradictory, in which case it is said to have purely logical meaning or significance" or "it is capable, at least potentially, of test by experiential evidence – in which case it is said to have empirical meaning or significance" (Hempel 1950: 41). A sentence such as "The President of the United States is a woman" can be judged as false, as it is analytical but is verified to not be true at the time of writing. But the sentence "The king of France is bald" cannot be easily judged – for France does not have a king at the present time – hence has generated a huge among of literature, without a definitive verdict among formal semanticists (Burton 1989; Chen 1991).

The inadequacy of the truth-condition analysis of meaning was challenged by many (e.g., Hempel 1950) and in various ways. Davis's (1991: 8–10) illustration is one of the most accessible. Consider (1).

(1) She is tired.

Since, as a personal deictic, *she* has no semantic referent (it does not by itself refer to a specific person), Example (1) requires a truth condition such as (2):

(2) "She is tired" is true just in case the person to whom the speaker refers in uttering this sentence is tired.

But – Davis points out – this will not work. In Example (3), the conclusion "Margaret Smith is tired" is valid if *she* and *Margaret Smith* are the same person and invalid if they are not.

(3) She is tired.
She is Margaret Smith.
Therefore, Margaret Smith is tired.

As a result, (3) would require a truth condition such as (4):

(4) "She is Margaret Smith" is true just in case the person to whom the speaker refers is Margaret Smith.

The problem with the truth-condition analysis, according to Davis, is that (4) still does not support the validity of (3), for "There is nothing in these truth conditions which guarantees that the speaker who uses the first and second sentences of the argument is the same" (Davis 1991: 9).

This sort of challenge to logical positivism focuses on a well-defined set of linguistic structures known as *deixis* or *indexicals,* including demonstratives (e.g., *this, that*), personal pronouns (*I, you, he, it*), specific time adverbs (*last week, yesterday*) and place adverbs (*here, there*), and verbs that are inherently tied to time (*following, preceding*) and place (*come, go*). I will not dwell much on this line of research but refer the reader to a comprehensive yet succinct survey of it in Levinson (1983, Chapter 2).

It is the second challenge to logical positivism, by John Austin and his students John Searle and H. Paul Grice, that was responsible for the creation of modern pragmatics. Calling themselves "ordinary language philosophers" (Hacker 2004), Austin and his students started a vibrant intellectual movement at Oxford University and began to build theories that were to form the backbones for pragmatics. The first open shot at logical positivism is probably Grice (1957).[1] In this paper, Grice distinguishes between natural meaning (meaning$_n$) and non-natural meaning (meaning$_{nn}$). Natural meaning is the meaning logicians had been analyzing, ones in which the meaning of the sentence coincides with the intention of the speaker. Non-natural meaning refers to speaker's intention when it is different from the (semantic) meaning of the sentence. Meaning$_{nn}$ is thus defined as "A uttered x with the intension of inducing a belief by means of the recognition of this intention" (Grice 1957: 76).

Grice's (1957) paper foretells several important developments in pragmatics that have by now unfolded. The first is the recognition of the fact that logic is not

---

[1] There is also his (1969) paper, a more elaborate account of the (1957) paper in which he spells out his views in more detail and defends his account against a few criticisms. However, the major arguments he makes in the (1957) paper remain.

the necessary condition for meaning. In fact, in the case of meaning$_{nn}$, it can be entirely irrelevant. So, the utterance

(5) Those three rings on the bell (of the bus) mean that the bus is full.

(Grice 1957: 72)

can occur inside

(6) Those three rings on the bell (of the bus) mean that the bus is full. But it isn't in fact full – the conductor made a mistake.

Thus, the meaning$_n$ of (5) is only part of the meaning$_{nn}$ of (6). But in logical terms, the truths of the two utterances are contradictory.

Second, Grice may be the first scholar to wrestle non-declarative sentences into the attention of language philosophers and later students of pragmatics. Of the four types of sentences – the declarative, the interrogative, the imperative, and the exclamatory – the declarative was the sole structure that language philosophers had been interested in for more than half a century. However, in real-life communication, the declarative is hardly the only type and the truth-condition analysis of language is apparently incapable of handling other types, for an interrogative such as "Are we there yet?" and an imperative such as "Come here" cannot be judged as experientially or evidentially true or false. But these types of sentences are indispensable in communication, particularly in face-to-face interactions. So, in his 1957 paper, Grice issues an unambiguous (and rather scathing) imperative: "Now perhaps it is time to drop the pretense that we have to deal only with 'informative' cases" – where "informative" refers to declarative sentences that assert – (Grice 1957: 76), an imperative that was soon heeded in pragmatics, helping to lay the foundation for the field.

Thirdly, Grice may be the first scholar to formally and explicitly bring the notion of context into the fold, although the idea of the notion is present in many previous works in the philosophy of language. The paragraph in which he introduces the term is worth quoting in full.

> Again, in cases where there is doubt, say, about which of the two or more things an utterer intends to convey, we tend to refer to the context (linguistic or otherwise) of the utterance and ask which of the alternatives would be relevant to other things he is saying or doing, or which intention in a particular situation would fit in with some purpose he obviously has (e.g., a man who calls for "pump" at a fire would not want a bicycle pump). Non-linguistic parallels are obvious: context is a criterion in setting the question of why a man who has just put a cigarette in his mouth has put his hand in his pocket; relevance to an obvious criterion in setting the end why a man is running away from a bull. (Grice 1957: 77)

Grice's, together with Austin's, Searle's, and possibly Brown and Levison's ([1978]1987) theories have been criticized for being "Euro-centric" and for neglecting the dynamism and fluidity of language use. I believe that a cursory reading of this quoted paragraph alone would go a long way to dispell these criticisms, a point I shall make more than once in the rest of the book.

It is in this backdrop – a virtual rebellion against logical positivism[2] – that the major theories of pragmatics came into being. The first is the speech act theory by Austin and Searle. In his (1962) book, which is a compilation of the William James Lectures he delivered at Harvard University, Austin put an end to the myth that Grice alluded to in his 1957 paper, "we have to only deal with 'informative' cases" when studying meaning (Grice 1957: 76, quoted above). He starts with "performatives" – a term that is "ugly" but advantageously "unprofound" (1961: 233) – sentences that explicitly performs a speech act. So, if I say "I promise you X", I am not just saying something, I am doing something that has consequences: you would have the right to hold me to X if I fail to deliver it. From performatives, Austin moves to other types of speech acts such as commissions, demonstrating the central thesis "saying is doing", i.e., by saying something, one is doing something.

Among the many aspects of the speech act theory, *felicity conditions* and the distinction between direct and indirect speech acts are the most pertinent for our purpose in this monograph. In essence, felicity conditions are rules of speech acts. Austin and Searle reason, if speakers do things with words, there have to be some rules to govern the doing of things so that a drunken sailor cannot name a ship in a way that happens to tickle his fancy, a well-meant person cannot marry two random persons without their consent, and I cannot promise that you will receive the Nobel in medicine. The felicity conditions of request, for example, can be simplified as (7). The failure to make sure that all of the conditions are satisfied will result in the request being "unfelicitous".

(7) *Felicity conditions of request*
    a. Hearer (H) is able to do Act (A).
    b. H is willing to do A.
    c. Speaker (S) wants A to be done.
    d. A has not been done yet.

The significance of felicity conditions is manifold. First, these conditions as "regulative" rules as opposed to "constitutive" ones (Searle 1965, 1969), a critical dis-

---

[2] Austin's critique of logical positivism is only thinly vailed: "The theory of truth is a series of truisms" (1961: 121).

tinction between what governs speech acts and what governs grammar. If I ask you to send me a check for the purchase of a new car, which would fail to satisfy Condition *b* above[3] and possibly Condition *a* in at least some cases, my request would fail. But that failure is different from the one resulting from using *they* to refer to myself as the speaker (a violation of the constitutive rule governing the use of pronouns). Second – and more importantly – these conditions are deeply embedded in context. H's ability and willingness, S's want, and the fact that A has not been done cannot be determined without weighing on the different factors about the speakers and hearers in a specific situation. These are therefore not rules of language, but "rules" of language use.

The third significance of felicity conditions is that these conditions establish a link between direct and indirect speech acts. In (8), below, A and B are members of the same household.

(8) A: The phone's ringing.
    B: I'm in the bathroom.

The utterances in the brief exchange take the form of assertions – statements about verifiable facts in reality – and indeed can be intended as such in a different context. A's utterance would be an assertion if it occurred in a description of sorts (e.g., "The phone's ringing; the kids're crying...".). However, as presented in (8), it is more likely to be interpreted as a request and B's utterance, a declination with the possibility of a counter request:

(9) A: Can you pick up the phone?
    B: I can't. (Can you pick it up instead?)

Example (8) presents things that are said; Example (9) presents things that are meant. The contrast between what is said and what is meant reveals an important fact about language use: that there can be (and often is) a discrepancy between what is said and what is meant. This discrepancy is the litmus test for the directness of speech acts: a direct speech act is one in which what is said and what is meant are similar (or the same); an indirect speech act is one in which what is said and what is meant are different.

The recognition of this discrepancy would seem to indicate that one can say anything to mean anything else. But that cannot be the case. It would be rather

---

[3] I am assuming that an average reader of an academic book is not willing to send funds to its author towards the purchase of a new vehicle.

difficult for me to make a request for a drink in a restaurant by saying "Donald Trump lost the 2020 election".[4] In other words, what would the theory of speech acts do to limit the range of possibilities for one to say A while meaning B? According to Searle ([1975]1991: 272), in order for one to mean B by saying A, A has to be connected with B via one of the felicity conditions. Such a connection is loose: by "stating a felicity condition" or "asking whether felicity condition obtains". If I want to request that you give me a ride, I can connect what I say (10) with the felicity conditions listed in (7), above.

(10) a. Can you give me a ride there?
    b. Would you give me a ride?
    c. I would like a ride from you.
    d. My ride there has not been arranged.

Each of the alphabetized utterances corresponds, respectively, to each felicity conditions listed in (7): Utterance a makes reference to Condition a: ability;[5] b to Condition b, willingness; and so on.

A bit more than a decade later,[6] Grice (1975) proposed the theory of Cooperative Principle (CP), also known as the theory of conversational implicature. Grice starts from the assumption that conversation – which has been taken to mean communication at large – is mostly a cooperative endeavor: "Make your conversational contribution such as is required, at the stage at which it occurs, by the accepted purpose of direction of the talk exchange in which you are engaged" (Grice 1975: 69). He then provides four maxims via which people communicate.

(11) *Quantity:* (=Be informative, give the right amount of information)
    a. Make your contribution as informative as is required.
    b. Do not make your contribution more informative than is required.

Quality: (=Be truthful)
    a. Do not say what you believe to be false.
    b. Do not say that for which you lack adequate evidence.

---

[4] Unless the server knew that I would come to the restaurant for a drink if Trump losed the election.
[5] See Morgan (1978) for a more nuanced analysis of *can* used to make a request.
[6] Grice's CP was first proposed at a William James Lecture at Harvard in 1969 but was not published until 1975 in the *Syntax and Semantics* series and then in the (1989) collection of his writings.

Relation: *Be relevant.*
Manner: *Be perspicuous (=Be clear)*
a. Avoid obscurity of expression.
b. Avoid ambiguity.
c. Be brief.
d. Be orderly.

Different from what was assumed in the literature for some time, these maxims – the connotations of the term *maxim* notwithstanding – are not meant to be hard and fast rules of conversation, as is seen in both Grice (1975) and his (1987) paper, "Further notes on conversational implicature". On the contrary, these maxims are flouted/violated very often, as seen below.

(12) A. Cindy was gossiping again.
B. Women are women.

(13) A. Tom flunked all his classes.
B. What a genius!

(14) A. Did you enjoy the play last night?
B. I thought the ice-creams they sold during the interval were quite good.

(15) [Wife to husband, on Christmas Eve]
Have you wrapped the you-know-what for you-know-who?

B's utterance in Example (12) violates the maxim of quantity by being tautological. B in (13) violates the maxim of quality by saying what is apparently not true. B's utterance in (14) violates relation by not answering the question. And the utterance in (15) violates the maxim of manner by being obscure.

A moment's reflection would tell us that these examples are not isolated instances. In fact, they occur more often than one may have realized. The question then is: are violations cooperative behavior? They are, Grice firmly tells us. They are cooperative because speakers generally get their message across when doing so. B's utterance in Example (12) expresses the speaker's sexist view that women are prone to gossiping; B in (13), an irony, expresses the opposite of what is said; B's utterance in (14) in essence reveals his low opinion of the play; and (15) is in fact quite clear (to her husband) about her intention of finding out whether her husband has finished gift wrapping for the children.

The seeming contradiction that both the adherence to and the violation of maxims are deemed cooperative is resolved by the notion of implicature, defined as a special meaning that results from the violation of a maxim that is intended to be recognized by the hearer. In (14), for instance, Speaker B wants A to realize the violation of relation so that his negative view of the play can get across. If the hearer does not, he could pursue: "But you did not answer my question about the play. Can you go back to my question again?" That, obviously, would be a breakdown of communication.

Implicature has several features, three of which we discuss here. The first is cancellability. Speaker B in (14), for instance, can cancel the implicature that he did not enjoy the play by adding something along the lines of "The play was just as good". Other types of meaning, however, cannot be taken back easily once expressed. Presupposition, for example, cannot be cancelled. If you say "All John's children are monks", you presuppose that John has children. Therefore, you cannot say "All John's children are monks but I know John doesn't have any children". Neither can entailment be cancelled. The utterance "John has five children" entails, among other things, "John has three children". You cannot say, therefore, "John has five children but he doesn't have three children" (Levinson 1983).

The second feature of implicature is non-detachability – that an implicature cannot be detached if certain words are changed. In other words, implicature has very little to do with the linguistic structure of the utterance. So, Speaker B in (14) can say a long list of things to generate the implicature that the play is not well thought of:

(16) a. I liked the costumes.
   b. I'm not convinced that was the best way to spend two hours of my evening.
   c. I had thought a theatrical experience was always a treat.
   d. The ticket for it was quite easy to obtain.

The third feature of implicature is calculability, that it can be "worked out". Grice outlines the following process for the "calculation" of an implicature.

(17) a. S said that p, which violates one or more of the conversational maxims.
   b. However, there is no reason to assume that S is not cooperative. Therefore, S must have meant something else.
   c. In order for S to be indeed cooperative and by the mutual knowledge between S and me, S must have meant q by saying p.
   d. S has done nothing to stop me from thinking that q.
   e. Therefore, S intends me to think that q, and in saying that p has implicated q.

The working out of B's implicature in 14 would be:

(18) a. B said that the ice creams were quite good, which is not relevant to my question (violating the maxim of relation).
b. However, there is no reason to assume that he is not cooperative. Therefore, he must have meant something else.
c. In order for B to be indeed cooperative and by the assumption that one would be reluctant to express negative opinions, he must have meant that he did not enjoy the play.
d. He has done nothing to stop me from thinking that he did not enjoy the play.
e. Therefore, he intends me to think that he did not enjoy the play, and in saying that the ice creams were quite good, he has implicated that he did not enjoy the play.

Both the speech act theory and theory of conversational implicature so far outlined have far reaching consequences for the field of pragmatics. First, the proposers of these two theories were trailblazers. While language philosophers of the time were avidly exploring ways to explain language in their respective intellectual tradition, Austin, Seale, and Grice saw the weakness of the approaches taken by their contemporaries. They were the first to openly challenge the truth-condition approach to language, convincingly demonstrating its many limitations. By calling themselves "ordinary language philosophers", they unambiguously turned their – and later many others' – attention from language itself to the use of it in real life. If Morris created the label of pragmatics, Austin, Searle, and Grice created the field of pragmatics.

Second, Austin and his students recognized the discrepancy between what is said and what is meant, a distinction that lies at the heart of pragmatics. Grice's non-natural meaning (as opposed to the natural), Austin's discussions on performatives and the classification of speech acts into the locutionary, illocutionary, and perlocutionary, and Seale's proposal of indirect speech acts are different manifestations of the same underlying idea: that in "ordinary language", what is said is not always what is meant.

Third, Austin, Searle, and Grice were fully aware of the role context plays in language use. Grice's notion of non-natural meaning firmly rests on context. His expositions of implicatures, in both his (1975) and (1978) papers, are replete with discussion of contextual factors. Take the definition of the Cooperative Principle, that the speaker's contribution being "required, at the stage at which it occurs, by the accepted purpose of direction of the talk exchange in which you are engaged". Its first element – "at the stage at which occurs" – is direct reference to the dynamic nature of communication. Its second element – "by the mutually accepted purpose of direction of the talk exchange" – is clear recognition of the negotiation between the speaker and the hearer in meaning making, a point that had remained neglected in the field for decades. The same is true of Austin and Searle. Austin's classification of speech acts could not have been done without context, neither can his definition of performatives. Searle's indirect speech acts are even more obvious. In (8), for example, "The phone is ringing" cannot have the illocutionary force – being the indirect speech act – of a request to pick up the phone without knowing the situation in which the conversation takes place.

Fourth, the Oxford trio's work has revealed important pragmatic features of language. The speech act theory changed the way in which not only language use but also language itself is viewed. Once seen as a means of doing, language should be analyzed as such and indeed has been thusly analyzed, as is seen in the rest of this monograph and in the pragmatics literature. The theory of conversational implicature further highlights the "implicating" function of language, pointing out the loose connection between language and meaning. Cancellability of implicature, which has been largely ignored in the literature, points out one reason why implicature is preferred in so many contexts.

These theories have met criticism galore to this day. These criticisms fall into two categories. The first category of criticisms is theory-internal. For speech acts, there were debates about what characterize a performative (Johansson 2003); there were disagreements about whether felicity conditions are constitutive or regulative (Hindriks 2007); there were complaints about the inadequacy of the theory in accounting for dialog (Levinson 1981), and there were alternative proposals for the classification of speech acts. For implicature, there were discussions about the logical problems of Grice's process of implicature interpretation (Hugly and Sayward 1979); there were suspicions about the assumption of cooperation in communication (Sampson 1982); there were arguments that the Cooperative Principle was not needed (Morpurgo-Tagliabue 1981); there were doubts about the four maxims – e.g., why four? Why those four but not others? – (Kempton 1975; Horn 1984, 2004); and there were regrets that Grice was "too inexplicit and informal" about the formulation of his maxims (Brockway 1981). While many of these theory-internal comments have demonstrated various degrees of validity, the major architectural structures of the two theories have remained intact.

The second category of the critique of speech acts and conversational implicature is theory-external – that the theories themselves are fundamentally flawed and hence should not be adopted in the study of language use at all. These criticisms are generally aired in vague terms, without specific analyses to show the purported vital failures of the targeted theories. A common accusation seems to be that these theories, together with others such as Brown and Levinson's politeness theory, are Euro-America centric, based on rationality, and miss the richness of linguistic reality. I disagree with these commentaries and will discuss them in various places where appropriate.

1.2 Expansion of the field

The last section outlined the trajectory of pragmatics in the early stage of its development, till the 1970s, which can be characterized as the foundation-laying period for the filed. The next decades witnessed the expansion of the field, an expansion that has to rank as the fastest in linguistics, if not in the more general areas of the humanities and the social sciences. For sake of convenience, I divide the expansion into expansion in theory and expansion in practice.

1.2.1 Expansion in theory

Formally establishing pragmatics as a legitimate study of language, the theory of speech acts and the theory of conversational implicature opened up a myriad of questions for students of language use. Grice's maxims, for instance, led to Sperber and Wilson's (1986) theory of relevance, as the authors believe that relevance is the only maxim (of the four maxims) that is needed to account for the processing of language use.[7]

The theories that came into being as a direct result of the Oxford trio's work are politeness theories. To my knowledge, Robin Lakoff (1973, 1976) is the first scholar to treat politeness as a target of linguistic investigation. In those papers, the author proposes her "rules of politeness": "don't impose, give options, and make the addressee feel good by being friendly". These rules, according to Lakoff, were motivations for language use in opposition to Grice's maxims: while Gricean maxims define directness and economy, politeness accounts for the opposite (1977: 88).

Leech's (1983) work is based on the same assumption as does Lakoff. In his papers on conversational implicature, Grice (1975) does not dwell much on why a speaker would choose to violate a maxim, except mentioning, in passing, the clash between maxims. Leech sees this as a drawback of the theory and argues explicitly that a theory of language should provide reasons for linguistic behav-

---

[7] "Relevance" is defined as contextual effects, hence a very different notion from that of Grice. However, the authors expressed their indebtedness to Grice in a paper (Wilson and Sperber 1980: 155–156) when they write that "the maxims are not all independently necessary for the generation of implicature: that they may in fact be reduced to a single principle . . . of relevance".

iors. His Politeness Principle, therefore, was proposed to "rescue Grice" by minimize the impoliteness of illocutions, with its mirror image of maximizing the politeness of illocutions (Leech 1983: 81, 83). The Politeness Principle (1983: 132) has the following maxims:

(19) *Tact maxim*
    a. Minimize cost to other
    b. Maximize benefit to other

    Generosity Maxim
    a. Minimize benefit to self
    b. Maximize benefit of other

    Approbation Maxim
    a. Minimize dispraise of other
    b. Maximize praise of other

    Modesty Maxim
    a. Minimize praise of self
    b. Maximize dispraise of self

    Agreement Maxim
    a. Minimize disagreement between self and other
    b. Maximize agreement between self and other

    Sympathy Maxim
    a. Minimize antipathy between self and other
    b. Maximize sympathy between self and other

At more or less the same time, Brown and Levinson were working on their (1987) theory of politeness.[8] Just as Leech bases his theory on implicature, Brown and Levinson base theirs on speech acts. The authors start by positing that members of a society have face, defined as wants and needs to maintain their public image approved of by other members of the society. The notion of face is further divided into negative and positive. Negative face refers to "the want of every competent adult member that his actions be unimpeded by others"; positive face refers to "the want of every member that his wants be desirable to at least some others"

---

[8] Brown and Levinson's (1987) book is a slight revision of their 1978 publication.

(1987: 62). On the other hand, however, speakers have to perform various speech acts in life. These acts very often threaten the face of the speaker or the hearer or both. Brown and Levinson hence call them Face Threatening Acts (FTAs). The authors then (1987: 65–68) provide a list of FTAs, which are categorized according to two parameters: whether the acts threaten negative or positive face and whether they threaten the hearer's or the speaker's face.

These two essential aspects of communication therefore create a bind for the speaker: she needs to figure out how to do FTAs in a way that they threaten face as little as possible (or, ideally, not at all). The way to do so, Brown and Levison argue, is politeness, broadly defined as a set of strategies to mitigate the threat to face. At the highest level, there are five super strategies:

(20) *Brown and Levinson's (1987) politeness supperstrategies*
    a. Without redressive action, baldly
    b. Positive politeness
    c. Negative politeness
    d. Off record
    e. Withhold the FTA

(Brown and Levinson 1987: 60)

The choice of a particular strategy is determined by the weightiness of an FTA. the weightier the FTA, the higher the number of strategies a speaker will choose. An FTA's weightiness is computed using the following formula:

(21) *Brown and Levinson's formula for computing the weightiness of an FTA*
$$Wx = D(S,H) + P(H,S) + Rx$$

about which, the authors explain:

> Wx is the numerical value that measures the weightiness of the FTA x, D(S,H) is the value that measures the social distance between S and H, P(H,S) is a measure of the power that H has over S, and Rx is a value that measures the degree to which the FTA x is rated an imposition in that culture. (Brown and Levinson 1987: 76)

As should be clear from the outlines of the two theories of politeness, Leech's theory was a reaction to Grice's theory of conversational implicature. He meant his theory to be an enhancement of – or addition to – Grice's. Brown and Levinson's theory was based on Austin's and Searle's speech act theory, offering a motivation for why speech acts are done the way they are in real life. As a result, both Leech and Brown and Levinson have been lumped together with the Oxford trio as the representation of Euro-America centralism, particularly rationality, and have faced widespread and pointed criticisms. I will discuss some of these critiques in later chapters, showing that many of them are inaccurate; a few misguided.

What cannot be denied, however, is the fact that these two theories are responsible for the vast amount of literature on politeness research, the discussions of which I delay till Chapter 3, and led to other theories of politeness. Some of these theories are proposed to replace them altogether while others, to expand on them.

Competing theories to Brown and Levinson's and Leech's theory include Hill et al.'s (1986) model of Discernment (Hill et al., 1986: 348; see also Ide, 1989), which has been developed into the construct of *wakimae* (Ide 1992); Fraser's (1990a) model of Conversational Contract; Escandell-Vidal's (1996) proposal of politeness that rests on cultural assumptions. I will outline below, however, Watt's (2003) model of politeness and Spenser-Oatey's (2007) treatment of politeness as rapport management.

Watts (1991, 1992, 2003) distinguishes between "first-order" and "second-order" politeness, with the former being a lay concept signifying various (disputed) notions of polite and impolite behavior and the latter being a technical term for discussion of particular features of language use in social interaction. His first-order distinction is one between behavior that is "politic" and behavior that is "polite". Politic behaviors are those that are "perceived to be appropriate to the social constraints of the ongoing interaction" and polite behaviors are those that are "perceived to be beyond what is expectable" (2003: 19). For him, Brown and Levinson's theory is static and much of what they had discussed – and of what others have investigated in the literature – are politic, not polite, behaviors. As the second-order distinction, Watts contrasts "emic politeness" with "etic politeness", with the former referring to the view of politeness held by actual speakers themselves and the latter, to views of politeness held by outsiders: theorists of politeness. The kind of politeness espoused by Leech (1983) and Brown and Levinson (1987) is therefore etic, seen as various constructs resulting from the introspection of theorists that is then imposed upon the study of language use or – worse – users: the native speakers themselves.

Watts's work on politeness is the most influential among its peers in opposition to the theories of Leech and Brown and Levinson. The notion of emic politeness is particularly noteworthy. Together with others' (e.g., Eelen 2001), Watts' work has given rise to the strand of "evaluation" in politeness research: what real-life speakers view the notion of politeness and how they judge a particular linguistic behavior in terms of politeness. My evaluation of politeness evaluation is presented in Section 3.5.

I now move to Spencer-Oatey's (2007, 2008) proposal that politeness be seen as rapport management. The thrust of Spencer-Oatey's argument is that a theory of politeness should not only account for considerations of face as interpersonal needs, but also sociality rights and obligations (as social expectancies) and interactional goals, which can be transactional and/or interactional. She divides sociality rights into equity rights and association rights: equity rights are the expectations in relation to what is fair or unfair in human interaction; association rights are the rights to relate to each other in light of the respective roles each participant plays in a given social activity.

Further, instead of classifying face into negative and positive, as do Brown and Levinson (1987), Spencer-Oatey divides face into quality face, referring to what is socially desirable, and identity face, referring to individual needs that arise from the roles speakers play in interaction. Rapport management, depending on all these factors, will lead to rapport enhancement, rapport maintenance, rapport neglect, or rapport challenge orientation (Spencer-Oatey 2008: 28).

Watts's and Spencer-Oatey's respective politeness theories represent a prevalent trend in pragmatics: a move away from what has been called "rationality-based" theories (see above). However, these often-criticized "rationality-based" theories seem to possess remarkable staying power. The position of the speech act theory and theory of conversational implicature appear to have been entrenched in the field. It would be fair to say – I am convinced – that the field of pragmatics would not easily continue its existence if the theory of speech acts and its accompanying notions were completely taken out of the literature. The theory of conversational implicature is similar. For one thing, the notions of Cooperative Principle, implicature, and maxims can now be used in the literature without being defined, an indication of theory's acceptance by practitioners. Similarly, Brown and Levinson's politeness theory has remained influential, guiding and spurring more research than any of its competitors.

There are also a few theories that are proposed in the spirit of Leech's and Brown and Levinson's work. Following and as a companion to Leech, Gu (1990) constructs a theory for Chinese politeness. Gu proposes four maxims to account for Chinese politeness: respectfulness (positive appreciation of others), modesty (self-denigration), attitudinal warmth (demonstration of kindness, consideration, and hospitality towards others), and refinement (behavior meeting certain social standards) (Gu 1990: 239). The most explicit "companion" theories to Brown and Levinson's theory are Culpeper's (1996) theory of impoliteness, the mirror image of Brown and Levinson's politeness, and Chen's (2001) theory of self-politeness, the mirror image of Brown and Levinson's "other-politeness". These two theories will be outlined in Chapter 3, when we discuss politeness in terms of MMP.

By way of concluding this section on theoretical expansion of the field, I note the larger scholarly backdrop against which these developments have taken place. The second half of the 20th century was a time of breaking down of boundaries, a time of emancipation in the political environment, and a time in which the intellectual movement of multiculturalism was launched, continued, and thrived. The most influential writers of that time in the loosely formed (and termed) discipline *cultural studies* are Lev Vygotsky (1987), Stuart Hall (1989, 1969a & b), and Michel Foucault (1976, 1984). These thinkers' interests are wide and their writings many, but their ideologies and philosophical underpinnings are consonant with each other's. To Vygotsky, social interaction places an important part in the cognitive development of a person, an argument that is pivotal to social constructionism. Hall's critique of cultural artifacts in different media leads him to deny the stability of identity and emphasize the fluidity of meaning. Foucault's works on power reveals how language can be used to form and consolidate power.

While most publications in pragmatics do not pay explicit homage to the likes of Vygotsky, Hall, and Foucault, the parallels between them appear to be more than historical accidents. In terms of theoretical orientation, it is common for writers in pragmatics to deny rationality as a foundation of theory building, for it is viewed as a Eurocentric notion, a point I will pick up in the next chapter. Instead, the notion of "cultural logic" (Blommaet 2005; Wierzbicka 1985, 1992, 2003, 2010; Ye 2004) has been put forward in place. In terms of research methods, introspection is now seen as the work of "armchair" (See Clark and Bangerter 2004; Jucker 2009) scholars and empirical research is seen by many as the only acceptable way of investigation. Writers pride themselves in promoting the "bottom-up" approach, implying that the "top-down" counterpart is a sign of intellectual naivete. Writers, too, are much keener on discovering differences between languages and cultures than similarities, tacitly advancing the multicultural dictum that "differences are good and should be celebrated". Lastly, the adjective *critical* has been in vogue, due largely to Fairclough's (1989, 1992, 1995) works on critical discourse analysis, so that it can be added to any area of research: *critical applied linguistics, critical pragmatics, critical genre analysis, critical sociolinguistics, critical stylistics, critical conversation analysis*. As will be seen in the rest of the book, I shall argue that this intellectual movement is a bit overheated and has led to unintended consequences.

1.2.2 Expansion in practice

It should be noted immediately that the term *practice* is unjustly inaccurate, as many of the practices cited below include clear theoretical elements. In addition, I will only outline the trajectory of this remarkable expansion, without in-depth analysis. More involved discussions on most of these topics shall be offered in Chapters 3–8.

The first expansion was the investigation of speech acts in all its facets. Speech acts were studied in particular languages as well as compared across languages as early as the 1970s, a decade after the publication of Austin and Seale's works. Most notable among the numerous publications were Blum-Kulka and colleagues' study on the speech act of request and apologies across eight (varieties of) languages (Blum-Kulka and Olshtain 1984; Blum-Kulka, House and Kasper 1989), leading to a sustained interest in speech act studies until this day. The number of publications on the speech act of compliment response alone, for example, is in the hundreds, as we shall see in Chapter 4.

Politeness is another area of pragmatics in which scholarly interest has only increased in the past three decades. The literature it has generated is mammoth. A glance at the table of contents of relevant journals alone tells the tale. The readers will also find, as they read on, politeness to be a common theme throughout this monograph.

The attention to lesser studied languages has led to a distinctive area of study: comparative/contrastive pragmatics. Languages and cultures are compared for similarities and differences, yielding a wealth of information. Such studies have also contributed to cross- and intercultural communication, a sister field of study to pragmatics from the very beginning.

Also worthy of note is historical pragmatics. Due largely to the work of Jucker and colleagues (Jucker 1995, 2008; Jucker and Taavistsainen 2008a & b, 2010, 2013; Taavitsainen and Jucker 2003, 2015), the study of how language use has developed and changed over time seems to be drawing more and more attention, adding a new dimension to the literature of language use.

If pragmatics is about language use and the teaching of a second or foreign language has much to do with enabling learners to use the target language, pragmatics should be relevant to language teaching. Indeed so: the field of applied linguistics and the teaching of a second/foreign language has been much influenced by pragmatics (Bardovi-Harlig 2010; Bardovi-Harlig et al. 1991; House 2013; Kasper and Blum-Kulka1993; Kasper and Rose 2001). The currently popular functional/notional syllabus, for example, is a direct consequence of the speech act theory, whereby learners are taught "how to do things in language" rather than the structural properties of language, as had been the case for much of the 20th century.

Discourse analysis started out as a field of study in its own right, as it stemmed from information packaging and thematic progression, strands of linguistics that were independent of pragmatics. However, discourse analysts have sought assistance from various pragmatic theories in their work, as discourse is just one way to categorize the use of language (Brown and Yule 1983; Strauss and Feiz 2014). In fact, argument can be made that discourse analysis is a branch of pragmatics, as its mission of studying language use in discourse is essentially the same with the mission of pragmatics.

Conversation analyses is a bit trickier. On the one hand, most conversation analysts, especially the first-generation scholars such as Sacks and Schegloff (Sacks [1964–72]1992; Sacks, Schegloff & Jefferson 1974; Schegloff 2002) would probably be reluctant to claim much affinity between pragmatics and conversation analyses.[9] On the other hand, most monographs in pragmatics devote sizeable space to conversation analysis (e.g., Chapter 6 of Levinson 1983; Chapters 10, 11, and 12 of Mey 1993), obviously assuming that conversation analysis is part of pragmatics. It should be noted, however, more recent works, particularly those by Heritage and colleagues (Heritage 2003, 2013; Heritage and Clayman 2010; Heritage and G. Raymond 2012; Heritage and C. W. Raymond 2016) have incorporated various pragmatic theories into their examination of social interaction. In my opinion, conversation analysis should indeed be housed under the tent of pragmatics. For it unambiguously studies how language is used in context, albeit in the context of conversation.

Studies in identity construction, an area of the social sciences, has also found itself to benefit from pragmatics. This is hardly surprising. Much of identity construction is done through language, and pragmatic theories have offered useful tools for analyzing how that is done. As indicated earlier, Spencer-Oatey's (2007, 2008) model of politeness – rapport management – connects identity with politeness. Chen and Chen (2020), a special issue of the journal *East Asian Pragmatics*, for example, include papers on how identity construction is studied based on theories and approaches in pragmatics.

Lastly, pragmatics has made its presence felt in the study of non-literal uses of language, the type that is called, in the parlance of rhetoric, *figure of speech:* metaphor, irony, sarcasm, and parody. The study of these uses of language had long been a purview of students of rhetoric and literary studies. But pragmatics has exerted its influence in these areas in two major aspects. The first is the scope of investigation. In the current literature, one finds an unmistakable interest in the study of how these devices are used by the ordinary folk (as opposed to them being used in exulted genres such as literature). The second is approach: these non-literal uses are analyzed in terms of identity, politeness, camaraderie, and relation-building (Carter and McCarthy 2004; Dynel 2013, 2018a & b, 2021; Gibbs 2000; Kwon et al. 2020; Varis and Blommaert 2015; Zappavigna 2011, 2014). These

---

[9] A glance at the references of these works reveals a complete absence of the pragmatic literature.

supposedly exalted uses of language, hence, have been returned to their rightful owner: ordinary language users.

Another way to appreciate the expansion of pragmatics is to take a cursory look at its output. There are more than a dozen handbooks of pragmatics, including a nine-volume tome by Publitz, Jucker, and Schneider (*Handbooks of Pragmatics,* de Gruyter Mouton) and the most recent by Barron, Gu, and Steen (2018). There are nearly a dozen journals dedicated exclusively to pragmatics: e.g., *Contrastive Pragmatics, East Asian Pragmatics, Historical Pragmatics, Intercultural Pragmatics, Internet Pragmatics, Journal of Pragmatics, Pragmatics, Pragmatics and Cognition,* and *Pragmatics and Society.* There are numerous papers published in journals that do not bear the term *pragmatics* in their tittles – which can be easily verified by skimming the table of contents in them – *Discourse Processing, Discourse Studies, Lingua, Journal of Language Contact, Journal of Sociolinguistics, Language in Society, Language Sciences, Linguistics, Linguistics and Philosophy, Modern Language Journal,* and *TESOL Quarterly,* to name just a few.

The reasons for the expansion of pragmatics are not hard to discern. In the very beginning of this section, I referred to Morris' initial tripartite classification of linguistics. In his definition of pragmatics, he sees pragmatics as a study of signs in relation to their interpreters, an investigation of the psychological, biological, and sociological phenomena involved in language use. The three adjectives – *psychological, biological,* and *sociological* – seem to include just about everything about the language user. And my brief and partial listing of the areas in which pragmatics has gotten into bears that out.

1.3 Further notes

The expansion of pragmatics as outline above has led to a remarkable diversity of the field. It is refreshing to see, for instance, the study of language focused not only on Indo-European languages (especially English) plus a few "exotic" languages that linguists happened to know but also others; it is encouraging to read research being published by an increasing number of scholars in traditionally under-represented regions; and it is certainly something we students of language use should take pride in that our discipline has been embraced by many of the sister disciplines.

On the other hand, the diversity of the field seems to have created some incoherence – and even confusion. In pragmatics, for instance, there is the area of interactional pragmatics and the area of variational pragmatics. The two areas are defined on different grounds: the former on interaction, and the latter on variation. They therefore cut across each other. If I were to study the interaction between English speakers and Chinese speakers, would that be interactional or variational? To make the matter more confusing, internet pragmatics seems to be defined by the mode (or venue) of communication. Should we therefore have other types of pragmatics also defined on mode: e.g., *academic writing pragmatics, telephone pragmatics, virtual meeting pragmatics*? Recent years have seen a new label, *emancipatory pragmatics,* whose political underdone is quite obvious. If we start to promote a particular ideology, are we opening the door for other ideologies? I can anticipate the answer from some readers: why is this a problem? It is not, for practical purposes. But would we, as scholars of a respected discipline, uphold some semblance of coherence in our shared field?

I am not the only, nor the first, to see a need to unify the field. Spinning off an endeavor to revise its scope statement in 2017, *Journal of Pragmatics* invited several board members to contribute to a "take stock" special issue of the journal. In the invitation email, the editors wrote:

> As pragmatics has been growing in new directions, both theoretically and methodologically, we believe the time is ripe for a public discussion that will help us trace both converging as well as diverging lines in the ways we conceive of what pragmatics is and how it should be practiced. Our hope is that the outcome will do justice to the polyphony of views within our field and will help identify both challenges to a unified view of the field as well as promising directions for future research. (Terkourafi and Haugh 2019: 1)

Eleven papers, which appeared in the eventual special issue entitled *Quo Vadis, Pragmatics*? (Issue 145), offer a glimpse of the "polyphony" of the field and the need to unify it.

This monograph is hence my attempt to provide a unified theory of pragmatics. Called "the Motivation Model of Pragmatics" (MMP), the proposal aims at being a framework that will subsume the findings in the literature, establish connections among the different subareas of the field, and seek deeper reasons for surface phenomena.

Chapter 2
A motivation model of pragmatics (MMP)

As indicated in the last chapter, MMP, advanced in this monograph, is meant to be a unified theoretical framework for the field. This chapter introduces the theory in full. The gist of the model is that language use can be adequately studied by looking at the motivation behind it. There are two levels of motivation in MMP. At the first level, motivations are categorized into the transactional (the transmission of information) and the interactional (the relationship between the speaker and hearer). At the second level, the transactional is divided into clarity and effectiveness; the interactional is divided into the maintaining of the public image of other and the maintaining of the public image of self. The two components of each pair are not meant to be dichotomic. Rather, they display a gradient relationship on a conflictive vs. assistive cline, i.e., depending on context, they can be in opposition; they can be mutually assistive; and they can be anywhere in between. It is hoped that MMP provide a framework in which connections between things that might otherwise appear unrelated be revealed; reasons for what we find in our empirical studies be identified, and the dynamic unfolding of communication be coherently accounted for.

I start with the definition of MMP in Section 2.1, move to its major elements in Section 2.2, and discuss the usefulness of the theory and other related issues in Section 2.3.

2.1 Definitional properties

MMP is defined as "the study of language use in context from the perspective of the motivation behind the employment of a linguistic device or pragmatic strategy." Three elements in this definition require explication: "language use in context", "motivation", and "a linguistic device or pragmatic strategy". They are discussed below and in that order.

I take "the study of language use in context" as the standard definition of pragmatics. Discussions about the definition of pragmatics largely took place in the 1970s and the 1980s, at a time when pragmatics was emerging and establishing itself as a discipline. Surveys of these discussions are found in Levinson (1983, Chapter 1), Mey (1993, Chapter 1), Green (1989, Chapter 1), and Davis (1991). It seems, however, that "the study of language use in context" has been the accepted definition of pragmatics in the literature.

The notion of context, too, has been debated for decades. In this study, it is defined as "any extralinguistic factor that bears on the expression of an intended meaning by the speaker and/or the interpretation of that intended meaning by the hearer". The lexeme "any" is meant to be encompassing and open-ended, so that context can include what we know as well as what we do not yet know.

What we know about context seems to fall into the epistemic, the physical, and the sociocultural. Epistemic context refers to the shared/mutual knowledge between the speaker and hearer. It includes knowledge of what has been said before, knowledge about each other's life, personality, and values and beliefs of all kinds, and knowledge about a mutual colleague or acquaintance. It, too, includes knowledge about shared assumptions, values, and conventions/rituals of a particular profession or workplace. It is uncontroversial that a piece of shared information will play a part in what one can say and how she says it. It also helps determine how she is interpreted by her hearer.

Physical context refers to the physical location in which communication takes place. What I can say in the classroom to my students would most likely be different from what I can say to them in a bar off campus. At the edge of cliff and about to fall, it may not do if I ask you to give me a hand by saying "Excuse me, I hate to be presumptuous, but is it at all possible that you extend your hand to me?". I would more than likely yell "Help!". The best illustration of this type of context, though, is perhaps ritualized events such as weddings, funerals, church services, or the birthday party for Queen Elizabeth of England (Kádár 2013; Kádár and House 2020a & b), whereby virtually everything to be said is scripted and monitored.

Sociocultural context is the most complex. It includes everything about the speaker and hearer as social beings: their values, beliefs, race and ethnicity, cultural heritage, position in society (both professional and cultural), and others. More importantly, social context covers the interactional aspect of language use, roughly what Brown and Levinson (1987) summarize into the distance between the speaker and hearer, the power the speaker has over the hearer, and the relative ranking of imposition of the speech act in question.

The three types of context clearly cut across each other. One can argue, for instance, epistemic context can cover all three as long as it is defined broadly enough. Indeed, such a view has been put forward: mutual knowledge, for instance, was proposed to replace context (Schiffer 1972; Chen 1990). The same can be said about social context, as it is possible to assert that everything is sociocultural. This logical inconsistency, as it has turned out, does not affect the validity of actual analysis, as long as we are cognizant that anything that is *not* derivative of the linguistic structure – be it morphological, semantic, or syntactical – but influences meaning making is contextual.

The key notion of the theoretical model I am proposing is "motivation". To use motivation as an anchor for a new pragmatics is grounded in the belief that human actions are motivated actions, a well-accepted principle in the social sciences (D'Andrade and Strauss 1992; Peters 1960; Weiner 2012).

The basic tenet of MMP is this. Humans have needs. These needs lead them to act. An action will further regulate behavior depending on its success or failure to meet the need. Take hunger for instance. Needing food, a person may endeavor to find some and then consume it. That would offer her satisfaction, leading to similar behaviors in future contexts. However, if she ends up eating something – out of desperation, due to a lack of knowledge of what he finds – that does not give her satisfaction or even get her poisoned, she will adjust her future behavior accordingly.

Two of the most influential models of motivation are Maslow's (1943) hierarchy of needs and Alderfer's (1989) Existence, Relatedness, and Growth model, commonly known as ERG. For Maslow, human need starts from the lowest level – basic needs – and keeps moving up as a lower-level need is fulfilled. These needs are seen in Figure 2.1.

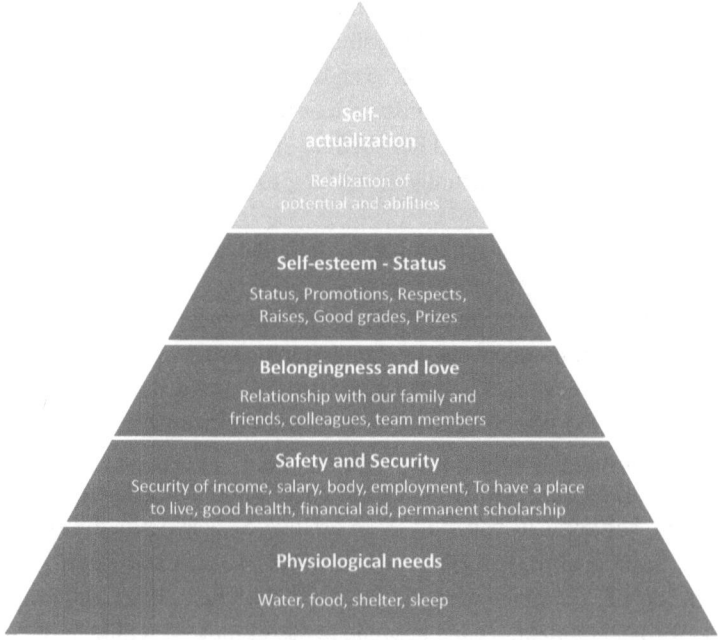

Figure 2.1: Maslow's model of needs.

Alderfer's ERG overlaps considerably with Maslow's model. His Existence group of needs includes the items in Maslow's physiological and safety and security needs – the lowest two levels in Figure 2.1. His Relatedness needs refer to the desire people have for maintaining important interpersonal relationships. These social and status desires require interaction with others if they are to be satisfied, and they align approximately with Maslow's social need and the external component of his esteem need (the second and third category in Figure 2.1). Finally, Alderfer's Growth needs refer to the intrinsic desire for personal development and correspond to the intrinsic component of Maslow's esteem category as well as his self-actualization category. In addition, Alderfer's needs follows a process of regression: when needs in a higher-category are not met, human beings will redouble the effort invested in a lower-category need.

These theories of motivation are about all human behavior. Being one kind of human behavior, the use of language is no exception. To put more simply, if human behavior in general is motived behavior, linguistic behavior must, by definition, be motivated behavior. This forms the theoretical underpinning for MMP.

In the pragmatics literature, terms such as "function" (Brown and Yule 1983; Cook 1989; Mey 1993; Strauss and Feiz 2014), "goal" (Grice 1975), and "intention" (Austin 1962, Grice 1975) have shown frequent appearances. Motivation is different from all of these, although it overlaps with them to various degrees. The concept of function refers to what something does. The function of a hammer is to drive nails but driving nails cannot be said to be the motivation of hammer as a tool. Instead, the need to drive nails is the motivation for *inventing* the hammer. Similarly, when I say "Hi" to you in the hallway, the function of "Hi" could be said to be greeting. The motivation for me to say "Hi", however, is deeper: to maintain relationship with you, which belongs to the "belongingness and love" need per Maslow, as seen in Figure 2.1. Goal is closer to motivation than function, as motivation is very close to goal-orientedness. However, a moment's reflection will reveal some differences. The first is consciousness. Goals are often conscious while motivation are often unconscious, particularly intrinsic ones. The goal of obtaining a degree via attending a university is perhaps conscious for most students. But the motivation – to fulfill the need for growth per Alderfer and the need for status and self-actualization per Maslow – are arguably less so. The same can be said about synonymous terms such as "purpose", "objective", and "intention", as appearing in Austin (1962), Grice (1975), and Seale (1965, 1969)[10] as well, for more or less the same reason.

The major difference between motivation and those other notions, however, is the level of generalization: motivation is a deeper notion about human action, a fundamental principle of agency. However, motivation has not been a favorite concept in linguistics. The mentioning of it, in its various morphological forms

---

[10] Challenges of the notion of speaker intention are seen in Kecskes and Mey (2008) and Wilson and Carston (2019).

such as "motivated by", is done frequently but only in passing. The only exception, to my knowledge, is Panther and Radden (2011), a collection of papers that demonstrate how various human cognitive and perceptive capacities (e.g., figure and ground) motivate linguistic constructions.

The third and last component of the definition of MMP that warrants exposition is "(behind the employment of) a linguistic device or pragmatic strategy". A linguistic device refers to anything linguistic: a word, a phrase, a sentence, however one defines it. "Pragmatic strategy" is added to cover things that speakers do that are not linguistic per se but are clearly relevant to meaning making. For instance, if I made a joke about you that is not to your liking, you could refuse to laugh, or laugh awkwardly, or look at me sternly. Any of these actions – none of them is strictly linguistic – would be "pregnant with meaning", as it were, and a theory of language use should not ignore them. Due to the decades of work by conversation analysts, we now have a good inventory of such non-linguistic strategies. Silence – the action of not making a sound where one is expected to at a particular juncture in a conversation – for example – has garnered considerable attention as is seen in the collection of papers in Murray and Durrheim (2019).

2.2 MMP

Based on the discussions in the last section, I present MMP in Figure 2.2.

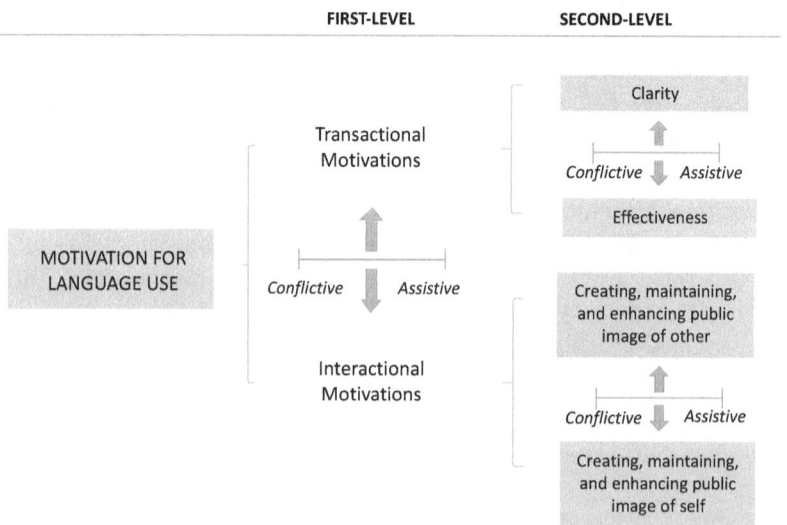

Figure 2.2: Motivation model of pragmatics (MMP).

The model has two levels of motivations. At the first level, motivations for language use are divided into the transactional and the interactional. At the second level, each of the two first-level motivations is categorized into two (sub)-motivations. In this section, I discuss these motivations in detail.

2.2.1 First-level motivations

For social scientists, human motivation comes in different stripes: social, psychological, emotional, and religious, as can be observed in both the two models of needs by Maslow and Alderfer outlined above and in other treatises on the subject (D'Andrade and Strauss 1992; Peters 2015; Weiner 2012). In MMP, which concerns only one kind of human action, motivation for language use is classified into transactional motivations and interactional motivations.

The terms *transactional* and *interactional* are taken from Brown and Yule's (1983) classification of language functions. Transactional language, according to the authors, is primarily "message-based" that is "used to covey factual or propositional information". Examples of transactional language use are a policeman giving directions to a traveler, a doctor telling a nurse how to administer medicine to a patient, or a householder puts in an insurance claim (Brown and Yule 1983: 2). Interactional language, on the other hand, is language used "to establish and maintain social relationships". The authors cite Pirsig's (1976) observations to illustrate their point. A woman on a bus describes the way a mutual friend has been behaving (getting out of bed too soon after an operation) and concludes her turn in the conversation by saying "Aye, she's an awfy [=awful] woman". Her hearer responds with the same exact utterance. There is no transfer of any information. The conversationalists go "on and on", seemingly "with no point of purpose" (Brown and Yule 1983: 34).

Brown and Yule's classification, proposed almost four decades ago, seems to be an apt system for the motivation of language use. The transactional captures the need for speakers to transmit factual information and intention, a view that has been held by most traditional language philosophers (see Chapter 1) and underlies the work by linguists in phonology, morphology, semantics and syntax. In other words, when we investigate the structural properties of language – be they sound, morphemes, word meaning, or sentence structure – we are assuming that language carries with it meaning and is used to get that meaning across. The interactional, on the other hand, captures what students of pragmatics have been discovering, that language is not only a conduit of information but also a means to manage our social life. This is akin, in particular, to the division of language into the ideational and the interpersonal by systemic functional linguistics (Halliday 2003, [1985] 2014).

The difference between the way these two terms are used by Brown and Yule and the way they are taken to mean in the present study is obvious: they are used by Brown and Yule to mean function but in the present study they refer to motivation. Compared to Maslow's and Alderfer's need models, we can say that language is an enabler for speakers to fulfill other life's needs. The two basic needs – physiological and safety and security – by Maslow (Figure 2.1) include examples such as water, food, shelter, income, health. Language can be a tool for us to obtain all of these things. A man searching for water in a desert has the motivation to seek information from the local folk about where to find it. To obtain an income from a business, I need to give that business information about what I can do for it. These are instances of the transactional motivation of language use. Moving up on Figure 2.1, we find other, and exceedingly higher, needs. One of these needs is belongingness and love: "relationships with our family and friends, colleagues, team members". These needs provide the interactional motivation for language use.

Some parallels may be drawn between MMP and other theories in terms of motivation. Speech acts can be seen as realizations of the transactional motivation. We do things with words because we *need* to do things with words. How to perform a speech act – e.g., directly or indirectly – however, seems to belong to the realm of the interactional. Grice's Cooperative Principle, likewise, can be said to be motivated by both: while the following of his maxims assists the fulfillment of the transactional, the reliance on implicature to get across one's message is more of a product of the interactional.

The relationship between transactional motivations and interactional motivations is complicated. On the one hand, there are situations in which they are conflictive. The example above about me standing at the edge of a cliff illustrates this. The need to survive is in conflict with the need to be "nice" and differential to you. Given that the need to stay alive trumps the need for social nicety, I would choose to yell "help". But the two can also be assistive. Suppose I want to ask you for a ride to a car mechanic, which is clearly transactional, saying "I am wondering if you have the time to take me to Bob's Garage" instead of "Take me to Bob's!" would reflect my interactional motivation. But that effort also enhances the chance to get an affirmative response from you (assuming, of course, that I am not in a position to issue orders to you). Similarly, if I know something you do not but knowing it would be advantageous to you, give you that information would enhances our relationship. The literature on gossip, for example, shows that this is indeed the case: gossip has been found to plays an important role in establishing and supporting group values and behaviors (Guendouzi 2020). The transfer of information in gossips (and possibly rumors as well) can be seen as being motivated by interactional needs. In Figure 2.2, this conflictive-assistive cline is schematized and placed between the two motivations.

In sum, then: the two first-level motivations – the transactional and the interactional – seem to be independent at first sight; but they are not. Instead, they are intertwined in intricate ways, reflecting the complexity of motivation at the deepest level. The recognition of this complexity in MMP will enable us to capture the varied nature of language use at all levels, as I shall endeavor to demonstrate in the remaining chapters.

2.2.2 Second-level motivations

Now we move to second-level motivations: clarity and effectiveness for the transactional; creating, maintaining, and enhancing the public image of other (hearer or a third party) or self (speaker) for the interactional. We start with the transactional.

The first transactional motivation, clarity, stems from the fact that language offers speakers more than one way to say the same thing. Other things being equal, clarity is a major criterion for speaker choice in a given situation or in the performing of a speech act. Take greetings for instance. One can say, "How're you?"; "How are you doing?"; "How's life treating you lately?"; "What's up?"; "Hey, long time no see!"; "What a lovely day, isn't it?"; "Hi"; "Hi Mr. Rodrigues. It is such a pleasure to run into you so unexpectedly", and any number of other possibilities. If you knew that I were an English speaker from rural South Africa, you may not use the Americanism "What's up?", as your intention might not be sufficiently "clear" for me. In this sense, the transfer of information – greeting – is more complicated than the transmission of physical goods. If I were tasked with delivering to you a packet, the packet will remain a packet however I get it into your hands. But if the "goods" I were tasked to deliver to you were a verbal message, that message may be different once delivered. Seen thusly, clarity has a great deal to do with accuracy.

Clarity has its origin in ancient philosophy. Aristotle declared, "Let the virtue of linguistic form be defined as clear" in his *Rhetoric* (III.2, 1404b1–4, see Garver 2009). Clarity also has a heavy presence in the English curriculum of U.S. secondary schools and colleges and has been codified by rhetoricians into a set of dictums for writers: "make sure each pronoun has a clear antecedent", "provide topic sentences for paragraphs", "try not to pack more than one idea in a paragraph", "provide cohesion among sentences and transition between paragraphs", and "avoid the passive voice".

Clarity is analogous to Grice's (1975) maximum of manner. The submaxims of the maxim – "avoid obscurity of expression, avoid ambiguity, be brief, and be orderly" – mirror some of the rhetorical dictums listed above. However, it is important to note that the notion of clarity in MMP is meant to be more encompassing, including violations of the maxims of quantity, quality, and relation as well. I copy Examples (12) through (14) in Chapter 1 below for easy reference.

(1) A: Cindy was gossiping again.
    B: Women are women.

(2) A: Tom flunked all his classes.
    B: What a genius!

(3) A: Did you enjoy the play last night?
    B: I thought the ice-creams they sold during the interval were quite good.

Speakers designated by "B" in the above examples violate the maxim of quantity, quality, and relation, respectively. As we discussed in Chapter 1, they do so for the purpose of creating implicatures. But implicatures are not models of clarity, as they leave more room for misinterpretation (Leech 1983; Levinson 1983). Example (4), below, illustrates the point.

(4) A: Should I call him right now?
    B: I would do that [Nodding gently]
    A: You would do that, for me? [A bit surprised but apparently thankful]
    B: No. *You* should call him right now.

Speaker A is an international student studying in a U.S. university. He asks B, his American roommate, for advice. B replies with an utterance that breaches the maxim of relation: "I would do that". But A takes it literally and verifies his understanding by asking "You would do that, for me"? Realizing that he has failed to get his message across, B changes his tactic, issuing a much clearer advice: "No. *You* should call him right now." Therefore, the notion of clarity as currently proposed is more encompassing than Grice's maxim of manner. In Chapter 6 when we move to MMP and discourse, we shall see that the transactional motivation of clarity provides a plausible explanation for the multitude of structures and systems in the organization of various types of discourse, including the moves writers of research papers make in academic writing, the turn-taking organization of conversations, and topic-management, thematic progression, and coherence in all discourse types.

The second motivation of the interactional, effectiveness, refers to the quality of a transaction: how successful an utterance is in achieving an end. If I asked my reluctant teenage son to help me do yardwork, he may go outside the house with me and get to work immediately; he may end up picking up the trimmer after a twenty-minute delay; and he may find a way to avoid assisting me at all. Knowing all these possibilities, I would be careful in the way I make the request. That means that what I say to him would be motivated by effectiveness – that it would succeed in achieving the intended outcome: to get the teenage boy out of the house into the blistering August southern California sun.

Theoretically, the notion of effectiveness would seem to have some affinity with Sperber and Wilson's (1986) notion of "cognitive effect". According to Sperber and Wilson's theory of relevance, speakers aim to achieve optimal relevance in communication by producing the most cognitive effect in the given situation ("cognitive environment" per Sperber and Wilson). What one says is effective if it produces the intended contextual assumptions *and* does not require the hearer to spend more effort than justifiable (by those contextual assumptions) to process. This affinity, I must point out, is more apparent than real. Effectiveness in MMP refers to the impact that what is said produces on the hearer (Chen 1993b), without explicitly taking into account of its processing cost on the hearer.

The relationship between the two transactional motivations is similar to the one between the two first-level motivations: it is a continuum from the conflictive to the assistive. At the conflictive end, we find types of discourse where the effectiveness motivation trumps the clarity almost entirely. The first is advertising (Amos 2020; Bhatia 2019; Cook 1988). On the one hand, the message of an ad is clear: buy X. On the other hand, just to say "buy X" probably will not work all the time. The challenge is to figure out how to get that message across most effectively so that X would come to the audience's mind when they need X type of products. Effective ads, as a consequence, are those that do not tell the audience to simply purchase X but say things in such a way that the audience will "get there" themselves. In an earlier but smart analysis, Cook (1988) shows how ambiguity is employed by Smirnoff (a brand of the Russian vodka) to create the perception that the product can enhance its consumers' life in numerous ways. In the context of the slogan "Walking the dog – with a dash of pure Smirnoff. Whatever you do with it, it's neat", the word *dash* has two possible meanings; the word *neat* has three possible meanings; and the pronoun *it* has eight possible referents. Multiply these three numbers (2x3x8) and we get a total of 48 interpretations – all could be intended by the slogan. What seems to be a simple slogan conveys dozens of meanings simultaneously. Similarly, the Nike slogan, "Just do it", invites the audience to interpret *it* to be anything and everything they do. Therefore, we see that clarity is not the motivation for ad writers. Effectiveness is.

Another type of discourse in which effectiveness is prominent is literature (Booth 1983; Leech 1985, 1992; Leech and Short 1983). If we assume that a piece of literature has a message – a *theme*, in the parlance of literary critics – to be clear about that message would probably not lead to literature. Take detective fiction, for instance. The writer of a detective novel knows precisely who committed a murder, but the revelation of the murderer's identity is invariably at the end. During the novel, in fact, the narrator may provide red herrings, intentionally misleading the reader so that the final revelation would be more unexpected. Therefore, the judgement of literature is not how clearly the message is expressed, but how effective it turns out to be, hence the sort of words critics – both scholars and ordinary readers – use to describe literature: "captive", "arresting", "page-turning", "profound", and "thought-provoking". One of the folksy yardsticks to judge literature is its staying power in our mind: whether it is recallable long after we read and, if it is, how detailed and vivid the recollection.[11]

Looking at the kind of discourse types in which effectiveness is the underlying motivation, we find persuasion to be the commonality among them. Besides advertising and literature, discourse that aims at persuasion also includes political discourse (Docherty 2019; Fairclough 1989, 1992, 1995, but see below) and religious discourse (Moratti and Goodblatt 2013). Persuasion presupposes reluctance on the part of the audience; its success depends crucially on how the message impacts that audience.

The importance of effectiveness as a transactional motivation could be seen in the universal existence of the non-literal uses of language: metaphor, irony, parody, and others. In Chapter 7, I will discuss in detail how metaphor is motivated by effectiveness, particularly in the area of politics. In Chapter 8, I will show how other non-literal uses of language enable the speaker to get across her message more effectively (among other motivations).

The right end of the conflictive-assistive scale – "assistive" – refers to cases in which a use of language is motivated by both clarity and effectiveness. There are a range of contexts in which the two motivations enjoy an assistive relationship. Political campaigns, particularly towards the final stretch, seem to encourage simple assertions (e.g., "The party of X is the party for the people" and "I, alone, can fix it"![12]) and order-like commissives (e.g., "Vote for me"! "Vote as if your life

---

11 My creative writer colleagues inform me that literary agents judge the marketability of the manuscript of a novel by whether they would want to continue reading after the first couple of pages. This coincides with our experience. Browsing the shelves at a bookstore in an airport terminal, we might purchase a paperback for the trip if it makes us "turn the page".
12 https://www.theatlantic.com/politics/archive/2016/07/trump-rnc-speech-alone-fix-it/492557/

depends on it"[13]). Emergency is another such context. The fabricated example of me standing on the edge of a cliff (above) yelling "help" to you would illustrate well how emergency suspends other motivations of language use, making the clearest utterance also the most effective.

I now move to the second-level motivations for the interactional. As Figure 2.2 shows, under the interactional, there are two sub-motivations: "Creating, maintaining, and enhancing public image of other" and "Creating, maintaining, and enhancing public image of self". I start with the notion of public image.

Public image refers to what a person is perceived by others. It covers elements of Maslow's top three needs: "self-actualization", "self-esteem", "and belongness and love". It also overlaps with Alderfer's relatededness and growth needs. The need to have the desirable public image, further, is taken to be universal across cultures (cf, Goffman [1955] 1967, 1974, 1979).

Apparently an umbrella notion, public image includes a long list of attributes. Here Brown and Levinson's notion of face provides a foundation for our discussion: public image in MMP includes negative and positive face per Brown and Levinson and all the sub-face wants listed under them (Brown and Levinson 1987: 65–68, see Section 1.2.1 above). But MMP moves beyond Brown and Levinson in three ways. First, based on recent literature, MMP adds a few sociocultural values and factors to public image such as ethics, morality (Haugh 2013, 2015, 2018; Kádár 2008, 2013; Kádár and Haugh 2013; Kádár, Parvaresh, and Ning 2019), and rights and obligations (Spencer-Oatey 2007, 2008). Second, MMP explicitly recognizes the interactional need in the content of public image. As is recalled from Chapter 1, Brown and Levison's theory of politeness has been challenged repeatedly for not taking into account the interactional nature of politeness. This criticism – I will argue below in Chapter 3 – ignores ample evidence that Brown and Levinson are aware of the interactionality of face and politeness. The issue for Brown and Levinson with regard to interactionality is not that they have turned a blind eye to it but that they should have given it more prominence. MMP, therefore, states that the need to belong (to a group) is part of the public image.

The motivational need to belong can take at least two forms. The first is the need to be recognized by others for the place one holds in society (Arundale 2013; Haugh 2013). The second is the need to belong to a group (Brown and Levinson 1983; Ide 2012). The need to belong has been found to regulate linguistic behavior in significant ways. Ran and Zhao (2019), for instance, provide evidence that the Chinese notion of face includes "relational face", referring to the connection

---

[13] https://www.npr.org/2020/10/06/920684113/michelle-obama-makes-final-pitch-vote-for-joe-biden-like-your-lives-depend-on-it

between speakers. Speakers therefore behave linguistically in accordance with the responsibilities and obligations resulting from it. If you have done me a favor, relational face will require that I return it. That favor may or may not be material. If you said something at the last department meeting in support of my view, I will feel obliged to support yours at the present meeting.

Coupled with the need to belong is the need for camaraderie. In Chapter 8 when we discuss non-literal uses of language, I will provide evidence that to establish camaraderie with the hearer is a major motivating factor for a host of things: irony, parody, sarcasm, teasing, and humor.

The third departure of the notion of public image in MMP from the notion of face in Brown and Levison is the most substantive – that the former is connected to self-interest while the latter is not, at least explicitly. This is due to two factors. The first is the connection of MMP to motivation theories. As is seen in Figure 2.1, much of human motivation is self-interest driven. The second is recent research findings. With the notable increase of attention paid to impoliteness, aggression, and conflicts, evidence emerged that linguistic behaviors are also connected to self-interest of the speaker. In Ran, Zhou and Kádár (2020), for instance, the verbal conflicts between speakers result from the conflict of clearly material interest such as whether a son should financially support his parents and who should legally own an apartment.[14]

The notion of public image, thusly seen, is encompassing. There are two advantages to this vagueness. First, a model such as MMP has to be able to explain variations. Speakers shall differ on what constitutes positive (or negative) public image. The same behavior might be seen differently from one culture to another, from one community to another in the same culture, and from one person to another in the same community. Humility, for instance, has been shown to be a value in Chinese society (Chen 1993a, 2020; Gu 1990), but at least in the area of academic writing, it is not as prominently valued in English (Chen 2020, Chen and Yang 2022). So does notions such as bravery. On the one hand, the admiration of bravery seems to transcend cultures. On the other, what constitutes bravery will differ. Suppose Marko jumps into a burning house to save his family photos but gets himself seriously injured without being able to save any. Some of us may view his deed as heroic, others may see it as a manifestation of his love of his family, and still others may walk away, after assisting him before the arrival of an

---

[14] The study also offers direct support for the prominence public image receives in MMP. During the conflict mediation meetings, the mediator is found to use public image as a means to persuade both sides to backdown from their respective positions. To a business owner who refuses to pay his employees in time, the mediator asks him to think about what his refusal will do to his image as a business owner, which will likely translate into business loses.

ambulance, wishing that he had exercised better judgement under the circumstance. The vagueness of the notion of public image will therefore allow us to apply it in all these situations.

Second, the vagueness of the notion of public image enables MMP to provide a framework for findings coming from different strands of pragmatics. In the above, we discussed the connection between MMP and Brown and Levison's theory of politeness. But the notion of public image subsumes politeness as envisaged by others as well. Watts' (2003) theory of politeness, which challenges Brown and Levinson's framework, also acknowledges public image as the core content of politeness, albeit with different terminology. His distinction between politic and polite behaviors is a distinction between two types of public image, with the latter being more desirable than the former. His promotion of evaluation of politicness or politeness is to let the participants be the judge about whether a behavior enhances or hurts the public image of the speaker and to what degree. Spencer-Oatey's (2007, 2008) rapport management theory of politeness likewise is based on the assumption of public image, albeit implicitly. To have rapport with our hearers is beneficial to our own public image as well as to that of our hearers'; to damage that rapport is not.

In Chapter 6, I will argue that much of a person's identity is public image, i.e., to maintain or construct the identity of X is the same as to maintain or to construct the public image of X. If identity is what a person is identified with or known for (Blommaet 2005; Ochs 2012; Tajfel 1974, 1981, 1982; Tracy 2002; Zimmerman 1988, 1992), it is not much different from public image. In the same vein, stance, referring to what academic writers do to establish credibility for both themselves and for their work (Hyland 1999, 2002, 2005), can also be viewed as public image in the context of academic writing, as it directly bears on how their work is received by peers. The various ways in which academic writers express their stance can plausibly be said to be motivated by their need to create and maintain their public image of a scholar.

Now we move to the distinction between other-image and self-image in MMP. Other vs. self has been a favorite topic in philosophy, psychology, sociology, and critical theory, although the two notions mean different things from one discipline to another. In the present study, other and self are taken to refer to real-life people, with *other* being the hearer and *self* being the speaker in most cases. In this sense, they are the same notions as used by motivation theorists. Maslow's model of needs – we go back to it once again – lists self-esteem and status as one of his five human needs. *Self* in "self-esteem" clearly refers to a real person.

In pragmatics, other vs. self has not received much attention. The first scholar to recognize it appears to be Leech (1983). His Politeness Principle, as presented in (19) in Chapter 1, sets up a dichotomy of other vs. self in some of his maxims. Brown and Levinson (1987) also make the distinction when they discuss face threating acts – some acts threaten the face of other; other acts threaten the face of self – but they discard the distinction altogether in the eventual and highly influential theory of politeness. Chen's (2001) work on self-politeness is possibly the first formal recognition of self in pragmatics. In it, I set up the dichotomy of other-politeness and self-politeness. As the model of self-politeness will be outlined in more detail in Section 3.3, suffice it to illustrate it with an example at this point. If I have a submission rejected by an academic journal and have to tell my department chair about it, I might say something like "That did not work out" as opposed to "The paper was not good enough". The use of the pronoun "that" would help me to avoid naming myself as the agent of the sentence (hence the failure in getting the paper accepted) and "did not work out" makes it sound as if the rejection was due to factors beyond my own control. So, what I say can be seen as being motivated by the need to protect my self-image, hence an act of self-politeness.

While *other* refers to the hearer and *self* to the speaker most of the time, we should note that both the hearer and speaker can be the representation of a group. The spokesperson of the White House speaking at a press conference does not speak for herself, but the U.S. administration. The self of a diplomat at the negotiation table is not the diplomat as a person but the country she represents. The self of an ordinary conversationist may include family and friends depending on context. Self, in addition, will surely vary cross-culturally. Li and Yue (1996) argue, for instance, that the Chinese self includes wife and children in the context of responding to compliments, which may or may not be the case in another culture.

We should also acknowledge that in displaced discourse – situations in which communication does not take place in real time – other is often imagined. A novelist's other is her future readership; the other of a post on Twitter is the poster's followers as well as all those who have a Twitter account; and the other of a textbook writer is the targeted body of students.

Lastly, about the relationship between other- and self-image. As is seen in Figure 2.2, the relationship between the two is the same as the relationship between others in the figure, i.e., it is one of a continuum of conflictivity vs. assistivity. On the conflictivity end, there seem to be two possibilities. The first is the inherent conflict of interest between other and self. Society is replete with such conflicts. In a lawsuit, the plaintiff and the defendant form a diametrical opposition, as the law does not allow both to be winners (Chen 1996b; Yuan 2019). In politics, different parties clash because there is only one office at each level of government to be occupied. The same is true with the daily life of ordinary speakers. In the case of bargaining in a market, for instance, the buyer of an item is expected to "run down" the value or quality of the negotiated item to justify a lower price while the seller would do the opposite. In the same vein, a husband may not agree with his wife about a familiar matter; a parent may differ with her teenage son about the purchase of a cellphone; and you and I may have different views about whether the distinction between other and self is worthy of debate. These inherent conflicts will manifest in language use, potentially leading to impoliteness (Culpeper 1996), a point to be picked up in the next chapter.

There are also situations in which confrontation results not from an inherent interest but from the motivation to self-defend, particularly when self-image is attacked. An aggressive speaker can cause an otherwise cordial exchange to become tense; the unintended mispronunciation of our hearer's name could cause friction. Such acts, either intentional or unintentional, may place the image of other and self in opposition, leading to confrontationality.

At the other end of the continuum – the end of assistivity – we find cases in which the image of other and self are either mutually assistive or one is assistive to the other. A party held by an organization to celebrate a collective accomplishment will likely generate congratulatory remarks among the attendees, which enhances the image of both of other and self. Casual greetings, even in a parking lot between strangers, create a desirable image for both. Even what might appear to be a "confrontation" could, in reality, be a negotiation for the benefit of the public image of both. In a phone call between two colleagues discussing a date for a meeting, for instance, we might find that both asks the other to name a date first ("I'm widely available. So, let's go by your schedule". "Well, I did that last time. Why don't we go by yours?"). The disagreement about who to decide is in fact an act of consideration and deference. This reciprocity is reflected in the cliché "I scratch your back and you scratch mine". After all, public image is *public*. To achieve, maintain, and enhance one's own public image is essentially the gaining of approval of others. This is the assumption of Grice's theory of Cooperative Principle. It also undergirds most other major theories in the field such as the linguistic adaptation theory (Verschueren 1999), the relevance theory (Sperber and Wilson 1987), politeness theories by Brown and Levinson (1987), by Fraser (1990), by Spencer-Oatey (2007, 2008), and by Watts (2003). "Co-construction" of meaning or identity, a term in vogue in the conversation analysis and identity construction literature, speaks directly to the reciprocal nature of much of human interaction.

The relationship between the public image of other and self is far more complicated than our discussions of the two-ends-of-the-continuum scenarios. Between the two ends are endless possibilities which, however, cannot be meaningfully explored without considering the nuances of the context wherein communication takes place. Some of these possibilities will come to the fore later in the monograph.

2.3 Further notes on MMP

2.3.1 "Top-down?": A rejoinder to an anticipated critique

MMP, as outlined so far in this chapter, may appear to be proposed in a top-down approach: two motivations are established at the "top", each of which leads to two more motivations at the next level. The top-down approach, in the current scholarly environment, is not popular. Its supposed opposite, the bottom-up approach, enjoys a much larger following. In this section, I offer a defense for the so-called top-down approach.

The unpopularity of the top-down approach is due in large part to the assumption that a theoretical model thusly constructed is not based on empirical evidence: the writer has not done the get-one's-hands-dirty type of necessary work of data collection and analysis but has "cooked up" her idea in an armchair. But that may not be always true. While a model may seem "top-down", the path of the model's constructing process oftentimes is not. The writer can survey the literature representative of the field by both herself and others and propose a theory based on that survey. In that case, it is actually bottom-up, although the "bottom" is not immediately obvious. This is precisely how the currently proposed theory has come about. As indicated in the Foreword, MMP is the result of learning about, as far as the writer can, the entire field of pragmatics from its birth to present. The idea of MMP, in other words, did not just appear in my brain. It is the accumulation of the combined work by all researchers that I have read and thought about. I am convinced that the same holds for many other writers similarly accused of being "top-down" in their approach.

The distain for the top-down approach, quite obviously, reflects a distrust of the writer's intuition and reflection. That mistrust has always been there in the hard sciences in which laboratory experiment is crucial. In the humanities and social sciences, the mistrust is less acute but has been intensified in the past decades. This can be seen as a result of the multicultural turn in the disciplines as discussed in Chapter 1 on the one hand and the rise of conversation analysis on the other. These intellectual movements have amassed a large amount of literature, pushing our discipline forward at a historic speed. However, the emphasis on the empirical approach may have been overdone, and I view the increasing mistrust on the validity of introspection as one of its consequences. I provide two arguments.

First, despite the rhetoric against introspection, a researcher cannot avoid it. We can spend months or years with a speech community of speakers, use appropriate methodology to collect data, and come back to our office to perform statistical and other types of analysis. But when we write up the project, our subjective views creep in. Some scholars prefer to stay with description, refraining from generalizing. But there is no commonly agreed-upon way even to describe, as the mere describing of a reality presupposes subjectivity of the describer. Moreover, description should not be the only objective for discovery. A reality needs to be understood – which necessarily requires subjective interpretation – and warranted generalization needs to be made. All this requires abstraction and introspection. So, even the so-called bottom-up approach is not a whole lot different from the purported top-down approach.

Second, too much emphasis on empiricism and on the minute details of language use has the potential to lead to overfocus on the trees at the expense of the forest. As students of language use – as is the case with students in any discipline – we need generalizations, which is what theory is all about, as much as we need knowledge of the reality we are studying.

Consequently, a theoretical model that is accused of resulting from a top-down approach should be evaluated on its merit, not to be dismissed outright. For instance, one typical claim against a theory is that, simply by being a theory of considerable generality, it cannot, *a priori*, handle the dynamic unfolding of communication. As I will argue in different places in the rest of the book, that claim needs more substantiation than has been hitherto offered.

2.3.2 MMP as a unifying framework

MMP hereby proposed has an ambitious aim: to provide a unified framework for pragmatics. In this section, I discuss how that can be achieved.

Because MMP stems from a well-recognized and intuitively plausible principle that human actions are motivated, it provides a framework to explore reasons for linguistic behaviors. As a result, it assists other theories, not replace them. The researcher can use whatever theory she sees fit for her investigation; but, with the help of MMP, she would be able to reveal underlying things that might otherwise be missed. MMP can, for instance, enable those who study speech acts to see why a particular speech act is performed in a particular context and why it is done the way it is. It helps those working in the framework of Grice's Cooperative Principle to explore reasons for (un)cooperation and for maxim violation. It is consonant with relevance theory in that the clarity motivation of the transactional is aligned with the "path of least effort" and the effectiveness motivation explains why a speaker would deviate from that path. It is in agreement with interactional pragmatics for its explicit recognition of interactionality. It explains notions such as ritual (Kádár 2013), because the conventionalization of ways of speaking results from their repeated occurrences (Morgan 1978), which is in turn the result of a common motivation "working behind the scenes" across discourse contexts.

MMP can be used also to make coherent sense of findings from different subareas of pragmatics. The remaining chapters are designed to do so. In Chapter 3, I will show that MMP will, at the highest level, propose that to be polite to others is motivated by the need to appear as face-sensitive members of a society, to be impolite to others is motivated by the need to protect self-image. As such, MMP works with existing theories. Culpeper's (1996) notion of impoliteness is seen in MMP as a result of the conflict between other-image and self-image: speakers attack the image of others because they want to protect the image of their own. When Spencer-Oatey (2007) says that politeness is a means of rapport management, she is essentially saying that face-work is motivated by the desire to establish and maintain rapport with others, which is part of the interactional motivation, as is seen in Figure 2.2.

Chapter 4 is on cross- and intercultural pragmatics, with two case studies. The first is on compliment responses. A comprehensive survey will be presented of the research that have taken place on the speech act of compliment response in the past three decades across more than one dozen languages. MMP will then be used to account for the findings, showing that it is capable of interpreting these findings coherently. The second case study is on the East-West divide debate. MMP will enable us to reveal the underlying similarities between "East" and "West" in politeness while at the same time account for the differences between the two large linguacultures. MMP, I will further argue, is useful not only for intercultural differences but also for other, more fine-tuned variational studies, those that focus on region, socioeconomic class, religion, gender, race, or profession. For it provides a framework, in the form of a continuum, in which differences can be seen as differences in degree, not in kind. This would help the field to discover underlying principles that transcend differences.

Chapter 5 demonstrates the efficacy of MMP for diachronic pragmatics. With two case studies that reveal changes in Chinese speakers' linguistic behaviors in compliment responses and in end-of-dinner food offering, I will show that MMP is capable of accounting for these changes as well.

In Chapter 6, I will demonstrate how MMP offers explanations for the reasons for a host of findings in discourse studies, including discourse analysis, genre analysis, conversation analysis, and identity studies. In discourse analysis, for instance, structural properties such as information packaging and thematic progression have long been recognized for their validity, but little discussion has been had on why these structures have emerged in the first place. MMP will offer a possibility – that these mechanisms of language use are motivated by the clarity consideration of the transactional. Similarly, different structures of conversation, such as the turn-taking system and adjacency pair organization, are also results of the clarity motivation exerting its force. Identity construction, on the other hand, is motivated by the interactional. Speakers endeavor to construct different identities in different contexts because they want to establish, maintain, or enhance the public image for themselves. I will also, in Section 6.4, offer a focused analysis of the discourse marker *so*, showing how MMP is capable of revealing a single function of the lexeme rather than a long list of disparate functions as has been seen in previous studies.

In Chapter 7, we will see how MMP accounts for metaphor. Once again, we will observe that MMP does not replace existing theories of metaphor, particularly the widely popular conceptual metaphor theory. Instead, it assists it by looking at the motivations of different metaphorists in different discursive contexts.

In Chapter 8, MMP is applied to the study of non-literal uses of language, resulting in a set of explanations that would not be arrived at without it. Take parody. With MMP, we are able to see how parody can establish camaraderie between the parodist and her audience in one context but attack a target in another, how it can help create, maintain, or enhance self-image, and how it helps enhance the effectiveness of the transaction of the message. Irony is similar. It can help the speaker to build relationship with the hearer in one context, to appear creative and humorous in another, and to damage the public image of the targeted victim in yet another. However, these different functions fall nicely under the motivations proposed in MMP.

In sum, the advantage of MMP lies in its depth of theoretical assumption and the resultant high level of generalization. Using a worn-out metaphor, we can say that MMP is a model of the "forest" that may be useful for both those who prefer to study the "trees" in the forest as well as the forest itself.

Chapter 3
MMP and (im)politeness

In the remaining chapters, MMP will be applied to different areas or strands of pragmatics. We begin our endeavor with politeness in this chapter and will make two major arguments. First, politeness is a principal interactional motivation, which often runs counter to transactional motivations, i.e., things said for the sake of politeness are often at the expense of transactional motivations, especially clarity. Second, politeness can be other-politeness or self-politeness based on orientation; it can be polite or impolite based on benefit. While the relationship among these four types of politeness is complicated, a simple proposal will be made that while politeness is the (interactional) motivation to be polite to others, self-politeness is the (interactional) motivation for impoliteness to others (Chen 2023).

The thesis of this chapter rests therefore on three types of (im)politeness: other-politeness, impoliteness, and self-politeness. They will be discussed first and in that order, in Sections 3.1 through 3.3. In Section 3.4, the three types of (im)politeness are put together to form an MMP-oriented (im)politeness framework, followed by detailed analyses of several types of (im)politeness. In Section 3.5, a critique of evaluation is provided, discussing the importance of politeness evaluation on the one hand and offering a cautionary note on its potential pitfalls on the other.

3.1 Other-politeness

Almost all theories that have been proposed on politeness are theories of other-politeness, including Brown and Levison's (1987) theory of universal politeness, Leech's (1983) Politeness Principle, Hill et al.'s (1986) model of Discernment (see also Ide, 1989), which has been developed into the construct of *wakimae* (Ide 1992, 2012); Fraser's (1990) model of Conversational Contract; Escandell-Vidal's (1996) proposal of politeness that rests on cultural assumptions; Spencer-Oatey's (2007) rapport management; and Arundale's (2013) face constitutive theory. There are also models of politeness for specific cultures, such as Haugh's (2005) notion of place for Japanese and Gu's (1990) Politeness Principle for Chinese. Of these theories, Brown and Levinson's theory has led to companion theories: Culpeper's theory of impoliteness and Chen's (2001) theory of self-politeness. It is therefore the fulcrum of the thesis advanced in this chapter.

I refer the reader to Section 1.2.1, in Chapter 1 for the basic tenets and elements of Brown and Levinson's theory. In this section, I focus on a few criticisms that have been leveled against it: its purported ethnocentricity and inability to handle context, among the many that are impossible to even list, let alone to review.[15]

Brown and Levinson's politeness theory is accused of being derived "directly from the high value based on individualism in Western culture" (Kasper 1990: 252–253). As a result, its claim of universality is cast in doubt. This criticism seems to have originated in Wierzbicka (1985), later followed by many others (chronologically): Wierzbicka (1991); Watts, Ide, and Ehlich (1992a, b); Janney and Arndt (1993); Chen (1996a); Kasper and Blum-Kulka (1993); Liao (1994); Eelen (2001); Locher and Watts (2008); Bousfield (2010); Arundale (2013); Xia and Lan (2019), to name a few. Typically drawing on data from non-English speaking cultures, these studies find that many speech acts are perceived differently on the dimension of politeness in different cultures. For example, an explicit performative is a typical way to give advice in Polish, while a bare imperative is "one of the softer options in issuing directives" (Wierzbicka 1985: 154). Similarly, Chinese speakers view as "polite" those imperatives which are used to make offers (Chen 1996a) and to invite the hearer to dinners (Mao 1992). Since Brown and Levinson categorize imperatives as a Bald on Record strategy, one that is the most imposing, hence most "impolite" – the critics reason – Brown and Levinson's claim of universality fails.

However, it is not at all clear that Brown and Levinson's theory is based on the Western value of individualism, at least explicitly. The authors' notion of negative face is defined as the want of freedom of action, which does seem to be "individualistic". But there is also positive politeness based on positive face: the want to be liked, to be appreciated, and to belong (to a group or community) – the kind of attributes that cannot be categorized as individualistic. Besides, the authors state – and as have been widely acknowledged in the literature – that they have adopted the notion of face in part from Goffman's (1967) work, and Goffman's notion of face comes from Chinese. There is another problem with this critique: If one assumed that individualism is a Western value, she would seem to imply that non-Western peoples do not value the freedom of action.

As for the observation that imperatives may be viewed in some non-Western cultures as polite, Brown and Levinson explicitly list a number of situations in

---

[15] Some detractors of Brown and Levinson's theory have gone as far as suggesting that politeness be gotten rid of altogether. Schneider (2012), for instance, argues that appropriateness is a more "salient notion" (1022) than politeness to capture the kind of linguistic behaviors under investigation, a view that appears to be shared by many in the theoretical orientations of variational pragmatics and relational pragmatics (Arundale 2013; Bousfield 2008, 2010; Bousfield and Locher 2008; Locher and Watts 2008; Watts 2003).

which imperatives can be used as politeness strategies in English as well (Brown and Levinson 1987: 94–101). The first is emergency, where "maximum efficiency is very important, and this is mutually known to both S and H", as seen in (1).

(1) Help!

(2) Watch out!

(3) Your pants are on fire!

(4) Give me the nails.
(Brown and Levinson 1987: 95)

More importantly, some imperatives are "oriented to face": (i) welcomings (or post-greetings), where S insists that H may impose on his negative face; (ii) farewells, where S insists that H may transgress on this positive face by taking his leave; (iii) offers, where S insists that H may impose on S's negative face (Brown and Levinson 1987: 99). The following are some of their examples:

(5) Come in, don't hesitate, I'm not busy.

(6) Don't bother, I'll clean it up.

(7) Leave it to me.

(8) Do come in, I insist, really!
(Brown and Levinson 1987: 99–101)

Assuming that Brown and Levinson's model of politeness is based on Western cultures and a set of predetermined values encapsulated in face, critics further accuse the Brown and Levinson model for being static, ignoring the dynamism of actual discourse and the diversity of discourse contexts. This, as it has turned out, is not a valid criticism either.

In Chapter 1, we discussed Brown and Levinson's formula for calculating the weightiness of the face threat of a speech act: $Wx = D(S,H) + P(H,S) + Rx$. Each of the factors to the right of the equation – the distance between the speaker and hearer, the power the hearer has over the speaker, and the ranking of imposition of the relevant act in a given situation – can be assigned a numerical value based on the specific context in which the analyzed conversation/discourse takes places. Later in the book (182–183), Brown and Levinson present an example for the use of *sir*, a term of deference. In a railway carriage where S and H are both well-dressed adult males, S offers H a sandwich with (9). Example (11) is a far more likely response than (10).

(9) Would you like/care for a sandwich?

(10) ?*Yes/thank you, Sir.

(11) (Oh/Yes) Please/thank you.

Suppose S later finds that his luggage has been moved. The use of *sir* would be appropriate in the following to match the heavily face-threatening context.

(12) A: Did you move my luggage?
B: Yes, sir, I thought perhaps you wouldn't mind and. . .

S can use *sir* to make a request, as in (13a), but not a simple statement meant to establish camaraderie, as in (13b).

(13) a. Excuse me, sir, but would you mind if I close the window?
b. *Goodness, sir, that sunset is amazing.

The use of *sir* in these examples – Brown and Levinson mean to illustrate – is determined by R, the ranking of imposition, as the social distance (D) between the two men (strangers) and the power (P) one has over the other are held constant throughout the train ride.[16] It seems that the more the imposition of the act, the more likely *sir* be used. For us, these examples, albeit fabricated, demonstrate that Brown and Levinson are fully aware of the constant and subtle changes that occur in an actual conversation. More importantly, they demonstrate that Brown and Levinson's model of politeness is capable of handling such changes: each change can be measured by one or a combination of more than one of the three determining factors – D, P, and R.

---

16 One can say that the three factors *interact with* each other dynamically. Take (13) for instance. The imposition in the request as expressed by the *a* version of the pair could be said to lead to a greater power differential, placing the hearer in a position (of power) to grant permission. In contrast, the *b* version of the pair – a commentary about a natural phenomenon – is less imposing, as it functions to reduce the distance between the participants. This observation would seem to be consonant with the spirit – albeit not the letter – of Brown and Levinson (1987).

Despite the many criticisms, Brown and Levinson's theory continues to be the most influential and versatile. To wit, Marsh (2019) uses it to analyze evasive answers to questions. Ghaleb and Rose (2020) use it to examines the apology strategies found in the speech of well-educated native Arabic speakers (Jordanian Arabic speakers) and native Mancunian English speakers (British English speakers). Hu and Chen (2017) use it to analyze backchanneling in Chinese TV talk shows. Larina and Ponton (2020) use it to analyze mitigating strategies utilized in negative recommendations in English and Russian blind peer reviews. Aisulu (2020) uses it to examine how two female Russian-speaking chairs (one of Russian and another of Kazakh origin) perform face-threatening acts of criticisms and directives during teacher meetings at a community college in Kazakhstan. Suau-Jiménez (2020) use it to analyze hotel websites.[17] This paradox – that the most criticized theory is at the same time the most used by practitioners – is indication not only of the theory's utility but also the invalidity of at least some of the criticisms leveled against it.

In the next chapter when we discuss MMP and cross-/intercultural and variational pragmatics, I will revisit the critiques of Brown and Levinson that are pertinent to the theme of that chapter. We now move back to our concern of the current chapter, discussing impoliteness and self-politeness.

3.2 Impoliteness

Culpeper's (1996) model of model of impoliteness is "parallel but opposite to Brown and Levinson's (1987) theory of politeness" (Culpeper 1996: 349), as presented in (14).

(14) *Bald on record impoliteness.* The FTA is performed in a direct, clear, unambiguous and concise way in circumstances where face is not irrelevant or minimized.

---

[17] On January 3, 2021, I searched Linguistics and Language Behavior Abstract (LLBA), a popular database of research among linguists in the U.S. The references cited here are from about two dozen publications using Brown and Levinson's theory to guide their research, more than the publications using other theories that are reviewed in this chapter combined. I also checked the citations of these theories on Google. Brown and Levinson's theory had, by that day, garnered 29,673 citations while the numbers for other theories are in the two- to three-figure range, with the exception of Culpeper's 1996 paper, which had by that day 9,876 citations. Since Culpeper's impoliteness is a spin-off of Brown and Levinson's theory, the endorsement for it implies endorsement for Brown and Levinson as well.

Positive impoliteness. The use of strategies designed to damage the addressee's positive face wants.
Negative impoliteness. The use of strategies designed to damage the addressee's negative face wants.
Sarcasm or mock politeness. The FFA is performed with the use of politeness: strategies that are obviously insincere, and thus remain surface realizations.
Withhold politeness. The absence of politeness work where it would be expected.

(Culpeper 1996: 356, with slight modifications)

Since the publication of Culpeper's (1996) paper, impoliteness research has spurred a great deal of research activity. Bousfield (2008) – possibly the first monograph on the topic – examines impoliteness in a host of situations: car-parking disputes, army and police training, police-public interaction, and kitchen discourse. Other notable works include (chronologically) Bousfield and Locher (2008), a collection of papers with a common thread of the relationship between power and impoliteness; Culpeper (2011), who provides detailed analyses of different kinds of realizations of impoliteness while discussing the various facets of impoliteness; Haugh and Schneider (2012), another collection of papers but with a focus on (im)politeness in Anglo varieties of English; Kádár (2013), in which impoliteness figures prominently in the author's proposal of the ritual theory of pragmatics, and Haugh (2015), who advances his theory of moral order in the analysis of impoliteness. Beyond this partial list of book-length studies, there are hundreds of papers published in journals such as *Journal of Pragmatics, Journal of Politeness Research, Pragmatics, Pragmatics and Society, Pragmatics and Cognition,* and *East Asian Pragmatics* and numerous presentations and talks at conferences.

As expected, the functions of impoliteness have been a favorite topic in the impoliteness literature. Culpeper summarizes impoliteness – in terms of function – into three types: affective impoliteness, coercive impoliteness, and entertaining impoliteness. Affective impoliteness helps the speaker to release/express anger or frustration, e.g., the use of expletives and the cursing of others. Coercive impoliteness refers to cases in which the speaker "seeks a realignment of values" between herself and the hearer so as to enforce or protect her own (Culpeper 2011: 226). Entertaining impoliteness occurs when a speaker uses impoliteness at the expense of a target for entertainment. In those cases, the target as well as the participants have to be aware that the impoliteness involved is not intended.

3.3 Self-politeness

The notion of self-politeness originated in my own work (Chen 2001). Since it will play an important part in our discussion of politeness within the framework of MMP, it is introduced here.

One of the key notions of Brown and Levinson's theory of politeness is the notion of FTAs (face threatening acts), defined as speech acts that threaten face (Goffman 1967, 1979). Brown and Levinson make two distinctions when listing FTAs. The first is the distinction between FTAs that threaten negative face and those that threaten positive face. The second is the distinction between the FTAs that threaten the speaker's face and those that threaten the hearer's face. On Pages 67 to 68, they provide six types of FTAs that threaten the face of the speaker and six types of FTAs that threaten the face of the hearer.

Brown and Levinson further argue that – as can be recalled from Chapter 1 and the last section in the current chapter – since face is important in social life, members of a society will find ways to mitigate the force of the threat of these FTAs. The way to do so is to adopt a strategy from a list of available strategies: without redressive action, baldly, positive politeness, negative politeness, off record, and withhold the FTA. Which of these strategies ends up being chosen depends on the speaker's assessment of the distance between her and the hearer, the perceived power the hearer has over the speaker, and the ranking of imposition (of the FTA) in that culture or in a specific situation.[18]

It is here that one sees a neglect by Brown and Levinson. If the speaker's face can be threatened in the same way a hearer's face can, as Brown and Levinson amply demonstrate, and if a speaker would take care to mitigate such a threat to the hearer's face when it is to be threatened, it stands to reason that a speaker would strive to protect her own face as well when *it* is threatened. Apology may be the best example here: isn't true that we at least sometimes (or rather often) hesitate to apologize? Even when we do, don't we work on how to apologize so that our face is somehow protected (or damaged less than otherwise)?[19] Heritage, Raymond, and Drew (2019) test Goffman's (1974) principle of proportionality – that apologies should be proportional to the offences they are designed to remediate – and found several instances in which the apologizers do less than

---

[18] This formula for the choice of strategy has, in my opinion, been ignored in much of the discussions of theory. If one applies this formula carefully to her analysis of data, one could discover that Brown and Levinson's theory may not be as hopeless as it has been portrayed to be in the handling of specific contexts (Chen, He, and Hu 2013, among many others).
[19] The most telling of all is probably the mantra of "never apologize" of Donald J. Trump, the 45th president of the United States.

the principle of proportionality would predict. One particular person, "Joyce", is the most notable. Her "apology for not going to a meeting is agentless, lacks any form of intensification, and noticeably involves the withholding of an account." With regard to the second virtual offense (not notifying Lesley), "Joyce neither mentions, apologizes, nor accounts for this lapse" (Heritage, Raymond, and Drew 2019: 196). The authors do not propose a reason for Joyce's behaviors, but it seems reasonable to say that her omission of the expected ingredients in an apology – taking responsibility of the wrongdoing and providing an account for it in the first case and her refusal to apologize at all in the second – are motivated by the need to protect her self-face.

In Brown and Levinson (1987), however, the need to protect the face of the speaker disappears immediately after they hint at it, in the entirety of rest of the book, from Page 91 through Page 279. None of the more than 400 examples they use to support their theory has to do with self-face. Brown and Levison's theory of politeness is therefore a theory of other-politeness.

Given the need to account for the many and unavoidable cases of communication in which what one says and how she says it are determined by the desire to mitigate the threat to her own face, a theory of self-politeness was proposed. Self-face is defined as the public image of the speaker. Self-politeness is defined as a set of strategies that a speaker adopts for the purpose of protecting, maintaining, or enhancing her own face, which fall under four board types.

(15) *Superstrategeis of self-politeness*
   a. Baldly
   b. With redress
   c. Off record
   d. Withhold the FTA (to self-face)

3.4 (Im)politeness seen in MMP

Based on the review in the last section, two distinctions have emerged in (im)politeness research: politeness vs. impoliteness and other vs. self. The former set of distinction is based on face: those acts that maintain or enhance face lead to politeness while those that threaten face lead to impoliteness. The latter distinction is based on participants: hearer (other) or speaker (self). So, what started as a single concept – politeness – has evolved into a two-orientation, four-possibility grid of (im)politeness, presented in Figure 3.1.

	POLITENESS	**IMPOLITENESS**
OTHER	1. Other-politeness	3. Other impoliteness
SELF	2. Self-politeness	4. Self-impoliteness

Figure 3.1: Kinds of (im)politeness.

The motivation for (im)politeness is uncontroversially interactional in all relevant theories. Other-politeness, according to Brown and Levinson (1987), is a set of strategies to mitigate the face-threatening force of certain speech acts. In MMP terms, other-politeness is motivated by the consideration to create, maintain, and/or enhance the public image of other (see Figure 2.2). The motivation for self-politeness, according to Chen (2001), is a set of strategies for the benefit of the public image of self. That leaves two types of (im)politeness to account for: other impoliteness and self-impoliteness.

The term "self-impoliteness" is not found in the literature, as it is not easy for one to imagine a speaker deliberately doing things to hurt her image. But we can imagine, at this stage, two broad categories of contexts in which self-impoliteness might arise. The first is coercion. In some cultures (Ran, Zhou, and Kádár 2020), persons can be forced to say things to publicly humiliate themselves. It is not clear whether such unintentional acts of self-impoliteness are indeed acts of self-impoliteness, although intuition seems to point to the negative. After all, speech acts have been assumed to be intentional, and the sense of fairness and justice suggests that we as members of a society should not always be held responsible for what we do under duress. The second possibility of self-impoliteness is the doing of certain self-face threatening acts. Admission of fault, for instance, threatens face of the admitter. But that act itself, like any other act, is complex. An admission of having committed a serious professional error is clearly different from one of having mispunctuated a sentence. Still, it seems justified to speculate that self-impoliteness is motivated by other-politeness, as to apologize benefits the hearer or some other party who has been negatively affected by the relevant act. To admit that I am a bad speller to Pamela whom I have asked to edit the draft of this monograph benefits her public image because her hard work is being tacitly acknowledged and appreciated. Therefore, if a motivation for self-impoliteness is to be proposed within the framework of MMP, it could be the need to benefit other-face.

What motivates other-impoliteness? There seems to have no attempt at addressing the issue. This is a bit unexpected. All theories of politeness in the literature either explicitly state or tacitly assume that to be polite is socially desirable: that it is a *good* thing. For Brown and Levinson (1987), politeness is good because it helps mitigate the face-threatening force of speech acts; for Leech (1983), politeness is good because it saves face for the speaker and hearer and helps Grice out of trouble (providing an explanation for the violation of his maxims); for Fraser (1990), politeness is good because it is a social contract that regulates speakers' behavior; for Spencer-Oatey (2007), politeness is good because it is a tool for the management of rapport; and – finally – for Schneider (2012) and Watts (2003), politeness is good because it is socially appropriate. If politeness is deemed good, impoliteness cannot be viewed as such. In the sense that human action is motivated action, there must exist reasons for speakers to volitionally do what appears to be *not* good.

Within the framework of MMP, it is proposed here (see also Chen 2023) that other-impoliteness is motivated by the interactional motivation to create, maintain, and/or enhance the public image of self. Putting all these together, we end up with Figure 3.2.

(IM)POLITENESS	MOTIVATION
Other-politeness	Creating, maintaining, and/or enhancing public image of other
Self-politeness	Creating, maintaining, and/or enhancing public image of self
Other-impoliteness	Creating, maintaining, and/or enhancing public image of self
Self-impoliteness	Creating, maintaining, and/or enhancing public image of other*

*Tentative, to be verified by future research

Figure 3.2: (Im)politeness and motivations.

Of the four sets of (im)politeness-motivation correspondences in Figure 3.2, the first and the second, about politeness oriented toward other and self, are seen respectively in Brown and Levinson (1987) and Chen (2001). The fourth set, about self-impoliteness, is a tentative postulate due to the absence of studies in self-impoliteness in the literature. The third, about other impoliteness, is explored in the rest of this chapter. However, I will revert to the conventions of the field – considering the fact that self-impoliteness is yet to become a topic of research – abandoning the lexeme *other* from "other-impoliteness", so that we will be speaking of "(other-)politeness", "self-politeness", and "impoliteness".

In the MMP politeness model presented here, the standard wording for the interactional motivations is "creating, maintaining, and/or enhancing public image". We will use the term *benefit* as a coverall term for economy and will use either of the three – "creating," "maintaining", or "enhancing" – when appropriate in a given analysis. Further, these motivations are stated in the affirmative. In the sense that the motivation to do something is synonymous with the motivation not to do its opposite, we will use the term *hurt* as the opposite of *benefit*. Lastly, to bring the model closer to politeness, we use *face* instead of *public image*, assuming synonymity between them. Our tweaking of terminology leads to Figure 3.3.

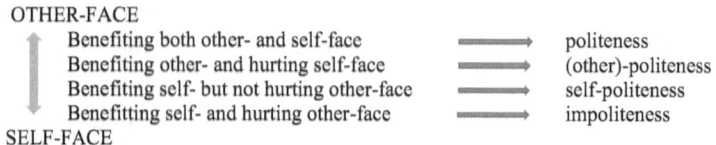

Figure 3.3: (Other)-politeness, self-politeness, and impoliteness.

On the left side of the figure are four types of relationships between other-face and self-face. Each of them leads to (indicated by the horizontal arrow) a particular type of politeness on the righthand side. The first relationship, "benefiting both other-face and self-face",[20] is meant to cover those speech acts that benefit both the self and other. Greeting, thanking, and complimenting are likely candidates that belong here.[21] The doing of these acts therefore leads to politeness (for both other and self). Greeting, for instance, enhances the face of other by indicating that other's presence is important enough to be acknowledged. It, too, benefits the face of self by appearing sensitive to and caring of other's face needs.

The second relationship, "enhancing other-face and hurting self-face", is a bit more complicated. On the one hand, it covers acts such as apology and admission of wrongdoing, which lead to politeness only to other (while being neutral to or hurting self-politeness, depending on context). On the other hand, it covers acts such as showing modesty or self-denigrating that, used in the right context, can lead to both self- and other-politeness. Leech's (1983) Modesty Maxim offers convincing evidence for this, so does the extensive research on compliment and compliment response (Chen 2010a). This ambiguity, expressed by the parenthesis around *other* in *(other)-politeness* on the righthand side, is being tolerated here, as it is not crucial for our subsequent analysis.

The third relationship between other-face and self-face, "benefitting self-face but not hurting other-face", refers to speech acts such as self-promoting and downplaying a wrongdoing. At a job interview, for instance, a candidate would tout her credentials and achievements. Someone talking about the failure of his

---

[20] "Politeness can be a good thing for both simultaneously, and it probably often is", Leech pointed out in 1982 (personal communication).
[21] I am ignoring the possibility that these acts, if not done "properly", may also threaten the hearer's face in some way. Unnecessary thanking may not be welcomed; complimenting someone on something that the complimentee is not proud of can cause discomfort.

business could say "It just did not work out" to (appear to) lay blame on external circumstances. In both cases, self-face is enhanced but not at the expense of other-face. More examples are found in Chen (2001).

Note that none of these three relationships leads to impoliteness. Therefore, I will not dwell further on them. The relevant relationship between other-face and self-face is the fourth in Figure 3.3: "benefitting self-face and hurting other-face". Intentional insult (as opposed to mock insult, which will be discussed in more detail in Section 3.4.4), for example, belittles and denigrates other and, by so doing, elevates self, which is the reason why it is listed in Brown and Levinson (1987) as an act that threatens other-face and is frequently used as an example of impoliteness (Culpeper 1996, 2011). It is on acts of this kind that the present proposal is built.

The rest of this section is divided into four subsections. In Section 3.4.1, I provide a few examples to demonstrate how self-politeness can be seen as a motivating factor for impoliteness. In Section 3.4.2, I discuss cases of impoliteness that have been grouped under the headings "moral order" and "morality". In Section 3.4.3, I turn to institutional impoliteness and entertaining impoliteness, aiming to show that these two types of impoliteness can be accounted for by self-politeness. The same argument is made in Section 3.3.4, that the current proposal is also consistent with the literature on mock impoliteness.

3.4.1 Impoliteness motivated by self-politeness

I have been speaking of the conflict between other-face and self-face as the cause of impoliteness (and the latter being the motivation for the former). However, conflict does not necessarily mean confrontation. Instead, conflict is better seen as the perception of the speaker. This, further, means that an act of impoliteness does not have to be triggered by or into a confrontation. As long as the speaker decides to benefit self-face in a way that will hurt other-face (Figure 3.3), impoliteness will result. So, the five examples discussed below are arranged to represent a full range of possibilities of triggeredness. Specifically, the first two are cases in which there is an obvious trigger for the act of impoliteness. In the next two examples, (20) and (21), the trigger for impoliteness is implicit: it is perceived by the person doing the act of impoliteness (self) but may or may not be intended by her target of impoliteness (other). In the last example, seen in (22), there is no trigger at all. The speaker simply decides to be impolite for reasons not easily discernible.

The first example is about a scuffle between former U.S. President Donald J. Trump on the one hand and the U.S. National Weather Service (NWS) and mainstream media on the other.²² In late August 2019, the southeast coastal states of U.S. were bracing for the upcoming hurricane Dorian. On September 1, Trump tweeted that Alabama would be among the states to be hit. About 20 minutes later, NWS Birmingham tweeted back:

(16) Alabama will NOT see any impacts form #Dorian. We repeat, no impacts from Hurricane #Dorian will be felt across Alabama. The system will remain too far east.²³

By the time of this tweet, Trump had been in office for more than two years. He had made it known that he does not tolerate differences of opinion very well (Chen 2019b). Still, NWS decided to contradict the president – hence hurting his positive face – in broad daylight and emphatically. Note the capitalization of the word *NOT* and the repetition of the assertion that Alabama was not in Dorian's path. The reason for its impoliteness to the president is obvious. As the weather agency in a time of a natural disaster, NWS cannot afford to allow misinformation to affect the life of people in Alabama. It is its obligation to correct the president and to protect its own image, as to maintain an image of credibility is key to what it does for the American public.

The former president was not to be outdone. He fought back, with the following tweet:

(17) . . .when in fact, under certain original scenarios, it was in fact correct that Alabama could have received some "hurt". Always good to be prepared. But the Fake News is only interested in demeaning and belittling. . . Bad people!²⁴

By this point, there was ample evidence that Dorian was never projected to hit Alabama. But to admit that would be an afront to his self-face. So, Trump continued to insist he was right, although in a much toned-down way: Alabama "could have received some 'hurt'" and "under certain original scenarios".

But, apparently, the forced toning-down has to be compensated by the turning-up of attack so as to satisfy his insatiable desire for self-face. So, Trump opens another front in his fight: against the U.S. mainstream media by calling them "Fake News" and "Bad people", although there was no evidence that "Fake News" had anything to do with the original tweet by NWS. The motivation for

---

[22] Chen (2019b), on Trump's (un)presidentialility, offers discussions on a host of aspects of Trump's behavior as president.
[23] https://twitter.com/NWSBirmingham/status/1168179647667814400
[24] https://twitter.com/realdonaldtrump/status/1168664116095082496?lang=fr

this is as clearly oriented toward self-politeness as his insistence on his mistaken assertion about Dorian: he needed to shift the blame to someone else, and the mainstream media, as is well known, has been his favorite – and easy – target. All mainstream media – *The New York Times, Wallstreet Journal, CBS, CNN, NBC, MSNBC* – joined in in the next two days, reporting that there was no evidence for Trump's "Dorian hitting Alabama" prediction.

Finally, on September 4th, 2019,[25] Trump showed a map in the White House (Figure 3.4 below) in front of the White House Press Corp, to support his original tweet about Alabama being in Dorian's path.

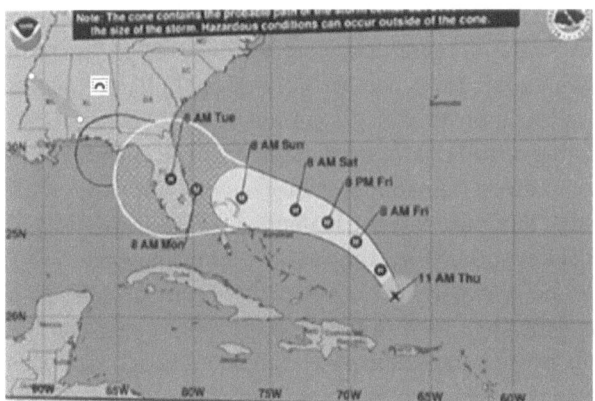

Figure 3.4: Map of Hurricane Dorian.

It did not take long for observers to notice that the dark half-circle that includes Alabama had been added to the original map using a Sharpie,[26] a brand of markers Trump uses as his favorite writing instrument. In one more tweet immediately after, he declares:

(18)   ... I accept Fake News apologies![27]

The series of back-and-forth dueling in the public eye about a relatively insignificant event can be seen as a dueling of self-face, particularly for Trump. His original tweet was mistaken, and he knew it was mistaken. A simple apology would have

---

[25] https://www.youtube.com/watch?v=HXkCZUAv_1A
[26] The incident hence became known as *Sharpie-gate*. https://www.vox.com/policy-and-politics/2019/9/6/20851971/trump-hurricane-dorian-alabama-sharpie-cnn-media
[27] https://twitter.com/realdonaldtrump/status/1169375550806351872?lang=en

put an end to it. But apology to Trump is so self-face threating that "never apologize" is believed to be one of his mantras in life.[28] As he has done for decades, he chose to double down, even doctoring a map. It is therefore fitting that he tweeted (18), suggesting that others should apologize to him instead.

The same is also true on the other side of the Dorian debate. The impoliteness (to Trump) in the NWS's contradicting the president in public and the mainstream media's reporting of the facts were motivated by the respective missions of their profession. For the NWS, that mission is to provide the most accurate information to the public possible. For the media, it is to discover and report facts. Trump's misinformation and attacks ran counter to these missions and would damage the public image – their self-face – they must maintain to do their job.

The second example is similar. It represents what has been called "coercive impoliteness" in the literature (e.g., Culpeper 2011). Coercion, Culpeper quotes Beebe (1995), achieves two kinds of results: "to get power over action (to get someone else to do something or avoid doing something yourself)" and "to get power in conversation (i.e. to do conversational management)" (Culpeper 2011: 227). To these Culpeper adds a third: to achieve a realignment of values (Culpeper 2011: 228). The heart of coercion is, therefore, imposition through power.

Power struggle in a conflict is largely[29] a relative concept. One person's gain is another's loss, which is equivalent to, in terms of politeness, saying that the enhancement of one person's face means damage to another person's face. This is illustrated in many previous works such as Locher (2004), Watts (1991), and Tedeschi and Felson (1994). Example (19) should suffice to show how coercive impoliteness helps the coercer to enhance his self-face.

(19)   A: Which lie are you telling me?
       B: I am not lying, Sir, I am just...
       A: Yes you are. Ran red light, no insurance and not wearing a seat belt. Sign right here. Court date's on the top.
       B: I did not pass the red light. I was holding the brake.
       A: Let me tell you something, (expletive). You cross that white line out there, that's running the red light. You want to argue with me or you want to go to jail.

---

[28] https://www.vox.com/2018/10/30/18037464/trump-rallies-apology-media-mobs
[29] Not always, though, as one can imaging situations whereby both sides of the power conflict "win".

This excerpt is part of an illustration in Culpeper (2011: 230), which records a policeman pulling aside a motorist. In subsequent paragraphs, Culpeper offers a detailed and careful discussion about how coercion takes place as a power play (my paraphrase), which I shall not repeat. What I would like to point out is how the police officer, A, employs obvious – and abusive, as Culpeper observes – impoliteness for the sake of self-politeness. As a police officer, authority is important. To maintain authority entails the putting down of the motorist. Employing an expletive, accusing the motorist of lying, and making allegations of driving offences without giving the motorist the opportunity to defend himself, the police officer is exercising his authority fully. If one has any doubt about his intention to enhance self-face, note his utterance "You want to argue with me or you want to go to jail": his image is being elevated to the level of someone else's imprisonment.

The above two examples are examples of conflict. But self-politeness can cause impoliteness even when there is no apparent conflict between other-face and self-face, as we are to see below.

In (20), B, a Chinese man visiting China after having lived in the U.S. for a long time, meets A, a female acquaintance. After the uncomfortable exchange recorded in (20), a third party broke up the conversation.

(20) A: Haven't seen you for years. You are still so thin!
     B: I know. You are still so fat!
                                    (Translated from Chinese)

I was able to talk to B afterwards. He admitted that A was very likely well-meant. "I understand that in this community, it is still common for speakers to comment on others' looks and body weight, particularly about their thinness, as a sign of showing care for their well-being". However, he said that he had heard one such comment too many on that day and took offence, as he "had grown used to the U.S. culture in which it is a taboo" to do so. He shot back, fully aware that what he said would be construed as "rude". So, the "trigger" for his impoliteness is an innocent expression of concern, but that did not prevent B from being impolite. He did what he did only because he decided to protect his self-face on that particular day.

The fourth example in this section involves even less threat to the self-face of the speaker. At a professional conference, a plenary talk got lukewarm reception. No one in the audience would ask a question or make a comment in the question-and-answer period. The speaker said:

(21) Don't worry. The stuff I've talked about today is new and is not very accessible. You can always contact me later after you've had the time to think more about it or read the paper I have published on the theory [Pointing to the reference of the paper on the screen].

The speaker does a number of things for her self-face. She reemphasizes the newness of her ideas, encourages her audience to contact her (so that she appears to be a congenial and helpful scholar), and promotes her paper one more time. These efforts for the sake of self-politeness, however, led to impoliteness to her audience of more than 200 scholars, a few of them more senior than her, by indicating that her ideas were beyond them.

The next and last example is a slightly alternated version of Kecskes' (2015), Ex. 1.

(22) [At a Chinese airport. A is a waitress. B is a traveler]
    A: Can I get you some more coffee, sir?
    B: Who is stopping you?
    A: You want to stop me?
    B: Oh no, just bring me the damned coffee.

I omit Kecskes' (2015) analysis, as his purpose does not concern us here. What does concern us is why B is repeatedly impolite to someone who is apparently trying to be nice. He could be a rude person – unfortunately there are rude people in our midst – or he could just be in a bad mood. Whatever the reason, the result seems to be the projection of an image of power and superiority. Could that result be the motivation? It is certainly possible, although we do not have conclusive evidence.

3.4.2 MMP and moral order, morality

In this section, I argue that the thesis of this chapter – that impoliteness is motivated by self-politeness – is in full agreement with the notion of moral order and the relationship between impoliteness and morality.

The theoretical construct of moral order (Davis 2008; Haugh 2013, 2015; Kádár and Haugh 2013) proposes that (im)politeness be analyzed based on "evaluative beliefs", which specify behavioral expectations in context. These expectations are grounded (Kádár and Haugh 2013: 94) in social values and beliefs that are, in turn, "dispersed to varying degrees across various kinds of relational networks, ranging from a group of families and friends, to a localized community of practice, through to a larger, much more diffuse societal or cultural group" (Kádár and Haugh 2013: 94).

A host of (im)politeness phenomena have been analyzed within the moral order framework. I will use one example, however, from Parvaresh and Tayebi (2018), to illustrate how the current proposal can provide an adequate explanation for the moral order approach of (im)politeness as well.

Parvaresh and Tayebi (2018) "examine the aggressive comments directed towards the official Facebook page of an Iranian actress, living in exile, after posting a nude photograph of herself" (91). These comments, according to the authors, reflect the commenters' moral order expectations, as seen in the following. The original posts are in Persian. The examples cited here are the translations provided by the authors.

(23) All women have those [breasts] that you are comfortably holding with your hands! But they protect [i.e. cover] them and do not reveal them. What you have done is done only by a few people whom we call whores. Real art is that derived from tact not from the body and sex organs. Other actresses are also artists but they play the roles they have been asked to with dignity and respect, and they also have what you have [i.e. breasts] but do not reveal them. Shame on you!

(Parvaresh and Tayebi 2018: 96)

(24) We should all be afraid of the day [such as today] when nudity equals civility and art. Ms Farahani when you were working in Iran I cried out of love for your beautiful performance in 'M for Mother' which I literally watched 100 times. But you should know that today [i.e. after posting the nude photo] 90% of your fans and followers no longer admire your art but rather are just attracted to you because you've become a whore and they're just curious to watch you. Your art was not like this before.

(Parvaresh and Tayebi 2018: 97)

(25) I pity you! You are no longer an Iranian! You are a traitor to your own country [of birth]! Traitors are not even human...They're not even animals...They're nothing...You are just a petty and weak creature. Do you think God loves you?! This behaviour [posing for a nude photo] would be acceptable from someone born in a different country with a different culture. But what about you? You were born in an Islamic country. [...] Wait to be tortured on the first night in your grave!

(Parvaresh and Tayebi 2018: 98)

Parvaresh and Tayebi's (2018) analysis of these Facebook posts are detailed, which I shall not repeat. The question before us is whether these posts could be seen as self-politeness driven. I argue they are.

What is implied in (23) is the value of keeping one's body private ("All women...protect and cover [their breasts]"); what is expressed in (24) are views of art vs. nudity ("We should all be afraid of the day . . . when nudity equals art"); and what is promoted in (25) is the dignity of the country ("You are a traitor of your own country"). The commentators are openly saying that they are being impolite because the artist has violated the beliefs and values they happen to hold dear. In the parlance of politeness theory, social values undergird a person's face ("public self-image", per Brown and Levinson 1987), which leads to (im) politeness. To state succinctly: the Facebook commentators opt to be impolite to the exiled artist because her posting of a nude photo is seen as a threat to their respective self-politeness, regardless whether that threat was intended or not.

A few more comments offer direct evidence that self-politeness is the reason for the commentator's outbursts.

(26) I pity you.. ... (104)

(27) Why do you have to stain the "face/reputation" of Iranian women? You are a bitch and lack honour. With God's help, these are your last days. There are many (good) people out there who won't let parasites like you stain the good image of chaste and innocent women of Iran. (102).

In (26), the commentator uses the word *pity* as a performative, delivering the act of pitying in the clearest manner.[30] Pitying, as a speech act, displays a moral superiority and elevates self to a higher moral ground and social position. In this sense, it helps the commentator to be self-polite and (other-)impolite at the same time. In (27), the commentator makes explicit reference to "face/reputation". According to Parvaresh and Tayebi (2018: 101, Note 13), the notion that underlies their English rendering of "face/reputation" is *âberu*, which "embodies the image of a person, a family, or a group, particularly as viewed by others in the society". Furthermore, since *âberu* is closely associated with people's sense of public worth and prestige, it should always be maintained and a speaker is expected to "do everything at his/her disposal not to damage" it (Tayebi 2016: 8, cited in Parvaresh and Tayebi 2018: 101, Note 13).

---

[30] This is not the only example in which the commentator "pities" the artist. There are two more examples in which *pity* is used and one example in which *despise* is used.

Note that there is a significant difference between the examples discussed in Section 3.4.1 and those discussed so far in the current section. In the former cases, the speaker and hearer either know each other and/or are face-to-face with each other. It is therefore easy to see how conflict arises due to the differing values, ideologies, personalities, interests, even communicative styles. In the latter cases, the commentators and the artist do not presumably know each other (although the commentators may know *of* the artist, for who, according to Parvaresh and Tayebi (2018), was popular in Iran). Neither were they face-to-face with each other. So, the conflict between the commentators and the artist can only be of values and beliefs, which tend to be strong and stubborn, causing the commentators to virtually "lash out" at a stranger.

Similar to the moral order approach is the discussion of the relationship between impoliteness and morality as seen in intervention (or bystander) implicitness studied by Kádár and colleagues (Kádár and de la Cruz 2015; Kádár and Márquez-Reiter 2015; see also Pizziconi 2012). Example (28) is from Kádár and Márquez-Reiter (2015: 250).

(28) [A couple is arguing in the park. Bystanders overhear the argument but seem conflicted over intervention. An elderly female bystander decides to intervene.]
Boyfriend: Stop crying. Shut up!
Elderly female: Hey buddy! Cool it!
Boyfriend: Ma'am, can you just let us do our own thing? It's my girlfriend. Can you just leave us alone?
Elderly female: No. That's not how to treat someone. How about I call the cops?

To Kádár and colleagues, intervention impoliteness is accounted for by moral alignment. In such a situation, the wrongdoer creates a conflict with the victim. The outspoken person intervenes and hence creates a second conflict, with the wrongdoer, who would "fight back". The back-and-forth exchanges are then seen as attempts for moral alignment. For the outspoken person, she tries to align with the victim and others present (bystanders). For the wrongdoer, he tries to align only with the bystanders.

The current proposal that self-politeness motivates impoliteness is consonant with the view held by Kádár and colleagues. Moral alignment between the intervener and the victim ties them together so that the notion of self includes both. Being a fundamental part of a person's being, morality can create strong bonds among us across chronological, geographical and social boundaries. An animal abused in one part of the world could cause strong indignation in – and possibly action by – animal rights activities in other parts of the world. The actions we take in defense of our morality is hence self-interest driven or, in the parlance of MMP, motivated by self-politeness. This is precisely what is happening in (28). Note that the victim in this case is the girlfriend. When she is told to "shut up" – an act of impoliteness – the morality against bullying is being violated. The elderly female obviously holds that morality dear, to the point of being willing to speak out against the boyfriend. To intervene is therefore to defend a morality that she subscribes to, and the impoliteness that results from the defense is a defense of her self-face, which happens to include the face of the victim.

3.4.3 Institutional impoliteness and entertaining impoliteness

This section attempts to demonstrate that self-politeness also motivates the kind of politeness that has been called "institutional politeness" and "entertaining politeness".

Institutional politeness includes impoliteness found in court (Kasper 1990), political debate,[31] and army recruit training (Harris 2001; Kaul de Marlangeon 2008; Culpeper 2011). The impoliteness in these institutionalized contexts is uncontroversial, as is seen below.

(29) The Government cannot even tell the truth about the duty on a litre of petrol.
(Harris 2001: 459)

(30) You haven't functioned as a human being I doubt since you were about thirteen you stopped being a member of the human race.
(Culpeper 2011: 248)

The utterance in (29) is from the Prime Minister's Question Time in the House of Commons of the British Parliament. Example (30) is said by the training officer of an army recruit training camp. In the former, the speaker accuses the Prime Minister ("The Government") of lying. The latter attacks the very humanity of the recruit. Both exhibit blatant impoliteness.

The key to institutionalized impoliteness is that such impoliteness is sanctioned by the very institution in which it occurs via formal rules (as is the case with the Prime Minister's Question Time, Harris 2001) or based on agreed-upon

---

[31] In the U.S., for instance, the debates by candidates for public offices presume that each candidate defends her views and policies, which necessarily leads to attacking others.

expectations (as is the case with army recruit training). If something is officially sanctioned or universally expected, would that thing be necessary impolite (or *rude*)? The very fact that the term used for this kind of (im)politeness is *impoliteness* suggests that we as students of (im)politeness have already made that judgement. But it is not at all clear if that judgement is valid. I can imagine myself being angry if I were told of (30), believing that the officer was extremely rude on the first day of the training. But would I continue to feel so at the end of the training camp? If I eventually accepted such treatment as normal and for a purpose that I accept, would I still call it "impoliteness?" Similarly, the Prime Minister of Britain gets attacked every time s/he faces the Question Time. Would the Prime Minister feel that her legislative counterparts in the parliament are impolite?

Relevant to the present proposal is the fact that institutionalized impoliteness is motivated by the mission of the institution to create, maintain, and enhance the public image of self. For politicians in contexts like the British Prime Minister Question Time, their mission is to gain advantage for their own party and constituents. At the time of writing this very paragraph (January 2021), the U.S. Congress was in the process of impeaching President Trump for the second time for his role in the January 6 Capitol riot. In the many hearings, the impoliteness readily employed by both sides – for and against impeachment – is not only expected but much needed: the highly consequential constitutional battle cannot be won without taking apart the argument of the opposite side. This applies to the army recruit trainers as well (Example 30), whose purpose it is to instill in the trainees the culture of the military, most notably the importance of discipline and hierarchy. This fact goes well with the thesis I am advancing: if the impoliteness we observe – if it should be called impoliteness at all, see above – is determined by the mission of the institution in which it occurs, then it is motivated by the maintaining of self-face, an important vehicle for the fulfillment of the mission in question. In this sense, institutional impoliteness is required impoliteness.

We move to entertaining impoliteness. Culpeper (2011: 236) demonstrates, with a letter written by a customer to a cable company, how impoliteness can be entertaining. But I use a more obvious type of entertaining impoliteness – late-night talk shows in the U.S. – to demonstrate how self-politeness, too, motivates entertaining impoliteness.

A late-night talk show is generally structured around monologues about the day's news, guest interviews, comedy sketches and music performances. There are dozens of them in the U.S., including "The Daily Show with Trevor Noah", "The Nightly Show with Larry Wilmore", "The Tonight Show Starring Jimmy Fallon", "The Late Show with Stephen Colbert", and "Last Week Tonight with John Oliver". Actual shows can be easily obtained via YouTube.

Much of the humor in these shows comes from impoliteness. The following excerpts, the first three of which are about Thanksgiving 2019 in the U.S., is a sampler:

(31) Even though it's Thanksgiving tomorrow, you can still go to Applebee's, Boston Market and Denny's. It's perfect if you just realized something's not working, like your oven, your stove or your marriage.

(32) Young people prefer Friendsgiving to Thanksgiving. In other words, they prefer fun drunk to angry drunk.

(33) President Trump this afternoon tweeted an image of his head on Sylvester Stallone's body from the movie poster for 'Rocky III.' So he's either trying to tell us how tough he is, or he's trying to explain his extensive brain damage".[32]

(34) [Supposedly talking to Melania Trump – Donald J. Trump's wife] Your unhappiness is obvious. You despise his creepy little monkey hands touching your fingers. . ... No more public embarrassment, no more porn stars, no more stealing your makeup. Toss his boxy clown suits on the front lawn. Just tell him "I'm leaving you with our child". He will be stunned: "We have a child?"[33]

The host of (31) attacks the positive face of all his audience by insinuating that their marriage is "not working". The host of (32) is being impolite to young people as well as Thanksgiving. The host of (33) insults Trump by implying that he has suffered "extensive brain damage". Example (34) makes reference to Trumps' marriage, Trump's alleged affairs with a porn star, the size of his genitals,[34] his not knowing the existence of his own child (which is not true), and Melania Trumps' reported unhappiness. It seems that the hosts of these shows are licensed to attack anyone's face and in any way they please.[35]

It is rather clear that self-politeness is precisely what is behind these acts of impoliteness. These shows, appearing at similar time slots, compete for rating fiercely. Unimpressive rating may lead to the demise of a show. Therefore, much

---

[32] All these three examples are from https://www.nytimes.com/2019/11/28/arts/television/thanksgiving-storm-turkey-trump.html.
[33] https://www.youtube.com/watch?v=2FwQBJIBuCg
[34] In the 2016 U.S. presidential campaign, the size of Trump's hands was a debating point. It provoked a folk belief that the size of a man's hands is indicative of the size of his genitals.
[35] Expletives such as *fuck* and *cunt* are uttered frequently in some of these shows.

rides on the image of each host and, to maintain and enhance that image, the hosts have to utilize everything there is in their toolboxes – and as creatively as possible (Culpeper 2011) – which certainly includes the institutionalized tools of impoliteness.

3.4.4 "Mock impoliteness"

Mock impoliteness refers to the kind of impoliteness "on the surface" because impoliteness is not intended by the speaker (Culpeper 1996: 352, see also Culpeper 2011), such as calling a friend "a son of bitch" as a sign of solidarity and intimacy. Because of the unintendedness of offence and the laugher that such an act often generates, mock impoliteness intersects with humor, banter, joking, irony, and even entertaining impoliteness as discussed above.

But is mock impoliteness impoliteness? Haugh and Bousfield (2012) call mock impoliteness "non-impoliteness", referring to "an 'allowable offence' that is evaluated as neither polite nor impolite, but . . . is closer in some respects, of course, to the latter" (Haugh and Bousfield 2012: 1103). Based on their analyses of attestable data of jocular mockery and jocular abuse, they conclude that mock impoliteness should not be judged on a politeness-impoliteness cline, because it does different things in different discourse contexts and for different participants, particularly in a multi-party interaction (Haugh and Bousfield 2012: 1104). Apparently, their argument caused Culpeper (2012: 1132) to declare that ". . .what we can say for sure is that politeness and impoliteness are not at opposite ends of a unitary scale". In other words, mock impoliteness lies outside the sphere of the notion of (im)politeness.

How is mock impoliteness treated in the current proposal that impoliteness is motivated by self-politeness? In Haugh and Bousfield's study, jocular mockery is considered by participants to be "supportive of their relational connection" (Haugh and Bousfield 2012: 1106). In one example, Participant A was complaining about a barman – who was not present – flirting with a woman costumer while he should be attending others. Participant B thought A's complaining was a bit overdone. Instead of pointing that out straightforwardly, B indicates that the barman's wife be contacted for threat, an apparent sarcasm. Haugh and Bousfield call this "non-impolite".

The MMP explanation for "mock impoliteness" agrees with Haugh and Bousfield's analysis but only partially: that "mock impoliteness" is not only "non-impolite" but *polite*. First, in all the cases of "mock impoliteness" cited in the literature, the speaker's own self-image is not threated. As is seen in Figure 3.3, impoliteness results from the motivation to "Benefit self-face and hurt other-face". If this motivation does not apply, there should not be impoliteness. To further illustrate the point, consider the following examples of "yo momma jokes":

(35) Yo momma is so stupid when an intruder broke into her house, she ran downstairs, dialed 9-1-1 on the microwave, and couldn't find the "CALL" button.

(36) Yo momma is so fat when she sat on Walmart, she lowered the prices.[36]

Such maternal insults typically accuse the hearer's mother of promiscuity, obesity, hairiness, laziness, incest, age, race, poverty, poor hygiene, unattractiveness, homosexuality, or stupidity. Given the widespread social value of filial piety, they are globally and deeply offensive taken at the face value. However, these insults are popular among male secondary school students in many U.S. communities. Instead of being insulting, this verbal trope is a tool for camaraderie, for ingroupness, and for creativity. The underlying assumption seems to be "we are such good friends that even insults targeted at hour mothers stop being insulting." In terms of MMP, when engaged in a "yo momma jokes" taunting match, the speaker is not hurting the hearer's face, hence no impoliteness either intended or received.

The MMP account of "mock impoliteness" departs from Haugh and Bousfield's (2012) analysis in that while Haugh and Bousfield do not see "mock impoliteness" as politeness, MMP does. This is because "mock impoliteness" fulfills the interactional motivation of relationship building, hence create, maintain, or enhance both other-face and self-face, as is verified by the many examples in Haugh and Bousfield (2012) and the "yo momma jokes" cited above.

In some cases, it appears that the speaker in a "mock impoliteness" situation enhances the hearer's face by choosing a less face-threatening utterance from possible alternatives. In Haugh and Bousfield's barman example above, Participant B's annoyance that A is over-complaining could have been done in a number of ways:

(37) Man, you're a whiner.

(38) I am tired of you making a big deal out of nothing.

---

[36] http://www.laughfactory.com/jokes/yo-momma-jokes

By choosing a sarcastic suggestion that B contact the barman's wife, hence appearing to be supportive of B's complaints, A can be said to have taken the least offensive option to mitigate the face threat of the intended speech act.

The same holds for jocular abuse. In one of Haugh and Bousfield's jocular abuse examples, Participant A calls Participant B "you big headed fucking bastard" and B responded, "yeah cos I were" (2012: 1110), accompanied by a lot of jovial laughter from the entire group of participants. Haugh and Bousfield comment that, although *bastard* is ranked high on the severity of offensiveness by Culpeper (2011), the insult it delivers is considered non-impolite as "it is ultimately evaluated as supportive of relational connection between not only David and Simon, but between all of the participants in this gaming group, as they once again reinforce their mutual commitment to not taking themselves too seriously" (1110). If Participant A wanted his utterance to be a sign of group solidarity and shared values, not an insult, and the rest of the group, including the target of the jocular abuse, perceived it as such, then clearly there is no conflict between self-face and other-face. According to MMP as well as Brown and Levinson (1987), these are cases of positive politeness.

The hesitance on the part of Haugh and Bousfield (2012) to deem "mock impoliteness" and "jocular abuse" politeness seems to result from the presumption that these things are impolite in the first place, which, in turn, seems to stem from Culpeper's view that some linguistic units are inherently impolite (e.g., expletives and anatomy-referring words). This is unfortunate. Haugh and Bousfield are among those who champions evaluation of politeness by the common folk and argue against imposition of theoretical constructs on empirical findings. But by assuming that certain things are inherently impolite, they help complicate what appear to be a simple situation. In other words, if we had refrained from deeming things polite or impolite out of context, the notions "mock impoliteness" and "jocular abuse" would not arise. Cases which are thusly called will remain what they are: if used to cause offense, they are impolite; if used to create camaraderie, they are polite.

As indicated earlier, both Culpeper and Haugh and Bousfield propose that, since "mock impoliteness" and the like are either impolite or polite, they are not at opposite ends of a unitary scale (quoted above). The very fact that mock impoliteness can be judged as polite (per Brown and Levinson) in some cases, as impolite in others (as hinted by Haugh and Bousfield), and – possibly – as either polite or impolite in still others suggest that it *should* be studied in terms of (im)politeness. For example, Haugh and Chang (2019) – to be discussed in some detail below – use a five-point Likert scale: *very impolite, impolite, neither impolite nor polite, polite,* and *very polite* in their study of evaluation of politeness. There does not seem to be an obvious reason why mock politeness would lie outside this scale.

By implying that if something is either A or B, it cannot be on the scale of A and B, the authors are saying that A and B are dichotomous, much like complementary notions such as marriage.

By way of summation of the above, we see that the MMP approach to politeness provides a coherent theoretical construct for (im)politeness. With motivation at the center, the four types of (im)politeness seen in Figure 3.3 are linked into a holistic system.

3.5 A note on evaluation studies

Evaluation – the metapragmatic awareness of politeness on the part of real-life speakers – is front and center in current politeness research. In this section, I discuss evaluation to demonstrate the general point that undergirds the proposal of MMP: that evaluation studies, at least as can be gleaned from the literature so far accumulated, have not yielded many insights for our understanding of (im)politeness.

The linguistic background for evaluation, according to Ogiermann and Saloustrou (2020: 3), is Trier's notion of *semantic field* and Jakobson's ([1957]1971) notion of *metalanguage*. It also seems to have a great deal of affinity with Wierzbicka and colleagues' theory of *natural semantic metalanguage* (Wierzbicka 1992, 2003, 2010; Wierzbicka and Goddard 2004). In the field of pragmatics, evaluation coincides with the discursive turn that started in the 1990s and is in full force currently. Culpeper (2011: 254–255) lists a host of factors for the "negative attitude" that defines impoliteness, including expectations, desires, beliefs, rights, power, intentionality, and perspectives. Since any number of these things are relative, particularly in specific discourse contexts in which communication unfolds dynamically and often unpredictably, the judgement of (im)politeness is brought to the fore and has generated a considerable amount of investigative activity (Blitvich and Sifianou 2019; Davies 2018; Eelen 2001; Locher and Watts 2008; Mills 2003; Ning, Kádár and Chen 2020; Ogriermann and Blitvich 2019).

On the one hand, evaluation is essential in the study of (im)politeness. There is little doubt that it is the discourse participants' judgement that counts in meaning making during the dynamic process of communication. Forgetting someone's name, ordinarily, would be considered impolite. However, if Bob, our colleague who we know is suffering considerable short memory loss, asks us to remind him of our names after he comes back from a year-long sabbatical, that would likely not be seen as impolite. To further illustrate the point, I present the following real-life incidence.

(39) [In a restaurant. B is talking and laughing loudly with his fellow dinners. A, sitting at the adjacent table with her friends, calls B out.]
A: Excuse me – do you see there are others in this place?
B: [Realized that he had been too loud]. I am so terribly sorry. I've just gotten a hearing aid [pointing to his right ear] and really did not realize how loud I was. I apologize indeed for being so loud!
A: Sorry – I did not know that. [Appearing embarrassed and trying to recover] Wish you the best with your new gadget.

Being loud in a public place in the U.S. is generally seen as a social transgression and A took offense. She pointed it out at the expense of B's image, only to learn that B was not aware of the assumed transgression, as he was adjusting to the newly-obtained hearing aid. This turn of events made A the "guilty party", showing obvious embarrassment in her voice and demeanor. He had to be comforted by her friends later. Therefore, B's loudness in a public place has to be considered not impolite, and the judgment of that depends crucially on context, particularly on the participants themselves.[37]

There appears to be two types of evaluation studies. The first investigates how speakers evaluate the (im)politeness of a given speech act or scenario. The second seeks speakers' opinions about what (im)politeness means for them. Both kinds reveal the need for caution. I will discuss them below, using Haugh and Chang (2019) as the representative of the former and Ogiermann and Saloustrou (2020) as the representative of the latter.

Haugh and Chang (2019) expand on Chang and Haugh (2011), studying the perception of (im)politeness of an apology for the failure to show up at an arranged dinner in a restaurant. They asked 80 Australian speakers of English residing in Australia (including the 25 in Chang and Haugh 2011) to rank the (im)politeness of the apology on a five-point Likert scale and conducted interviews with 25 carefully selected respondents afterward. Their results show a great variability in the evaluation of (im)politeness ("very impolite" 6.3%, "impolite" 22.5%, "neither impolite nor polite" 40%, "polite" 27.5%, and "very polite" 3.7%) (Haugh and Chang (2019: 211). Of all the factors about the respondents – gender, educational variables, occupation, language backgrounds, and age – only age is shown to be significantly related to the variability of the (im)politeness ranking.

---

37 Also relevant is the discussion of the use of *cunt* by Culpeper (2001: 1116). A young person, who is known to use the word in place of *guy* or *dude* in his own speech community, uses the word in front of a different group who would ordinarily view *cunt* as extremely offensive. How would one evaluate this apparent unintentional behavior? Culpeper's hesitancy to call it straightforwardly impolite is well taken, as he recognizes the unintended nature of the act.

The authors therefore conclude: ". . .evaluations of (im)politeness necessarily involve some form of agency on the part of the evaluator. . ... This agency is exercised in two ways: (1) making different contextual assumptions about the event in question, and (2) drawing on different rationales to ground their respective classifications" (Haugh and Chang 2019: 218). I agree with the authors on these fronts but add one more point: that the findings do not tell us much about how the respondents evaluate. If we use a typical graph to represent the results of the study, we end up with Figure 3.5.

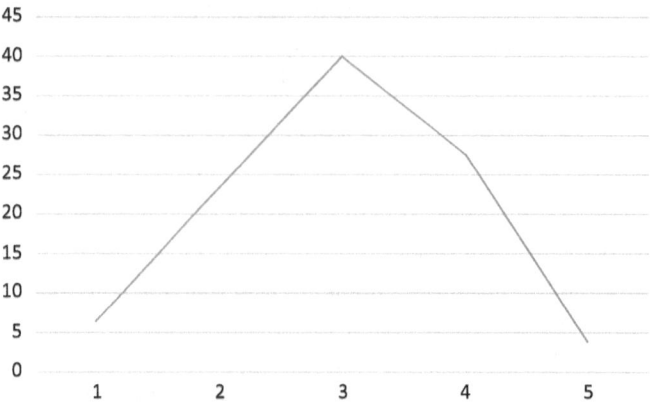

Figure 3.5: Near-bell curve.

Figure 3.5 is close to being a bell curve ("normal distribution"), which means that the participants, as a group, show no opinion about whether the apology is impolite or polite. As cited above, 40% did precisely that, giving the prompt a rating of "3": neither impolite nor polite. Only 3.7% thought it was "very polite" and 6.3%, "very impolite". The study, therefore, reveals very little about what it purports to investigate.

But why? Note that the authors of the study provided to their respondents a scenario without instructions on what *polite* or *impolite* mean. If we, as students of (im)politeness, can agree on anything about (im)politeness, it must be that we do not agree on what it is. If we cannot agree, how can we expect the general public to agree?

The second kind of evaluation studies point to the same direction. Ogiermann and Saloustrou (2020) study the notion of politeness among Greek and U.K. English speakers. They asked respondents in each group (N-100) five questions, three of which are seen below.

(40) a. What other words would you use to describe a polite person?
  b. How would you define politeness?
  c. Can you think of a situation in which somebody behaved in a particularly polite way?

(Ogiermann and Saloustrou 2020: 6)

The most frequent politeness concepts in the British data are (ranked in descending order of frequency: respectful, respectable, respect; well-mannered, (good) manners; considerate, consideration, to consider; kind, kindness; friendly, in a friendly manner; socially savvy, adhering to social norms; saying "please" and "thank you"; thoughtful, thinking of others (before yourself); and nice (Ogiermann and Saloustrou 2020: 8). Those from the Greek data are Βοήθεια, (το) να βοηθάς, προσφορά βοήθειας 'help, helping, offering help'; (Το) να λες ευχαριστώ και παρακαλώ 'saying please and thank you'; Σεβασμός, (το) να σέβεσαι 'respect, respecting'; Το να μιλάς όμορφα 'speaking nicely'; (Το) να χαμογελάς, χαμόγελο 'smiling, smile'; (Το) να ακούς 'listening'; Ηρεμία 'calmness'; Ενδιαφέρον, (το) να ενδιαφέρεσαι 'interest/care/consideration'; and Υποστήριξη, (το) να υποστηρίζεις 'support, supporting' (Ogiermann and Saloustrou 2020: 9).

There are clearly differences between the two groups of corresponds. However, Ogiermann and Saloustrou (2020) discuss several difficulties with such studies. The first is the lack of pattern in the findings so that "it seems tricky to interpret these findings beyond providing a descriptive account" (Ogiermann and Saloustrou 2020: 12). The second is that their findings do not agree – even conflict – with those of other studies in the literature.

The review of these two studies suggests that we need to rethink the purpose of politeness evaluation. The metapragmatic research of (im)politeness have been in existence for more than two decades and what we have discovered shows no patterns but variability. If the decades' work has shown us that there is no agreement on what (im)politeness is across languages (Fukushima 2019; Fukushima and Sifianou 2017; Grainger and Mills 2016; Sifianou 1992; Sifianou and Tzanne 2010), across generations (Bella and Ogiermann 2019) and even across varieties of the same language (Culpeper, O'Driscoll, and Hardaker 2019), then it may be time for us to acknowledge that evaluation studies do not serve a much greater purpose than description, a point that is consonant with Haugh and Chang:

> Moral rationales can be construed in multiple different ways, in part because they are explicated by observers to varying degrees of generality-specificity for particular locally situated purposes, and in part because they are not mutually exclusive. It follows that the rationales provided by observers cannot be used "as is" for typological purposes by analysts. They . . . cannot in themselves stand in place of a theory of (im)politeness.
> (Haugh and Chang (2019: 217)

The findings of evaluation studies, indeed, "cannot in themselves stand in place of a theory of (im) politeness". Furthermore, these studies are typically conducted without an underlying theory for guidance in research design or interpretation of findings. Little wonder that the findings have not proven particularly useful.

    The relevance of these somewhat critical comments on politeness evaluation studies to the present monograph is a philosophical one, i.e., empirical studies are not meant to be mere fact collectors. Facts are interesting so far as they inform us of things beyond the factual. MMP, advanced in this book, is meant to provide a framework that might guide empirical investigations.

Chapter 4
MMP and cross-/intercultural variation

Cross-/intercultural pragmatics came into being right after the inception of pragmatics in the second half of the 20th century. The contributions cross-/intercultural pragmatics has made to pragmatics, to linguistics, to the mutual understanding between peoples, to the teaching of a second or foreign language, and to neighboring fields such as cultural studies and intercultural communication are manifold and profound.

In this chapter, I demonstrate that MMP provides an elegant baseline account for the findings in cross-/intercultural pragmatics by looking at two focused topics. The first is the cross-cultural investigation of the speech acts of compliments and compliment responses. The second is what has been dubbed as the debate on a purported East-West divide.

4.1 Compliments and compliment responses

Cross-/intercultural pragmatics has been carried out on many dimensions of language use, but speech acts have remained the most adopted units of analysis, sparked by the seminal work by Blum-Kulka and colleagues (Blum-Kulka and Olshtain 1984; Blum-Kulka, House, and Kasper 1989). The speech acts that have attracted the greatest attention from practitioners are requests and compliments/compliment responses, followed by apologies and refusals. Compliments and Compliment responses are chosen in this section as an illustration of how MMP can account for cross-/intercultural variations due to the amount of research that have been generated on them and the complexity that has been exhibited in the findings about them.

4.1.1 Survey of research

The interest in compliments and compliment response started with Pomerantz (1978) and has not waned till this day (Danziger 2018; Rodriguez and Fernando 2020). In this section, I provide a detailed survey of this decades-long research tradition, with the aim to show its coverage and complexity.[38]

---

[38] Information in this survey before 2009 is taken from Chen (2010a).

I begin with English. Pomerantz (1978) is the first pragmatic study on complimenting and compliment responding, followed by a series of papers in the 1980s, most of which investigate the two speech acts in the English language spoken in America (Herbert 1986, 1990, 1991; Manes 1983; Manes and Wolfson 1981; Pomerantz 1984; Wolfson 1981, 1983, 1989), South Africa (Herbert 1989; Herbert and Straight 1989), New Zealand (Holmes 1988), and Ireland (Schneider and Schneider 2000).

Complimenting in American English is primarily studied by Manes and Wolfson (Manes 1983; Manes and Wolfson 1981; Wolfson 1981, 1983, 1989; among others). The authors find that, like other well-studied speech acts such as requesting, apologizing, and greeting, complimenting is done through formulaic utterances. Syntactically, English compliments are confined to a small set of structures, most often the NP *is/looks (really) Adj* type (e.g., "Your blouse is/looks (really) beautiful!") and the *I (really) like/love* type (e.g., "I like/love your car"). Lexically, the adjectives used in compliments are mostly *nice, beautiful*, and *good*; the verbs used are primarily *like* and *love*. In addition, the things that compliments are paid on (in the rest of the section, these things will be referred to as the *topics, objects*, or *targets* of compliments) are also predictable, belonging to two broad categories: appearance and/or possession and ability and/or accomplishments. With regard to interlocutors, compliments are paid mostly to people of equal status – colleagues, acquaintances, and casual friends – not nearly as frequently among intimates such as family members. These findings by Manes and Wolfson are later confirmed by Herbert (1986, 1989, 1990, 1991) and have since been used as starting points for research on complimenting in other languages.

These authors also discover a great deal of subtleties in the compliment behavior of Americans. They find, for instance, that while compliments on appearance and possessions can be delivered quite freely, compliments on ability and accomplishments are limited to situations of unequal status and, in these situations, compliments flow from those in higher status to those in lower status, not vice versa, as is commonly assumed (Manes and Wolfson 1981; Wolfson 1989). These findings enable the authors to conclude that the most important function of compliments is to establish and/or enhance solidarity and camaraderie (Manes 1983; see also Herbert 1990).

The relationship between gender on the one hand and the compliment and compliment response behavior on the other is yet another topic of investigation for these pioneer researchers. Manes and Wolfson show that women pay and receive more compliments than men and that women's responses to compliments are more geared towards social harmony than men's. Herbert (1990) is a more focused study on gender-based differences in compliments and compliment responses. He discovers, from his corpus of 1062 compliment events, that men's compliments are twice as likely to be accepted as women's, that women are twice as likely to accept compliments as men, that compliments given by men are far more likely to be met with agreement – particularly by a female responder – and, among all interactional pairs (men-to-men, men-to-women, women-to-women, and women-to-men), men-to-men compliments are the most likely to be met with no acknowledgement (Herbert 1990: 213).

While Wolfson and Manes are credited for their original work on the speech act of complimenting, Pomerantz (1978) is the first study that brings the speech act of compliment responding to the fore of pragmatics. The most notable contribution Pomorantz makes to the field is her recognition of two conflicting constraints on speakers' compliment responding behavior, presented in (1) below:

(1) *Pomerantz's (1978: 81–82) constraints in compliment responses*
   a. Agree with the complimenter
   b. Avoid self-praise

Constraint *a* explains compliment acceptance, often expressed by appreciation tokens (e.g., "Thank you"). Constraint *b* is the motivation for a set of strategies that downgrade the value of the object of the compliment (e.g., "That's a beautiful sweater!" "It keeps out the cold") or to shift the credit away from the responder herself (e.g., "That's a beautiful sweater!" "My best friend gave it to me on my birthday").

These two general principles are the basis for Herbert's (1986) three categories of compliment responses: Agreement, Nonagreement, and Other Interpretations, each of which includes several sub-types. Applying this schema to his corpus of 1062 instances of compliment responses gathered from an American University, Herbert finds that his subjects overly accept compliments 36.35 % of the time (Herbert 1986: 80) and overly disagree with the compliment 9.98 % of the time. The rest of the responses lie in between, belonging to types such as Comment History ("That's a cute shirt". "Every time I wash it the sleeves get more and more stretched out"), Reassignment ("That's a beautiful necklace". "It was my grand-mother's"), Return ("You are funny". "You are a good audience"), and Qualification ("You look good in a moustache". "Yeah, but it itches").

Placencia, Lower, and Powell (2016) examine the responses to compliments made on Facebook (FB) by a group of women within an FB network in the U.S. While these women received 1057 compliments, they produced only 205 responses. Regarding compliments which were responded to, acceptance predominated over rejection, in line with previous work within English-speaking communities discussed above and will be discussed below.

Compliments and compliment responses in English spoken in New Zealand and South America were also investigated. Studying New Zealand English is Holmes (1988), who confirms the formulaic nature of compliments with her corpus of 517 tokens of compliment and compliment response. She proposes a new system for categorizing compliment responding strategies: *Acceptance*, *Rejection*, and *Deflect/Evasion* and finds that New Zealand English speakers accept compliments 61.1 % of the time, reject them 10 % of the time, and deflect/ evade them about 28.8 % of the time. In addition, she is the first researcher to connect complimenting and compliment responding with Brown and Levinson's (1987) and Leech's (1983) respective politeness theories, although no rigorous attempt is made to test the soundness of these theories against her data. Investigations of South African English compliments and compliment responses are Herbert (1989) and Herbert and Straight (1989), both contrastive studies between American English and South African English. Herbert reports significant differences between the two speech communities: White South African English speakers pay compliments less but accept them more than their American counterparts. Herbert and Straight (1989) attribute these differences to the following factors. The first factor is psycholinguistic: the South African compliment behavior is governed by a speaker-based stance – "Don't offer (many) compliments" – whereas the American behavior is governed by a listener-based stance – "Don't accept (many) compliments". The second factor is functional: South Africans use compliments and compliment responses to affirm a confidently assumed social solidarity with their (white, middle-class) status-equals whereas Americans use the two related speech acts to establish, maintain, and otherwise negotiate such solidarity or seeming solidarity.

Lastly, compliment responding in Irish English is investigated by Schneider and Schneider (2000) in a contrastive study among Chinese, American English, German, and Irish English. The authors find that, compared to Americans, Irish speakers of English employ more strategies (15 as opposed to 10 by Americans) and favor compliment rejecting far more than their American counterparts. Based on Chen's (1993a) proposal that compliment rejection is motivated by Leech's (1983) Modesty Maxim and compliment acceptance is motivated by Leech's Agreement Maxim, Schneider and Schneider report that overall compliment responses in Irish English give approximately equal weight to these two maxims (cited in Barron and Schneider 2005: 4), as about 43% of the responses are categorized as Modesty-driven and 57 % as Agreement-driven (cited in Jucker 2009: 21).

Studies on compliment and compliment response in English discussed above led researchers to turn their attention to other European languages: Polish, German, French, Spanish, Icelandic, and Greek.

Complimenting and compliment responding in Polish are studied by Herbert (1991) and Jaworski (1995). Herbert (1991) finds that Polish compliments are very similar to English: they display a very small set of syntactic patterns and semantic formulae, although the exact syntactic structures used differ from those found in English due to typological differences between the two languages. However, while English compliments are more first person-based (e.g., "I like your shoes"), Polish compliments are more second person-based (e.g., *Masz bardzo ładne buty* "You have very pretty shoes"). In addition, Polish compliments are more about possession (49 %) than any other categories of topics, which is a significant departure from what is reported about American English (Wolfson 1981) and New Zealand English (Holmes 1988). Herbert speculates that the focus on possession in Polish compliments is due to the scarcity of material goods Polish speakers faced at the time of his fieldwork – 1983–1988 – when Poland was still under the communist government.

Jaworski (1995) concentrates on the functions of Polish compliments. He distinguishes between two types of solidarity – procedural and relational – and argues that "many Polish compliments which are used in a manipulative or instrumental way are only procedurally solidary but not relational solidary" (Jaworski 1995: 63). Such compliments are often met with suspicion, joking, even sarcasm. Looking deeper, Joworski finds that a compliment often has a next-step function – the complimenter intends her compliment to lead to something beyond the mere praise of the target of the compliment. One such function is to encourage like behavior in the future (e.g., A husband complimenting on his wife's cooking); the other is to lead to the disclosure of information regarding the source of complimented object so that the complimenter can obtain it herself (e.g., compliment on a blouse is often intended to be a trigger for vital information for obtaining one).

We move to German. Golato (2002) focuses on compliment responses in German using data collected from natural interactions in different parts of Germany and compares her findings strategy by strategy with American English compliment responses as reported in Pomerantz (1978) and Herbert and Straight (1989). While the two languages are strikingly similar at the macro-level of comparison – e.g., compliments in both languages are met with frequent acceptance, although no numerical data are provided – they differ in specific strategies speakers use in like situations. To accept a response, for instance, Appreciation Token is a favorite device for Americans but it is non-existent in Golato's German data. Likewise, Americans can express their agreement with a same-strength adjective, but Germans are found, correspondingly, to agree with a compliment via a confirmation marker. Golato (2005) extends her analysis of German compliments and compliment responses further, looking at the position of a compliment in the sequential organization of the conversation in which it occurs. She argues that the placement of a compliment in a larger context is relevant – even crucial at times – to its interpretation. Specifically, compliments can occur in a preferred environment (e.g., after the complimentee has just deprecated herself) or a dispreferred environment (e.g., before a criticism). These two types of context will lead to differences in the face-threatening force the compliments respectively carry.

According to Schneider and Schneider (2000), however, Germans reject compliments significantly more than Americans. In their contrastive study of compliment responses (cited above), they find that close to 40 % of the German responses are motivated by Leech's (1983) Agreement Maxim while only about 24 % of the American responses belong to that category (cited in Jucker 2009: 21). This is in sharp contrast with Golato's findings cited above. Jucker (2009: 22) appears to attribute this discrepancy to the different research methods the respective researchers adopt: Golato uses natural data while Schneider and Schneider use the Discourse Completion Test (DCT).

Wieland (1995) audio-recorded seven dinner conversations among French speakers and advanced learners of French whose native language is (American) English. She finds the assumption that French speakers do not compliment much is not borne out in her data. There are noticeable gender differences in compliment topics and the frequency of compliments: appearance is complimented only between women and more compliments are given by women. As for compliment responses, Wieland claims that responses that agree with the complimentee are rare, as "they violate the law of modesty" (Wieland 1995: 806). So the subjects routinely reject compliments, often prefaced by *non*. In addition, the French speaking subjects use a variety of mitigating devices such minimizing the compliment (Herbert's Scale-Down type) and displacing the compliment (Herbert's Reassignment type).

Spanish, Icelandic, and Greek have received some attention as well. For Spanish, Cordella, Large, and Pardo (1995) collect compliments from spontaneous interactions among Australian English speakers and Australian Spanish speakers who had immigrated to Australia from Uruguay, Chile, and Argentina and analyze their data using the framework from classical studies by Manes and Wolfson. Their findings, first, reveal similarities between the two groups. Both English and Spanish speakers compliment more among females than males and more among friends than among intimates and strangers. For Australian English speakers, Cordella, Large and Pardo (1995: 245) find that speakers under the age of 30 tend to be complimented on their appearance and those above 30, on their skills. There is no reportage of data about the Spanish group on the topics of compliments. Lorenzo-Dus (2001) contrasts compliment responses between British English and Spanish speakers. Using a DCT, Lorenzo-Dus solicits data from students studying at Cardiff University (UK) and Valencia University (Spain).

She finds that both groups reassign compliments on targets such as talent or intelligence to avoid self-praise. She also finds both groups use humor regularly, although English speakers combine humor with various types of agreeing strategies such as Comment Acceptance, History, and Returning. There are also differences: 1) English speakers question the value of compliments more than their Spanish counterparts; 2) Spanish speakers frequently ask for repetition of the compliment, something English speakers are not found to do. In a more resent study, Mir and Cots (2017) find no significant differences between their English and peninsular Spanish subjects. Both groups accept compliments about 48% of the time, evade the about 46%, and reject the about 5% of the time. Maiz-Arevalo (2013), however, reveals deviations from these findings in her Spanish Facebook data, most notably the high no-response rate (30%) and high non-verbal response rate (e.g., smileys, emoticons, onomatopoeia or the "Like" option) rate (41.3%), which the author attributes to "disembodiment" of the online mode of communication.

Rodriguez and Fernando (2020) are the sole study on compliment responses in Icelandic in current literature. Using role-play data, the authors demonstrate that Icelanders prefer non-agreement with the compliments they receive, with a majority of 64% deflating, evading or ignoring compliments.

Investigation of Compliment and compliment responses in Greek was commenced by Sifianou (2001). Based on 450 compliment exchanges collected ethnographically, Sifianou makes several qualitative observations about Greek compliments. First, since compliment is "personal assessment of a situation", it is "likely to be viewed suspiciously as expressing insincere feelings and flattery" (Sifianou 2001: 392–393). This leads to exchanges in which the complimenter provides disclaimers to diminish the possible negative connotation of a compliment ("It's true". "I'm telling the truth"). Second, compliments can be used together with, instead of, or in response to other speech acts such as congratulating ("Well, O.K. you've surpassed everybody, what else can I say?") and thanking ("You are a gem! What would I do without you", said after the complimentee had collected and brought the complimenter's ticket from the agent). Third, Sifianou's Greek data confirms findings in previous studies about gender-differences. Of the 450 compliments, 79 % of them are paid by women and 83 % are received by women. In contrast, only 5 % of these compliments are between men. Besides, compliments paid to women are mostly about appearances while those paid to men are mostly about ability (Sifianou 2001: 401).

Sifianou also finds that Greek compliments are often seen as information seekers, in much the same way as in other languages such as Polish (see above). ("This dress also suits you a lot". "Do you like it? Laura Ashley"). Obviously, to provide information about how to obtain the object of the compliment assumes that the complimenter is interested in the complimented object. Hence Greek speakers may simply offer the object of the compliment to the complimenter. ("Nice brooch!" "Do you like it? Have it").

Lastly, Sifianou reports that although there are a few formulaic utterances Greeks use to pay "routine" compliments – compliments resulting from social obligations to say something nice to an acquaintance or friend – Greek complimenting displays an array of creative utterances in non-routine, unexpected situations. The following is a sampler from Sifianou's data, with the author's original Greek orthography omitted:

(2) A: My dear mother, I split up with Alexander.
    B: So what? A doll like you will find a thousand like him and even better (ones).

(Sifianou 2001: 418)

(3) A: Have I ever told you that you are the best (thing) that has ever happened in my life?
    B: Only when you want to ask for a favor.
    A: And the most witty?
    B: Come on tell me more. I like it.

(Sifianou 2001: 422)

Traveling to Asia, we find that Chinese is among the best (if not the best) studied language(s) in compliments and compliment responses.

Chen (1993a), the first study on the subject, uses the DCT method to collect data from college students in Missouri, USA and Xi'an, China. The results about American compliment responses confirm previous studies on American English (Herbert 1986, 1989) and New Zealand English (Holmes 1988) – that Americans accept compliments outright 39 % of the time, return them 18 % of the time, deflect/evade them 29 % of the time, and reject them 13 % of the time. The findings about the Chinese compliment responses are drastically different: Chinese reject compliment 95 % of the time, accept them 1 % of the time, and deflect/evade them 3 % of the time. In terms of theoretical framework, Chen (1993a) represents the first serious attempt to use politeness theories to inform the study of complimenting and compliment responding (cf. Holmes 1988). Brown and Levinson's (1987) theory of politeness, Leech's (1983) Politeness Principle, and Gu's (1990) notion of Chinese politeness are then applied to the findings strategy by strategy. Brown and Levinson's theory is found to explain only the American data, Gu's only the Chinese data, and Leech's Agreement Maxim explains the American data and his Modesty Maxim explains the Chinese data.

Since Chen (1993a), studies on Chinese complimenting and compliment responding flourished. These studies cover a wide variety of Chinese populations – Mainland Chinese, Hong Kong Chinese, Taiwanese Chinese, Chinese residing in America, Australia, and the United Kingdom, as well as Chinese immigrants in America (Fong 1998) – and an equally wide range of facets of the speech acts of complimenting and compliment responding.

About compliments, these studies show that Chinese compliments are also formulaic, although the structures of actual utterances are different from those found in other languages. Recall that Wolfson's (1981) identifies three syntactic structures that account for 85 % of her American English data, Yuan (2002: 207) finds that four structures account for 94 % of her Chinese data. Ye (1995) shows similar results, although there is a noticeable difference in the percentage of verbs used between the Chinese data (2.3 %) and Wolfson's American English data (16 %). With regard to compliment topics, both Ye (1995) and Yuan (2002) identify ability/accomplishments (which Ye calls "performance") as the most preferred for their respective subjects. Yuan (2002), furthermore, discovers that child is also a frequent compliment topic in her corpus (18.36 %), a topic that does not seem to have appeared in compliments in any other language.

However, it is the findings about compliment responses in Chinese that have turned out to be the most fascinating, as results by researchers have varied considerably. Table 4.1 is a tabulation of those studies that have provided quantitative data on the frequency of occurrence of compliment response types: Chen (1993a) on Xi'an Chinese; Loh (1993) on Hong Kong Chinese (quoted in Spencer-Oatey and Ng 2001); Schneider and Schneider (2000, cited in Jucker 2009), who do not reveal where their subjects were from; Yuan (2002) on Kunming (Mainland China) Chinese; Yu (2004) on Taiwanese Chinese; and Tang and Zhang (2009) on Chinese residing in Australia. Because the taxonomy each author uses differs from the next, it is difficult to compare their findings accurately. However, since Chen's (1993a) finding that Chinese compliments are characterized by rejection has been used as a baseline by all other studies, I extracted two types of compliment responses from these studies – acceptance and rejection – for comparison purposes. Those compliments that do not belong to either of the two are left out. In addition, Yuan (2002) uses a triangulation of data colleting methods – DCT, natural conversation, and interview – and reports the DCT and natural data separately. Hence there are two rows presenting her study. In addition, Chen and Yang (2010) is a replication of Chen (1993a). It will be discussed in detail in the next chapter, on diachronic pragmatics.

Table 4.1 shows remarkable variability among the different groups of Chinese in their compliment responding behavior. The column on acceptance, for instance, ranges from 1% to roughly 62%. The column on rejection varies from 24% to 95%.

Table 4.1: Chinese compliment acceptance and rejection.

	Subjects	Acceptance	Rejection
Chen (1993a)	Mainland Chinese (Xi'an)	1.03	95
Loh (1993)	HK Chinese in Britain	41	22
Schneider & Schneider (2000)	Unknown	20	80
Yuan (2002) DCT	Mainland Chinese (Kunming)	7.00	28.93
Yuan (2002) Natural	Mainland Chinese (Kunming)	15.63	33.98
Yu (2004)	Taiwanese Chinese	13	24
Tang and Zhang (2008)	Chinese in Australia	49	38
Chen and Yang (2010)	Xi'an Chinese	62.6	9.13

There are two more studies that add to the complexity of the Chinese compliment responding picture: Rose and Ng (1999) and Spencer-Oatey and Ng (2001). Rose and Ng have Cantonese subjects studying in Hong Kong rate compliment responses belonging to the three broad categories: Accepting, Deflecting(/Evading), and Rejecting on a 1–4 scale, with "1" being the most preferred and "4" the least preferred. The mean for accepting is 1.79; the mean for deflecting is 2.24; and the mean for rejecting is 2.25. Spencer-Oatey and Ng, likewise, have Shanghai and Guilin (both Mainland) Chinese and Hong Kong Chinese evaluate acceptance and rejection responses on a 5-point Likert-type scale in terms of appropriateness, conceit, and impression conveyed (favorable/bad). They find, first, that mainland Chinese and Hong Kong Chinese evaluate acceptance responses in similar ways but their respective evaluations of rejection responses are significantly different, with the Hong Kong group finding rejection responses more acceptable than their main-land counterparts. Second, both groups rate acceptance responses as more preferred than rejection responses. "Agree", an acceptance strategy, for instance, produced a mean of 3.6 on appropriateness, a mean of 3.5 for impression (clearly towards the "favorable" end of the scale), but a mean of 3.23 for conceit, the lowest of the three sets of scores. "Disagree", on the other hand, generated the highest score on conceit and the lowest on appropriateness.

Putting these two studies together with those presented in Table 4.1, we find that the compliment responding behavior of Chinese differs drastically from group to group. The differences among the findings of these studies beg for explanation and explanations, at this stage, seem hard to come by. Geographical region and contact with Western cultures are obvious possible reasons, both of which have been suggested (Spencer-Oatey and Ng 2001: 193–195; Yuan 2002: 214–215).

While the Chinese language has taken the center stage in compliment and compliment response research, a few other Asian languages have also received attention: Japanese, Korean, and Thai. Research on these languages is discussed below.

The first work on Japanese compliment responses published in English is Daikuhara (1986). Using naturalistic data collected from Japanese who had resided in America for less than two years, Daihuhara finds that her subjects compliment frequently on appearance and abilities, much like Americans. But the similarity between the two languages stops here. While compliments in English have been treated as a means of building solidarity by Pomerantz, Wolfson, and Manes, compliments in Japanese function to show respect and deference. The showing of respect and deference in turn creates distance, which in turn leads to denial of compliments by the complimentee. This is claimed by Daikuhara to be the reason for her findings that Japanese favor compliment rejection: 95 % of the responses in the author's data are self-praise avoidance (Pomerantz 1978) utterances and only 5 % are appreciation tokens. Of the 95 % compliments that help the responder to avoid self-praise, 35 % are flat-out rejections, characterized by utterances such as "No, No" or "That's not true".

The next notable work on Japanese compliment responses is Saito and Beecken (1997). The authors used role play to collect compliment response data from 10 Japanese speakers, 10 American English speakers, and 10 Americans learning Japanese in America, with the aim to study transfer of compliment responding strategies from English to Japanese. As can be gleaned from their tabulation (Saito and Beecken 1997: 369), the Japanese speakers in the study accept compliments (which the authors term "positive") about 57% of the time, reject them (the authors' "negative" category) 15% of the time, and deflect/evade them (the authors' "avoidance" category) 28% of the time. Compared to Daikuhara (1986), Saito and Beecken (1997) thus paint a very different picture of Japanese compliment responses. But the authors do not discuss possible reasons for this obvious discrepancy. They only cite Yokota's (1986) findings that 21 % of the responses fall under Acceptance, 20 % of the responses fall under Rejection, and 59 % under Deflection/Evasion to demonstrate the complexity of the issue.

Compliments and compliment responses in Korean are studied by Han (1992) and those in Thai are studied by Cedar (2006) and Gajaseni (1995). Han (1992) collected data from real-life conversations by 10 Korean female students studying in America and conducted interviews with them afterwards. Statistically, Han's subjects are found to accept compliment 20 % of the time, reject them 45 % of the time, and deflect/evade them 35% of the time. These percentages bear much resemblance to the many studies on Chinese compliment responding, as cited above, and Daikuhara's (1986) study on Japanese compliment responding, in that rejection, although differing widely among these studies, seem to be a key feature in compliment responses in these three East Asian languages.

Working on compliment responses in Thai, Gajaseni (1995) used a DCT to solicit oral data from 40 Americans (students at University of Illinois, Urbana-Champaign) and 40 Thais (three universities in Bangkok, Thailand). There were 20 males and 20 females in each population. She finds compliment acceptance to be the most preferred strategy for both Americans and Thais, although more for the former than the latter. Likewise, compliment rejection is the least preferred for both subject groups, although Americans reject less than Thais. In terms of the relationship between the complimenter and the complimentee, Gajaseni discovers that the direction of a compliment is a factor in both American English and Thai: a compliment that flows from someone in higher social status to someone in lower status is more likely to be accepted while a compliment that flows in the opposite direction is more likely to be rejected. This difference, however, is more pronounced in the authors' Thai data than American data.

The last group of languages in which compliments and compliment responses have been investigated are those spoken in the Middle East: Turkish, Persian, Israeli Hebrew, and Arabic.

Ruhi (2006)'s study of Turkish compliment responses is based on 830 naturally occurring compliment exchanges. Her subjects are found to accept compliments 61% of the time, reject them 23% of the time, and deflect/evade them 16 % of the time. Following Chen (1993a), Ruhi subjects Leech's (1983) Politeness Principle and Brown and Levinson's (1987) theory of politeness to a rigorous application to her data. Recall that Chen finds Brown and Levinson cannot explain his Chinese data, so does Ruhi, finding Brown and Levinson wanting as an explanatory tool for Turkish compliment responses. Differing from Chen (1993a), who finds Leech's Agreement Maxim sufficient for accounting for American English compliment responses and his Modesty Maxim sufficient for accounting for Chinese compliment responses, Ruhi finds Leech equally wanting. For instance, the strategy of Upgrading, whereby the responder increases the complimentary force of the compliment, cannot be adequately explained by either the Agreement or the Modesty Maxim. Likewise, Leech's theory would be hard pressed to explain some rejecting strategies that border on impoliteness, as seen in the following exchange (Ruhi's original Turkish orthography is omitted):

(4) A: Your eyes look so much like F's. (F: a famous pop star)
    B: You can't be serious.
    A: Why?
    B: Because I hate them that's why.

(Ruhi 2006: 70)

B's second utterance is clearly impolite as it threatens A's positive face per Brown and Levinson. Neither does it fit Leech's Agreement Maxim nor his Modesty Maxim. Based on examples like this, Ruhi proposes a construct of self-politeness (see also Ruhi 2007), which draws on Chen (2001). She then applies the three superstrategies of self-politeness – Display Confidence, Display Individuality, Display Impoliteness – to the compliment responses in her data to demonstrate that self-politeness has greater explanatory power than classical politeness theories for explaining compliment responses in Turkish.

Persian is studied by Sharifian (2005, 2008), from the perspective of cultural schemas, defined as "conceptualizations that act as dynamic templates in people's interaction with others and with the external world". These schemas "emerge as the group's collective knowledge and thought" after repeated and shared experience in relevant social contexts (Sharifian 2005: 338). The specific schema for accounting for Persian compliment responses is *shekastehnafsi*, "broken-self", literally glossed as "self-breaking" or "doing self-broken" and approximately meaning "modesty" or "humility" (Sharifian 2005: 342–343). This schema motivates Persian speakers to respond to compliments in various ways – and oftenfro in ways different from Australian English speakers in the author's data – such as downplaying the compliment, elevating the complimenter, and reassigning the credit. The following three examples illustrate these types of responses respectively and in that order (AES=Australian English speaker; PS=Persian Speaker):

(5) (Your friends praises your child by saying "you have a very smart child".)
 AES: And he's nice as well, thanks.
 PS: *loft daarin bacheyeh aziat kono sheitunieh*
  'You are kind (to say that) (but he) is troublesome and mischievous'.

(6) (A family friend compliments your cooking after dinner by saying "Your food is so delicious. You're a fantastic cook!")
 AES: Thank you.
 PS: *vali beh paayeh dast pokhteh shomaa nemireseh.*
  'But not as good as yours'.

(7) (You have received a prize for your outstanding work and your mother says to you, "congratulations! Well done!")
 AES: I know mum, I'm a champ, check me out!
 PS: *Maamaan in jaayezeh moto'alegh be shomaast*
  'Mum, this prize belongs to you'.

Eslami, Jabbari, and Kuo (2015) study compliment responses on Facebook by Persian-speaking Iranians. Just as does Maiz-Arevalo (2013), cited above, the authors find no-response to be the most frequent. Further, compared to face-to-face interaction, fewer complimentees on Facebook evade and reject compliments. This leads the authors to conclude that the cultural schema of *shekastehnafsi*, that "motivates the speakers to negate or scale down compliments, downplay their talents, skills, achievements, etc., and return the compliment to the complimenter" (Sharifian, 2008: 55) is not "materialized when responding to compliments online" Eslami Jabbari, and Kuo (2015: 273).

Israeli Hebrew is investigated by Danziger (2018). Using DCT data, Danziger finds that Hebrew speakers accept compliments most and that the object of the compliment has the most influence on the choice of responding strategies, with "external compliments" (appearance, performances, and possession) more welcomed than "internal compliments" (physical appearance, talent, and personality).

Lastly, different varieties of the Arabic language have been investigated for their respective pragmatics of complimenting and compliment responding: Jordanian Arabic by Farghal and Al-Khatib (2001) and by Mohammad, Norsimah, and Khazriyati (2016); Egyptian Arabic by Morsy (1992), Nelson, El Bakary, and Al-Batal (1993), and Mursy and Wilson (2001); and Syrian Arabic by Nelson, Al-Batal, and Echols (1996). The findings of these studies have revealed two important features of complimenting and compliment responding in the language. First, Arabic speakers favor acceptance the most when they respond to compliments, more so than American English speakers. Using data gathered via interviews conducted in America and Syria (whereby subjects were paid unexpected compliments), Nelson, Al-Batal, and Echols (1996), for example, find that 50% of the compliment responses by American English speakers belong to acceptance, 45% to mitigation, and 0.3 % of them belong to the category of rejection. Their Syrian subjects, on the other hand, accept compliments 67% of the time, mitigate them 33% of the time, and there are no instances of rejection. Similarly, Morsy's (1992) Egyptian subjects accept compliments 72% of the time, deflect them 20% of the time, and reject them 8% of the time. Farghal and Al-Khatib's (2001) Jordanian subjects display analogous behavior: they accept compliments 84% of the time. The percentages of the rest, non-acceptance responses are difficult to discern, as they are lumped together under a category of "Downgrading", which include instances of deflecting/evading as well as instances of rejecting.

The second notable feature of Arabic compliment responses is the strategy of "offering", as is seen in (8):

(8) (Responding to a compliment on necklace)
Shukran ruuHu' m'addam, maa b-yighla 'aleeki shu
'Thank you my dear [It is] presented [to you]. Nothing can be too precious for you'.
(Adapted from Nelson, Al Batal, and Echols 1996: 425, Example 20).

The offering of the compliment object, however, is only "lip service" (Farghal and Haggan 2006: 102) – the responder does not intend to "present" it to the complimentee, neither does the complimentee take the offer seriously. This is in part seen in the formulaic nature of the utterances speakers use to make the offer: *m'addam* 'I proffer it to you', as is the case in (8); *halaalic˘* 'It's all yours'; or *mayiëla 'aleec˘* 'You are worth it' (Farghal and Haggan 2006: 102).

4.1.2 MMP and compliments/compliment responses

The survey of the research on compliments and compliment responses in the last section demonstrates the complexity of the speech acts involved. After almost more than four decades of sustained efforts (if we count Pomerantz 1978 as the commencement of this long research endeavor), we have looked at myriad dimensions of compliments and compliment responses. About compliments, we have looked at their structural properties and their objects, the frequency of compliment received by men vs. women, and the relationship between the object of compliment and the sex of the complimentee. About compliment responses, we have looked at their functions from a variety of angles; we have tried to make sense of our respective findings in different ways; and we have examined the sociocultural factors that might affect the strategies that a complimentee adopts in a given situation. In terms of representation, our research has covered more than two dozen languages from four major regions: Asia, America, Europe, and the Middle East, making compliment and compliment response research possibly the most representative strand in pragmatics. On the one hand, we can say we know a lot about compliments and compliment responses. On the other hand, what we do know is messy and at times conflicting. Below, I argue that this "messiness" can be both accounted for and sorted out by MMP.

First, about compliments. we can say that complimenting is a speech act motivated by the interactional motivation. A compliment typically does not have "useful" information to convey but to play into the hearer's interactional need to to have her public image enhanced. This explains the choice of what to compliment about: appearance, possession, ability, and accomplishment: things that are intimate and which members of a society tend to take pride in. In the parlance of MMP, these things are generally – if not universally – shared components of public image. In this sense, compliment goes to the heart of that interactional need to establish, maintain, and enhance public image by essentially saying to the hearer that "I know you like your looks, possessions, abilities, and accomplishments – or anything else about you. So I will say things to indicate my liking of these things via a compliment". It also provides a reason for variation: since one expects the content of public image to differ on various dimensions, one can expect that a particular thing be complimented about in one culture more than others, on one occasion more than others, and to one person more than others, as clearly demonstrated in the studies discussed above.

The importance of the interactional motivation for compliments is also seen in the limited number of syntactic structures and lexical items used for complimenting across languages, although languages differ in the kind of structure and lexical item they respectively choose due to typological reasons. This formulaic nature is significant, as it suggests a conventionalization of the complimenting and compliment responding practices. For conventionalization can only come through repeated use, and repeated use is sure evidence for the entrenchedness of the meanings they express.

In the survey above, we saw that gender difference in compliments has been investigated in several studies. A pattern seems to have emerged: women are found to be complimented more on appearance (looks and attire) while men, more on accomplishments and ability. Also, women are found to pay compliments more but receive compliment less. The possibility of gender-bias that underlie these behaviors aside, these differences reflect the different content of public image in a culture. Compliments on appearance to women, for instance, could be motivated by the (surely sexist) assumption that appearance is an important component of the public image of them.

The job of the complimentee to respond to a compliment, however, has turned out to be considerably less straightforward than that of the complimenter. A compliment is a semantic proposition that involves a positive evaluation. A complimentee is bound to address that proposition in her response based on Grice's Cooperative Principle. However, the truth conditions of a compliment are often difficult to verify. When I say "You look fantastic in that new sweater" or "That was a smart representation", whether you look "fantastic" or your presentation was "smart" is difficult to measure, as an evaluation of the kind is necessarily subjective. That leads to the possibility that I was "just saying it" to make you feel good and, on rare occasions, the possibility that I am engaged in flattery. This explains why affirmation (e.g., "Really?") and expressing doubt (e.g., "I thought the presentation could be better in some ways") are found in many cultures in the survey above.

The complimentee is thusly placed in a bind. To agree with the complimenter upholds her public image, seemingly affirming her sense of judgment. At the same time, however, it indicates that the complimentee is taking what may be a social nicety as true, going against the notion of humility and modesty, a value built in the public image of many cultures (Brown and Levison 1987; Chen 2020; Gu 1990; Leech 1983). To reject the compliment, on the other hand, would benefit her own public image by appearing modest but will run the risk of hurting the complimentee's desire to be agreed with. In Chapter 1, we discussed the possible conflict between other-public image and self-public image. Compliment responses are an example of that conflict. Speakers make different choices in a conflict, and the findings of the studies surveyed above shows many such choices.

In the above survey, we observed that, while the taxonomies of compliment responses differ widely from researcher to researcher, a pattern seems to have emerged. Recall Pomerantz's (1978) two constraints on compliment responding: agree with the complimenter and avoid self-praise. Herbert (1986) develops a 12-type classification and Chen (1993a) devises another set of strategies. However, Holmes' (1988) three-pronged system – Acceptance, Deflection/Evasion, and Rejection – which is also endorsed by Chen (1993a) and Chen and Yang (2010) – seems to have been well-received by scholars in the next two decades, as shown by the many references cited above. These three major strategies, upon closer examination, can be nicely mapped with the two interactional motivations: to benefit the public image of other and to benefit the public image of self (Figure 2.2). This mapping is schematized in Figure 4.1, in which the arrows are read as "motivated by".

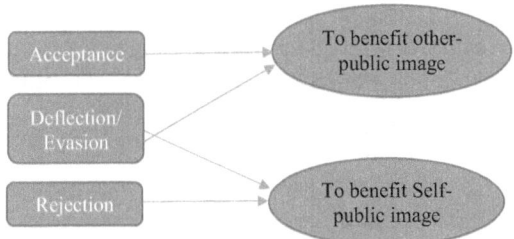

Figure 4.1: Compliment responding strategies and interactional motivations.

Obviously, Acceptance, Deflection/Evasion, and Rejection are umbrella terms, under each of which is a long list of substrategies, as can be seen in (9).

(9) *Acceptance*: thanking and agreeing with the complimentee, returning compliment ("You look nice, too"), offering the object of compliment to the complimenter "(It's yours now")
Deflection/Evasion: Giving credit to others ("I got it from my mom"), downplaying ("It is Okay"), attributing to hard work ("I spent three whole nights on that presentation"), doubting sincerity ("Really? I did not expect you would like it"), joking ("What do you want from me today?")
Rejection: disagreeing ("I don't think so"; "Not really"), rejecting outright ("No. I look really awful")

The studies that categorize compliment responding strategies in this three-part framework show more strategies for the Deflection/Evasion group, which finding is explained by the fact that Deflection/Evasion is an in-between category, akin to the region in the middle of a continuum. This region provides space for complimentees to maneuver, many of whom end up "hitting two birds with one stone": combining several strategies into one response. In addition, this in-between region also provides room for the complimentee to display creativity, again as shown above.

The conclusion summarized into Figure 4.1 is also supported by findings about compliment responses in computer-mediated communication. Three such studies on Facebook compliment responses were discussed above: Placencia, Lower, and Powell (2016) on American English, Eslami, Jabbari, and Kuo (2015) on Persian, and Maiz-Arevalo (2013) on Spanish. Two pattens are found in them: that a large number of compliments are unresponded to and – among those that are – there are less deflections/evasions and rejections than in face-to-face communication. These patterns fit the MMP framework well. The absence of face-to-face interaction on Facebook means that the complimentee is relieved from the pressure of having to respond and, if she chooses to respond, which could happen much later in time, from the pressure of maintaining the self-image of humility and modesty.

Applying MMP to compliment responses also reveals the pros and cons of different data collecting methods. Clark and Bangerter (2004) classify data used in pragmatics into three kinds: intuited, natural (e.g., collected via the ethnographic approach), and laboratory (artificially designed methods such as the DCT and role-play). Jucker (2009) offers a detailed analysis of the advantages and disadvantages of each. Of all the studies cited above, Golato's work (2002) work on German and Yuan's (2002) work on Chinese are notable for their natural data. One of their findings that cannot be gained via a laboratory approach is that complimentees often do not just do one thing – accepting, deflecting/evading, or rejecting – in a response. A natural response tends to be longer than the designed choices in a DCT and often does more than one thing. It can accept a compliment and then evade/deflect it by various means. In rare cases, a natural response can accept a compliment and then immediately reject it "I like it too and I really appreciate it, but . . . well. . . on second thought, I could have done better. I was under pressure to turn it in before the due date". This type of natural data further indicates the "pull" of the two international motivations in opposite directions.

Based on the Acceptance-Deflection/Evasion-Rejection classification of compliment responses (Figure 4.1), we seem to be in a position to measure languages in terms of their pragmatics towards compliments. As the above survey shows, Arabic speakers accept compliments the most, followed by English speakers in South African, America, and New Zealand. Then come non-English European languages such as Germany and Spanish, with the possible exception of French (Wieland 1995). In the middle is Irish English, Persian, and possibly Icelandic. Turkish and East Asian languages – Chinese, Japanese, and Korea – seem to cluster together towards the rejection end of the scale. Obviously, this is a very crude comparison that should only be used for observations at the highest level of generalization.

Then we seem able to have a bird's-eye view of the behaviors in compliments and compliment responses summarized in Figure 4.2.

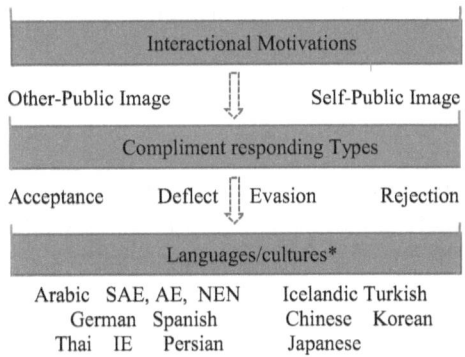

*Notes: Positioning of languages not meant to be accurate
  SAE: South African English
  AE: American English
  NEN: New England English
  IE: Irish English

Figure 4.2: Motivation, strategy, and language.

There are three continuums in the Figure. The top presents the two interactional motivations: the need to benefit other-public image and the need to benefit self-public image. In the middle is the region representing the many possibilities of both other-image and self-image being relevant in a given context. The second continuum is the three types of strategies that have been found in the literature on compliments and compliment responses. In the third continuum are placed languages and cultures. The three continuums are "mapped" with each other so that they form a parallel relationship: the strategy continuum is a linguistic realization of motivations; the languages/cultures continuum lists language/cultures according to the strategies they are found to favor.

To summarize this section: a detailed survey of research on compliments and compliment responses was first provided. MMP was then applied to the findings. The result shows that MMP can account for the complimenting and compliment responding behaviors at the highest level of generalization while allowing for the subtleties in these behaviors to fall in their proper places.

4.2 MMP and the East-West Divide

This section continues the discussion on cross-/intercultural pragmatics within the framework of MMP. The focus is on what has been dubbed the West-West divide, a divide between Western European languages, particularly English, and East Asian languages. I will first summarize research on the topic and then discuss how this lively debate can be cast in the framework of MMP.

4.2.1 Setting the scene

As is clear from the last section on compliments and compliment responses, the late 1980s saw concerted efforts by students of pragmatics to investigate language use in non-Western languages. The investigation of language use in Middle Eastern languages, for instance, have made strides: Persian by Eslami (2005) and Sharifian (2008); Jordanian Arabic by Migdadi (2003) and Farghal and Al-Khatib (2001); Syrian Arabic by Nelson, Al-Batal, and Echols (1996); Egyptian Arabic by Nelson, El Bakary, and Al Batal (1993) and Nelson *et al* (2002); Kuwaiti Arabic by Farghal and Haggan (2006); Greek by Sifianou (2015, 2019) and Bella and Moser (2018); Turkish by Ruhi (2006) and Ruhi and Islk-Güler (2007).

The other major group of Eastern languages – Asian languages – have generated a greater amount of scholarship. The pragmatics of Korean is studied by Yoon (2004), Miyahara *et al* (1998), and Idemaru, Wintre, and Brown (2019); Nepali in Upadhyay (2003), and Thai in Gajaseni (1995). However, the most privileged languages in this aspect are no doubt Japanese and Chinese. Cross-cultural pragmatic research on Japanese began in the 1980s (Hill *et al* 1986; Hiro 1986; Ide 1982; Kitagawa 1980), saw important works come out by Matsumoto (1988, 1989) and

Ide (1989), and has continued with a high level of activity until this day (Coulmas 1992; Fukushima 2019; Haugh 2007; Ohashi 2008). The Chinese language began to draw the interest of pragmaticians in the 1990s (Chen 1993a, 1996a; Gu 1990; Mao 1992, 1994) and seems to be surpassing Japanese of late (Kádár and Zhou 2020; Leech 2007; Ran, Zhou, and Kádár 2020; Rue and Zhang 2008; Spencer-Oatey and Ng 2001; Ye 2019).

This impressive amount of research in cross-cultural pragmatics has produced a vast reservoir of knowledge about the pragmatics of Eastern languages. We now know far more than ever before about how a great many Eastern languages do various speech acts such as complaining, refusing, thanking, apologizing, requesting, and responding to compliments. We are better informed about some key cultural concepts that underlie the doing of speech acts in those languages. For instance, the notion of one's place in the complicated web of social relationship appears to be an important yardstick in East Asian languages – Japanese, Chinese, and Korean – and the constructs of modesty and care for others have been found to determine the way a number of speech acts are performed in these languages, particularly Chinese. We also have a better understanding of how honorifics function in Korean and Japanese and the greater degree of interconnectedness in those cultures.

There has emerged from this strand of research a debate whether East and West are similar or different in pragmatics, particularly in politeness, to a point the term "East-West Divide" was coined by Leech (2007) and the debate has continued till recently (Ly 2016; Ye 2019). In this section, I follow Chen (2010b), abbreviating the view that East and West are fundamentally similar in their respective pragmatics as *the Similar Position* and the view that they are essentially different as *the Different Position*. I will focus on Japanese and Chinese, solely due to the fact that they are the best studied Eastern languages. As such, they seem to have been thrust into the position of representing East and have hence been time and again invoked to defend either of the two positions.

In the rest of the section, I discuss Japanese first, followed by Chinese. I will then discuss how the two positions – the Similar Position and the Different Position – are reconciled in the framework of MMP. Lastly, I discuss theoretical implications of this debate in pragmatic theorizing in general.

4.2.2 Politeness Japanese and West: Similar or different?

The debate about whether Japanese pragmatics is similar to or different from the pragmatics of a Western language such as English is a good representative of the East-West debate in general. The central issue has been whether Brown and Levinson's (1987) politeness theory applies to Japanese politeness. It started out with researchers applying Brown and Levinson's theory to Japanese and finding it inadequate. These researchers hence advance the position that Japanese is much different from Euro-American pragmatics, on which Brown and Levinson's theory is believed to be based, and propose their own theories to account for the Japanese data. This Different Position has been later challenged, however, by a few scholars who instead argue that the apparent differences between Japanese pragmatics and Western pragmatics can be satisfactorily accounted for by existing theories or some slight revisions of these theories.

The position that Japanese pragmatics is essentially different from the pragmatics of Euro-American languages have been held by many. However, the most influential scholars are Matsumoto (1988, 1989) and Ide (1989), who independently proposed the concept of discernment to account for Japanese pragmatics (but see Hill *et al*'s 1986 paper, which proposes the notion of discernment a few years earlier). The spirit of their work was later carried on by Haugh (2005, 2007, among others) and Ohashi (2003, 2008). I start with Matsumoto (1989), whose arguments are shared by Matsumoto (1988) and Ide (1989) as well.

Matsumoto's view that Japanese pragmatics is essentially different from Western pragmatics is based on two major arguments: the use of honorifics and the formulaic expression *yoroshiku onegaishimasu*. Matsumoto shows how the simple statement *Today is Saturday* can be said in different ways, as seen in (10) through (12):

(10) *Kyoo wa   doyoobi da*
      today TOPIC Saturday COPULA (plain)

(11) *Kyoo wa   doyoobi deso*
      today TOP Saturday COPULA (ADDRESSEE HONORIFIC)

(12) *Kyoo wa   doyoobi degozai-masu*
      today TOP Saturday COPULA (ADDRESSEE HONORIFIC, formal)
                                               (Matsumoto 1989: 209)

Which of the three one uses in conversation depends on the relationship between herself and the hearer. In the sense that a Japanese speaker has no choice but pick one from the available allomorphs according to her perception of the position the hearer occupies in the social hierarchy, Matsumoto argues that Brown and Levinson's (1987) theory of politeness does not apply, as Japanese communication depends more on the shared social norms than on the effort to mitigate the force of face threat of a given speech act.

Second, the utterance *yoroshiku onegaishimasu* is typically used upon meeting someone for the first time. Although it can be glossed as "Nice to meet you" in

English, its literal meaning is analogous to "Please treat me favorably" or "Please take care of me", which, being imperative in structure, is "imposing", per Brown and Levinson (1987). However, it is viewed by Japanese speaker not as imposing but polite. Therefore, Matsumoto concludes, Japanese politeness is a different kind of thing from Western politeness.

Based on these arguments, Matsumoto (1989) concludes that Brown and Levinson's (1987) politeness theory, which is believed to be a theory about Anglo cultures, does not capture the essence of Japanese. Japanese politeness, Matsumoto argues, is centered on discernment (*wakimae*), defined as a "sense of place or role in a given situation according to social convention" (Matsumoto 1989: 230). This view is also defended in Ide (1989) and Ide (1992), who categorizes politeness into the discernment type, in the same sense as Matsumoto's, and the volitional type, characterized by speaker's own individual face needs.

Matsumoto (1989) and Ide (1989) are among the first to openly challenge Brown and Levinson's politeness theory, hence starting the debate about whether East and West are similar or different in pragmatics. Their theory of discernment enjoyed considerable currency in the 1990s and their respective papers have become the "standard reference" (Pizziconi 2003: 1472) of Japanese pragmatics, widely cited as evidence that Japanese politeness is very different from Western politeness and – quite unwittingly, see below – as evidence against Brown and Levinson's (1987) theory of universal politeness (Chen 1996a; Janney and Arndt 1993; Kasper 1990; Lee-Wong 1994; Mao 1994; Skewis 2003; Yabuuchi 2006; Ye 2019).

The new millennium has seen a few more notable papers further defending the Different Position. Responding to Pizziconi (2003), who offers the most comprehensive critique of Matsumoto (1989) and Ide (1989) and whom I will discuss in detail below, Haugh (2005) strengthens Matsumoto's and Ide's arguments about Brown and Levinson's (1987) alleged inability to account for Japanese politeness. The use of the different allomorphs within the Japanese honorific paradigm, as illustrated in (10) through (12), above, Haugh argues, "is not a matter of showing concern for the address's desire to be free from imposition, nor does it involve showing approval for their wants" (Haugh 2005: 44). Therefore, Haugh extends Matsumoto's and Ide's discernment into the notion of place "to encompass all politeness phenomena in Japanese, rather than leaving Brown and Levinson's notion of face to deal with politeness strategies" (Haugh 2005: 45).

According to Haugh (2005), place is composed of two aspects: the place one belongs and the place one stands. The place one belongs reflects the value of inclusion: to be part of a group. The place one stands refers to distinction: to be different from others. At the next level, the place one stands is divided into one's rank, circumstance, and public persona/social standing (Haugh 2005: 48). Elsewhere, Haugh defines place "as encompassing one's contextually-contingent and discursively enacted social role and position" (Haugh 2007: 660). To Haugh, place does not only include facets of Japanese politeness that can be subsumed under Brown and Levinson's positive politeness but also facets that are clearly negative face-based, involving imposition on other's territory:

> what defines imposition, in relation to politeness in Japanese at least, is the place of the interactants rather than individual autonomy. That is to say, something is only an imposition when it falls outside the place (or more specifically the role) of the interactants in question. If the place of the interactant does encompass the action in question, then it does not constitute an imposition. (Haugh 2005: 59)

In other words, Haugh seems to be saying that if one insists on using imposition as a yardstick for politeness, it would have to take on an entirely different meaning, redefined in relation to the notion of face instead of "individual autonomy". Thus, Haugh's stance against Brown and Levinson is more explicit and forceful than Matsumoto's (1989) and Ide's (1989).

Note should be taken that although they have been frequently cited as works against Brown and Levinson, Matsumoto and S. Ide may not have held as strong a position against Brown and Levinson as have been believed. Hill *et al* (1986), of which S. Ide is the second coauthor, for instance, indicate that the notion of discernment is proposed to be complementary to Brown and Levinson, and a careful reading of the paper, a contrastive study of requests between English and Japanese, reveals that there is much support in the findings for Brown and Levinson. For instance, the authors posit that politeness, at the macro level, can be either volition-based or discernment-based. Their data suggest that American English is primarily – not entirely – volition-based while Japanese is primarily – again, not entirely – discernment-based. Similarly, Matsumoto (2003) states that her 1989 paper was not meant to replace Brown and Levinson, but to offer an alternative to it for the purpose of accounting for Japanese politeness.

While Matsumoto (1989), Ide (1989), and Haugh (2005) are significant works that have proposed theoretical constructs for Japanese pragmatics at the macro level, one should not ignore studies that support the Different Position using data from a particular type of communication. Ohashi (2003, 2008), for instance, discusses the credit-debt equilibrium in Japanese pragmatics: how Japanese speakers negotiate with each other to achieve a balance between credit and debt. The typical structure of such a conversation is that the beneficiary of a favor initiates the conversation to thank the benefactor. The benefactor rejects. The beneficiary insists on thanking and asserting how much effort the benefactor must have made to do her the favor in question. The benefactor denies. Along the way, the beneficiary may even apologize (cf. Kumatoridani 1999; Ide 1998) for the trouble the benefactor had been put into. Such an exchange can go on for as long as a dozen turns until the balance of credit-debt is achieved, most often indicated by a change of topic in the conversation. As a result, Ohashi concludes that Brown and Levinson's definition of thanking – expression of gratitude – does not work for his data and the speech act of thanking needs to be re-examined.

The dominance of the Different Position in Japanese pragmatics remained virtually unchallenged for about a decade. At the turn of the century emerged studies that advance the Similar Position, chiefly Usami (2002), Pizziconi (2003), and Fukada and Asato (2004). Fukushima (2000) could also be seen as a sympathizer with the Similar Position, although she discussed a number of differences in the output strategies for requests between Japanese and British English.

These writers have made four counter arguments against the position that Japanese is different from Western languages in its pragmatics. First, the use of honorifics has been proven to be sensitive to Brown and Levinson's three factors – the power of the hearer over the speaker (P), the social distance between the hearer and the speaker (D), and – albeit to a much lesser degree – the degree of imposition of the relevant speech act in the relevant culture (R) (Fukada and Asato 2004; Pizziconi 2003; Usami 2002). Specifically, when the addressee is a person of higher status, D and P will be given higher values, which will then lead to a higher value of W(x) (Fukada and Asato 2004; Fukushima 2000). This argument, it should be noted, is assumed in a recent study on Koran and Japanese honorifics by Idemaru, Wintre, and Brown (2019), although the authors do not reference the East-West debate in their work.

Second, Japanese honorifics are also sensitive to factors arising from the specific context in which they are used. It is true that the speaker in a given conversation will use or not use honorifics according to convention; she is also found to alter her usage according to the dynamic change in the relationship between herself and the hearer. Fukada and Asato (2004: 1998–1999) illustrate this point with several examples: a lecturer using honorific expressions to an intern – a person of lower status – because she is asking the intern for a favor; a village chief using honorific language to a villager, also of lower status, due to the extreme formality of the context; and college professors switching between honorific and non-honorific languages with each other according to the formality of the situation at hand (honorific language in formal situations and plain language in informal situations). In the sense that the use of honorifics is sensitive to the changing relationship between the speaker and the hearer at a given time, honorific expressions in Japanese are not much different from verbal strategies in a language without an honorific system such as English (Pizziconi 2003).

The third argument of the Similar Position is made by Pizziconi (2003), concerning the greeting expression *yoroshiku onegaishimasu*. Recall Matsumoto's

(1988, 1989) contention that *yoroshiku onegaishimasu* is polite and imposing at the same time. But Pizziconi argues that this expression can very well be seen as "deferential begging" semantically, used to express gratitude for the exalted party, treating her as "a person of prestige and authority that has the power to bestow favors" (Pizziconi 2003: 1485). As such, it "can more intuitively be interpreted as an implicit – yet transparent – message of the speaker's appreciation of the hearer's social persona, a very clear instance of politeness strategies" (Pizziconi 2003: 1485).

The fourth argument of the Similar Position is also advanced by Pizziconi (2003). Since most of the authors defending the Different Position focus on positive face – how Japanese speakers say things in such a way as to protect the hearer's wants of being liked, appreciated, and respected, either claim or imply that Brown and Levinson's negative face plays little role in Japanese. Pizziconi, however, cites extensive literature to show that negative face is just as valid in Japanese as it is in Western cultures – that Japanese speakers are found to use euphemisms, hedging, questioning, and apologizing to signal their respect for the hearer's territory and that negative face considerations are found to "constrain the use of declaratives, emotive/affective terms, the expression of the speaker's intentions, or questions on the hearer's skills and abilities" (Pizziconi 2003: 1479).

4.2.3 Politeness Chinese and West: Similar or different?

The emergence and continuation of the East-West debate in Chinese pragmatics are analogous to what had taken place in Japanese pragmatics. That is, scholars apply classical pragmatic theories to Chinese, find them wanting in their explanatory power, and then take the position that Chinese pragmatics is different from Euro-American pragmatics. The Different Position could have started with Gu (1990) and later Mao (1994). Like those working on Japanese pragmatics, Gu finds Brown and Levinson inadequate, for their individual-based approach does not address the normative constraints society endorses on its individuals. Gu then proposes four maxims to account for Chinese politeness: respectfulness (positive appreciation of others), modesty (self-denigration), attitudinal warmth (demonstration of kindness, consideration, and hospitality towards others), and refinement (behavior meeting certain social standards) (Gu 1990: 239).

Mao's (1994) challenge of Brown and Levinson is more direct than Gu's. Mao argues, first, that while face *à la* Brown and Levinson is individual-based, constant and predetermined, Chinese face "encodes a reputable image that individuals can claim for themselves as they interact with others in a given community; it is intimately linked to the views of the community", "emphasizes ... the harmony of individual conduct with the views and judgment of the community", and "depends upon, and is indeed determined by, the participation of others" (Mao 1994: 460). Second, Mao proposes that Chinese face differs from Western face also in content. Whereas Euro-American face may be composed of positive and negative face, Chinese face "identifies a Chinese desire to secure public acknowledgement of one's prestige or reputation" (Mao 1994: 460).

The influence of Gu's and Mao's respective papers on the East-West debate can very well match that of Matsumoto (1988, 198) and Ide (1989), as they have become the flag bearers of the Different Position concerning Chinese pragmatics, being frequently cited as the key representatives of the Different Position. In the next 30 years also, research on Chinese pragmatics flourished, making Chinese the most studied Asian language. (In fact, it might be the second most studied of all languages, next only to English.) Most of these works have taken the Different Position, albeit to different degrees. The series of works on Chinese compliment responses, for instance, have typically yielded findings that Chinese speakers tend to reject compliments and denigrate themselves when responding to compliments. Since rejection runs counter to Brown and Levinson's positive face by disagreeing with the complimenter and self-denigration threatens the responder's positive face, the compliment responding behavior has been seen as strong evidence for the position that Chinese pragmatics is essentially different from Western pragmatics.

Students of Chinese requests have likewise been aligned with the Different Position. Lee-Wong (1994) finds little evidence for indirection in her subjects' requesting behavior and comments on the Chinese dislike of circumlocution thusly: "Anything that can be expressed directly is preferred" (Lee-Wong 1994: 511). Similarly, Skewis (2003) studies directives by 18th century men using dyads from *Hong Lou Meng* "Dreams of the Red Chamber" and finds that direct imperatives account for 90% of all strategies in the classical novel, although he also identifies a large number of mitigating linguistic devices such as downgraders, subjectivisers, grounders, disarmers, and sweeteners – the kind of devices originally discussed in Blum-Kulka and Olshtain (1984). Since indirection in requests is believed to be motivated by negative face considerations, both Lee-Wong and Skewis view their findings as evidence against Brown and Levinson, particularly their concept of negative face. This general view has been shared by other researchers (Gao 1999; Huang 1996; Rue and Zhang 2008).

The strongest evidence that researchers on Chinese pragmatics have offered in support of the Different Position, perhaps, has come from studies on what can be called "benefit offering": gift giving, dinner invitation, and food-plying at a dinner, as these events all involve the speaker offering something – a gift, a dinner, or food at a dinner – to the hearer. Invitations have been investigated by Mao (1992, 1994) and Tseng (1996); gift giving by Zhu, Li, and Qian (2000), and food offering by Chen (1996a).[39] These studies have yielded similar findings about the complicated structure of the negotiation between the speaker and the hearer. Typically, the recipient would decline the offer and, along the way, state how much trouble the favor must have cost or will cost the offerer. The offerer insists on offering, emphasizing that little effort is involved in the offer. This cycle repeats itself several times until the recipient eventually accepts the offer. (But see Tseng 1996, who finds that single inviting-accepting sequence exists between speakers who are familiar with each other). The gift-giving event, for instance, displays the following structure (where A=gift offerer; B=gift recipient):

(13) *The structure of gift-giving*
    A: Presequence (Optional)
    B: Presequence (Optional)
    A: Offer
    B: Decline
    A: Offer repeated
    B: Decline repeated (Optional)
    A: Offer repeated (Optional)
    B: Acceptance

                                  (Adopted from Zhu, Li, and Qian 2000)

Food-plying at the end of a dinner is found to go through the same cycle of negotiation as demonstrated in Chen (1996a). Following Mao (1992, 1994) and Zhu, Li, and Qian (2000), I argued that these findings constituted evidence against Brown and Levinson's (1987) politeness theory, for, by plying guests with food (to the point of forcing food down their throats), Chinese hosts would be threatening the negative face of their guests, imposing on their freedom of action. This constitutes evidence for Gu's (1990) concept of attitudinal warmth. Then I wrote the following:

> [T]his study seems to suggest that not only is Brown and Levinson's universality claim questionable, but also that the prospect of arriving at a unified theory of politeness, one that is able to explain the politeness phenomena across cultures, is far out of sight.
>   (Chen 1996a: 153)[40]

---

39 This study will be discussed in detail in the next chapter on diachronic pragmatics, as it is the first of what has turned out to be a longitudinal study on food offering at the end of a invited dinner (with a gust and a host).
40 As should be clear by now, I no longer hold the view herein expressed.

The Difference position, since then, has been either assumed (Ran and Zhao 2019; Ren 2019, Zhou and Zhang 2018) or explicitly promoted. Ye (2019) belongs to the latter and is reviewed below.

Following (and quoting heavily) Mao (1994) and Matsumoto (1989), Ye goes further than Mao and Matsumoto. To her, Western politeness is based on "society of strangers" while Chinese politeness is based on "society of intimates". Using Google Ngram Viewer, Ye shows how the frequency of appearances of the term "politeness" correlates better with the term "strangers" than it is with "friends", "families", and "acquaintances" in English. The notion of politeness in English, further, is supposed to be heavily influenced by commerce and characterized by the relationship between an innkeeper and shopkeeper with their customers. So, Ye writes:

> Politeness itself does not imply depth of relationships between interlocutors. If anything, it keeps them at a safe distance. Yet it is an important cohesive mechanism that connects people to each other in a society where each person is also an autonomous being who is entitled to privacy and thinking in their own way. (Ye 2019: 9)

In Chinese society, on the other hand, "strangers are largely irrelevant, because the primary concerns in Chinese social interaction lie somewhere else and are linked to the set of fundamental cultural values that are drastically different from those in Anglo linguacultures". These values start from the key notion of *shúrén* 'familiar people', which Ye sees as an "important instrumental social category" through which the dynamics of Chinese social interaction are created, maintained, and achieved. A *shúrén* is someone you know for a length of time, someone with whom you are mutually obligated, someone you can greet by asking personal questions. Correspondingly, there are two derived opposites: *zìjǐrén* 'in-groupers/insiders/one of us' and *wàirén* 'out-groupers/outsiders', whom one should treat differently, as dictated by the age-old dictum: *nèi wài yǒu bié* 'insiders and outsiders should be differentiated' (Ye 2019: 5–6).

Ye seems to be suggesting that a Chinese has different relationships with others. If we view a Chinese as at the center, there will be different circles around her, one inside another, with the most inter circle being her immediate family, followed by groups of decreasing familiarity, all the way to the most outside circle – "outsiders". She will then treat them differently. With those in the most inside circle – Ye describes – there is no need to be "polite", which would be seen as "standing on ceremony".

To account for this network of relationships, Ye invokes the Confucius notion of *he* 'harmony'. A primary concern in Chinese interpersonal relations is hence to avoid conflict and preserve group harmony. As a result, members belonging to the "society of intimates" are demanded not to voice their needs and wants. "This is in stark contrast with the interactional model based on the society of strangers, in which politeness is a linguistic device for mitigating conflict" (Ye 2019: 6).

What seems to underlie all these studies in defense of the Different Position is the view that Chinese, being a collectivist society, values harmony and connectiveness with each other. As a result, the speech of Chinese is "assumed not to be motivated by the desire for freedom (negative face), but instead to seek the respect of the group" (Yu 2003: 1685. See also Yu 2004). This group-orientedness is believed to have led to key notions that underlie the linguistic behaviors of the speakers. It explains the demonstration of warmth and care toward others, as is seen in benefit offering events; it explains modesty, for to denigrate oneself is to elevate others, as is seen in compliment responses; it also explains the lack of indirection in requests, as imposition is believed not to play an important part in Chinese pragmatics. All this has been treated as evidence that Chinese pragmatics is essentially different from its Euro-American counterpart.

The Similar Position has been argued by far fewer researchers: Chen (2005), Chen, He, and Hu (2013), and Ly (2016). In Chen (2005), I offered a reanalysis of the findings about food-plying as reported in Chen (1996a), arguing that the repeated offering of food at the end of a dinner is in fact in consonance with Brown and Levinson's notion of positive face. Brown and Levinson, for instance, state that "in positive politeness the sphere of redress is widened to the appreciation of alter's wants in general or to the expression of similarity between ego's and alter's wants" (Brown and Levinson 1987: 101). These wants include the "wants to be liked, admired, cared about, understood, listened to, and so on" (1987: 120). Such positive polite strategies include offer (Brown and Levinson 1987: 125) and gift-giving (Brown and Levinson 1987: 129). In a speech community such as Xi'an before the mid 1990's, food-plying was clearly a social norm, as suggested by the repeated offering of food by the host and the repeated refusal by the guest. As a norm, both sides of the plying event would expect it to happen for the purpose of maintaining and enhancing their respective face. For the guest, it is her positive face want of being cared about that is enhanced; for the host, it is also the positive face that is at stake, although a different dimension of it, that of showing warmth and care for her guests. Such a norm may be very different from the norm of a Western culture in an analogous social context. But that does not suggest that Westerners do not care about being cared about or being shown warmth. In other words, the position that Westerners do not value being cared about or being shown warmth has to be demonstrated, not assumed.[41]

Chen, He, and Hu (2013) ostensibly aim to test if English, Japanese, and Chinese are similar or different in their respective doing of the speech act of request, replicating Hill et al.'s (1986) study of request in Japanese and English. The purpose of Hill et al. (1986) is to provide evidence for the notion of discern-

---

41 Chen (1996a) will be discussed in more detail in Chapter 5.

ment, a key notion of Japanese politeness. They draw on a comparison of the requests of borrowing a pen between college students in America and Japan with a three-stepped methodology. (1) Subjects rated a list of expressions they might use in borrowing a pen on a scale of being the most uninhibited (casual, informal, and direct) to being the most careful (opposite of uninhibited). (2) Subjects rated a list of people they would borrow a pen from on the same scale. (3) The subjects were asked to match each type of people with expressions (subjects could match as many expressions as they saw fit with each "people"). The authors find that "the fundamental pattern for the Japanese and American subjects is the same; that is, both groups show graded responses in which choice of request forms correlates with person/situation" (Hill et al.1986: 357–358). There are differences, too: Japanese request forms are more different from one another in terms of politeness than those used in English and that Japanese subjects perceived a greater degree of difference between various types of people than Americans (Hill et al.1986: 359). As a result, Hill et al. conclude that Japanese politeness is more discernment-based and American politeness, more volition-based.

To replicate Hill et al. (1986) as close as possible, My colleagues and I first asked respondents – also college students – to provide expressions they would use to borrow a pen, the result of which was very similar to the list used by Hill et al. We then asked them to rate these expressions and then people on the uninhibited-careful scale. Finally, the same group of respondents matched expressions with people. This multi-step survey was done among 207 students at Xi'an International Studies University and generated 17,638 responses (due to crosstab possibilities). Two findings are the most significant. The first is the matching between expression and people, which is seen in Figure 4.3.

In Figure 4.3, the expressions used for borrowing a pen are listed on the left, from the most uninhibited to the most careful, and the people to borrow a pen from are listed on the top, based on the same sale. The size of a dot represents the number of ratings: the larger the dot, the high the number. The general patten is clear: the more uninhibited the people, the more uninhibited the expression speakers would choose to use when making a request. These are the same findings in Hill et al. (1986), about their Japanese and English respondents (their figure, arranged in similar fashion, about Japanese is seen on Page 357 and about English, on Page 357).

The second finding in the study is about the rating of people, as seen in Table 4.2.

Comparing the findings in Table 4.2 and their counterparts in Hill et al. (1986, the details of which are omitted), we observe that the orders for the three groups of respondents are different. The first five for Japan are Professor, Mid-

104 —— Chapter 4 MMP and cross-/intercultural variation

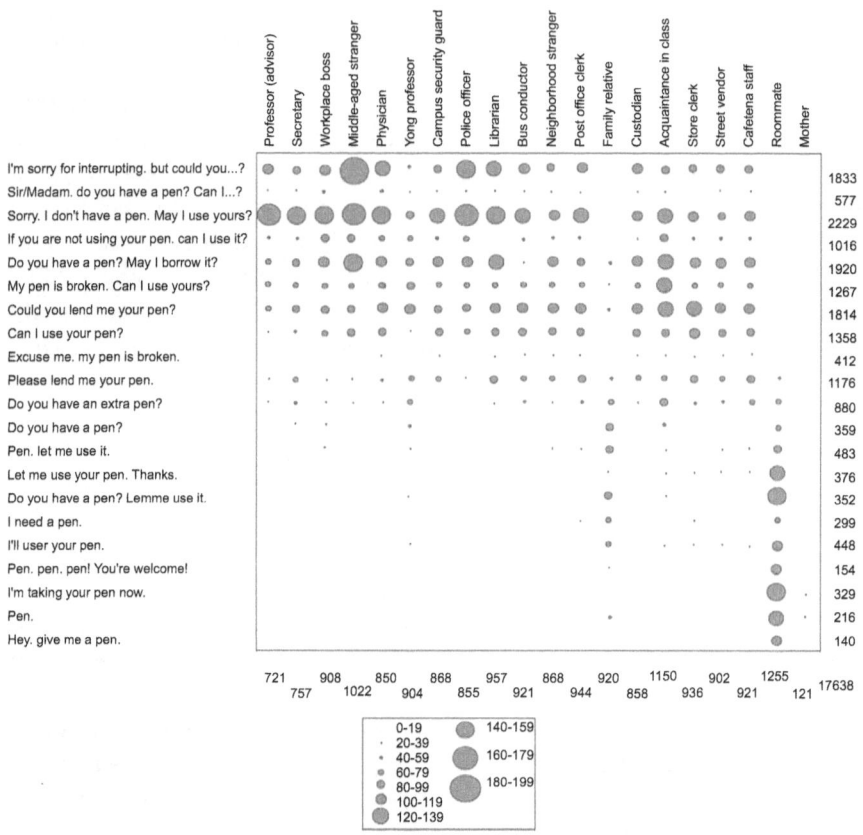

Figure 4.3: Matching of expression and people.

Table 4.2: Category of people and ratings, China.

Professor (advisor)	3.94	Stranger in neighborhood	2.70
Secretary	3.50	Post office clerk	2.64
Workplace boss	3.39	Family relative	2.45
Middle-aged stranger	3.39	Custodian	2.38
Physician	3.30	Acquaintance in large class	2.35
Young professor	3.07	Store clerk	2.30
Campus security guard	2.87	Street vendor	2.19
Police officer	2.85	Cafeteria staff	2.17
Librarian on duty	2.79	Roommate	1.40
Bus conductor	2.70	Mother	1.27

dle-aged stranger, Physician, Workplace Boss, and Secretary. The first five for China are Professor, Secretary, Workplace Boss, Middle Aged Stanger, and Physician. The first five for America are Professor, Police Officer, Workplace Boss, Physician, and Middle-Aged Stranger. This different ordering suggests the different relationships in the respective cultures. Police Officer, for instance, does not make it to the top five in Japan and China, indicating that American students view a police officer as more "careful". Secretary is ranked as the second highest by Chinese respondents but the fifth by Japanese and the seventh by Americans, which, again, is indicative of how support staff in a university is perceived in the three cultures.

The scale of uninhibited to careful in Hill et al. (1986) is intended to measure the "perceived distance" between speakers, a notion that is key to their theory of discernment. However, that distance, as they point out, is a combination of Brown and Levinson's P, D and R (Hill et al., 1986: 351–352, n. 6), particularly P and D, as R is held independently in the borrowing of a pen. This can be easily verified by a look at the people categories. For all three groups, those types of people listed at the top of the rankings are either those who hold considerable power over the subjects (e.g., professor, physician, police officer, and workplace boss) or those who are socially distant from the subjects (e.g., middle-aged stranger) or both. Similarly, one finds the opposite at the bottom of the scale: sibling, mother, roommate, or meaningful other. This is evidence that Brown and Levinson's P and D are relevant factors in determining speakers' choices of expressions when making requests. Put it in other words, for subjects from all three groups, the way they requested a pen depends on how much power their hearer has over them and how socially distant the hearer is perceived to be from them. Based on these findings, my colleagues and I conclude that our study lends support to the Similar Position in the East-West debate.

We now move to Ly (2016), another study that pertains directly to the East-West Divide debate. To investigate email interaction in a multinational shipbuilding and maintenance company, Ly created three scenarios .

(14) *Ly's (2016) scenarios*
 Scenario 1. You are working on a project with a Chinese colleague in China. Last week, you asked him to send you a report, X, but he did not do it. Write him an e-mail to ask him again.
 Scenario 2. Your colleague in China has eventually sent you the report. You have read it with attention but have found out that some of the data is incorrect. Write him an e-mail informing him that you have received the report.

> *Scenario* 3.   On Monday, you sent a drawing to your colleague in China. This morning, you received an e-mail from him asking you to make modifications to the drawing. You think that the drawing is fine and disagree about making the changes. Write him an e-mail to inform him.

Scenario 1 is meant to solicit emails of request, Scenario 2 to solicit emails of criticism, and Scenario 3, emails of disagreement. The activity was distributed to 130 participants (trained engineers) of a business seminar, and 63 e-mail sets were collected: 18 in Norway, 21 in Sweden, and 24 in Germany. From this total, Ly selected four examples of different levels of directness used by her European informants. The request e-mail, for instance, included examples of requests formulated with the imperative, a query preparatory, a hint, and a white lie. These three sets of emails were then incorporated into a questionnaire that asked the respondents to choose the example they liked the most – i.e., they would react most positively to by being clear, polite, friendly, and short – from the four proposed, and the one they liked the least. The questionnaire was distributed to Asian employees of the company. Seventeen responses were collected in China, and 14 in Korea.

Ly finds that when expressing in English a work-routine request, criticism, or disagreement directed to their Asian colleagues, the European informants use a broad portfolio of directness strategy types. Further, while requests are expressed in a slightly more direct way, criticisms and disagreements are predominantly expressed indirectly. In terms of perception of the request e-mails, the Asian informants prefer a clear, direct, and short e-mail from their colleagues. However, when a criticism or a disagreement is expressed, an indirect strategy is preferred. In addition, the use of negative evaluation to express a criticism or disagreement is disliked, as such utterances are perceived to be too harsh, patronizing, and somewhat arrogant, in spite of the mitigation used to soften the message. Ly's discussion with the Asian participants show that they had no problem coping with disagreement or criticism, as long as it is expressed in a friendly and polite way.

In sum, Ly observes a correlation between the English-speaking Europeans' production and Asians' perception of criticism and disagreement, that is, both groups of informants prefer indirection. For example, the second most used strategy by the Westerners to criticize is "expression of difference" (20%), which is also the most liked strategy by the Asian informants (15/31). Similarly, "request for information/clarification" is the second most used strategy (30%) and also the second most liked (11/31) by the Asian employees (Ly 2016: 64). Therefore, the author argues, "Popular work in intercultural business communication depicts

Europeans as direct and Asians as indirect". However, these depictions are "simplistic", "essentialist", and "stereotyped" (Ly 2016: 63). Her study is thus "in favor of the Similar Position" (Ly 2016: 65) in the East-West debate.

4.2.4 MMP and the debate

The survey above shows a rather complex picture of the debate on East-West Divide. In this Section, I discuss how MMP can provide an adequate framework for the debate and can even provide guidance for those who are interested in carrying on with the debate. Two points will be made. First, MMP is capable of subsuming the range of aspects of politeness that have been uncovered in the East-West debate. Second, MMP is also capable of accounting for the differences between East and West.

Recall that under interactional motivations, which is what the East-West debate is about, there are two sub-motivations: to create, maintain, and enhance the public image of other and to create, maintain, and enhance the public image of self. The purported Western politeness that values avoidance of imposition would be motivated by the need to benefit other-image, reflecting the recognition of other's freedom of action. As to the purported Eastern politeness, I re-examine the proposals by previous researchers in terms of MMP.

The first is the Japanese notion of place and discernment. The sensitivity that members of a hierarchical society have towards the place of other is analogous to the sensitivity they display towards the public image of other. If the place (and standing) of person is recognized in a society, it must have built-in power and status, which will translate into a sort of public image the person holding the place strives to keep. So, if A is higher than B and B uses more deferential forms of speech, including appropriate honorifics, when speaking to or with A, there would be little doubt that such treatment is expected by A and accepted by society, for not doing so would lead to inappropriateness.

Relevant to this is the honorific system in Japanese. As discussed earlier, scholars differ on whether such a system supports the Similar Position or the Different Position in the East-West debate, with the latter view being more prevalent. In the framework of MMP, the honorifics in the Japanese language are seen as being motivated by the need to establish, maintain, and enhance the public image of other. According to Kim (2010, 2014, unpublished paper), the morphological encoding of honorification did not exist in the beginning of Japanese (or Korean). Instead, it has been gradually formed via a process of grammaticalization from different sources. This fits well with MMP. That is, the need to benefit other-image (the image of both the hearer and a third party) pressured the language to gradually build a system in its morphology. If scholars are right in their observation that the Japanese society can be characterized as "hierarchical" in which a great deal of attention is given to the notion of place and the discernment of it, MMP provides the missing link between this observation and the honorific system: the former is the motivation for the latter.

Further, the pressure to benefit other-image, according to MMP, is present not just in languages such as Japanese and Korean but in other languages as well. Take English. Although the honorific distinction in its pronoun system – *thou* vs. *thy* – has disappeared, the language has kept other means of honorification. For the royal family, terms such as *Your Majesty* and *her Highness* are still in use. In the U.S., the Congress has kept much of lexical honorication in English: a congressperson is referred to as "The gentleman/woman (from a particular state)", a high-level government official attending a hearing is referred to as "honorable X". Therefore, we seem to be in a position to say that Japanese and English are similar in that they both have linguistic structures to recognize the position or place – which is part of the public image – of other but differ in terms of *the kind of* linguistic structures and in terms of *the degree* to which it is done.

About the interconnectedness that has been demonstrated repeatedly by students of Chinese politeness, let us use Ye's study to illustrate. Ye's observation rings true to this native speaker of Chinese: that a Chinese does seem to live in a tighter community. I, too, agree that a Chinese generally does not thank a family member for a small favor such as bringing a cup of tea[42] (Ye 2019: 6). If so, however, it must be true that not to be thanked for a favor is part of the public image of the person doing the favor – the image of "intimate" – in Ye's terms.

In the last section, I discussed the findings of a series of studies that Chinese seem to be "imposing" in invitational/offering acts – that a Chinese speaker might repeatedly offer a drink to a guest, who repeatedly declines before eventually accepting it. This, too, is consonant with MMP. In a community in which this occurs, there is only one explanation: that the guest expects to be offered more than once and the host expects the guest to decline a few times before she accepts. Thus the repeated declination and repeated offering will be part of the image for both. For the host, to stop after the first offer would hurt the image of both: the guest may not get the drink she is actually planning to get, the host may create the impression that she is not considerate and caring (cf, Chen 1996a). The same is true for the guest, albeit in a reversed direction.

In a recent paper, Ran and Zhao (2019) bring to our attention one more aspect of Chinse politeness: *qingmian*, "affection-based face". *Qingmian* refers

---

[42] I do not recall, for instance, to have ever thanked my parents for anything, big or small.

to the part of Chinese face that a speaker needs to return a favor. If you have done a favor for me, I will be obliged to return it in some way either at the time the favor is done or later. For Ran and Zhao, *qingmian* is a source of interpersonal conflict in two ways. The first is when the speaker fails to return the favor while his hearer expects it. The second is when the speaker wants to return the favor – and insists on returning – while his hearer does not want it. This is again accounted for by MMP. To return a favor is part of the public image, reflecting a value of appreciation. The conflict that might arise based on *qingmian* considerations could be a conflict of different expectations of the favor-returning public image or a tug-of-war between the need to benefit other-public image and self-public image.

To be able to subsume under it these important aspects of pragmatics as discussed above, however, does not mean that MMP ignores differences. Before I discuss how MMP accounts for differences, it is important to highlight one point, that few if at all of the findings about either the East or the West is unique, i.e., what is found about one is true also of the other. We start from what has been argued about West first.

Western pragmatics has been argued by many (see above) to be based on rationality, on individualism, on "a society of strangers". It is no doubt that the theory of conversational implicature, of speech acts, of politeness (by both Brown and Levinson and by Leech), and of relevance are rationality-based. Rationality, for these scholars, it should be pointed out, is not the complicated philosophical notion we find in the treatises of western philosophers such as Kant (See Grandy and Warner 1986), but is narrow in scope and specific in application. Brown and Levison (1986: 64), for instance, write:

> We here define 'rationality' as the application of a specific mode of reasoning – what Aristotle called 'practical reasoning' – which guarantees inferences from ends or goals to means that will satisfy those ends.

One of the examples they provide is:

> If I want a drink of water, and I could use the tap in this room or the tap in the bathroom or the tap in the garden, it would sure be 'irrational' to trot out into the garden unnecessarily (provided that I have no secret want to be in the garden, etc.).

Simply put, rationality is the ability to choose the best means to an end from an array of options, an understanding also shared by Grice for his theory of conversational implicature (Grandy and Warner 1986) and by Sperber and Wilson (1986) for their theory of relevance.

Seen in this light, it is very difficult for one to say that rationality is a uniquely Western mechanism of thought. Those who argue that rationality does not apply to non-Western cultures are essentially saying that members of non-Western cultures could go to the tap in the garden – using Brown and Levinson's example above – for water while there is one a few feet away inside the room she is in. I am quite convinced that that is *not* what these scholars have in mind, even those who appear to be quite strident in the expression of their views (Kopykto 1995a; Shi-Xu 2005; Ye 2004).

Neither is individualism a uniquely Western value, for saying so is to say that in a non-Western culture, there is no constraint on the imposition of others. For this is, again, an awkward position: it is difficult to imagine a culture whereby members can impose on each other freely. In fact, those who blame Brown and Levinson's theory for being based on individualism provide example to the contrary at the same time. Ye (2019), for example, argues that in a society of intimates such as Chinese, members withhold their own wants for the sake of harmony with others. That seems to be a typical case of imposition avoidance, and to avoid imposition – ironically yet convincingly – proves the existence of it.

In the same vein, many aspects of pragmatics found in Eastern languages turn out not to be unique either. The notion of discernment/place that have been dubbed as a hallmark of Japanese politeness has to hold also in Western cultures. In American English, for instance, an employee speaks differently to her supervisor from the way the supervisor speaks to the employee, and a driver pulled over by a police officer will surely speak differently from the way she does at home to her children. In other words, it seems that "Westerners" are as conscious of the place each other holds in society as their "Eastern" counterpart.

The same holds for the many features of pragmatics identified for Chinese. The most salient of these features is the interconnectedness of members of the society (Gu 1990), which results in the interdependence on (Mao 1994) and the mutual obligation to face maintenance and enhancement (Ran and Zhao 2019, Ye 2016). Although none of these authors has claimed that the interconnectedness is *only* true of Chinese, casting it as an argument against a purported Eurocentric theory of language use is prone to creating that impression, and it indeed has, as Mao's views have been widely used against theories supposedly EuroAmerican in origin.

The flip side of the argument about the Eastern interconnectedness is that it suggests little or no interconnectedness in Western societies. In Ye's (2019) paper, the notion of society of strangers is said to have been based on commence in the colonial period of England, citing a couple of sources. To me, to dub a society a "society of strangers" would need a bit more evidence than Ye provides. I am not entirely sure a society of strangers, taken in its extreme sense, can exist as a human society. Below I provide an example of the interconnectedness observed among Americans.

In January 2021, the U.S. House of Representatives impeached the former president Donald Trump for the second time. Adam Kinzinger, one of the ten Republican congresspersons who voted to impeach the leader of their own party, was sent a letter from his family members, expressing their extreme displeasure with Kinzinger's vote.[43] The following is part of the letter.

(15)   It is now most embarrassing to us that we are related to you. You have embarrassed the Kinzinger family name!

The family connection is clearly seen here. Are the Kinzingers an exception to the norm? Subsequent tweets suggest otherwise. Kinzinger, for one, clearly does not think his family is not the only one that values interconnectedness:

(16)   I'm ok, more sad that someone would be willing to choose a man over family. And sad that it's happening to so many.[44]

There are dozens of tweets in response lamenting the breakdown of families due to politics. Many posters extend their support by welcoming Kinzinger to their owe families. A Dave Kitzinger offers up his thusly:

(17)   If you change 1 letter in your name you can be in my family (followed by a winking emoji).

To comfort Kinzinger's loneliness, another poster tweets:

(18)   You are being embraced by a much larger family of cousins all across America (ending with a U.S. flag).

These tweets are evidence that interconnectedness may not be as non-existence in Western societies as we have been led to believe. One member's action is tied to the reputation of the rest of the family; the breakdown of the family (and friends) over politics is seen as being a significant social issue; people – supposedly strangers – on Twitter explicitly say how important such interconnectedness is to them. One Canadian expressed surprise that Americans would talk about politics among the close circles of family and friends. He claims that he

---

43 https://www.msn.com/en-us/news/politics/gop-rep-adam-kinzingers-family-bashed-him-for-voting-to-impeach-trump-we-are-thoroughly-disgusted-with-you/ar-BB1dIzN5 (accessed 17 February 2021).
44 https://twitter.com/RepKinzinger/status/1361470740340482051?s=20 (accessed 17 February 2021).

does not know the political orientation of his family members. But he, as the same time, states that avoidance of politics within a group is not indication of looseness of the members of the group. On the contrary, it is a conscious effort to keep the group close.[45]

How about the purported feature of imposition in Chinese culture? First, we should emphasize that Chinese are found to be "imposing" only on specific situations such as invitations and dinners. None of the studies discussed above indicates that Chinese are impositing on all social occasions. Looking at Western cultures, we find that the same holds. In Chapter 3, I discussed Brown and Levinson's full recognition of cases in which imposition is viewed as polite. Example (19), from Tannen (1986), demonstrates the point well. The conversation takes place at Bill's home. Ethel and Ben are Bill's parents. Max is Ethel and Ben's stepfather, who has been recently widowed.

(19) Ben: You have to uh... uh... uh – Hey, this is the best herring you ever tasted. I'll tell
you that right now.
Ethel: Bring some out so that Max could have some too.
Ben: Oh, boy.
Max: I don't want any.
Ben: They don't have this at Mayfair, but this is delicious.
Ethel: What's the name of it?
Ben: It's the Lasko but there's herring snack bits and there's reasons why – the guy told me once before that it was the best. It's Nova Scotia herring.
Bill: Why is it the best?
Ben: 'Cause it comes from cold water. 'Cause cold-water fish is always
Max: [?] when they... uh... can it.
Ethel: Mmmm.
Ben: Cold-water fish is –
Ethel: Oooo, Max, have a piece.
Ben: This is the best you ever tasted.

---

45 Much has been discussed about Chinese's readiness to share information about their family members, income, and other things that a "Westerner" would find private in an effort to demonstrate the communality of Chinese culture (e.g., Mao 1992; 1994; Ye 2004, 2019). But that would, again, be what is on the surface. One can say – if the two societies are eventually found to differ on this – that the sharing of private information in one culture is motivated by the need for interconnectedness; the avoidance of such sharing in another culture is motivated by the need to prevent disintegration of interconnectedness.

Ethel:	Geschmacht. Mmm. Oh, It's delicious. Ben, could you hand 'me a napkin, please.
Bill:	Lemme cut up a little piece a' bread.
Ben:	Innat good?
Ethel:	Delicious. Geschmacht, Max.
Max:	What?
Ethel:	Geschmacht. Max, one piece.
Max:	I don' want.
Ben:	You're gonna be – You better eat sump'n because you're gonna be hungry before we get there.
Max:	So?
Ben:	C'mo. Here. I don't wancha to get sick.
Max:	Get there I'll have something.
Ben:	Huh?
Max:	When I get there I'll eat.
Ben:	Yeah, but you better eat something before. You wanna lay down'n take a nap?
Max:	No.
Ben:	C'mon. You wanna sit up and take a nap? Cause I'm gonna take one.
Max:	[?]
Ben:	– in a minute. That's good. That is really good.
Ethel:	Mmm.
Ben:	Honestly. C'mon.
Max:	I don't [?] .
Ben:	[?] Please, I don't wancha to get sick.
Max:	I don't get sick.
Ben:	'Ooo, that's so –
Ethel:	It's just sorta –
Ben:	Innat – Innat –
Ethel:	– tickles the tongue, doesn't it?
Ben:	Mmm. Maybe we oughta take one – take one home with us.
Bill:	Where dju get it.
Ethel:	Alpha Beta [up here].
Bill:	Right here?
Ethel:	Mmm.
Bill:	Hm.
Ethel:	Hm – you better put some more in the dish, Ben. Would you be good enough to empty this in there and then I'll fill it *up* for you again.
Ben:	Yeah, I know.
Ethel:	Thank you.

Ben: Max doesn't know what he's missing.
Bill: *He* knows.
Ben: I don't want him to get sick. I want him to eat.

(Tannen 1986: 106–108)

In the conversation, Ethel and Ben are trying to get Max eat herring and Max refuses to eat it throughout. What is remarkable is the length Ethel and Ben go to to achieve their end: they force him with straightforward imperatives, they cajole him with seemingly denigrating remarks ("Max doesn't know what he's missing"), they lure him with the taste of herring, and they insist on the benefit of eating ("I don't' want him to get sick"). This is a far more elaborate sequence of offering than what is reported in the literature on offering and inviting in Chinese. But a resolute Max stands his ground.

Tannen asked Harvey Sacks – one of the founding fathers of conversation analysis as will be seen below in Chapter 6 – to analyze the conversation. Sacks saw the tug-of-war as resulting from a conflict between independence and solidarity. For Max, he has been told what to eat and what not to by his wife for 35 years. Now he feels it is time for him to to eat what he wants. If he gives in, he would subject himself to the will of others again. For Ethel and Ben, they feel responsible for Max, an elderly man who needs to be cared for. For us, though, the issue is imposition: it demonstrates that American English speakers can be just imposing on each other's individual freedom in situations that call for imposition.

One may say that (19) represents a rare case of imposition in English, a view I used to hold myself. But that view needs to be demonstrated, not assumed. On January 6, 2021, a mob breached the U.S. Capitol building, the seat of the U.S. Congress, while the Congress was in the process of certifying the election of the new president, Joe Biden. The speaker of the House of Representatives, Nancy Pelosi, reported on TV a short conversation between her and a Capitol police officer, who came to the House chamber to protect and then evacuate the lawmakers. Pelosi reported that the officer told her to leave. The following exchange took place:

(20) Pelosi: I want to stay here.
     Police: No. You must go.

A police officer bluntly telling the Speaker of the House to leave has to be "imposing", but few would blame the officer of imposition, as the urgency of the situation – the mobs were right outside the House Chamber – relieved the officer of the burden to be deferential, a point I made earlier with the about-to-fall-off-a-cliff scenario.

Example (21) was heard between two young men in their late teens.

(21) A: I've run out of cigs.
B: [takes out a half-full packet of cigarettes and hands to A]. Take the whole thing.
A: Sure? I just need one.
B: I have another pack.
A: Just one...
B: Take the whole damn thing, bro, and shut up!
A: As you say.

B's utterance "Take the whole damn thing, bro, and shut up!" is not taken as impoliteness, A told me later, "That is the way we talk". But the imposition is there nonetheless, and such imposition may not be uncommon among "intimates" in Western societies as well.

Based on the above, MMP leads to the following with regard to the debate about the East-West Divide.

(22) *East and West are similar*
   a. They have similar interactional motivations (benefit public image of other and self)
   b. In both, the public image includes the desire for freedom of action and the desire for solidarity and connection.
   c. In both, the motivation to benefit other-public image and the motivation to benefit self-public image may coincide or clash, leading to different degrees of politeness or impoliteness.

East and West may be different (where *one* and *the other* refers to either East or West)
   a. on the content of the public image (e.g., One may value solidarity/freedom of action more than the other).
   b. on what value is salient in a given context (e.g., When someone is in financial difficulty, a friend may lend him money in one but not in another).
   c. on the power one social status may hold over the other. (e.g., A parent may hold more power over a child in one than in the other. Age may hold more power in one than in the other.)
   d. on the judgement of social distance (e.g., A colleague may be seen as more intimate in one than in the other.)

These points can be further summarized into two simple statements: East and West are similar at the highest level of generalization. They may differ at lower levels. Further, the differences would be differences in degree, not in kind, as is seen in the "more than" syntax in the difference part of (22).

4.2.5 Further notes

In the past decade, a new strand of research interest has emerged: variational pragmatics. Variational pragmatics is defined as "the study of how language use varies within one language as a result of such macrosocial factors as region, gender, age, ethnic identity, and socioeconomic class" (Schneider and Barron 2008). It is thus a combination of pragmatics and Labovian sociolinguistics. While we are not going to have space for a chapter on it (which it richly deserves), it is believed that the analysis conducted in this chapter on cross-/intercultural pragmatics will be applicable to variational pragmatics as well.

As we depart this section, a few more notes are necessary. First, while the East-West Divide debate has been cast as a binary, grouping students of cross-/intercultural pragmatics into two opposing camps, we should not ignore the fact that many scholars are situated in the middle (Chen 2010b: 169) and their voices are possibly not adequately heard when the two ends of the Different-Similar continuum are picked out as prototypical (and easy) representations of each camp.

Second, the debate between the two opposing campus is often not about facts but about how to interpret facts, indicating that the debate is as much philosophical as it is empirical, if not more philosophical than empirical. This may be analogous to a medical diagnosis. One doctor might be content to see different symptoms as different diseases and treat them accordingly. Another doctor might prefer to determine if the different symptoms are different manifestations of the same disease before treating them as different diseases. It is here we see the advantage of MMP: it recognizes these differences but accounts for them as variations of similar motivations at the deeper level.

At the same time, the debate about the East-West Divide should be seen not as an isolated pursuit but as a product of the larger intellectual environment in the social sciences and humanities. In one sense, any cross-cultural pragmatic study entails comparison and/or contrast. You look at a particular pragmatic phenomenon in language X and you are almost bound to compare your findings with those from a different language. What makes the East-West debate special is the fact that East, typically presented by Chinese, Japanese, and Korean, has been perceived to be the opposite of West in pragmatics. This is in part influenced by sister disciplines of study, particularly sociology, intercultural communication, anthropology, and psychology. In these fields, East and West have been cast as opposites: East is portrayed as collectivist (Miyahara et al. 1998) while West, individualist. Eastern cultures are dubbed "high context" cultures while Western cultures, "low context" ones. In terms of psychology, East is believed to exemplify "shame culture" while West, "guilt culture" (McNamee 2015). In terms of social relationship orientation, Eastern cultures are considered "vertical" (or "hierarchical", as seen in Yabuuchi 2006) while West, "horizontal". In terms of social distance among members, East is said to be a society of "intimates" while West, of "strangers" (Ye 2019).

These assertions are intuitively valid and the labels in them are useful for their own right. However, problems arise when these assumptions are taken a bit too far. When we say that East is X and West is Y, it seems necessary to clarify that what we really mean is that East is more X and West is more Y. It seems seldom the case, in the study of language use, that East is X, *not Y*. For example, the statement that Western cultures are more individualistic than Eastern cultures seems to possess more intuitive validity – and possibly more empirical evidence – than the statement that West is individual-based and East is not. Sweeping statements have the potential to stereotype. Part of the mission of us students of language use is to break stereotypes, not to perpetuate them.

In addition, the difference we have uncovered between East and West in the use of language has been used against the existence – or even the possibility – of universal theories. This, again, may have to do with the "multicultural turn" in cultural studies (Koyama 2003) and critical discourse analysis (Gee 2005), the "quantitative turn" in areas such as cognitive linguistics, and the "discursive turn" in pragmatics. This emphasis on empiricism is a justifiable reaction to the earlier research paradigm in which introspection and intuition ruled the day. Have we gone a bit too far here as well? Quite possibly. We may not have a universal theory in pragmatics at this point, but it does not seem prudent to say that we will never have one or there should not be one. Denying universality in language use is close to denying humanity that transcends boundaries between language users.

The framework of MMP also points to a direction for how to account for differences. There is no denying of differences among any groups, even between identical twins who have grown up together on a day-to-day basis. To study these differences are no doubt important. But it may just be important not to overstate what we discover. It may also be important for us to discern similarities, which has the potential to achieve the kind of understanding that we may not achieve if we focus our eyes entirely on differences.

Chapter 5
MMP and diachronic pragmatics

In this chapter, I discuss the connection between MMP and diachronic pragmatics, with an aim to demonstrate that MMP offers us a useful lens through which to view developments and changes in language use. MMP will be shown to be a flexible construct that allows for such changes at the second level of the interactional, i.e., at the level of the public image of other and self.

In Section 5.1, I offer a quick sketch of historical/diachronic pragmatics. In Section 5.2. I review two cross-generational studies. In Sections 5.3 and 5.4, I present two longitudinal case studies in Chinese that my colleagues and I have conducted. The first is the study of the changes seen in the behavior of responding to compliments over a seventeen-year time span. The second is the study of how the offering of food at the end of a dinner seems to have changed also, between 1995 and 2019. In Section 5.5, MMP will be applied to the findings of these studies, showing that the changes that have been identified are changes of the content of the public image of other and self.

5.1 A sketch of historical and diachronic pragmatics

Diachronic pragmatics is part of historical pragmatics. Historical pragmatics emerged in 1995, with the publication of Jucker's (1995) edited volume entitled *Historical Pragmatics: Pragmatic Developments in the History of English*. Since then, the field has progressed through "the changes in terms of shifts in thought styles and . . . seven different turns – the pragmatic turn, the socio-cultural turn, the dispersive turn, the empirical turn, the digital turn, the discursive turn and the diachronic turn" (Taavitsainen and Jucker 2015: 1) – and has produced a large amount of literature. A review of the literature is not offered here but readers are referred to studies by Jocker and colleagues (Jucker 1995, 2008, Jucker and Taavistsainen 2010; 2013; Taavitsainen and Jucker 2003) and others (Brinton 2006, 2008; Traugott, 2008; Traugott and Trousdale 2010).

Historical pragmatics, according to Jucker, is a field of study that "wants to understand the patterns of intentional human interaction (as determined by the conditions of society) of earlier periods, the historical developments of these patterns, and the general principles underlying such developments" (Jucker 2008: 895). Of the three aspects of historical pragmatics – the pragmatics of a language in earlier periods, the historical development, and the reasons for such developments – diachronic pragmatics is tasked with the last two: to study the development of pragmatic patterns and to explore the reasons for these patterns (Brinton 2001; Jacobs and Jucker 1995).

For students of diachronic pragmatics, the major focus on the development of patterns of language use has been form-to-function mapping. Brinton, for instance, traces the discourse markers in English and demonstrates how they have become what they are today through changes of various kinds (Brinton 1998, 2006, 2008). What is the most relevant to us (see below) are a series of studies on speech acts or speech events. Arnovick (1999) explores the evolution of such speech acts as promises, curses, blessings, and greetings and such speech events as flyting and sounding. Flyting of the Anglo-Saxon warrior, for one, developed into the competitive sounding of African-American youths. Similarly, the utterance in early Modern English "God be with you" entailed an explicit blessing and an implicit parting but has by now changed into "good-bye" in present-day English, with its meaning of blessing lost (cf, Morgan 1978). There are also cases of consistency over time, as exhibited in speech acts such as compliments (Taavitsainen and Jucker 2008) and apologies (Jucker and Taavitsainen 2008a). Other studies on speech acts and speech events are seen in Jucker and Taavitsainen (2008b).

Politeness has also been a focus for diachronic pragmatics. For instance, Kohnen (2008) discusses how politeness was seen in address terms in Anglo-Saxon England. Brown and Gilman (1989) and Kopytko (1995b) investigate the preferences for negative and positive politeness in Early Modern English (1400–1600). Culpeper and Demmen (2011) trace the emergence of the concept of negative politeness (in particular the use of ability questions for requesting) back to the Victorian era.

All of the studies cited above concentrate on specific areas of language use in historical periods of time. There are studies – it should be noted – that contrast two languages in the same period of time, such as Ruhi and Kádár (2010), who investigate the use of the notion *face* in late 19th and early 20th century Turkish and Chinese. There are also studies that investigate language use *over* time. Allen (2018), for example, compares lexical bundles found in the language input of a selection of historical (1905–1907) documents with current (2004–2014) English language teaching material. Pan and Kádár (2011) investigate politeness in Chinese, contrasting historical and contemporary periods. The offering of tea at a wedding by the bride to her parents-in-law – an example of contemporary Chinese politeness – for instance, is till ritualized but different from historical Chinese politeness: honorifics are no longer used and the offer sounds "more direct" (Pan and Kádár 2011: 76–77). The collection of papers in *Popular News Discourse in American and British newspapers 1833–1988,* a special issue of the *Journal of Historical Pragmatics*, compare and contrast "the various strategies employed by popular newspapers to articulate an idealized version of the interests and language of their readers for profit and political influence" (Conboy 2014).

For diachronic pragmaticists, one obvious challenge is the authenticity of data. Due to the fact that there is no data of spontaneous communication in the bulk of human history, scholars can only rely on written accounts of spoken language or recreations in literary works of poetry, drama, and fiction. Arguments can be made that such texts – particularly court records – are good enough, but they are records, replicas, representations, or recreations nonetheless. Even transcriptions of a court proceeding miss many important clues such as gestures, facial expressions, and phonological features (stress, pitch, and intonation). A detailed discussion of the advantages and disadvantages of the various kinds of texts is seen in Jucker and Taavitsainen (2010).

The "bad data" issue in diachronic pragmatics, according to Jucker and Taavitsainen (2010: 16–23), has led to several problems for the field: pathways to change problem (how to generalize the pathway of a change that can account for a large number of linguistic units that may seem disparate), meaning problem (how to determine the precise meaning of a unit of language without requisite contextual clues), identification problem (how to decide on the intended speech act), categorization and inventory problem (how to group the different linguistic units into a coherent system for the language concerned), and contextualization problem (how to contextualize the study, which is critical to a pragmatic analysis). As we will see below, the four studies discussed help alleviate some of these concerns.

5.2 Cross-generational pragmatics

In this section, I review two cross-generation studies in pragmatics. The first is Fukushima (2011). Fukushima used questionnaires to collect quantitative data from three groups of respondents – Japanese university students, Japanese parents, and American university students – followed by interviews with some of them. The questionnaire includes six situations. Her Situation 1 is below:

(1) You are sitting in a train, reading a book. There are many standing passengers, but there is a vacancy in a priority seat in the same car. At the next station, A, your acquaintance, gets on the train. A is carrying a lot of baggage. You do not have any heavy baggage.

To which the respondents were asked to rate the following options on a 5-point Likert scale:

(2) What would you do in this situation?
   a. You offer A a seat. Or you hold A's baggage.
   b. You tell A that there is a vacancy in a priority seat.
   c. You keep reading a book.
   d. Other (write what):

Of the six situations, the only situation in which the three groups exhibit differences in their choices of what to do is Situation 5.[46]

(3) *Fukushima's Situation 5*
   You have attended a lecture at the university and are about to go home. There were presentations from every group in the class. There has been a huge amount of papers submitted to the professor from every group. You do not have any urgent appointment after class.

Fukushima does not provide choices that she provided to her respondents for this situation in the paper. But as is gleaned from the interviews, it seems that the issue centers on whether one should help the professor to carry the papers. Japanese parents favor the option of helping, American students are split but lean towards not helping, and Japanese students are split but lean towards helping. If one can draw any conclusion from this single example, it might be that the younger generation of Japanese are moving away from positive politeness, as helping others is a positive politeness strategy per Brown and Levinson (1987).

The second cross-generation study is conducted by Bella and Ogiermann (2019). The authors interviewed 40 (23 female and 17 male; aged 30–45) native speakers of Greek residing in the capital city of Athens and the third biggest Greek city of Patras. The interview had two parts: the first eliciting memories involving evaluations of impoliteness made during interactions with members of the older generation and the second explicitly engaging with the concept of politeness, "eliciting the informants' definitions of politeness and the characteristics of a polite person" (Bella and Ogiermann 2019: 169).

The first part of the interview resulted in three types of impolite behaviors by older-generation, as seen below.

---

46 Fukushima does not provide statistical significance for the scores in her Table 4.2 (Fukushima 2011: 560). So, I estimated the significance of these situations based on the sizes of the differences in the table.

(4) [Numbers in parenthesis are frequencies of mention by interviewees; *the types* are my relabeling for ease of reference]
   a. *Non-verbal*
      Disregarding queues (19)
      Invading privacy, e.g., entering rooms, opening bags, drawers, etc. (21)
      Being too intimate, e.g., passing on personal information to third parties, engaging strangers in lengthy conversations (7)
      Acting in an authoritative way, e.g., prescribing others what to do, demanding a seat on public transport (4)
   b. *Verbal*
      Asking indiscreet personal questions (17)
      Making inappropriate comments (6)
      Sharing intimate details in public places (3)
   c. *Not as expected*
      Not saying "thank you", "please" or "I'm sorry" – or reserving the use of politeness formulae to strangers only (11)
      Being overly familiar by using the T-form where the V-form is expected (7)
      Impolite speech act realization: use of imperatives in requests, high degree of insistence in offering (7)
      Prosodic features, such as loudness (7)

(Bella and Ogiermann 2019: 171)

Based on the second part of the interview – on why the interviewees thought the examples they had provided were "impolite" – the authors summarize the generational change into the following. First, the older-generation speakers of Greek do not express gratitude ("My parents take it for granted that, since we live in the same house, we do things for each other and politeness is redundant") and appear imposing among ingroups ("When my dad asks for something, it always sounds like an order"). Second, they have different ideas about privacy, as one interviewer reports:

> When I was still living at home and had friends over, I didn't dare to invite them to the living room because my dad would sit with us for hours asking them all kinds of questions about their lives, their jobs, their parents. So embarrassing. When I confronted him about this, he said that it would be rude to have people in his home and not talk to them or show interest. I tried to explain the limits – but in vain. (Bella and Ogiermann 2019: 174)

Third – with regard to behaviors in public – the older-generation Greeks are seen as assuming more intimacy, are readier to divulge private information, and ignore queues. The following quote is from another interviewee.

> This generation has no manners. They behave to complete strangers as if they were their assistants. No "please", no "I am sorry", no nothing. The other day a woman my mother's age hit me badly with her elbow in the street and she just stared at me. Especially if you are younger, you have no hope of getting an apology. (Bella and Ogiermann 2019: 179)

Bella and Ogiermann (2019: 164) conclude: "While Greece has been unanimously characterized as a positive politeness culture in previous research, the present study illustrates an increasing emphasis on values and norms associated with negative politeness".

These two cross-generational pragmatic studies both identify changes in language use by their respective targeted population. Despite the difference in methodology, the two studies were carried out in one period of time. By looking at how speakers of different generations behave in the same context, changes (or lack of them) of a particular language use can be validly identified. This helps resolve the "bad data" problem in diachronic pragmatics. In the following sections, we will review two longitudinal studies by me and my colleagues. The first study is on the diachronic change of the speech act of compliment responding in Chinese, drawing on Chen (1993a) and Chen and Yang (2010). The second is on the diachronic change of the speech event of end-of-dinner food offering, also in Chinese, based on Chen (1996a) and Chen and Hu (2020).

5.3 Compliment responses

As we have seen in Chapter 4, compliment responding has been one of the most studied speech acts in pragmatics, particularly in cross-/intercultural pragmatics. The Chinese linguaculture has figured prominently in this scholarly landscape, which has also been used for the evaluation of theories and research methodologies (Juker 2009).

As is recalled from Section 4.1, while scholars in compliment responses research have adopted a range of taxonomies, there has appeared a convergence in the way compliment responses are categorized, i.e., the tripartite system – Acceptance, Deflection/Evasion, and Rejection – originally proposed by Holmes (1988), supported by Han (1992) and Chen (1993a), and adopted by many (Ruhi 2006; Tang and Zhang 2009; among others). This taxonomy, first, reflects the insights of Pomerantz's (1978) constraints of "agree with the complimenter" and "avoid self-praise". For the need to agree with the complimenter motivates the acceptance of a compliment; the need to avoid self-praise motivates the rejection of a compliment, while the need to strike a balance between the two constraints leads to utterances that deflect or evade the compliment.

Chen (1993a) used a DCT – a questionnaire containing four conversational situations – for data collection. A compliment was paid in each situation. The subjects were asked to write down as many utterances as they thought they would use to respond to the compliment in each situation. The four situations have to do with appearances (Situation 1), clothing (Situation 2), achievement (Situation 3), and possession (Situation 4), respectively. The relationship between the complimenter and the complimentee in these situations is limited to friends and acquaintances, based on earlier works (Homes 1988; Manes 1983) about the most likely complimentees in actual conversations.

As a contrastive study, the English version of the questionnaire was distributed to 50 Missouri College (U.S.) undergraduate students and the Chinese version to 50 Xi'an International Studies University (XISU, China) undergraduate students. The actual time for this data collection was January 1991. Data in the collected questionnaires were coded into strategies, which were then grouped under several superstrategies.

The American subjects in the study used altogether ten strategies, grouped under four superstrategies: Accepting, Returning, Deflecting, and Rejecting. If we convert these four into the tripartite structure outlined in Section 1, Accepting and Returning can be grouped together. Therefore Americans are found to accept compliments 57.78% of the time, deflect/evade compliments 29.50% of the time, and reject compliments 12.70% of the time. The Chinese subjects, on the other hand, reject compliments 95.73% of the time, accept compliments 1.03% of the time, and deflect/evade them 3.41% of the time. Applying politeness theories to these findings, I argued that Brown and Levinson's (1987) theory accounts for the English data but not the Chinese data. Gu's (1990) notion of modesty accounts for the Chinese data but not the English data. Leech's (1983) Politeness Principle, on the other hand, accounts for both sets of data: his Agreement Maxim explains the American data and his Modesty Maxim explains the Chinese data.

Seventeen years later, another study was carried out, replicating Chen (1993a) to assure compatibility. The Chinese version of the 1993a questionnaire was administered among 160 undergraduate students at the same site – XISU – in June 2008. The subjects were instructed to write down as many responses as they wanted. In the 160 questionnaires collected, there are a total of 1501 compliment responses, grouped into 16 strategies. These 16 strategies are further grouped into the three categories (the equivalent of Chen's term "superstrategies") Accepting, Evading/Deflecting, and Rejecting. Under each of these categories are also a great number of responses that combine two or more strategies. They are grouped under "combination". The comparison of the two groups is seen in Figure 5.1.

Table 5.1: Comparison of Chinese compliment responses between 1991 and 2008.

		1991 (N = 50)		2008 (N = 160)	
		No.	%	No.	%
ACCEPTING	1. Agreeing	0	0	76	5.07
	2. Thanking	3	1.03	184	12.27
	3. Expressing gladness	0	0	47	3.13
	4. Returning	0	0	107	7.13
	5. Encouraging	0	0	92	6.13
	6. A-Explaining	0	0	42	2.80
	Combination	0	0	391	26.07
	Total	3	1.03	939	62.60
DEFLECTING/ EVADING	7. Offering	0	0	49	3.27
	8. Using humor	0	0	31	2.07
	9. Seeking confirmation	0	0	23	1.53
	10. Doubting	0	0	9	0.60
	11. Deflecting	0	0	65	4.33
	12. D/E-Explaining	0	0	82	5.47
	Combination	10	3.41	165	11.00
	Total	10	3.41	424	28.27
REJECTING	13. Disagreeing	0	0	31	2.07
	14. Denigrating	0	0	41	2.73
	15. Expressing Embarrassment	76	26.21	23	1.53
	16. R-Explaining	55	18.83	7	0.47
	Combination	148	50.70	35	2.33
	Total	279	95.73	138	9.13
TOTAL		292	100	1501	100

Table 5.1 reveals important differences between the two respondent groups. Respondents in 1991 reported that they rejected compliments 95.73% of the time while the those who were surveyed in 2008 rejected them only 9.13% of the time. Similarly, the 1991 group accepted compliments 1.03% of the time while the 2008 group accepted compliments 62.60% of the time. Besides, the latter group also reported a large percentage of Deflecting/Evading strategies, which are absent in the 1991 group.

What are the reasons for the drastic change in Xi'an Chinese' behaviors within a span of 17 years? We proposed that the contact Chinese in Xi'an had with Western cultures is the major reason. The cite of the research – XISU – is largely a regional university. While it enrolls students from all parts of China, XISU takes by far the majority of students from the Northwest Region of the country that covers five provinces along the Yellow River, an area known as the cradle of ancient Chinese civilization. It is commonly believed that the ancientness of the region, together with its inland location, has made it the most socially conservative region of the country.

China remained a closed society from 1949 till the early 1980s, when the government began a political and economic reform. This reform started in the southeastern coastal cities such as Guangzhou and Shenzhen and spread gradually along the coast upwards. In the early 1980s, therefore, the Northwest Region of China by and large continued with the old economy and maintained its social conservatism while the coastal cities were experiencing drastic reformation in all facets of society.

The average age of the 1991 survey respondents was 22. These students were born between 1968 and 1971, spent their childhood still under Mao Zedong's time (Mao died in 1976), and grew up in the 1980s. However, since Xi'an and its surrounding communities were still relatively closed to the outside world, these subjects probably represented the traditional social values such as modesty, which caused them to reject compliments.

The much-touted reform in China eventually made its way into the inland region in the 1990s and flourished at the turn of the century. This reform brought to the region capitalist economy, leading to remarkable economic growth. It has also brought business, tourism, and technology, resulting in the increasing presence of speakers of other languages in Xi'an and its neighboring cities. The relative easing of government control of the media has made available to the people in the region a host of TV programs, films, music CDs, and books from the outside. The city of Xi'an and the Northwest Region it represents were fast transforming, both economically and socially.

The respondents of the 2008 study are largely a product of this historic change. Their average age was 21, which means that they were born in the late 1980s and grew up in the 1990s, a time of change for the communities in which they have lived. Therefore, although the two studies have been carried out with a time span of seventeen years in between, the respondents happen to have grown up in two very different times, hence representing two very different generations. It is therefore possible that the major difference between the two groups in their compliment responding behavior is a result of the societal changes that have taken place in the region.

This hypothesis seems to agree with findings of other studies on the compliment corresponding behaviors of Chinese in different locals of the country. Yuan (2002) studies compliment responses by Chinese Kunming, also an inland city (but in the Southwest Region) that was late (albeit not as late as Xi'an) in its exposure to Western cultures. Yuan's work is estimated – she does not provide the time of her field work for the study – to have been carried out around 2000. So, we would have three studies on Chinese compliment responses with roughly the same amount of time span in between: the 1991 Xi'an study, the 1999–2000 Kunming study, and the 2008 Xi'an study. Placing the three studies together, we find a progression of compliment acceptance.

Table 5.2: A longitudinal comparison.

Year of study	Acceptance	Deflection/Evasion	Rejection
1991 (Chen 1993a)	1.03%	3.41%	95.73%
2000 (Yuan 2002)	31.26%	34.76%	33.98%
2008 (Chen and Yang 2010)	62.6%	28.27%	9.13%

Table 5.2 reveals that, longitudinally, the compliment responding behavior of Chinese is moving from rejection to acceptance: as the time progresses, they reject less and accept more over the 17-year period. Like our study, Yuan also identified contact with Western cultures as a reason for change. One of Yuan's interviewees, for example, said:

> Well, the influence is rather big, indeed it's big. Like there were some expressions in the past, right, for example, from Western civilizations, through all kinds of channels, their languages, have had great influence on people like us, people everywhere. For example, our say of compliment is totally different from that of people who are a few dozens of years older than we are. Their attitudes towards people have all kinds of impact, in fact. From things like video games, in all aspects, even a popular pet phrase, things like that, right, from Hong Kong and Taiwan movies, from the West, when you hear them, you'll learn to say them. (Yuan, 2002: 215)

A comparison between the Xi'an studies and Tang and Zhang (2009) may offer further support for the hypothesis that the change identified in the compliment responding behavior of Xi'an Chinese is a result of changes in culture. Tang and Zhang (2009) study compliment responses by Chinese in Australia, who are found to accept compliments 48.82% of the time, deflect/evade them 36.66% of the time, and reject them 14.55% of the time. These numbers are quite similar to our 2008 Xi'an study (Chen and Yang 2010), as presented in Table 5.2, at least in the order in which they use these strategies: Accepting, followed by Deflecting/Evading, with Rejecting as the least favored category of strategies. Secondly, the percentages in the frequency of occurrence for each of the three categories are somewhat similar: Tang and Zhang's subjects, for instance, accepted compliments most of the time. Since the actual data collection for both studies were done at more or less the same year (2008), there seems to be reason to believe that similar sociocultural factors are responsible for these findings.[47]

The findings of the 1991 Xi'an study may be best interpreted in terms of Leech's (1983) Politeness Principle: that X'an Chinese rejected compliments overwhelmingly because they want to be modest. Modesty, however, is not only an other-oriented value (e.g., to lower self for the purpose of elevating other) as believed by Leech. It is also part of the public image of members of the Chinese society (Chen and Yang 2022; Gu 1990; Zhou and Zhang 2018). In other words, the rejection of compliments by Chinese speakers in 1991 could be said to be due to the interactional motivation of establishing, maintaining, or enhancing the public image of self. A similar argument is made in Ruhi (2006, 2007), about Turkish compliment responses.

This proposal, however, does not explain the findings in the 2008 Xi'an study, whose respondents accept compliments most of the time. A possible explanation will be provided in Section 5.5. wherein I explore the connection between MMP and diachronic pragmatics.

5.4 End-of-dinner food offering

5.4.1 Introduction and methodology

The longitudinal studies on end-of-dinner were conducted with 24 years apart: in 1995 and then in 2019 and, like the compliment response study, reveal drastic differences in the two groups. The 1995 study was originally reported in Chen (1996a) and the 2019 study, in Chen and Hu (2020).

End-of-dinner food offering refers to hosts asking their guests to eat more food when the latter signal that they have finished eating. While offer as a single speech act has drawn considerable attention from students of language use – see Barron (2017) for a comprehensive review – offer as an event has not been extensively studied, with possibly only two studies in the literature: Grainger, Mansor, and Mills (2015) and Zhu, Li, and Qian (2000).

Grainger, Mansor, and Mills (2015) compare how an offer is conducted in Arabic and English. They find that Libyan Arabic speakers make the same offer at least twice. The first time the offer is made, it is generally refused. The host

---

[47] We emphasize the tentativeness of this view, as there is little discussion on the relationship between CRs and culture in Tang and Zhang (2009) and likewise little information about the geographical and other backgrounds of their subjects.

then offers again (and sometimes more than once) before the offer is eventually accepted or refused. In one of their examples, the host of a party offers a piece of cake three times, before eventually giving up. To the authors, the reason for this repeated offer is the importance of hospitality, that is, "the host's need to conform to the social convention of appearing generous and the guest's need to not appear greedy" (Grainger, Mansor, and Mills 2015: 67). As a result, "the host's behavior typically conveys generosity and warmth, whilst the guest's refusal displays humility and self-restraint". British English speakers, on the other hand, may repeat the offer, but much less persistently, which the authors attribute to "the rights to autonomy" (Grainger, Mansor, and Mills 2015: 66) in British culture.

Zhu, Li, and Qian (2000) study gift offering in Chinese within the framework of conversation analysis. The majority of their ethnographical data displays the following sequential structure, which is a representation of (13) in Chapter 4 for ready reference.

(5) A: Presequence (Optional)
 B: Presequence (Optional)
 A: Offer
 B: Decline
 A: Offer repeated
 B: Decline repeated (Optional)
 A: Offer repeated (Optional)
 B: Acceptance

(Zhu, Li, and Qian 2000: 98)

This structure is similar to that in Arabic: the offering event is composed of several adjacency pairs (about three in each case) and a set of fixed speech acts, most notably the act of offering and of refusal ("decline", according to them). However, they do not consider politeness when accounting for their findings. Instead, they propose that the notions of sincerity and balance are responsible for the offering behavior of their subjects. The rather complicated sequence helps to ensure the sincerity of the offer. It also provides an opportunity to balance conflicting needs. For the gift giver, that balance is "between not imposing an unwanted gift onto someone and protecting the recipient's face by not suggesting that the recipient is in need of certain things". For the gift recipient, the balance is "between not hurting the gift offeror's feelings by rejecting the offer outright, and not showing greediness by accepting it straightaway" (Zhu, Li, and Qian 2000: 99–100).

In 1995, the first study of end-of-dinner food offering was conducted in the city of Xi'an, China, the same city the longitudinal studies on compliment responses were carried out as discussed in the last section. The data came from dinners that involved hosts and guests. The hosts either invited the guests to dine in a restaurant (and paid for the dinner) or to their homes and prepared the dinner themselves. These dinners were provided for primarily two reasons: to express gratitude for a favor done by the guests or to maintain/enhance the relationship, either familial or professional, with the guests. The food offering events occurred at the end of the dinner, typically when the guests put down their chopsticks (or silverware) and pushed the bowl/plate slightly away to indicate that they had finished eating. The aim of the study was to determine whether the host would ask the latter to eat more and, if so, how such an offering would be performed. The data were obtained from eight actual end-of-dinner conversations: five held in restaurants and three held in the hosts' homes. The findings of the study are presented in Table 5.3 below.

Table 5.3: Frequency of occurrence of Adjacency Pairs (AP) in all eight events.[48]

	RESTAURANT (1–5)					HOME (6–8)			TOTAL
Conversation	1	2	3	4	5	6	7	8	8
AP1	1	1	2	1	2	2	1	1	11
AP2	1	2	1	1	2	0	1	1	9
AP3	1	1	1	1	1	1	1	1	8
AP4	1	0	1	0	1	1	0	1	5
TOTAL	4	4	5	3	6	4	3	4	33

From Table 5.3, we can observe that at the end of a dinner involving a host and a guest, there is a lengthy back-and-forth flow to the food offering (which I called "food-plying") that includes an average of 4.0 adjacency pairs. The coding of the data led to the following structure for the end-of-dinner food offering.

Table 5.4: Structure of end-of-dinner food offering by Xi'an Chinese in 1995.

AP	TURN, SPEAKER	SPEECH ACT
1&	1, host	Offering
	2, guest	Refusing
2&*	3, host	Asserting that G has eaten little
	4, guest	Asserting that she has eaten much.

---

48 Taken from Chen (1996a: 145) with slight formatting alterations.

5.4 End-of-dinner food offering

Table 5.4 (continued)

AP	TURN, SPEAKER	SPEECH ACT
3*	5, host	Denigrating food or skill, offering
	6, guest	Praising food or skill, refusing
4+	7, host	Offering, "threatening" with offence
	8, guest	Accepting

Notes: &: repeatable; *: position not fixed; +: optional

This structure is illustrated by Example (6).[49]

(6) AP1 T1: H: 老王，再吃一点.
Lǎo wáng zàichīyīdiǎn
'Lao Wang, eat some more'.
T2: G: 不用客气，我吃好了。
búyòng kèqì wǒchīhǎole
'Don't stand on ceremony. I've had enough'.
AP2 T3: H: 你才吃了那么一点。
nǐ cái chī le nà me yī diǎn
But you've had so little".
T4: G: 不，不. 我吃了很多.
bú bú wǒchīlehěnduō
'No, no. I've had a lot'.
AP3 T5: H: 饭不好吃，但总得吃好啊。
Fànbúhǎochī dànzǒngdéchīhǎo ā
'The food is not good. But you have to have enough'.
T6: G: 饭很好吃。我再也吃不下了。
fànhěnhǎochī wǒzàiyěchībúxià le
'The food is delicious. But I can't eat anymore'.
AP4 T7: H: 不行。你得再吃点。要不我就生气了。
bùháng nǐdézàichīdiǎn yàobúwǒjiùshēngqìle 。
'No. You have to eat more. Otherwise I'll be offended'.
T8: G: 好吧。我再吃一点。
hǎo ba wǒ zài chī yī diǎn
'Ok. I'll have a bit more'.

---

49 Example (2) taken from Chen (1996a: 145) with slight formatting alterations and the addition of Chinese typographical characters.

Several generalizations emerge from this study about food offering at the end of a hosted dinner in Xi'an, China. First, the food offering event is a lengthy and repetitive process, lasting an average of eight conversational turns, organized into four adjacency pairs. Second, the internal structure of the event is rather "tight" and predictable, although there are variations in terms of the positioning and repeatability of some APs. The event starts with the host offering food (AP1 of Table 5.4), moves on to whether the guest has eaten enough (AP2) and whether or not the food is good (AP3), and may or may not include AP4, in which the host threatens that he will be offended if the guest continues to refuse the food being offered. Invariably, the guest accepts the offering, oftentimes only one small bite of food.

The predictability of the food offering event is also seen in the internal structure of the APs. In the classical conversation analysis literature, the second part of an adjacency pair is either preferred or dispreferred. Agreement is the preferred second to an assertion, while disagreement is the dispreferred second. In the food offering speech event, however, most seconds (as seen in APs 1 to 3) are dispreferred. In AP1, the offer is met with a decline; in AP2, the assertion that the guest has eaten little is met with disagreement; and, in AP3, the host's denigration of the food is met with the guest praising it.

An obvious similarity is observed across the Chinese end-of-dinner food offering event as shown in (6), the typical offering event in Arabic (Grainger, Mansor, and Mills 2015) and the Chinese gift giving reported in Zhu, Li, and Qian (2000): the structure of all three is complicated and involves a number of adjacency pairs. However, there is a notable difference between the findings on offering in Arabic and English on the one hand and offering in Chinese on the other: in the former, the offer may or may not be eventually accepted; in the latter, the offer is *always* accepted. This suggests that offering in Chinese – at least when the offered "goods" are gifts or food at the end of a dinner – are more "ritualized" than "conventionalized" (Kádár 2013).

To offer an account for his findings, an interview with a group of seven speakers in the same city were conducted. During the interview, the informants were asked to express their opinions on why the host repeatedly offered the guest food, whether such an offering sounded "pushy", and why the guest did not accept the food earlier. The interviewees converged on the view that the repeated offering of food by the host, as well as the repeated rejection of the offering by the guest, is due to warmth (Gu 1990). In other words, the repeated and forceful offering of food, which would appear to be particularly imposing to the guest in the eyes of a cultural outsider, serves the purpose of demonstrating care about the guest's wellbeing – that the host wants the guest to eat well and enjoy the occasion.

Twenty-four years later, the second study on end-of-dinner food offering was conducted. The study included data about end-of-dinner food offering by Americans and Chinese. The primary purpose of the study was longitudinal, but American data were included to provide a basis for synchronic cross-cultural comparison, due to the paucity of research on the topic. The American dataset was collected in Southern California during dinners at home. A total of 10 conversations were collected, only eight were randomly chosen to match the number of conversations used in the 1995 study on Chinese offering. The food for the dinner was either prepared by the host or ordered from a restaurant. The absence of restaurant dinners is due to the way food is served in American restaurants: each diner orders their own food, which is then served on plates specifically for that order. It would therefore be very unlikely that the host would offer his/her guest(s) food at the end of the dinner (except for making enquiries about dessert). Data on the food offering behaviors of the Chinese living in the Xi'an area were collected in a similar way, except six of the conversations took place in Restaurants and two, at the hosts' homes.

Also to replicate the 1995 study, the native speakers' views on their food offering behavior were obtained from face-to-face interviews and email surveys. In both the interview and email survey, the findings of the study were presented. The participants were asked to comment on these findings. For the American group, three interviews were conducted with eight dinner participants and the questionnaire was sent to all 29 dinner participants, with 21 returning the survey. For the Chinese group, two interviews were conducted with a total of seven dinner participants and the questionnaire was sent to all 31 dinner participants, with 23 responding.

5.4.2 Findings and discussion

Table 5.5 presents the findings about the number of adjacency pairs obtained from the American data.

Table 5.5: Findings obtained from the American data.

Conversation	1	2	3	4	5	6	7	8	AVERAGE
Number of APs	1	0	2	0	0	1	0	1	5/8=0.63

Of the eight end-of-dinner conversations in the data, there were only five instances of food offering occurring in four of the eight conversations. This suggests that food offering is not a particularly frequent occurrence during dinners hosted and attended by the American residents of Southern California. In addition, when Americans do offer food on such occasions, the offering event tends to be succinct, as shown in Example (7) below:

(7) [Thanksgiving party. There are four invited guests: two married couples. The host is female and she has cooked the meal.]
Host: [Seeing that one guest, John, has put down his fork] More turkey, John?
Guest: Oh no. Thanks.
Host: Okay. [Resumes the prior topic of conversation concerning the quality of local public schools.]

(American Conversation 1)

The offering of food is achieved with "More Turkey" and the declining of the offer with "Oh no", followed by "thanks". The host immediately stops.

In Example (8), the offer of food is carried out indirectly.

(8) Host: [To all the five guests at a birthday party for her husband Josh]: Hope y"all like the food.
Guest: [While other guests simultaneously praise the food with exclamations ("yum yum"), gestures (thumbs up, okay sign), and nods of heads] I did not know you are such a good cook – everything's delicious! Josh is a lucky man indeed.
Host: I'm glad. There is more – a lot more. Nobody is stopping you from getting a second or even a third serving.
Guest: I would love to, but there is no space left in the stomach [slightly massaging his stomach with both hands].

(American Conversation 6)

This excerpt of conversation begins with the host enquiring about the quality of the food. While all the guests compliment the food in different ways, John goes further by praising the food with lengthy utterances ("I did not know. . ."). This creates the opportunity for the host to offer him food. However, she does not make the offer directly, e.g., with an imperative sentence such as "Take more then", but instead says, "Nobody is stopping you from getting a second or even a third serving". This statement is what Searle (1975) would call the indirect speech act of offering and Brown and Levinson (1987) would call an "off-record" politeness strategy for the purpose of mitigating the face-threat entailed in the act of offering. Indeed, the guest takes it as such and declines the offer with the account, "No space left in the stomach".

The most elaborate form of food offering in the American data is shown in Example (9), in which two adjacency pairs are devoted to the act offering.

(9) [A get-together of friends after one of them – *guest*, – has been away for two years. The food is a takeout from a local restaurant, which has been placed in the kitchen adjacent to the dining room.]
Host: [Seeing that the Guest puts down his fork and pushes his plate slightly away] Hey, don't stop yet. There's plenty of food there. You got to help me with all that good stuff.
Guest: [Hesitates] Well. . ... But. . ... Not sure it'll be a wise thing to do.
Host: Look at you – a couple of more pounds will make you look even more attractive.
Guest: That is itself an attractive proposition. For the heck of it. [Stands up and walks to the kitchen for another serving.]
(American Conversation 3)

The first adjacency pair starts with the host offering food in a "bald-on-record" way, with imperative sentences such as ". . . don't stop yet" and "You got to help me with all that good stuff". The refusal of that order-like offer comes after a slight hesitation on the part of the guest, who seems to be between two minds about the offer: "Not sure it'll be a wise thing to do". The host starts the second adjacency pair with "Look at you. . ." and then makes the second offer attempt by making a veiled reference to the guest's supposed thin figure. The guest takes the food, agreeing that eating more food is good for his appearance ("that is itself an attractive proposition"). These two adjacency pairs reflect the participants' efforts to create positive politeness between themselves, hence reducing the face threatening force of the offer by the use of a joke, a strategy that often helps create camaraderie and in-groupness (Brown and Levinson 1987).

The behaviors exhibited by the Southern Californians in the study during end-of-dinner food offerings appear to be accountable by Brown and Levinson's politeness theory. According to Brown and Levinson (1987: 66), offering is a face-threatening act (FTA) in that it forces the hearer to decide whether to accept or refuse an offer. Accepting offer indebts the recipient; refusing it makes one appear disagreeable.[50] Therefore, it seems justifiable to propose that the food offering behavior exhibited by the Americans is due to the interactional motiva-

---

50 An offer may not always be this face-threatening, as it also depends on whether the hearer needs the goods being offered and how the offer is performed. In a London subway station, the first author was struggling with luggage and was on the verge of asking for help, when a young man came over and asked: 'Would you be happy if I carried this for you [pointing at a piece of

tion to benefit the public image of other. The indirectness in their offering is hence strategies to mitigate the face threatening force of the offering act. This is in agreement with Grainger, Mansor, and Mills' (2015: 66) finding about the British offering behavior, which is said to be motivated by the speakers' "rights to autonomy".

This conclusion is supported by the interview and survey data as well. First, almost all the 29 respondents – eight interviewees and 21 email survey respondents – expressed surprise when they were presented the findings of the 1995 Xi'an study, with "Wow" being a common exclamation. However, one interviewee noted that he had actually experienced the repeated offering himself while travelling in China during the late 1980s: "Yeah. My host pressed and pressed and I realized I was not to be let go without eating a bit more", he recalled. "I really appreciated my host's good intention: to make sure I was taken care of".

The interviewees and survey respondents provided several reasons as to why they did not frequently engage in end-of-dinner food offering themselves. Firstly, the main reason was that "There doesn't seem to be a need". Thirteen of the survey respondents reported, in different ways, that dinner is not a "big deal" in their culture. "You invite someone. They come, eat, and talk. When they finish, it means they have had enough. Why bother to ask them to eat more?" one respondent wrote in her email. Others echoed that food is only one part of the dining event: "Talking, catching up, enjoying the company are just as important". One interviewee and two survey respondents did say, however, that they would offer food to their guests "just to make sure that they are not being bashful" about eating in front of others. Two survey respondents reported that some occasions might call for the offering of food more than others. One of these respondents emphasized that "If I am hosting a dinner to thank someone for a favor, I think I might just ask if they want more of something".

Secondly, not to offer food can be regarded as being "considerate" of other people's tastes. One of the interviewees said the following, winning nods of approval from two others present.

> I think there is also a matter of. . . well. . . if your guest likes the food. Eating is a private experience, I think. We like vastly different things. We don't want to force our guests to eat something they are not particularly fond of. If they don't like what you want them to eat, they cannot say "Sorry, I hate it", right?

---

luggage], would you?' The first author did not feel that his face was threatened and we doubt that anyone would.

The same view was also expressed by the email survey respondents. One of them jokingly wrote: "Remember the cliché "One man's meat is another man's poison"? You never know. What you like can be absolutely disgusting to someone else".

If that is the case, why did the host in Example (9) offer her guest food the second time? We asked the host this question during one of the face-to-face interviews. After the host was shown the transcript of the conversation, she recalled: "Oh, I got it. He [the guest] was hesitant in his refusal, indicating that he *could* eat more". The host was then asked, "Are you saying that if he assertively refused your offer, you would not have attempted a second try?" "I believe so", she replied.

Thirdly, one should not be offering food because "You just don't know that some people may be dieting or have health reasons".

We now move to the findings from our Chinese data. The findings on food offering by the Xi'an Chinese are given in Table 5.6.

Table 5.6: Findings obtained from the Chinese data.

Conversation	1	2	3	4	5	6	7	8	AVERAGE
Number of APs	0	1	2	0	1	2	0	1	7/8=0.88

The Xi'an Chinese are found to offer their guests food by using an average of 0.88 adjacency pairs per dinner. Of the eight conversations in the data, it can be observed that food offering does not take place in three of them (Conversations 1, 4 and 7). Of the five that do include food offering, the number of adjacency pairs ranges from one (Conversations 2, 5 and 8) to two (Conversations 3 and 6). In the following, four examples are provided, two with one adjacency pair and two with two adjacency pairs.

(10) [A get-together of five participants. The dinner is prepared by the host at his home.]
Guest: [Puts down his chopsticks, signaling he has finished eating.]
你的饭 做的 真好.
nǐdefàn zuòde zhēn hǎo
'You are such a good cook'.
Host: 好吃 就要 再吃 一些。 来, 我 给你 夹。 [Starting to serve food.]
hǎochī jiùyào zàichī yīxiē lái wǒ gěinǐ jiá
'Since you like it, you should have more. Come on. We will get more for you'.
Guest: 好. 谢谢。 就 再来 一点。
hǎo xièxiè jiù zàilái yīdiǎnr
'Sure. Thanks. Just a little bit'.

(Chinese Conversation 2)

In this example, the offering of food appears to be precipitated by the guest's compliment of the host's cooking skills. The host tacitly accepts the compliment and uses it as a reason to offer the guest more food. It should be noted that the host begins serving before his offer is accepted, but the guest accepts the offer without much hesitation.

The offering in Example (11) also has one adjacency pair, but this time the offer is not accepted.

(11) [At a restaurant. Two participants are invited by the host]
    Host: [Seeing both guests stop eating and push their plates slightly away.]
        吃好 了 吗？再来一点 吧？
        chīhǎo le ma zàilái yīdiǎnr ba
        'Have you had enough? A bit more'?
    Guest1: 好啦。谢谢。
        hǎolā xièxiè 。
        'I'm good. Thanks'.
    Host: [To Guest2]
        你哪？
        nǐ nǎ
        'How about you'?
    Guest2: 我 也 吃好 啦。不 客气。
        wǒ yě chīhǎo lā   bú kèqì
        'I have had enough as well. Thanks'.
    Host: 好。那就 边 喝茶 边 聊 吧。
        hǎo nàjiù biān hēchá biān liáo ba 。
        'Ok. Let's continue to talk while drinking tea'.
                      (Chinese Conversation 8)

The host offers food twice because there are two guests. Since each guest is offered food only once, this conversation is counted as having one adjacency pair. When the host notices that the guests intend to stop eating, he asks both of them to have some more food. Both guests decline and the host stops the offering and asks the guests to continue drinking tea.

The following examples illustrate two adjacency pair food offerings.

(12) [In an upmarket restaurant. The dinner was intended to be a token of appreciation in return for a sizeable favour that the guest has done for the host.]
    Host: 我们 说话 不要耽误 吃饭。我 来 给您 再夹些鱼。
        wǒmen shuōhuà búyàodānwù chīfàn wǒ lái gěinín zàijiáxiēyú
        'Let's not allow talking to hinder eating. Let me serve you more fish'.

Guest:	不用了。我吃好了。 búyòngle wǒchī hǎo le 'No. I have had enough'.
Host:	李先生，再来点吧.您为这事累了一整天。多吃一点, OK? lǐ xiānshēng zàilái diǎnba nín wéizhèshi lèile yīzhěngtiān duōchī yīdiǎn OK 'Mr. Li, just a bit more. You have been working on this for the whole day. Just a bit more, OK'?
Guest:	好吧。一点就行。 hǎoba yīdiǎn jiùxíng 'Ok. Just a bit'.

(Chinese Conversation 3)

In the first food offering adjacency pair, the host's offer of more fish is refused (Guest: "No. I have had enough"). The host tries once more, this time with a reason: "You have been working on this for the whole day". The guest relents and accepts the offer by saying, "Ok. Just a bit".

(13) [At the host's home. A small alumni gathering of five in honor of the guest who has been away from the group for nine years.]

Guest:	谢谢李学姐，做了这顿美餐。太好了。 xiè xiè lǐ xué jiě, zuò le zhè dùn měi cān tài hǎo le 'Thank you so much, Sister Li.[51] You have cooked such a fantastic dinner. Wonderful'.
Host:	好吃就要多吃。接着来。 hǎo chī jiù yào duō chī。jiē zhe lái 'Since you like it, eat more'.
Guest:	好了。就此打住。 hǎo le jiù cǐ dǎ zhù 'I'm good. I'm stopping'.
Host:	你叫我姐姐，我就要照顾你。听话,啊？ nǐ jiào wǒ jiě jiě wǒ jiù yào zhào gù nǐ tīng huà ā ? 'As your sister, I should take care of you. Listen to your sister, ok'?
Guest:	亲爱的姐姐，饶了我吧，真不行了。 qīn ài de jiě jiě, ráo le wǒ ba, zhēn bú háng le 'My dear sister, please forgive me, I really can't'.
Host:	好吧，饶了你。

---

51 "Sister Li" is a case of using kinship terms to address non-kins.

>hǎo ba, ráo le nǐ。
>'Ok. You are forgiven'.

(Chinese Conversation 6)

In sum, the Xi'an Chinese in the 2019 study are found to offer food much less often than their counterparts did in 1995. As shown in Table 5.6, they now use on average less than one adjacency pair (0.88) in the end-of-dinner food offering (as opposed to 4.0 in 1995, Table 5.3). Even though the number of conversations recorded is too small to draw statistical significance, the decrease in the number of adjacency pairs from 4.0 to 0.88 is rather substantial.

The manner in which the offering is performed has also changed. As shown in Table 5.4, the structure of food offering at the end of a dinner in the 1995 study includes adjacency pairs such as "host asserting that guest has eaten little/guest asserting that she has eaten much"; "host denigrating food or skill, offering/guest praising food or skill, refusing"; and "host offering, "threatening" with offence/guest accepting". However, none of these three types of adjacency pairs occurs in the 2019 dataset. Instead, the way in which food is offered is much less direct. In Example (11), for instance, the host offers food by asking the question "A bit more"? (rather than "You must eat more!") and, after the guest declines the offer with "I'm good. Thanks", the host unceremoniously stops offering. Even in the two conversations that have two adjacency pairs, the tone is much different. In Example (12), the second offering is performed by the host asking "Ok?", leaving the guest some room to refuse. In Example (13), the first offer is dovetailed with the host's compliment of the food, "Since you like it, eat more". In the second adjacency pair, the offer is rendered in a joking manner, "As your sister, I should take care of you. Listen to your sister, Ok"? The use of the kinship term and the jocular tone are typical of positive politeness strategies, serving to establish in-groupness and hence reducing the threat to the guest's negative face.

Lastly, the result of the offer is also different in the two groups of Chinese participants. As shown in Table 5.4, the guest always accepts the offer in 1995. This indicates that both the host and guest are aware that the lengthy offering sequence – particularly the refusals in it – are for ritual purposes (Kádár 2013). However, in the 2019 data, several offers end up with the guest not accepting the offer. This process of deritualization coincides with a pattern identified by Pan and Kádár (2011) regarding the general notion of Chinese politeness.

How can one explain these changes in the end-of-dinner food offering behavior of the Chinese living in the greater Xi'an area? The interviews and email surveys we conducted provide some answers.

The first reason was the availability of food. Seven of the interviewees – all in their late 50s and early 60s – commented on the findings of the 1995 study by saying that "People were offered food in that way in the 1990s because the country was just beginning to get out of poverty" and "People had not had enough to eat for a long time, and they needed to make sure that their guests were having enough at their dinners". By the time of the second leg of the study, "Food is everywhere and nobody is starving anymore", one interviewee confidently declared, with five other survey respondents making similar observations.

Second, if the Chinese valued the demonstration of warmth and care for their guests in 1995, they are shown to do much less in 2019. Several respondents wrote in their email surveys that "there doesn't seem to be a need to show so much hospitality nowadays, as people are more casual in their relationships".

Third, Western cultures may have influenced the linguistic behavior of the Chinese public. Five respondents who had lived outside China, particularly in Europe and America, admitted that they had changed their verbal behaviors in noticeable ways, towards being less "pushy" and more individualistic. The majority of the email survey respondents and the interview participants agreed. During one of the interviews, a participant – not one of the five who had lived overseas – observed:

> I remember those old days when we literally forced people to eat, particularly in rural areas. But that seems to be old-fashioned now. You now see all kinds of "foreigners" on the streets of Xi'an and everywhere. Their way of doing things is influencing us. Your figure shows that Americans do not offer food at the end of a dinner very much, and it makes sense, as American culture is exerting its influence on Chinese culture. . . films, songs, clothing, technology, you name it.

Like the American respondents, the Chinese respondents mentioned the need to consider the guests' food preferences. Three respondents commented on the possibility of food restrictions or diets: "Women, especially young women, are careful about what and how much they eat". Two respondents also mentioned "greenness": "You never know. Some people are picky about eating 'green' food. You don't want them to feel they have to eat what they find morally objectionable".

As alluded to earlier, serving food onto each guest's individual plate occurred during six of the eight conversations in our data. Several respondents opined that this is also a way of demonstrating warmth and care. Two respondents added that when doing so, they would only serve food that they knew the guest liked. If they were not sure of the guest's food preferences, they would inquire before serving. Indeed, in the six conversations during which serving took place, there were three instances where the hosts asked their guests whether they liked a particular dish before serving. In two of these instances, the hosts later responded that they only served those foods which they knew their guests "liked". As one of the respondents explained, "I knew their habits well".

It is evident that the ritual of food offering in Chinese settings had significantly weakened in the 24 years between the two studies, almost to the point of non-existence,[52] as can be clearly seen in Figure 5.1 below (in which the numbers above the bars are numbers of adjacency pairs for each group).

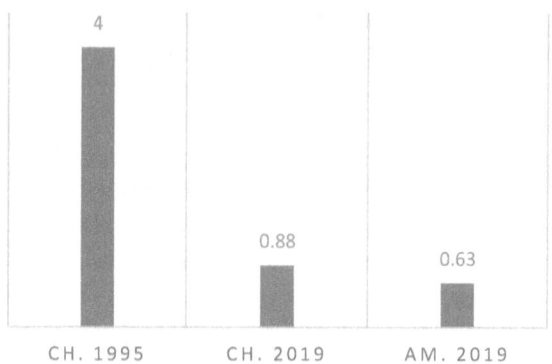

Figure 5.1: A three-way comparison.

In Figure 5.1, each column represents the average number of adjacency pairs that occurred in the food offering event for each studied population group. Two generalizations can be made from this graph. First, the food offering behaviors of the Chinese appear to have undergone a significant change, from having 4.0 adjacency pairs in 1995 to 0.88 adjacency pairs per dinner conversation in 2019. Second, in comparison to the Chinese, Americans conduct fewer food offerings, with an average of 0.63 adjacency pairs per dinner conversation.

The findings on Chinese food offering in 1995 can be attributed to the notion of showing warmth and care, as indicated above, which are hallmarks of Brown and Levinson's (1987) positive politeness. The findings obtained from the American group suggest that the American act of food offering (or the lack of it in half the dinners in the data) is motivated by a need to avoid and mitigate the threat that the speech act of food offering entails to the negative face of the guest, that is, the desire to be left alone. The Chinese offering behaviors as of 2019, therefore, suggest a change in politeness: more weight is now being given to negative politeness.

---

52 Whether this ritual still exists is a matter of debate.

5.5 MMP and diachronic changes

The four studies discussed in this chapter all identify diachronic changes in the pragmatics of the linguacultures involved: Japanese, Greek, and Chinese. How do MMP account for these changes? In this section, I argue that these changes are seen primarily as changes in the *content* of the public image of other and self.

In the Japanese cross-generational study, Fukushima (2011) finds that younger Japanese offer help less than the older generation. If the older Japanese see their boss having difficulty carrying papers to their offices, they will voluntarily extend a helping hand. Younger Japanese are more hesitant: some will and others will not help. So, we can say that to appear ready to help others was an important element of older Japanese's self-image but not so for younger Japanese. Similarly, Bella and Ogiermann's (2019) younger-generation Greeks judge the linguistic behaviors of older Greeks to be "impolite", e.g., their sense of privacy (or lack thereof), their assumption of intimacy (not expressing gratitude for a favor), and their seemingly readiness to impose (ordering others to do things). The authors interpret these changes as a move away from positive politeness. This is akin to the Japanese generational change, that the content of the self-image has experienced a lessening of in-groupness and considerateness towards respect for others' freedom of action.

The two longitudinal studies about Xi'an Chinese's behaviors in compliment responding and end-of-dinner food offering can also be seen as illustrations of the change in the content of public image of self. In the compliment responses study, the earlier behaviors of Xi'an Chinese are interpreted as stemming from modesty, a notion that is recognized as an important aspect of Chinese politeness. In the second leg of the study, they are shown to accept compliments more and reject less, suggesting a weakening of modesty but a strengthening of consideration for the complimenter's wish to be agreed with. Changes in the end-of-dinner food offering behaviors in Xi'an Chinese can be accounted for in similar ways. In 1995, Xi'an Chinese appeared keen on projecting a self-image of warmth and care for the guests' wellbeing. The guest, likewise, projected the self-image of being considerate of the host's display of warmth by refusing the offer several times before accepting it. In 2019, 24 years later, the hosts seem to have become more attune to appearing respectful for their guests' freedom of choice and food preferences resulting from dietary or moral considerations.

The change in self-image necessarily entails a change in other-image. In the Japanese study, the younger generation's less readiness in helping their professor means that they assume more independence on the part of the latter, for needing help could be seen as a sign of weakness. In addition, helping others without their consent could be seen as encroaching on their personal space. In the Greek study, the younger generation view as impolite the older generation's loudness in speech and ordering around instead of requesting. This again is the reflection that the Greeks' perception of other-image has changed, towards personal territory and freedom. The changes in self-image as noted above in the two Chinese studies, too, are linked with changes in other-image. When Xi'an Chinese reject compliment less, they end up agreeing with the complimenter, hence respecting his or her opinion. When they offer food less at the end of a dinner, it means necessarily that they have changed what they think their guests would want under the circumstances – that, instead of wanting to be cared for, they now prefer to be left alone.

In sum, in the framework of MMP, the changes in the pragmatics identified in the four studies discussed in this section are seen as changes in the content of the public image in a given culture. Recall that MMP has two levels of motivation. The public image of other and self are under the interactional motivation. The content of the public image is therefore at the lowest level of the model. As such, the changes in it are perfectly allowed by MMP, hence demonstrating the explanatory power of the model.

5.6 Further notes

In this section, I make a few notes about the four diachronic pragmatics studies discussed above.

In Section 5.1, it was pointed out that diachronic pragmatics is inherently disadvantaged by not having authentic data. The two cross-generational studies, by Fukushima (2011) and by Bella and Ogiermann (2019), help alleviate this problem. Comparing the linguistic behaviors of different generations in the same speech event, Fukushima is able to identify a difference between the two generations. Bella and Ogiermann's (2019) asked younger Greeks' views of the linguistic behaviors of older Greeks. They, too, discover some important generational differences. Clearly, the generational differences can be used as evidence for diachronic change, albeit not entirely directly.

The two longitudinal studies my colleagues and I conducted offer more direct evidence for diachronic pragmatics, as the two legs of each study adopted the same methodology at different times. The DCT method, used in the compliment response study, is essentially a "laboratory" method and does not collect natural and spontaneous data. However, it is still an improvement over other diachronic studies that relying on written records, representation, or recreation of real language use. The method of data collection in the end-of-dinner food offering study gathered data from spontaneous language use, which is obviously an even better alternative than traditional diachronic studies.

Another aspect of the two longitudinal studies is also worth noting, i.e., interviews with respondents. We intended the interviews as a way of data triangulation, but ended up benefiting more from them than we had originally anticipated. There was not a whole lot we could think of in terms of methodology that can compete for authenticity with talking to native speakers face-to-face about their own linguistic behaviors. As I have indicated at different times in this section, it is the native speakers themselves that led us to our conclusions about both studies. All these research methods, I am convinced, help solve most of the problems in diachronic pragmatics as noted by Jucker and Taavitsainen (2010: 16–23, see 6.1 above): pathways to change problem, meaning problem, identification program, and contextualization problem.[53]

Looking back at the history of pragmatics (see Chapter 1), pragmatics probably can no longer claim to be "a new kid on the block". After the collective effort by its practitioners over half a century, strides have been made on all fronts. One of these achievements is the availability of data. Beginning from the 1980s, we began to have more and more empirical studies carried out on different topics, and the replication of these studies would yield insights about language change, insights that should be verifiable, more reliable, and hence more valuable. It is hoped therefore that more study be done in this direction. Zhu, Li and Qian (2000), for example, find that the gift offering and acceptance sequence in Chinese follows a similar pattern – that the giver and recipient undertake several rounds of negotiation before the gift is eventually accepted. But this study was conducted two decades ago. Wouldn't it be interesting to establish whether the Chinese have changed their linguistic behaviors in gift offering and acceptance as well?

There are notes of caution, too. Any change that one can identify about a particular speech act or other type of linguistic behavior should not be taken out of context or to be a basis for unwarranted generalizations. In the two longitudinal studies discussed in this chapter, there seems to be a trend of decrease in self-denigration. In the compliment responding study, for example, respondents do significantly less of compliment rejection. In the end-of-diner food offering study,

---

[53] The two remaining problems – categorization problem and inventory problem – exist only for students of linguistic units, not for studies of speech events.

respondents are found not to say things such as "I know the food is not good" or "You know I am not a good cook" as much as they did in 1995. This, however, is not evidence that self-denigration, as part of the self-image of Chinese, is being weakened in general. In a recent paper, for example, Kadar and Zhou (2020) demonstrate that self-denigration is much alive in Chinses culture.

Chapter 6
MMP and discourse

The "discursive turn" has been widely accredited to the most recent advent in pragmatics, leading to what has been dubbed "the second generation (or wave)" in both theory building and empirical investigation. This is a turn away from theories that presuppose the stability of meaning or are general in nature and toward the particularity of language use. The new emphasis is on the "here and now" of communication, on the dynamism of meaning making, and on the fleeting nature of social norms and values. Methodologically, the discursive turn is a turn toward a distrust in – in some corners, a disdain towards – introspection. Highly valued is empiricism in its many manifestations: microscopic scrutiny of details, emphasis on what real-life speakers think about the issue under investigation (e.g., evaluation of politeness as we saw in Chapter 3), and a reluctance to seek deeper reasons for surface phenomena.

In this chapter, we look at how these issues are seen from the perspective of MMP. I will demonstrate that the structures of discourse are motivated by the clarity consideration of the transactional, including information structure – which applies to all types of discourse – moves that writers make in academic writing, and the turn-taking system in conversation. Other aspects of discourse such as identity, stance, critical discourse analysis, and the preference of a second in an adjacency pair, are argued to be realizations of interactionally motivations. The major thesis of the chapter, therefore, is that a general theoretical model such as MMP is capable of subsuming a multitude of findings under it, hence providing a coherent framework for the vast and varied field of discourse studies.

Section 6.1 provides a historical background in the area of discourse studies. Section 6.2 is devoted to the discussion of how structural properties of discourse are motivated by the clarity need of the transactional motivation. Section 6.3 advances our discussion to the interactional, arguing that identity construction, stance expression, and other speaker-oriented features of discourse are all parts of the interactional motivation at work. Critical discourse analysis, too, belongs here: to use language as a means of social power is motivated by the need to enhance self-image and self-interest.

Section 6.4 represents a case study on the discourse marker *so*. The purpose of the case study is to demonstrate the advantage of MMP – that looking at the underlying motivation of a linguistic construction can help us capture the higher level of generalization. Section 6.5 summarizes the chapter and Section 6.6 discusses a few important theoretical issues with regard to theorizing and empirical investigation in discourse studies.

6.1 Setting the scene

Discourse is a convenient label for the *type* of language use. As such, it is meant to cover all types of language use with any defining feature. A type of discourse can be as large as literature, news media, legal writing, and can be as specific as classroom interaction in a kindergarten in a particular locale, highway signage in a particular state in the U.S. (as highway signage is known to differ from one state to another), or posts on Tweeter or Facebook. To make it more complicated, larger discourse types have their subtypes. In literature, there are drama, poetry, and fiction. In poetry, there are the sonnet, free verse, visual poems, and many others. Advertising can be in print, on TV, and on social media. These subtypes are called "discourse" as well.

The reason why the notion of discourse is useful is that the type of discourse creates specific expectations and exerts specific constraints on how language is used and understood in it. When you converse with your family, you might be casual in your word choice and in tone. When you post on Twitter, you cannot go beyond 282 characters (141, formerly) per post. When you are driving on a U.S. highway, the ability to understand the signs may prevent you from getting off at a wrong ramp (or worse).

Discourse, too, is closely related to context. As students of language use in context, we pragmaticists have spent a great deal of energy defining context. We seem to have come to the conclusion that the notion is too illusive to be characterized in a way that is both precise and agreeable to most, save the general idea that context can be anything that has to do with meaning making on the part of the hearer as well as the speaker. However, discourse is another way to define context, as discourse, broadly speaking, can include all the factors that affect meaning making. Take the discourse of business letters for instance. The structure of the letter is determined by the profession: the business letter in the law profession may be significantly different from one in the retail industry; a business letter between the royal family and the executive branches of the British government is perhaps different from the business letter between the U.S. President and his governor. Even the language of a letter could vary from writer to writer – a writer will gear the tone of her language toward who she is writing too (e.g., subordinate vs. supervisor). In this sense, discourse is synonymous with context, and is intended to be so in this study.

The study of language use in relation to discourse started at the same time pragmatics was emerging, in the second half of the 20th century. In the following paragraphs, I provide a sketch of the development of this line of inquiry.

In the 1970s, the Prague School's Functional Sentence Perspective (FSP) brought to linguists' attention the fact that the organization of a sentence does not only depends on its syntax. A sentence, according to Firbas (1962, 1974, 1992. See also Daneš 1974) is divided into a theme and a rheme, with the former referring to what the sentence is about and the letter to the aboutness of theme. Hence, in the English sentence *John is from Ireland*, *John* is the theme and *is from Ireland* is the rheme. While the theme/rheme division is not much different from the topic/comment dichotomy that had existed in American structuralism (Bloomfield 1933), Firbas and colleagues' FSP gained far more prominence than its American twin sister: it was (and still is) used to analyzed language (e.g., Chen 1995; Potter 2016) while the topic/comment contrast seems to have been met with passing interest (Chomsky 1957), being relevant only when it gets in the way of the generative analysis of language.

More importantly, however, is the fact that the Prague School's attention to "aboutness" in the study of sentences was expanded to the analysis of chunks of texts beyond the sentence, leading to three related topics of research. The first is thematic progression (Cummings 2003; Daneš 1974), which, in turn, is synonymous with the notion of topic continuity (cf, Section 6.4 below). Specifically, Firbas' notion of theme of a sentence is extended to the theme of a discourse. What comes first in a discourse (theme) is vital for readers' processing of the discourse due to culturally-primed expectations about the rheme (Hoey 2005). As the text unfolds, new themes are introduced in connection with a theme or a rheme in the preceding text, picking up or repeating the important concepts and developing them further. The second is textual cohesion (Halliday and Hasan 1976). In order for a text to hang together ideationally, there must be "cohesive ties". In this paragraph, for instance, the first sentence mentions "three related topics of research". The next sentence is "The first is. . .", followed, a few lines down, by "The second is. . ..". I am pretty sure that you are expecting something like " The third. . .", which will begin the next paragraph.

The third is information structure. In a series of works, Haviland and Clark (1974) and Clark and Haviland (1975) categorize the information carried by a linguistic unit, most often a noun phrase, as either *given* or *new*. Given information is information that is supposed to be known and shared by the speaker and hearer and new information is information that is not. The simplest example would be that the pronoun *he* in "He lives in New York" must refer to *John* if the sentence follows "John is from Ireland". Seen in this way, a piece of discourse is structured also on information status, with the expected pattern that it moves from given information to new information.

Prince (1981, 1992), however, may have done more than Clark and Haviland to thrust information structure onto the center stage in the study of discourse. In her (1981) paper, Prince proposes that information status is better seen not as a given-new dichotomy but as a hierarchy of entities as presented in Figure 6.1, with further modifications appearing in her (1992) paper, which we omit.

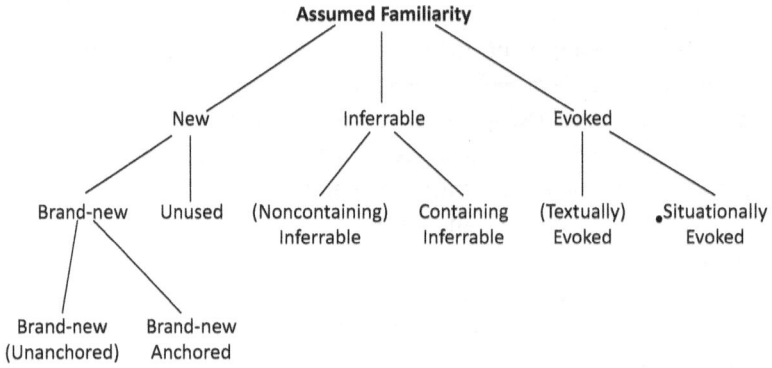

Figure 6.1: Prince's given-new information.

This taxonomy has been used extensively in the study of language and is shown to be versatile in its ability to account for a host of phenomena, such as marked constructions and language processing.

As is clear, the three aspects of discourse – thematic progression (or topic continuity), coherence, and information packaging – are all based on the principle that language use is not based on grammar alone and meaning making is a process that transcends sentence boundaries and over the course (and often the entirety) of discourse.

At more or less the same time when discourse was recognized as a key notion for the study of language and language use, another movement was taking place: conversation analysis. Based on the ethnographic tradition, actual conversations were picked up and zeroed in on as specimens of social interaction. The most notable studies in this research program are Sacks ([1964–72]1992), Sacks, Schegloff, and Jefferson (1974), and Schegloff (2002, 2007). These early scholars (known as "the first generation/wave conversation analysists") came from sociology rather than linguistics. They share a suspicion of the quantitative approach in their own field and largely shunted existing theories in both sociology and linguistics, which they believed to be an arbitrary imposition on the data of "objective categories" (Levinson 1983: 295). For conversation analysts, then, data speak for themselves and the analysts should not be influenced by pre-existing theoretical constructs.

The contributions conversation analysis has made to the study of language use is at least twofold. First, it has introduced to the field a set of well-defined methodology: actual conversations are recorded and painstakingly transcribed, with a set of notations to mark the phonetics of speech. Second, it has acculminated a large body of knowledge about the structure of conversation: how turn-taking is managed via turn construction unit, how an error made in conversation is corrected via different kinds of repair, and how utterances form adjacency pairs (e.g., apology/acceptance). We will discuss all of these below in light of MMP later in the chapter.

Now we move to the third notable episode in the study of discourse: genre analysis, initiated by Swales and his students at the University of Michigan. Genre analysis originated in Swales' Creating a Research Space (CARS) model of the introduction part of a research article. Based on research articles published in academic journals, Swales (1981, 1990) shows that the introduction of a research article is composed of three moves, each of which includes a number of steps. Move 1 is "establishing a territory", in which the writer claims centrality of her views, makes topic generalizations, and reviews previous items of research. Move 2 is "establishing a niche", which the writer can do via one of these four mechanisms: "counter-claiming, indicating a gap, question raising, and continuing a tradition". Move 3 is "occupying the niche", which may be accomplished by outlining purposes or announcing present research, announcing principal findings, and indicating the structure of the research. This general pattern that research article writers follow, Swales argues, is due to the competition for presence within a particular domain of research and the need to attract readers into the rhetorical space that the writer creates.

Although focusing on one part of a specific type of writing, genre analysis has turned out to be consequential in the study of discourse in general. It is closely related to the field of English for Specific Purposes (Hyon 1996, 2018), a field originally growing out of teaching English in specific disciplines such as science, and extends to the study of discourse in different professions. Internally, genre analysis has gone beyond the patterns in the organization of academic writing into academic speaking and then into writer stance, a point we will spend more time on below. It served also as a precursor for discourse of the profession (Bazerman 1994; Hyon 2008; Chen and Hyon 2007).

The fourth milestone in the study of discourse is the establishment of critical discourse analysis, whose origin was Fowler's (Fowler et al. 1979) critical linguistics but whose leap into popularity came from the series of works by Fairclough (1989, 1992, 1995), although others such as van Dijk (1988) and Wodak (2001) have also made significant contributions to the maturity of the strand. The major tenet of critical discourse analysis is its focus on how societal power relations are established and reinforced through language use. As such, it highlights issues of power asymmetries, manipulation, exploitation, and structural inequities in domains such as education, media, and politics. In this sense, critical discourse analysis can be better seen as an ideology, which sets itself apart from these other theories and approaches outlined above.

Proponents of critical discourse analysis have proposed methods for analysis. For Fairclough, such a methodology is a process of mapping three separate forms of analysis onto one another: analysis of (spoken or written) language texts, analysis of discourse practice (processes of text production, distribution and consumption), and analysis of discursive events as instances of socio-cultural practice. For van Dijk (1988), cognitive theories should be combined with linguistic and social theories. He believes that, by integrating a cognitive approach, researchers are better able to understand how larger social phenomenon are reinforced through popular, everyday discourse. Wodak (2001), on the other hand, highlights the interrelationship between discourses. She argues that looking at social practice in a collection of sample texts on a topic offers a global view of the macro-structures of inequality so that the analyst can see how an ideology permeates across social practices.

The ideology against inequality and for social justice, which is very much Marxist and liberal in orientation, has been welcomed in both the humanities and the social sciences. This can be seen in the readiness to add the term *critical* in front of one's field of study. There is *critical pedagogy;* there is *critical stylistics;* there is *critical literary criticism;* there is *critical sociolinguistics;* and there is *critical media studies.* This readiness, however, may not be always justified and at times led to superfluity. *Critical literary analysis* and *critical sociolinguistics,* for instance, make one wonder why: literary analysis has always been critical and looking at the ideology of a piece of literary work has always been part of what a literary critic does. Sociolinguistics has, likewise, been looking at issues of ideology and has been a champion of ethnic and racial equality. In fact, one can even say that sociolinguistics was founded on such liberal principles and has done much towards the worthy end of social justice, as is seen in a series of works by Labov ([1966] 2006, 1969, 1970, 2001, 2012), albeit less explicit in argument and less strident in tone.[54]

---

[54] And maybe more in action. To wit, in a court case filed with the U.S. federal court in Detroit, Michigan, in 1979 on whether Black English can be considered a barrier to learning standard English and, if so, whether a school system has a legal responsibility to help students overcome the barrier, three sociolinguists – Roger Shuy, William Labov, and J. L. Dillard – testified on behalf of the plaintiff, helping Black students to win the case (https://www.nytimes.com/1979/06/12/archives/court-to-decide-if-black-english-is-a-language-and-a-learning.html) that proved influential in subsequent debates on similar topics, e.g., the 1996 debate about "Ebonics" in the Oakland, California school district (https://www.latimes.com/archives/la-xpm-1996-12-20-mn-11042-story.html).

In the few pages above, I have sketched the four major milestones in the development of discourse studies: information packaging (including thematic progression and cohesion), conversation analysis, genre analysis, and critical discourse analysis. Some colleagues in these fields may resist including their field in pragmatics. But it is uncontroversial that these fields, despite the diversity in their respective assumptions, arguments, and methodologies, share the common aim to study how language is used in context. In the next section, I argue that MMP is capable of coherently accounting for the findings in all these subfields of discourse studies.

6.2 Transactional motivations

This section is devoted to transactional motivations. I will, in Section 6.2.1, argue that information structure, which has been believed to hold across types of discourse and languages, is the manifestation of the clarity transactional motivation at work. In Section 6.2.2, I turned to the structural properties of genres and discourse in relation to profession, with the aim to demonstrate that the different clarity expectations in different professions or genres undergird their respective discursive structural properties and conventions. In Section 6.2.3, I move to conversation analysis, with the same argument that the structures of conversation are also a result of the pressure for clarity at work.

6.2.1 Information structure

In this section, I argue that information structure/packaging is motivated by clarity considerations of the transactional motivation. The key to information structure is the general pattern in the order of given-new information: *given before new*. Consider the following.

(1) *How to turn off your water*
    Turn off Procedure
    Locate *your customer valve. . . The valve* is usually located on a hose bib where the plumbing service line enters the house. A hose bib is an exterior water faucet with a threaded end to connect a lawn or garden hose. Turn *the gate valve* clockwise.

    (Strauss and Feiz 2014: 144)

While a great deal can be said about information packaging based on this example, we focus on the references to *valve*. When first appeared, in "your customer valve", *valve* is inferrable per Prince (1992), as one can reasonably assume that a regular homeowner knows that there must be a valve to control water flow. The second appearance of *valve* comes right after, modified by the definite article *the*, indicating that, by now, the referent of *valve* is "given" to the homeowner audience. But knowing what a value is does not mean that one can locate it. So, the writer of the text spends the next two sentences on how to find it. In the last sentence, *valve* makes its third appearance, in "the gate valve". By now, the audience is supposed to know what the valve is but also to have actually located it in the water meter assembly. So, the entire discourse progresses in the from-given-to-new order and – equally importantly – new information can become given in that process.

Secondly, the presence of information packaging in language use is believed to be universal. Prince is not alone when she writes:

> One presumably universal feature of natural language is that the objective information conveyed is not conveyed on a single plane... and perhaps this is not only universal, but also distinctive of human languages – the crucial factor appears to be the tailoring of an utterance by a sender to meet the particular assumed needs of the intended receiver. That is, information-packaging in natural language reflects the sender's hypothesis about eh receiver's assumptions and beliefs and strategies. (Prince 1981: 224)

Her view seems to be supported by the fact that information status is prominent at different dimensions of language: phonology (Halliday 1967), lexicon (Halliday and Hasan 1976), as well as syntax (Clark and Haviland 1975), as illustrated in (2) through (4), respectively.

(2) Halfway down the page (0.3) draw (0.6) a red (0.4) horizontal line (0.2) of about (0.5) two inches (1.6) on eh (1.1) the righthand side just above the line (1.9) in black (0.1) write ON (3.2)

(Brown and Yue 1983: 162)

(3) John is from Ireland. He's now living in New York.

(4) What he overheard surprised him.

Example (2) comes from an experiment by Brown and Yule. They had their undergraduate students giving directions and found that in those directions, students inserted pauses of various lengths, as indicated by the numbers in parenthesis (in seconds). They conclude that the pauses represent termination markers for chunks of texts, each of which presents a definable piece of information. The length of a pause seems to match the weightiness of information a chunk of text carries. Example (3), as we indicated above, shows how a pronoun – *he*, referring to John – presents given information. In a *wh*-cleft construction (as in many others) seen in (4), the part of the sentence led by *what* presents given information by default.

In other words, the codification of information status in language is indicative of its entrenchedness. This matches MMP well, as the motivations proposed in it – including clarity of the transactional – are meant to be factors that underlying surface linguistic phenomena.

To say that information packaging helps clarity is to say that the violation of information packaging patterns will result in unclarity. This turns out to be the case. In (5), from Chen (2003), Sentences *a, b, c,* and *e* are all inversions – the order of the subject and verb are revered. Sentence *c*, for instance, is of the order of adverbial + verb + subject instead of the canonical order of subject + verb + adverbial ("Eddie sat behind Ben"). However, these inversions result in a from-given-to-new order in terms of information status: every sentence in the example begins with given information and ends with new information. In Sentence *a*, "right-hand side and the copilot's seat" are given because they appears in the previous paragraph that is omitted. The adverbial *then* in Sentence *b* is semi-new (inferrable), as the reader expects more descriptions to come. In Sentence *c*, *Ben* is given because *Ben* is introduced in the rheme of Sentence *b*. So, we observe a regular pattern. The initial element of each sentence refers back to a part of the previous sentence (so that it is treated as given). The verb is in the middle, linking that given unit to the new unit after it.

(5) [The original is written as a paragraph. Sentences are alphabetized for sake of easy reference.]
   a. On the starboard, right-hand side, immediately behind the copilot's seat, was the staircase that led down to the passenger deck.
   b. Then came the radio operator's station, where Ben Thompson sat facing forward.
   c. Behind Ben sat Eddie.
   d. He faced sideways, looking at a wall of dials and a bank of levers.
   e. A little to his right was the oval hatch leading to the starboard wing crawlway.

(Chen 2003: 211)

Turning all the sentences in (5) into the supposedly more "normal" SV(O) word order, we would end up with (6).

(6) a. The staircase that led down to the passenger deck was on the starboard, right-hand side, immediately behind the copilot's seat.
b. The radio operator's station, where Ben Thompson sat facing forward, came then.
c. Eddie sat behind Ben.
d. He faced sideways, looking at a wall of dials and a bank of levers.
e. The oval hatch leading to the starboard wing crawlway was a little to his right.

(Chen 2003: 213)

I presented (5) and (6) to both graduate and undergraduate students to read and then decide which is "clear" and "easy to understand". Of the 256 students I asked over a period of two years, an overwhelming 89 percent judged (5) to be clearer and easier to process than (6). They reported that (6) is "confusing" and "disorienting", as they found themselves going back and forth in an attempt to figure out the layout of the starboard of the airplane being described.

Similarly, a more given unit is found to be more easily understood than its less given counterpart.

(7) Mary got some beer out of the car. The beer was warm.

(8) Mary got some picnic supplies out of the car. The beer was warm.

Haviland and Clark's (1974) subjects took longer time to process the second sentence in (8) than the second sentence in (7). The word *beer* in (7) is repeated ("second-mentioned") in the second sentence. The word *beer* in (8) is inferrable from the noun phrase *picnic supplies*.

As indicated earlier in the last section, I view information structure, thematic progression, and cohesion as variations of the same underlying principle about how information is presented. Thematic progression is similar to information structure in that the progression of a theme is essentially the progression of the given-to-new progression of information. Cohesion is similar in that the linkage between linguistic units with what Halliday and Hasan (1976) call "cohesive ties" such as anaphoric (looking backward in discourse, e.g., "In the last conversation. . .") and cataphoric references (looking forward in discourse, e.g., "What follows is. . ."), ellipses, and second mention are essentially linkages of information. Therefore, if information structure is motivated by clarity considerations under the transactional motivation in MMP, so, too, should be thematic progression and cohesion, the discussions of which I omit.

There appears to be something fundamental about information packaging. If we look more deeply into the way humans learn, we find that information packaging goes hand in hand with the principle that we learn about what we do not know based on what we do know. There are at least two parallels. The first is analogy, which allows the application of preexisting conceptual structure to new problems and domains. It hence facilitates the rapid learning of new systems. Of all the learning processes, analogy is the only one that offers a mechanism for the acquisition of substantial knowledge structures in a brief span of learning. The second is conceptual metaphor theory, which we shall discuss in detail in Chapter 7. According to cognitive linguists (Lakoff and Johnson 1980; more references to follow), metaphor is a process of mapping a source domain with a target domain. By doing so, speakers will be able to understand the thing in the target domain in terms of (the thing in) the source domain. Information packaging can be viewed as a cousin to these two well-established theories, as it allows speakers to acquire new information based on the given.

6.2.2 Genre structures

Genre, as indicated above in Section 6.1, in the term *genre analysis*, refers to academic research article per Swales. It is taken here to be a general term, referring to a subtype of discourse, very much in line with its use to refer to a subtype of literature (e.g., *poetry, drama, fiction*), of art (*oil painting, baroque, landscape*), or of music (*classical, rock, hip hop*). In this section, I show that the structures of genres are motivated by the transactional consideration of clarity as well.

In our discussions to follow, we will also take advantage of the notion *discourse community*. Discourse community refers to a group of people involved in and communicating about a particular topic, issue, or in a particular field. According to Swales (1981), a discourse community has a broadly agreed-upon set of goals. It has mechanisms of intercommunication among members for information and feedback. A discourse community may utilize one or more genres in the communicative furtherance of its aims and has its special lexis. Lastly, a discourse community has a threshold level of members with a suitable degree of relevant content and discoursal expertise. Members often join the community as novices and are then initiated into it gradually and through practice, via informal mentoring rather than explicit instruction.

We start with the research article genre. According to Swales (2011), the CARS model of the research article introduction, in which the writer establishes a territory, locates a niche, and then occupies the niche, results from the competition for presence within a particular domain of research and the needs to create a rhetorical space and to attract readers into that space. This is perfectly in line with the clarity consideration of the transactional motivation in MMP. To publish is to participate in knowledge making; to make knowledge assumes that there is a need for it; and to demonstrate that need requires the carving out of the area in which the knowledge is to be made. In other words, the three moves in the CARS model reflects the shared goals of the speech community of scholars.

The three major moves in the CARS model, further, are the expectations for writers. If we imagine a published research article to be a storage of information (which is in turn stored in what we call "literature" abstractly or physically (in print and/or in electronic form), we can say that the reader is some one to go to the storage to find the information she needs. Suppose the reader wants to know whether an article is relevant, which would lead to her decision either to read with care or skim it, or not read it at all. Given that a research article is often complex and includes information of various kinds, she needs to know where to find what, and quickly, as she often does not have the time to read the article word for word. The three moves in the introduction part of the article are therefore useful for her: she would know where precisely to find the needed information – the kinds that are summarized in the CARS. Analogously, to find information in an article is akin to find a hammer in a crowded and messy garage: if you and I have agreed that that the hammer is always going to be stored in the top drawer on the righthand side of the workbench, we will pull out that drawer automatically when we need the hammer. Without that agreement, it would be an entirely different task to locate that hammer. This explains why, I believe, we as readers of research articles sometimes feel frustrated if one of these three moves is not in the right place, not clearly stated, or simply missing.

The value of agreeing on where to store what was discovered by Swales' CARS explains why the initiation process for new members of academia includes the mastering of such discourse conventions. In the U.S., how to write research articles is an important topic for the mentoring of graduate students. It is also present in the curriculum of many graduate and undergraduate programs, typically taught in research methodology or academic writing classes. Swales' CARS model, which started out as a research finding, is becoming increasingly popular in the classroom: novices to academia are explicitly trained to follow the three moves in actual writing. At the time of writing, I googled CARS and found it to be adopted by academic writing labs and centers in many U.S. universities, including Purdue University, Emory University, University of Southern California, and University of Massachusetts.

The pressure for clarity seen in the following of CARS is also manifested, albeit anecdotally, in the review process of journal submissions. As beginning writers, we may have received comments from reviewers about these moves (e.g.,

"You need to be clearer about the gap in the literature you are trying to fill"). As reviewers, we may make similar comments in addition to comments and suggestions on the content and substance of the manuscript we review.

In his original work on CARS, Swales (1981) based his discovery on research papers in the general area of arts and humanities. Later research in genre analysis affirmed that the CARS model applies to other disciplines as well, with differences at the lower level (Samraj 2002). More importantly, CARS are found to exist in research papers in other languages than English, e.g., Chinese (Loi and Evans 2010), Hungarian (Arvay and Tanko 2004), Korean (Lee 2001), Malay (Ahmad 1997), and Spanish (Dueñas 2007), although differences exist in how each move is linguistically executed. While there is always the possibility of borrowing due to language contact, it is difficult to assume that all these and other languages have "learned" the English way to structure the introduction of a research paper. It is more likely that these languages have arrived at the same destination independently. This – if true – has to be remarkably profound, as it is indication that there is something deeply natural about the CARS structure. That naturalness, according to MMP, comes from the pressure for clarity by the research paper genre.

The clarity consideration of the transactional motivation pressuring the academic community to agree on the structure of a genre goes beyond the introduction part of a research article. Spurred by Swales' seminal work, other parts of the genre have been investigated in different scientific disciplines. While different in their findings about specifics, the overall pattern is clear: each discipline has its shared conventions about how its genre should be structured at the macro level. We discuss one example to demonstrate the point.

Based on 60 articles published in core journals in the discipline of biochemistry, Kanoksilapatham (2005) finds that the macro structure of the genre is Introduction, Method Design, Results, Discussion, Conclusion. Across these sections, the author identified 15 moves, from Move 1 (Asserts the importance of the topic of study) to Move 15 (Suggesting further research). Of these 15, only two moves appear in less than 50% of the articles: Move 6 (Detailing equipment 10.00%) and Move 7 (Describing statistical procedures, 13.32%), which the author call "optional". All the rest appear in the dataset from 55% to 100% of the time (Kanoksilapatham 2005: 86).

The author does not discuss why research articles in biochemistry are structured in such uniformity; but the same point we made about the introduction part of the research article in arts and humanities should hold: the structure of biochemistry research paper is a response to the need for clarity in the field. A hard science, biochemistry makes knowledge largely via experiment, and experiment requires the description of research design, upon which the validity of the findings depend. Once an experiment is conducted, there will be findings. Once there are findings, there will be interpretation and discussion. It is small wonder, therefore, that moves that do these (and other) necessary things – establishing a topic, introducing the resent study, describing materials, describing experimental procedures, announcing results, and consolidating results – are found to appear in all the 60 articles surveyed (Kanoksilapatham 2005: 86).

The clarity consideration, if it is as prevalent and undergirding as it is argued here, should not only motivate the macro-structures of research articles in academia but also the structures of other genres. An academic book, for instance, seems to have an expected structure. It is typically divided into chapters (some have "parts" above chapters), which is further divided into headings and (layers of) subheadings. In each chapter, there is an introduction and conclusion of sorts, although they may not appear as such in headings. Across all disciplines, there is an agreed-upon practice that works cited be listed, but each discipline may have its own conventions on *how* they are listed. These expectations, too, seem to exist at lower levels such as a paragraph: a paragraph generally has a "topic sentence", which presents the gist of the paragraph and occurs at the very beginning of it. There are non-structural conventions in the academic world also. Each discipline has its acronyms, which, for one thing, helps save time and space. Each discipline has a set of terminology that do not need definition. Each discipline may have its own way to evaluate the work of its members.

How about genres outside academia? While the discourse/genre analysis literature on the different genres and in different professions is rich – some of it investigate the kind of language used and sociocultural factors with regard to the discourse participants (see Bhatia and Bhatia 2011 and Kurzon 1994 for legal discourse; Gotti and Salager-Meyer 2006 for medical discourse); others investigate issues of multimodality, identity construction, and politeness (see Bou-Franch and Blitvich 2019 for digital discourse) – few studies focus on the structures of genres beyond those in academia. However, it may not be too implausible to suspect that the structures and conventions of genres in general are motivated by clarity. The terminologies our doctors and nurses use among themselves during a conversation we overhear may not make much sense to us, but these terminologies have precise meanings to them. The same holds for artists, cyclists, and auto mechanics. In the digital world, texting has posed a distinctive set of expectations for clarity, such as the use of emojis and the liberty of not to be elaborate in salutations. The genre of tweets leaves us no choice but to stop the expression of our thought at the 182nd character. These conventions aid the processing of information, which is what the motivation for clarity is about.

6.2.3 Conversational structures

Conversation analysts,[55] as discussed in the last section, have been active and have contributed a great deal to the understanding of the structure of conversation and social interaction in different speech communities. I will show, in this section, that the structure of conversation, like the structures of other genres discussed in the last section, is motivated by the clarity motivation of the transactional in MMP. We will look at two such structures – turn-taking and presequencing – in this section. The other two systems – adjacency pair and repair – will be discussed in Section 6.3.4, under the interactional motivation of MMP.

Conversation, which assumes at least two participants, is at the most basic level composed of turns. Unless in highly specialize situations such as a religious service, a panel discussion on TV, or an academic conference, turn-taking – who speaks next – is seldom predesignated but negotiated. The general rules of turn taking are the following (Sacks, Schegloff & Jefferson 1974: 704).

(9) *Rule 1.* When the current speaker selects the next speaker, the next speaker has the right and, at the same time, is obliged to take the next turn
 Rule 2. If the current speaker does not select the next speaker, any one of the participants has the right to self-select.
 Rule 3. If neither the current speaker selects the next speaker nor any of the participants become the next speaker, the current speaker may resume his/her turn.

These rules, which have been debated about (e.g., Oreström 1983: 29) but have largely held, are rules to make sure that there is only one person speaking at a time. But "one person speaking at a time" seems to have physiological (auditory) and neurological basis. Physiologically, the human auditory system is not equipped with the ability to perceive multiple stimuli at one time (Bess and Humes 2008; Broadbent 1958; Karns et al. 2015), which explains why the ability

---

[55] The following symbols are used in transcriptions.
  - abrupt cutoff, stammering quality when hyphenating syllables of a word
  ! animated tone, not necessarily an exclamation
  ::: elongated sounds
  (.) micropause
  // overlapping speech
  [ ] transcriber's comment or transcription
  ( ) non audible segment
  = no interval between adjacent utterances
  @ Laughter

to keep out background noise is an important factor when we select an earphone. Neurologically and cognitively, the human mind works the best when focused on one thing (Chen 2003, 2022; Posner 2011; Talmy 2000). In a word, to allow more than one interactant to speak at the same time will be counterproductive to the very purpose of conversation. The rules of conversational turn taking are, thus, rules for clarity.

What is remarkable about these rules is that conversation participants know how to uphold them via various means. First, when the current speaker is about to finish speaking, she is found to signal it, which serves as an invitation for the next turn, via intonation, pitch or loudness, drawl, body motion, eye contact, discourse markers ("but uh", "or something", "you know"), or full sentence.[56] These signals are subtle but are usually picked up by the hearer so that the average time between turns is just a few tenths of a second (Ervin-Tripp 1979). Second, these rules offer convincing explanations for deviations. Overlaps (marked by double slashes below), for example, occur at predictable places: either as competing first starts, as allowed by Rule 2:

(10) J: Twelve pounds I think wasn't it.
     D: //Can you believe it?
     L: Twelve pounds on the Weight Watchers' scale.
                    (Adopted from Sacks, Schegloff, and Jefferson 1978: 16)

or in situations in which the turn taking is mis-signaled, as illustrated in (11):

(11) A: Uh you been down here before //havenche
     B: Yeah.
                    (Adopted from Sacks, Schegloff, and Jefferson 1978: 17)

Sometimes participants interrupt intentionally, which is "caught" readily by speaking at times when their turns are unexpected. In (12), for example, B cuts in with an accusatory remark in the middle of A's word "reasonable".

(12) A: We:ll I wrote what I thought was a a a
            rea:s'n //ble explanatio:n
     B: I think it was a very rude letter.
                    (Adopted from Sacks, Schegloff, and Jefferson 1978: 17)

---

56 The points at which these devices occur are called TRPs (transitional relevant places).

Third, conversation participants uphold these turn-taking rules by dropping out of the competition for turns usually quickly, as B does below.

(13) A: ...he's got to talk to someone (very sor)
         supportive way towards you (.)
     B: //Greg's (got wha)*
     C: Think you sh*   think you should have one to:hold him
                                    (Adopted from Atkinson and Dew 1979: 44)

Besides, as soon as one speaker thus emerges into "the clear", she recycles precisely the part of the turn obscured by the overlap, as C does in (13).

Conversation analysts, as alluded to earlier, are generally not interested in finding out reasons for what they discover, particularly in the early days (Cook 1989; Coulthard 1985; Sacks 1992; Sacks, Schegloff, and Jefferson 1974; Wardhaugh 1998). Levinson (1983: 30) is the first author, to my knowledge, to discuss the importance of the *why* of conversational structures. About the turn-taking rules, he writes that they are undergirded by "an intrinsic motivation for participants to both listen and process what is said". As is clear, his view is in line with what I am arguing in this section: "to both listen and process what is said" is no doubt part of clarity.

Pre-sequence – the second and last structural aspect of conversation that we are discussing under the transactional – is motivated by clarity, too, but in a different way from the way turn-taking is motivated. While turn-taking ensures that a message is delivered without interruption and competition, a pre-sequence enhances clarity by preparing for the upcoming speech act. Consider the following examples.

Pre-invitation:

(14) A: Whatcha doin'?
     B: Nothin'
     A: Wanna drink?
                                    (Atkinson and Drew 1979: 253)

(15) A: Hi John
     B: How ya doin' = say what'r you doing
     A: Well we're going out. Why?
     B: Oh, I was just gonna say come out and come over here an' talk this evening, but if you're going out you can't very well do that
                                    (Atkinson and Drew 1979: 143)

Pre-request:

(16) A: Do you have hot chocolate?
  B: mmhmm
  A: Can I have hot chocolate with whipped cream?
  B: Sure [leaves to get it]

(Merritt 1976: 337)

Pre-arrangement:

(17) A: Erm (2.8) what what are you doing today?
  B: Er well I'm supervising at quarter past (1.6)
  A: Er yuh why (don't) er (1.5) would you like to come by after that?
  B: I can't I'm afraid no

(Levinson 1983: 348)

Pre-announcement:

(18) A: Didju hear the terrible news?
  B: No. What.
  A: Dan died in an automobile accident.

These examples vary in terms of speech acts, a term early conversational analysts generally stayed away from; but there is something in common in all of them: that the pre-s *prepare for* the upcoming act, be it inviting, requesting, arranging, or announcing. Seen within the framework of the speech act theory (Searle 1969, 1991), these pre-s function to make sure that a particular felicity condition is met. In order for an invitation to be successful, the invitee has to be available to attend the invited event. So, A in (15) asks B's availability in the first TCU (turn construction unit). Similarly, the success of a request has the felicity condition of the requestee being able to fulfill the request, which explains why the costumer in (16) checks the availability of hot chocolate before ordering it. The same is the case with arrangement (17) and announcement (18). Such preparations ensure clarity in two ways. If the needed felicity condition is met, as is the case with (14), (16), and (18), the intended speech act will be carried out smoothly. If it is not, as is the case with (15), the speaker can withhold the doing of the intended act.⁵⁷ Either case is in line with the clarity transactional motivation (Figure 2.2).

6.3 Interactional motivations

In this section, we discuss how the interactional motivations of creating, maintaining, and enhancing the public image of both other and self are responsible for speakers' effort to construct a desirable identity for herself, to express her stance, and to manage adjacency pairs and repair in conversation.

A note of terminology is in order before we start. In the literature on identity construction and conversation analysis, the term *identity* and *stance* are used interchangeably. I will not attempt a delineation of the two in either Section 6.3.1 or Section 6.3.2. The two sections are entitled the way they are because the literature discussed in Section 6.3.1 primarily comes from conversation analysis and the literature discussed in Section 6.3.2, from genre analysis.

6.3.1 Identity construction

The study of identity construction is taken here to refer to the study of how speakers create image/identity for themselves as desired in a given context. This strand of pragmatics originated in conversation analysis. I will not delve into social theories of identity, such as the type of identity: identity of the self (Erikson 1968; Marcia 1980) or identity as defined by age, sex, class, economy, ethnicity, profession, and others (Horowitz 1985; Tajfel 1974, 1981, 1982). Neither is it relevant for us to discuss developmental identity formation: how a person is molded in and by society – passively and unconsciously (Côté 2006: 5; 2000) – from childhood (Luyckx, Goossens, and Soenens 2006) to adolescence and then to adulthood (Rorty 1976; Stryker 1987). Instead, we will be looking at how identity emerges from the dynamic communitive event via (co-)construction⁵⁸ (Blommaet 2005; Bucholtz and Hall 2004, 2008, 2010; Butler 1990; De Fina 2010; De Fina, Schiffrin, and Bamberg 2006; Ho 2010; Locher and Hoffmann 2006; Tracy 2002; Zimmerman 1988, 1992, 1998). My overall argument is that identity construction is motivated by the interactional motivation to establish, maintain, and/or enhance

---

57 It also serves to maintain the inviter's positive face, as it is better for him to withhold inviting than having his invitation rejected.
58 See Chen (2019b) for a summary discussion about whether identity is emergent or preexisting.

the image of self. The hearer's effort to help the speaker for the latter's identity construction is motivated by the interactional motivation of benefiting the image of other. Our discussion is based on a survey of findings in the literature.

The first group of findings come primarily from conversation analysts. Inspired by a series of works by Ochs (1990, 1993, 2012), researchers have turned their attention to identity construction and stance expression via *indexicals*: linguistic devices that point to or having a semiotic relationship with the social identity of a person, either a participant of the conversation or someone outside the immediate context. In the following paragraphs, I demonstrate that the identities that are constructed are coherently included in the public image of self.

In Bucholtz and Hall (2005: 589–590), the authors report two case studies. The first is about *hijras*, a transgender category in India who are predominantly born male but identify as neither men nor women. Bucholtz and Hall provide an excerpt from a transcription of an ethnographic interview in which a *hijra* (fictitiously named "Sulekha'") uses the feminine case marking to refer to herself. However, she recounts that her estranged family members referred to her in the masculine gender.[59] Based on this, Bucholtz and Hall (2005: 590) conclude that "Under these circumstances, gender marking becomes a powerful tool used by Sulekha to construct herself as feminine in opposition to her family's perception of her gender. Such identity positioning is, therefore, occasioned by the interactional demands of her narrative". The second example from Bucholtz and Hall (2005: 592–593) has to do with teenagers' use of *go, be like* and *be all* as quotative verbs (e.g., *say*). Of the three, the last one, *be all*, is the most marked form. Ethnographic data collected by Bucholtz and Hall demonstrate that an academically oriented teenager uses the first two while a less "nerdy" girl uses the last.

From the perspective of MMP, Bucholtz and Hall's subjects are both using indexicals for self-image. Sulekha uses the case marking in the language to signal her unmistaken desire to be seen and treated as a woman. The academically oriented girl uses the more former quotative verbs to create the image that fits her desired goal while the less "nerdy" girl uses *be all* to create a different kind of image.

Style, too, has been investigated. In a fascinating study, Kiesling (2004) analyzes the use of *dude*, a common slang form in American English, by American youth. Originated from African Americans and later appropriated by European Americans, especially young men, the address form *dude* is currently used primarily (though not exclusively) by younger white male speakers. Drawing on discourse data among university fraternity members, Kiesling argues that, interactionally, *dude* creates an "intersubjective alignment of friendly nonintimacy" and

---

[59] Hindi requires the marking of gender obligatorily.

projects a "stance of cool solidarity" (2004: 282). As Kiesling puts it: the term is used mainly in situations in which a speaker takes a stance of solidarity or camaraderie, but crucially in a nonchalant, not-too-enthusiastic manner. The following are two examples.

(19)   Pete: Fuckin' ay man. Gimme the red Dave. *Dude*. (1.0)
      Dave: No.
      Pete: Dave *dude, dude* Dave hm hm hm hm
      Dave: I'll give you the purple one
      Pete :   Oh that's a good trade
(Adopted from Kiesling 2004: 294)

(20)   Dan: I love playin' caps.
             That's what did me in last-| |last week.
      Pete: |that's-|
             Everybody plays that damn game, dude.
(Adopted from Kiesling 2004: 295)

In Example (19), Pete and Dave are playing the board game Monopoly. Pete uses the term *dude* in his first turn to mitigate his initial unmitigated command to Dave to give him a piece of property, but to no avail. He then says "Dave dude, dude Dave…", an obvious attempt at alliteration (repetition of consonants), as a means to get what he wants. He does get something ("a purple one") as a result. In (20), Dan expresses his strong liking of the drinking game – "caps". Pete, however, undercuts his enthusiasm with *dude*, saying the game is widespread and hence implying that it is not particularly remarkable.

Kiesling argues that the reason young men use the term *dude* is that the term indexes the stance of cool solidarity. Such a stance is especially valuable for young men as they navigate cultural discourses of young masculinity, which simultaneously demand masculine solidarity, strict heterosexuality, and nonconformity (2004: 282). He maintains, further, that the term's indexical meaning in the social realm derives from its various discourse functions in the interactional realm, marking discourse structure, exclamation, confrontation mitigation, agreement, affiliation, and connection.

Another study of indexicals of style is Bucholtz (2009). The author investigates the use of *güey* by Spanish speaking youth in a high school in California, U.S. *Güey*, Bucholtz notes, is a widespread term of affiliative address term, comparable to *dude*, *bro*, and similar slang items in English. In (21), for example, Chilango's greeting on the cell phone of the caller is populated by *güey*, signaling Chilango's awareness of the caller's identity and inviting the initiation of the interaction.

(21) [Chilango's phone rings. He takes it out of his pocket, puts it to his ear.]
    Chilango: *¿Qué pedo, güey?* (2 sec.)
                  'What's going on, güey'?
                  ¿Qué pedo, güey?
                  'What's going on, güey'?
[Chilango lowers the phone.]
    Chris: *¿Quién era?*
                  'Who was that'?
    Chilango: *¿Qué onda, güey?*
                  'What's up, güey'?
    Caller: #
    Chilango: *¿Qué onda?*
                  'What's up'?
    Caller: (A::h,)

(Adopted from Bucholtz 2009: 252)

Bucholtz identifies several uses of the term: as an insult (Bucholtz 2009: 253) ("Hey, idiot. This *güey* can't go here", Spanish version omitted), to highlight important information and to maintain solidarity (Bucholtz 2009: 154), to be boastful (Bucholtz 2009: 155), and to lodge disagreements (Bucholtz 2009: 156). To summarize her study, the author writes that the slang term

> allowed these boys to do something of much greater immediate importance: to interact with one another, to greet their friends, to brag, to undercut a friend's boasting – in short, to establish both status and solidarity in relation to their social group – and to index a cool, nonchalant stance all the while. In turn, the habitual use of these practices by male speakers to perform these and other interactional and social actions could create an indirect indexical link to masculinity... (Bucholtz 2009: 165)

The conclusion of Bucholtz's study of *güey* is similar to the conclusion of Kiesling's study of *dude*. Used by late teens, both slangs perform a specific set of local functions, indexing camaraderie, solidarity, and, eventually, masculinity. Adolescence is an important period for identity formation, a time when youth are conscious of obtaining identity of adults but, at the same time, have difficulty doing it (Marcia 1980, Rorty 1976; Stryker 1987; Tajfel 1974, 1981, among others). This is what MMP predicts: these youth have the intrinsic need to create a public image for themselves, an image that they believe is deemed desirable by both their speech community (toughness, brotherhood, straightforwardness) and the society in general (masculinity).

We now move to another important identity – ethnicity – by reviewing De Fina (2000), who looks at the construction of ethnic identity in an all-male card playing club, *Circolo della Briscola*, operating in the Washington D.C. area of the United States. We will focus specifically on how code-switching from English to Italian is utilized as a central category for the creating and negotiation of the collective identity for the club.

The club members are largely monolingual speakers of English, with a few bilingual speakers of English and Italian. However, the club has a distinctive Italian orientation and identity. Therefore members sprinkle their conversations, either at the card table or elsewhere, with Italian. There is also the initiation process that teaches the newcomers some Italian. In example (22) – in which the line numbers are provided – Carl, a new member who does not speak Italian, has trouble recognizing Italian cards and is asking his companion to clarify what each card is (lines 01–09). In Line 05, he makes a gesture of desperation and asks disapprovingly why people do not use American cards (Line 10). Paul responds by explaining that it is not *"tradizionale"* (line 13), making explicit the connection between playing Briscola and Italian traditions, a basis for the ethnic allegiance of the Circolo. Later Paul makes a point of translating the names of the cards into Italian (Lines 15 and 19) despite his limited competence in the language.

(22) 01 Carl: [pointing at card] What the hell is this? Is that a queen?
      02 Paul: No that's a horse.
      03 Carl: You don't have a queen in there.
      04 Paul: No.
      05 Carl: [holds his head with his hands]
      06 [pointing] That's three,
      07 Paul: Three.
      08 Carl: That's two,
      09 Paul: Two.
      10 Carl: [Shakes head] Why don't you use American cards?
      11 Paul: That's not=
      12 Carl: =What's that thing?
      13 Paul: That's not *tradizionale*! [traditional]@
      14 Carl: @@[annoyed] What's that thing there?
      15 Paul: That's the ace of *spade, spada*.
      16 Carl: That's ace?
      17 Paul: Now this is (.)
      18 Al: A horse.
      19 Paul: Cavallo, *cavallo di spada*.

The result of the teaching is that Carl starts accepting not only the need to recognize Sicilian cards, but also the need to learn their names, as is shown in (23), which takes place later in the same game.

(23) Carl: [addressing Paul] *Cavallo bastoni* [knight (of)clubs] ah?
      Paul: [Nods] *Cavallo bastoni*.
      (.)
      Paul: [addressing researcher] *Come si dice*? [How do you say?]
      Res.: *Questo e ii* (.) *fante di coppa* [This is the jack of cups]
      Paul: *Fante di coppa*.

(De Fina 2000: 387)

To the author, "the use of Italian is enforced in socialization practices through code-switching into Italian and the learning of target words". Such strategies enable the members of the club to create "an association between good card playing and the ability to speak some Italian" and "expectations about characteristics defining a good player's identity". They, too, "affect the community in that they reinforce a collective sense of respect for tradition" (De Fina 2000: 389). To us, code-switching that occurs in the club is motivated by the interactional motivation of establishing, maintaining, and enhancing the public image of the club. It should be noted that De Fina uses the term *image* also in the paper (De Fina 2000: 312) to refer to the ethnic identity of Italian. As is recalled in Chapter 2, the term *self* may refer to an entity the speaker represents. De Fina's study thus reviewed is clear evidence for the efforts members of a group make to benefit the public image of the group they represent (and belong in).

There have been other studies on group identity. The papers included in Bhatia and Allori (2011) are a good representation. In it, advertising discourse is found to build the advertised companies' identity and reputation of cleanness (Chapter 2); pragma-dialectic strategies are responsible for the pharmaceutical company Novartis to re-establish its identity of social responsibility (Chapter 4); weblogs are utilized to construct a company's choice of identity (Chapter 5). There are also studies in the volume about how group identity is constructed in the legal profession as well as by government agencies (e.g., the White House).

In the identity studies literature, there is the emphasis on the co-construction of an identity – that the speaker and hearer help each other to create a desired image. In the above *dude* example, for instance, the person being called "dude" dose not protest but goes with it. In Example (23), the identity of members of the club – being able to speak some Italian – is co-constructed for Paul, the new member, by both others and Paul himself. The motivation for doing so is the interactional motivation to create the expected and desired image for both the club member being initiated and the club itself.

There are also cases in which an identity is being constructed for an expedient purpose. Yuan (2020) explores ways in which Chinese pharmaceutical company representatives construct the identity of medical experts on radio so as to sell medicine. Ye, Cheng, and Zhao (2020) discusses strategies used by telecom and internet gang members to commit fraud. Zhong and Zeng (2020) demonstrate how con artists pretend to be acquaintances and friends of their victims for the purpose of swindling money out of them. In these cases, the motivation is clearer: in order to achieve their specific ends, the speakers try to imitate the identity – or image – of what they are not. The success of their efforts depends on the success of creating the intended image. In addition, since the success of the construction of the fake identity – in the case of a fraud at least – incur tangible material loss to hearer, they belong to the "benefit self and hurt other" category of the interactional motivation, as we discussed in Chapter 3. In all these cases, we see how the interactional motivation is assistive of the transactional motivation: the creating of an image serves the purpose of achieving a preplanned transactional task.

6.3.2 Writer stance

Now we move to stance expression and identity construction in the area of genre analysis, with the aim of demonstrating that academic writing is motivated by interactional motivations as well as by the transactional. When they express a stance or construct an identity, academic writers end up establishing, maintaining, or enhancing the expected public image for themselves. This, in turn, helps them fulfill the effectiveness motivation of the transactional.

Stance refers to the academic writer's views of, attitudes towards, and positioning on issues they write about and the relationship they wish to establish between themselves and their readers (Du Bois 2007: 139; Harwood 2005; Hyland 2005, 2008; Hyland and Tse 2005a & b; Hyon 2008; Hyon and & Chen 2004; Kuo 1999; Strauss and Feiz 2014). It has received considerable attention in genre analysis in recent years. For example, individuality is found by Abbamonte (2008) to be achieved via praising and other means by cognitive neuroscientists. Cultural identity may be constructed via argumentative style in legal studies (Sala 2008). Readers' attention could be attracted via evaluative *that*-clauses in conference abstracts (Hyland and Tse 2005a, 2005b). Similarly, attitude, certainty, and allusions to common knowledge are investigated by Koutsantoni (2004); expressions of possibility by Marques-Aguado (2009); and – finally – how insights from studies on identity construction and stance are related to teaching and learning a second language (Chang and Schleppegrell 2011; Ouellette 2008). In this section, I will focus on how academic writers establish, maintain, and enhance the public image for themselves via the way they refer to themselves as single authors.

In general, there are four ways for single authors to refer to themselves: the 1st-person singular pronoun *I*, the 1st-person plural *we*, 3rd-person NPs (e.g., *the/this author/writer*), and inanimate NPs that typically refer to the work as opposed to the writer (e.g., *this paper/book/study*). An author can also hide her identity via linguistic devices such as the passive voice (e.g., *It is argued that..*). However, our purpose in this section is *not* about whether authors refer to themselves or not, but about how to refer to themselves when they do (Chen 2020; Chen and Yang 2022).

Hyland (2001) may be the first study on author self-reference. In the study, the author surveyed 240 research articles in eight disciplines: physics, biology, electrical engineering, and mechanical engineering (hard fields); marketing, philosophy, applied linguistics, and sociology (soft fields). He finds (2001: 214) that writers in hard fields use less pronouns for self-reference ("self-mention", in his words) – averaging 11.9 per paper – than those in the soft fields – 33.6 per paper. The reason for this difference, Hyland proposes, is that the former group of writers are motivated by the disciplinary expectations of objectivity, as the avoidance of direct self-mention suggests that "research outcomes would be the same irrespective of the individual conducting it" (Hyland 2001: 216). Those in the soft fields, which include a wider range of disciplines with defused boundaries among them, on the other hand, rely more heavily on the personal pronoun to establish "an appropriate authorial persona" and to maintain "an effective degree of personal engagement with one's audience" (Hyland 2001: 216).

There is also a clear difference between the hard and soft fields in the use of the singular vs. the plural 1st-person pronouns. In the hard knowledge corpora, there are 16 single-authored papers in which are found "only a handful of singular forms. but 80 plural first person pronouns" (Hyland 2001: 217). The reverse is true in the soft fields: there are only eight plurals in the 75 papers while the rest – a clear majority, as can be gleaned from his Table 4, on Page 214 – are singulars.

Dueñas (2007) studies author self-reference based on a comparison between English and Spanish in the area of business management, a soft field according to Hyland's (2001) classification. Most of the articles that are included in the corpus (11 out of 12 in English and four out of 12 in Spanish, see Dueñas 2007: 128) are bylined by multiple authors. The pronoun used for self-reference are predictably plural. Also predictable is the sole self-authored article in English: all the 17 instances of self-reference (as is seen in Dueñas 2007: 146) are 1st-person singular (Dueñas 2007: 155).

At the same time, both Hyland and Dueñas identify deviations from the general practice of using the singular for self-reference. The eight uses of the plural found in Hyland (2001) by single authors – a clear minority – "suggest how writers can simultaneously reduce their personal intrusion and yet emphasize the importance that should be given to their unique procedural choices or views" (Hyland 2001: 217). The use of the plural in Dueñas (2007) occurs in academic writing in Spanish: all instances of self-reference in the four single-authored articles are plural. Dueñas follows Hyland in her accounting for this semantic misalignment, seeing it as a middle ground between personal intrusion and authorial voice.

In the following pages, I discuss a series of studies reported in Chen (2020) and Chen and Yang (2022). To prepare for these studies, we conducted a survey of journals published in English in the area of language studies. Of the two years' worth of publications in *Language in Society, Linguistic Inquiry,* and *PMLA: Publications of the Linguistic society of America,* there are 245 articles by single authors (articles by multiple authors were excluded) and 3,726 instances of self-reference. Of this total, 3,577 (96%) are instances of the 1st-person singular (*I* and its morphological variations *me* and *mine;* 48 (1%) instances of the plural (*we* and its variations *us* and *our*), zero instances of 3rd-person NPs (e.g., *this writer*), and 101 (3%) instances of inanimate NPs (e.g., *This paper*). It is thus clear that that English academic writers use the 1st-person singular for single-author reference predominantly. Moreover, the plural that is being used, upon closer examination, actually does not refer to the author but to a group of people of which she is a part. The writer of (24), for example, is the editor of a special issue of the journal, writing the introduction to the issue. Therefore, *our* refers not to herself (although it includes herself) but to the collective of writers in the entire special issue.

(24) In that context, *our* four-part title may sound like a union of opposites.

Likewise, a writer may refer to the entire research group of which she is a member, although her name is the only name appearing on the byline. In (25), for instance, the author reports the findings of a study that was done by a group of researchers, of which she is the leader:

(25) To date, we have looked at two heroin epidemics, the crack cocaine epidemic and recent increase in use of the drug known as ecstasy.

A similar survey was conducted on Chinese academic writing at the same time and the results are reported in Chen and Yang (2022). Two years' worth of six academic journals in the area of language studies were used as the data base. Of the 6,657 instances of author self-refence in 653 single-authored articles, 365 (5%) are instances of the 1st-person singular; 4,435 (67%) are instances of the plural; 483 (7%) 3rd-person NPs; and 1,374 (21%) are uses of inanimate NPs. The following are examples of each use, in the order of singular, plural, 3rd-person NP, and inanimate NP.

(26) 我分析过...
   Wo fenxi guo
   'I *have* analysed....'.

(27) 按照认知语法的这一语义观，我们提出如下假设。
   Anzhao renzhiyufa de zhe yi yuyigan, *women* tichu ruxia jiashe
   'Based on the perspective of cognitive semantics, we *propose* the following hypotheses'.

(28) 作者详细分析了相关文献
   Zuozhe xiangxi fenxi le xiangguan wenjian
   'The author/writer carefully examined the relevant literature'.

(29) 本文思考了语言和文化的相互关系
   Benwen sikao le yuyan he wenhua de xianghu guanxi
   'This paper has thought about the relationship between language and culture'.

The findings about single-author self-reference are summarized into Table 6.1.

Table 6.1: Single-author self-reference.

	1ST SINGULAR	1ST PLURAL	3RD NP	INANIM. NP
English, hard fields	"a handful"	80	N/A	N/A
English, soft fields	67	8	N/A	N/A
English, management	17	0	N/A	N/A
English, language studies	3,577 (96%)	48 (1%)	0	101 (3%)
Chinese, language studies	365 (5%)	4,435 (67%)	483 (7%)	1,374 (21%)

It seems that the key to our attempt to make sense of these findings lies in what authorship means. To scholars such as Ivanić (1994, 1995, 1998), authorship entails power. The fact that one is writing on a topic entails that she has something new to inform her readers about that topic, hence placing her in the position of authority. More specifically, Tang and Suganthi (1999: S27–S29) break the author identity into six "roles", as seen below.

(30) Author as a representative
      Author as the guide through the essay
      Author as the architect of the essay
      Author as the recounter of the research process
      Author as the opinion-holder
      Author as the originator

To Tang and Suganthi, these author identities display an ascending order of authority. The first, author as representative, entails the least power and the last, author as the originator, the most power.

But power seen in the form of authority, at the same time, entails accountability and, subsequently, vulnerability. In the academic world, there is no absolute authority, as any theory is open to scrutiny, criticism, and – sometimes – attack. So, it seems that authors in different disciplines and languages will make that "hard" choice between appearing authoritative and tentative, and the choice they end up making will be based on the agreed upon values of the speech community in which they belong. These values will undergird the eventual public images practitioners create for themselves, the second interactional motivation of MMP.

Hyland (2001, quoted above) attributes hard fields writers' preference for the plural for single-author self-reference to the need for objectivity, based on his interviews with scientists. The appearance of objectivity is therefore an image that writers create for themselves. The preference of the singular pronoun by writers in soft fields, Hyland proposes, is indication that soft fields practitioners want to appear engaging. That again, can be seen as an image, one that has been agreed upon collectively and over time.

The most surprising finding of all is Chinese academic writers' near complete refusal to refer to themselves as single writers, Instead of saying *wo renwei. . .* 'I believe. . .', they are found to say *women renwei. . .* 'we believe. . .' or *zuozhe/benwen renwei. . .* 'This writer/this paper believes. . .'. According to interviews and questionnaire surveys (Chen and Yang, 2022), we concluded that the self-referencing behaviors of Chinese academic writers in the general areas of language studies are motivated by modesty. In the parlance of MMP, modesty is also an image.

In sum, self-referring in academic writing is motivated by the interactional motivation of establishing, maintaining, and enhancing the public image of self. The differences found in the way writers self-refer in their academic writing between disciplines and languages are differences between public images resulting from the different values that exit in different discourse communities.

6.3.3 Critical discourse analysis

In this section, we discuss MMP and critical discourse analysis, a strand of pragmatics whose presence has been growing. Surveying the literature in it, one finds that critical discourse analysis has been applied to virtually every conceivable type of discourse in every conceivable areas of study, e.g., multicultural language policy in Eritrea (Asfaha 2020), conflicts about a test of English in Korea (Dongil and Cho 2020), former U.S. President Donald J. Trump's tweets (Ross and Rivers 2020), the rhetoric of recruitment propaganda by contemporary fascism in Sweden (Westberg 2021), school curriculum (Qin 2020), social justice issues with first peoples in the Caribbean area (Steele 2020), a TV show in Turkey (Er 2020), and the use of modals in pro- and anti-Trump comments on Facebook (Knoblock 2020).

Various as they are, the findings of these studies lend themselves to be nicely accounted for by MMP. In other words, I argue in the following paragraphs that the interactional motivation of establishing, maintaining, and enhancing the public image of self is the underlying factor for speakers to do what they are found to do by critical discourse analysts. Two studies are reviewed in some detail below.

Ross and Rivers (2020) analyze Trump's tweets on immigration across the border between the U.S. and Mexico. Specifically, Trump was promoting the building of a wall on the border, a campaign promise that he would "build a wall and Mexico will pay for it". To achieve that end, Trump is found to use several strategies on Twitter, his favorite avenue of communication with the American republic before being permanently banned by the microblogging website, including appealing to emotion (Ross and Rivers 2020: 630):

(31) The most important way to stop gangs, drugs, human trafficking and massive crime is at our Southern Border. We need Border Security, and as EVERYONE knows, you can't have Border Security without a Wall. The Drones & Technology are just bells and whistles. Safety for America!

creating hypothetical futures:

(32) The Democrats will probably submit a Bill, being cute as always, which gives everything away but gives NOTHING to Border Security, namely the Wall. You see, without the Wall there can be no Border Security – the Tech 'stuff' is just, by comparison, meaningless bells & whistles

appealing to rationality:

(33) We will be forced to close the Southern Border entirely if the Obstructionist Democrats do not give us the money to finish the Wall & also change the ridiculous immigration laws that our Country is saddled with. Hard to believe there was a Congress & President who would approve!

(Ross and Rivers 2020: 632)

appealing to experts:

(34) General Anthony Tata: "President Trump is a man of his word & he said he was going to be tough on the Border, and he is tough on the Border. He has rightfully strengthened the Border in the face of an unprecedented threat. It's the right move by President Trump". Thanks General!

(Ross and Rivers 2020: 633)

and, finally, invoking altruism:

(35) I do have a plan on the Shutdown. But to understand that plan you would have to understand the fact that I won the election, and I promised safety and security for the American people. Part of that promise was a Wall at the Southern Border. Elections have consequences!

(Ross and Rivers 2020: 634)

Trump's rhetoric is dubbed "anti-intellectualism and informality" and believed to be evidence for his authenticity (Ross and Rivers 2020: 635). In terms of MMP, however, we see the former president as a skilled politician and communicator. These strategies can be seen as dexterous manipulations of images, of both himself and others. The appeal to emotion is to create an image of scare and anger (31) for the public. Creating hypothetical futures (32) is to establish a negative image for his opponents ("Democrats... will ...gives everything away but gives NOTHING to Border Security"). Sounding rational (33) establishes an image of reasonability. Quoting a general (34) enhances his self-image of having made the "right move". Making himself look altruistic ("I won the election, and I promised safety and security for the American people") (35) brings his effort to enhance his own public image into sharp focus.

Looking more closely, we find that some of these tweets are motivated doubly. As is recalled in Chapter 2 (Figure 2.2), to benefit self-image is one of the two interactional motivations. But to benefit self-image in a political context can also increase the chances of one's ideas, policies, or ideologies being accepted, hence helping the effectiveness of the transactional consideration.

Our second example of critical discourse analysis is Knoblock (2020). Knoblock examines the use of the modal auxiliaries *must* and *have (got) to* in politically charged online communication. Comments from Donald Trump's official Facebook page are categorized according to the ideological position of the commenters into pro-Trump vs. anti-Trump. The uses of modals under each of the two camps are then divided into deontic or epistemic. Her findings about *must* are seen in Table 6.2.

Table 6.2: Use of *must*, from Knoblock (2020: 525, Table 4.1).

All MUST (excluding unclear)	Pro-Trump		Anti-Trump	
	378		111	
	Frequency	Percentage	Frequency	Percentage
Deontic MUST	324	85.7	63	56.8
Epistemic MUST	54	14.3	48	43.2

And her findings about *have to* are presented in Table 6.3.

Table 6.3: Use of *have to*, from Knoblock (2020: 525, Table 4.2).

All HAVE TO (excluding unclear)	Pro-proposal		Anti-proposal	
	409		141	
	Frequency	Percentage	Frequency	Percentage
Deontic HAVE TO	401	98	131	92.9
Epistemic HAVE TO	8	1.9	10	7.1

The differences in the use of the two modals between the two political groups are stark. The pro-Trump group is found to use far more of *must* and *have to* than the anti-Trump group. Pro-Trumpers also used far more deontic versions of the two modals than their political opponents. A few examples help illustrate the difference (Knoblock 2020: 527–529). The use of *must* comes first.

Pro-Trump, deontic followed by epistemic:

(36) If you don't know what's coming through your Borders they *must* be closed until we do that's not hard to understand.

(37) You *must* have an IQ smaller than your shoe size. Wake up!

Anti-Trump, deontic followed by epistemic:

(38) We must never remain silent in the face of bigotry. We *must* condemn those who seek to divide us. In all quarters and at all times, we *must* teach tolerance and denounce racism, anti-Semitism, and all ethnic or religious bigotry . . .

(39) To all Muslims in United States, hope you guys don't end like the Jews in 1943! Trump *must* be related to Hitler.

Knoblock notes that in the deontic versions of *must*, there is also a qualitative difference: while the pro-Trump group tend to use the modal to promote their ideology such as closing the borders, as is seen in (36), the anti-Trump group tend to affirm "the US principles of democracy, equality and freedom" (Knoblock 2020: 527), as is the case in (38). When it comes to the use of *have to*, the pro-Trumpers are more likely to target their criticism at their Facebook opponents whereas the anti-Trumpers, at the president himself.

Pro-Trump, deontic followed by epistemic:

(40) [. . .] since Muslims are the ones that become radicalized over Islam then they are the ones we *have to* block until we have a way to know who is and who is not been radicalized.

(41) How stupid can you be to believe it is okay to allow Muslims in this country at this time. You *have to* be crazy.

Anti-Trump, deontic followed by epistemic:

(42) Americans who cheer him *have to* be the dumbest race in the world I'm convinced of that how can you cheer such a bigot.

(43) Americans who cheer him *have to* be the dumbest race in the world I'm convinced of that how can you cheer such a bigot.

Semantically, the modals of *must* and *have to* express conviction and assertiveness demonically (e.g., "You must go now" is noticeably stronger than "You could/can/may go now") and certainty and confidence epistemically (Compare "He must have been at the party" with "He could have been at the party"). Knoblock therefore concludes about the pro-Trumpers thusly:

> They were more confident and unequivocal, less likely to consider possibility or likelihood of events and actions, and more likely to assign necessity or duty....These results may point to the feeling of superiority by the nativist communicators who are convinced of their right to maintain a superior standard of living and defend it from newcomers, as well as to ensure the dominant position of their culture. (Knoblock 2020: 535)

Knoblock's findings about Facebook posters' use of the two modal auxiliaries in relation to their political views seem to offer convincing support for MMP. Both pro-Trumpers and anti-Trumpers are motivated by the need to enhance their own image. On the opposite sides of the issue – the Muslim Ban that the Trump administration put in place in 2017 – for instance, both groups would be motivated to defend their own views and to create for themselves the images in their favor. In such confrontations, the images of self and other are diametrically opposed. To maintain the image of one means the hurting of the other. Therefore the two semantically strong lexemes become handy tools for members of both groups.

The different frequencies of use by the two opposition groups – the fact that the pro-Trumpers are more frequent users of *must* and *have to* than their anti-Trump counterparts – reveal the kind of image each group end up establishing. The pro-Trumpers appear stronger in language and conviction and readier to attack fellow citizens on the social media platform. The anti-Trumpers, on the other hand, appear more reasoned, for they shy away from direct engagement with their Facebook opponents, and are less willing to impose their views. They direct their critical commentary at Trump – not his supporters – as Trump was the responsible person for the Muslim Ban in the first place.

MMP can also explain other studies carried out in the critical discourse tradition. Dongil and Cho (2020) find that Korean government's implementation of a high-stakes English language test is geared toward those who comply and to curb the private education sector. The authors argue that the government's action stresses market-friendly state interaction, which serves to perpetuate neoliberal conditions. The government's position is hence self-interest (or self-image) driven. Westberg (2021), studying contemporary fascism in Sweden, finds that the most prominent Swedish Nazi movement recruits new members by offering an affective script of feeling angry, insulted, and ashamed, as well as courageous, proud, and hopeful. In other words, the propagandists try to create a negative image for the readers but promise a positive one should they join the movement. This is precisely what MMP would predict: the effectiveness in getting the message across motivates the manipulation of image.

Investigating the curriculum in secondary schools, Qin (2020) finds that about 42% of the 1,560 sentence starters and example sentences designed by a teacher for vocabulary-building activities had an implicit subjectivation goal: directing students to get good grades, to understand school procedures or classroom rules, to be "good learners".[60] Er (2020) finds the discussion of a segment from the Turkish adaptation of the global television format, *The Voice*, to be indicative of the inherently asymmetrical nature of the show: the contestant's highly non-standard language and manners are demonized (multimodally) while the coaches and the host find a relatively less judgmental environment as the "authority" in the show. Note that both studies reveal an asymmetry of power, and both show what those in power do for their own interest. The teacher uses the classroom curriculum to instill qualities that she believes good students should possess; the coaches and the host use that power to create a better environment for themselves. The key, according to MMP, is that the actions of the powerful is motivated by their own interest, which translate into both the transactional and the interactional considerations. Transactionally, the teacher in Qin's study, for example, gets across to her students her own expectations of good students; interactionally, she establishes for herself the image of influence. The same can be said about the coaches and the host in Er (2020).

6.3.4 Conversation analysis revisited

In Section 6.2.3, we looked at two of the four major structures of conversation: turn-taking and pre-sequencing. I proposed that these two structures are conventionalized mechanisms motivated by the transactional need for clarity. In this section, we move to the two remaining major structures of conversation: adjacency pairs and repair, with an emphasis on interactional motivations. Adjacency pair is discussed first.

An adjacency pair is a sequence of two turn construction units (TCUs) that are adjacent in time and produced by different participants. The first TCU is called the first of the pair, and the second TCU is called the second. Adjacency

---

60 The criticism the author lodges of the teacher appears a bit too critical, which we omit here.

pairs are typed in such a way that a particular first requires a particular second or a range of seconds, e.g., question/answer; offer/acceptance or rejection. The rule of adjacency pair is quite simple: having produced a first part of some pair, current speaker must stop speaking, and next speaker must produce at that point a second part to the pair (Atkinson and Drew 1979; Coulthard 1985). A greeting of "Good morning!" would lead to a greeting-back: "Good morning!" from the other person. A refusal to greet back would be seen as an anomaly. This obligatory nature of the adjacency pair reflects corporation and is transactional: if speech acts such as greeting that benefit other are viewed as goods, the deliverer will have reasons to expect some sort of return. The cliché "one good turn deserves another" seems apt. Furthermore, adjacency pair is part of the turn-taking structure discussed in Section 6.2.3. So, the structure of an adjacency pair is as transactional as turn-taking is.

It ought to be noted that sometimes a second does not immediately follow its first.

(44)   A: Are you coming tonight?   Q1
       B: Can I bring a guest?   Q2
       A: Male or female?   Q3
       B: What difference does that make?   Q4
       A: An issue of balance.   A4
       B: Female.   A3
       A: Sure.   A2
       B: I'll be there.   A1

In Example (44), there are four "adjacency pairs" embedded inside each other, as marked by Q and A on the right. However, this complicated structure is deployed for a good reason: the embedded answers are pre-answers to a preceding question: A4 answers Q4 as well as prepares for answering A3; A3 answers Q3 as well as prepares for the answering of A2; and A2 answers Q2 as well as prepares for the answer to A1. Put it in a different way: each question cannot be answered without knowing the answer to the next. Therefore, an exchange like this is also motivated for the clarity consideration of the transactional consideration, in the same way pre-sequencing is, as we discussed in Section 6.2.3.

However, the seconds of adjacency pairs are not always fixed. In fact, most are not. Questions, for instance, can take many responses besides answer, such as protestations of ignorance ("I don't know"), re-routes ("Better ask Henry"), refusal to answer ("I am not interest in that"), and challenges to the presupposition or sincerity of the question ("You really want to know?").

Conversation analysts therefore provide us with another set of terminology: preferred and dispreferred seconds, a sampler of which is seen in Table 6.4.

Table 6.4: Preferred and dispreferred seconds.

FIRSTS	SECONDS	
	PREFERRED	DISPREFERRED
Request	Acceptance	Declination
Offer/Invitation	Acceptance	Declination
Assessment	Agreement	Disagreement
Question	Expected answer	Unexpected answer
Apology	Acceptance	Rejection

In conversation, preferred seconds are typically simpler and without hesitation or delay.

(45) A: How 'bout a coffee at the Starbucks?
     B: Wonderful idea!

(46) A: T's it's a beautiful day out isn't it?
     B: Yeah it's just gorgeous . . .

(Pomerantz 1975: I)

Dispreferred seconds, on the other hand, display many features: delay, prefaces with discourse markers ("uh" and "well"), token agreements before disagreements ("I agree but. . ."), appreciations for offers and invitations ("Nice of you to invite but. . ."), hesitations in various forms ("Let me sleep on it"), accounts ("That was due to unforeseeable circumstances"), and declination components ("I'd love to come but I have an event that had been scheduled for several months now") (Atkinson and Drew 1979; Pomerantz 1975). The following are three examples of how dispreferred seconds are delivered.

Preface and account:

(47) A: What about coming here on the way (.) or doesn't that give you enough time?
     B: Well no I'm supervising here.

(Levinson 1983: 335)

Delay, Preface, and declination component:

(48) A: Um I wondered if there's any chance of seeing you tomorrow sometime
(0.5)
morning or before the seminar
(1.0)
B: Ahum (.) I doubt it.

(Levinson 1983: 335)

Delay, marker, appreciation, declination, and account:

(49) A: Uh if you'd care to come and visit a little while this morning I'll give you a cup of coffee.
B: hehh Well that's awfully sweet of you. I don't think I can make it this morning. .hh uhm I'm running an ad in the paper and-uh I have to stay near the phone.

(Atkinson and Drew 1979: 58).

The difference between the way a preferred second is delivered and the way a dispreferred second is delivered is sharp. A natural question to ask is why. As indicated earlier, conversation analysts have been reticent about the why of a phenomenon. But students of language use should not shy away from such questions, and MMP is capable of providing an answer.

The key to the question, first of all, is why some seconds are preferred and others are dispreferred. Let's take requests for example. To make a request is to lower oneself, hence hurting self-image. To be refused of the request is worse, as it deals a further blow to the requester's public image. Being aware of such consequences, the requestee is under pressure to mitigate the impact of a rejection. She is motived to maintain the public image of the requester as much as she can, thus using all these tools (delay, providing accounts, expressing hesitation) available to that end.

The way in which a second is delivered presents yet another case of conflict between motivations. According to the clarity transactional motivation, the invitee, B, of (49) should say, simply, "No. I cannot make it". However, the interactional motivation of maintaining the image of the inviter is obviously too strong to allow a straightforward refusal, resulting in what appears to be a pains-takingly delivered second to the first of the adjacency pair.

Pomerantz (1975) reveals several interesting features in the agreement/disagreement adjacency pair. One of them is about responding to self-denigration. Self-denigration takes disagreement as its preferred second. But to disagree implies criticism. This conflict results in the delivery of the preferred second (disagreement) with mitigating devices, as seen in (50) and (51).

(50) A: ... I'm so dumb I don't even know it. hhh! Heh
     B: Y-no, y-you're not du:mb...
                                                        (Pomerantz 1975: 93)

(51) A: You're not bored (huh)?
     B: Bored? No. We're fascinated.
                                                        (Pomerantz 1975: 94)

Levinson (1983: 338–339) points out "an asymmetry in the significance of a pause after an ordinary assessment" like (52) and after a self-deprecating assessment like (53):

(52) A: God isn't it dreary!
     B: [Silence = disagreement]

(53) A: I'm gettin fat hh
     B: [Silence = agreement]
                                                        (Levinson 1983: 339)

To Levinson (1983: 339), this is due to "different cross-cutting principles at work: a preference for agreement with the compliment, and a norm specifying the avoidance of self-praise". Within the framework of MMP, however, the explanation is once again straightforward: in (52), the public image of A – having her assessment valued – demands agreement. Refraining from saying anything is naturally seen as the opposite. In (53), on the other hand, the public image of A demands disagreement. Refraining from saying anything will likewise be seen as its opposite: agreement.

Moving to repair, we also find that MMP provides a coherent framework in which the different facts that have been revealed in the conversation analysis literature can be coherently accounted for. Repair refers to the correction of an error or a clarification of a view. Schegloff, Jefferson, and Sacks' (1977) paper lays the foundation for the repair system, which has remained valid till this day. Our discussion below will be based on it, although we will be omitting a great deal of details – such as how repair is initiated via a host of phonetic, kinetic, lexical, and discourse making devices – from this substantive and consequential work.

Repair has two components: initiation and repair. Each of the two can be done by self or other. Putting the two parameters together, we have four types – self-initiation and self-repair, other-initiation and self-repair, self-initiation and other-repair, and other-initiation and other-repair – respectively illustrated below.

Self-initiation and self-repair:

(54) A: She was giving me a:ll the people that were go:ne this yea:r *I mean this quarter y'// know*
B: yeah

(Schegloff, Jefferson, and Sacks 1977: 364)

Other-initiation and self-repair:

(55) A: Is Al here today?
B: Yeah
(2.0)
C: He is? hh eh heh
B: Well he was.

(Schegloff, Jefferson, and Sacks 1977: 364)

Self-initiation and other-repair:

(56) A: He had dis uh Mistuh W- whatever K- I can't think of his first name, Watts on, the
wone that wrote //that piece,
B: Dan Watts

(Schegloff, Jefferson, and Sacks 1977: 365)

Other-initiation and other-repair:

(57) A: Where didju play ba:sk//etbaw.
B: (The) gy:m.
A: In the gy:m?
B: Yea:h. Like grou(h)y therapy. Yuh know =
A: Oh :::.
B: Half the group thet we had la:s' term wz there en jus' playing arou:nd.
A: Uh – fooling around.
B: Eh – yeah...

(Schegloff, Jefferson, and Sacks 1977: 365)

Schegloff, Jefferson, and Sacks (1977) show various ways in which self-correction (both initiation and repair) is encouraged. The speaker of the trouble source, for instance, is provided the opportunity to self-initiate in a number of ways, although the other participant clearly knows how to repair the trouble herself. Examples of encouraging self-initiation are pauses (waiting for the speaker of the trouble source to realize the need then to repair and to repair voluntarily), as is seen in (55) and (58), and expression of doubts (59).

(58) A: Hey the first time they stopped me from sellin cigarettes was this morning.
 (1.0)
 B: From selling cigarettes?
 A: From buying cigarettes. They // said uh Uh huh
 (Schegloff, Jefferson, and Sacks 1977: 370)

(59) A: It's just about three o'clock, so she's probably free. I'll call her now.
 B: What time is it?
 A: Three, isn't it?
 B: *I thought it was earlier.*
 A: Oh, two. Sorry. (Cf. also 58 above.)
 (Schegloff, Jefferson, and Sacks 1977: 377)

Example (60) demonstrates how a conversationist provides her hearer the opportunity to self-repair by locating the trouble source.

(60) A: 'E likes that waiter over there,
 B: Wait-er?
 A: Waitress, sorry,
 B: 'ats better.
 (Schegloff, Jefferson, and Sacks 1977: 377)

In (61), the children playing the game of water tag refuse other-repair and insist on self-repair:

(61) [Three children playing water tag; Steven has been tagged, and is now "It"]
 Steven: One, two, three, [pause] four five...
  six, [pause] eleven eight nine ten.
 Susan: Eleven? eight, nine, ten?
 Steven: Eleven, eight, nine, ten.
 Nancy: Eleven?
 Steven: Seven, eight, nine, ten.

Susan: That's better.
[Game continues]

> (Schegloff, Jefferson, and Sacks 1977: 373)

Other-repair seems to be the last resort. When it does occur, it tends to go with "modulators" like *I think* and *y'mean*:

(62)   A: But y'know single beds'r awfully thin to sleep on.
      B: What?
      A: single beds. //They're
      B: Y'mean narrow?
      A: They're awfully narrow yeah.

> (Schegloff, Jefferson, and Sacks 1977: 378)

The preference for self-correction over other correction is most convincingly and carefully demonstrated in Schegloff, Jefferson, and Sacks (1977), although the authors are characteristically cautious about the reasons why conversationalists are so keen on avoiding self-correction:

> Even casual inspection of talk in interaction finds self-correction vastly more common than other correction. In locating a strong empirical skewing, the relevance of the distinction is afforded some initial rough support; the direction of the skewing toward self-correction affords one sort of evidence for the preference relationship of its components. We are, therefore, encouraged to explore the organizational mechanisms operating in any particular sequential environment, which, by their case-by-case operation, produce the observed over-all skewed distribution. (Schegloff, Jefferson, and Sacks 1977: 362)

The preference for other-correction, to the authors, is an "observed over-all skewed distribution" based on a "case-by-case" basis. This preference is a mechanism for social interaction and social action that is "organizationally designed" (Schegloff, Jefferson, and Sacks 1977: 372). The authors seem to sense an inherent contradiction in their philosophical positioning. On the one hand – quite possibly compelled by their theoretical orientation – they emphasize the localness, the case-by-caseness, and the dynamic and fluid nature of social interaction. On the other hand, by discovering an obvious pattern of reality, which they believe to be an indication of something deeper, they seem to be aware that an explanation is in order for the reasons for that pattern. Without an explanation, it is very difficult to reconcile the two opposing prerogatives.[61]

---

[61] The authors write elsewhere that the "skewing towards" self-correction is an "organization, operative in local environments and on a case-by-case basis, which cumulatively produced the aggregate orderliness of repair phenomena" (Schegloff, Jefferson, and Sacks 1977: 374). But one

To explore the why of an important social reality requires some sort of theory. The authors realize it, as seen the following quote:

> However, the organization of repair is the self-righting mechanism for the organization of language use in social interaction. If language is composed of systems of rules which are integrated, then it will have sources of trouble related to the modes of their integration (at the least). And if it has intrinsic sources of trouble, then it will have a mechanism for dealing with them intrinsically. An adequate theory of the organization of natural language will need to depict how a natural language handles its intrinsic troubles. Such a theory will, then, need an account of the organization of repair.
> (Schegloff, Jefferson, and Sacks 1977: 338)

Note, however, that Schegloff, Jefferson, and Sacks believe the reasons for the organization of repair should come from "the organization of natural language". If what they mean by "the organization of natural language" refers to the structure or architect of language, such as morphology, semantics, and syntax – I admit that I am not sure that *is* indeed what they mean – I cannot agree with them. The preference of self-correction in conversation is social, and a theory of it can only come from one that deals with the use of language, not the internal architecture of it.

We are back at MMP, which *is* a model of language use. Conversationalists prefer self-correction, MMP would say, because other correction hurts the public image of (the speaker of) the trouble source. One of the important aspects of public image, as we discussed in Chapter 2, is not to make mistakes. To appear "correct" about facts and to be agreed with by others are included in Brown and Levinson's (1987) positive face and are part of the image of self. If you, therefore, correct an error I have made, you would hurt my image, as you would be appearing critical about my ability, judgement, or character, depending the nature and gravity of the error.

MMP, too, seems capable of accounting for two more facts about repair. The first is other-correction, which is covered by Schegloff, Jefferson, and Sacks (1977). As is seen earlier, the authors show that other correction is done often with "modulators" such as *you mean* or *I think*. The most "unmodulated" other-correction in the paper, however, is (63).

---

wonders how things "in local environments and on a case-by-case basis" can produce an aggregate orderliness" randomly.

(63) A: ... I was thinkin this morning, I was having a little trouble in the bathroom, an' I thought 'Oh, boy, I- n- I- uh- uh this business of getting up at six o'clock'n being ready t'eat, is uh- is not fer me'// I heh heh
B: Uh huh
B: Well, uh th- [clears throat]
A: Somehow you // endure it.
B: There's 'n- There's 'n answer to that too.
(2.0)
B: hhhh a physical answer t(hh)oo hhh
A: You mean takin laxative at night.
B: *No, suppositories.*

(Schegloff, Jefferson, and Sacks 1977: 379)

The other-repair in this example, "No. Suppositories", is delivered without modulation. However, Schegloff, Jefferson, and Sacks (1977: 379) observe that in cases like this, other-repair, which typically occurs after a checking of understanding, will be "(either) invited, and/or reject a modulated other-correction in prior turn". In sum, the authors conclude that other-correction is both "restricted" and, in the rare case in which it does occur, it will behave differently from self-correction, much like the behaviors of dispreferred seconds we discussed earlier in the chapter (Section 6.2.3).

It is purely by accident that I came upon the following, from *Morning Joe*, a political talk show aired on MSNBC in the U.S. Mika and Joe, who are married to each other, are two of the three cohosts.

(64) Mika: [Monologue] How a congressman set off the metal detector at the door of the House of representatives and was investigated about whether he had tried to carry a gun into the House chamber.
Joe: Look, I have done that thousands// of times..
Mika: No. You haven't.
Joe: I have voted on that floor. . .
Mika: *Yeah. You didn't take a gun. . .*
Joe: Yes. I. . .[62]

---

[62] https://www.msnbc.com/morning-joe/watch/jaime-harrison-organize-organize-organize-will-be-the-dems-strategy-99858501557 (accessed January 22, 2021).

There are two other-repairs in this example. The first, "No. You haven't", is delivered in the most unmodulated way possible. After Joe has accepted her correction with "I have voted on that floor. . .", Mika reaffirms: "Yeah. You didn't take a gun. . .". While it is difficult to predict what Schegloff, Jefferson, and Sacks might say about this example, MMP has its explanation: Mika delivers other-correction so readily and directly because it is beneficial to both the image of Joe – of the trouble source – and the image of the organization they represent on national TV. A bit explanation is in order.

As many readers might be aware, former president Donald Trump called mainstream news media "the enemy of the people". MSNBC is one of these targeted media outlets. Being openly anti-Trump, *Morning Joe* was constantly\in Trump and his allies' crosshairs. What the hosts say each day is scrutinized, sometimes intentionally twisted, and a few times attacked. In this segment, however, Joe misspeaks. By saying "Look. I have done that thousands of times. . .", he implies that he has "tried to carry a gun into the House chamber" thousands of times, the only possible antecedent of *that*. Mika, Joe's wife and often the "cooler head" of the couple, realizes the mistake instantaneously and interrupts Joe in the middle of the phrase *thousands of times* to correct him in the most straightforward way possible: "No. You haven't". Joe realizes his mistake and corrects it: "I have voted on that floor. . .". Mika continues to repair: "Yeah. You didn't take a gun. . ." until Joe accepts the repair one more time.

Mika's unmodulated other-corrections would provide a challenge to conversational analysts. However, they follow naturally from MMP. That is, they are motivated by the need to protect the image of both Joe and the program. In an ordinary context, Mika might not correct Joe in such a straightforwardly. However, on national TV, she knows the consequence of letting Joe's misstatement uncorrected: Joe would be said to have admitted trying "to carry a gun into the House chamber thousands of times". She therefore chooses "the lesser of the two evils," damaging Joe's image to avoid greater damage to it (as well as the image of MSNBC).

The second issue about repair is that there seems to be a category in the repair system that conversation analysts have not discussed: withholding correction. It should be immediately acknowledged that such withholding must be conditioned, as it cannot apply to all withholding. Many "errors" we make are inconsequential: slightly mispronouncing a colleague's name, calling something "dark read" instead of "maroon", saying that the lunch cost five dollars while it in reality cost four dollars and ninety-nine cents. The hearers of these "errors" probably often do not correct them. But there are at the same time errors that are significant but speakers consciously ignores them. Such withholding may be so conscious that the hearer debates about whether to correct the error but decides not to. It therefore should be part of the repair system.

How do we know that a needed correction was withheld since it did not happen? Fortunately, the former president Donald Trump has provided us much fodder. According to the *Washington Post,* Trump made 30,573 misstatements during the four years of presidency. Some of these misstatements are surely inconsequential; some may even be "innocent". But some *are* consequential and those around him *were* considering correcting but decided not to. Let's use one of the best-known things Trump has said as a president in April 2020: that injection of disinfectants and light rays into the human body might be effective to kill the coronavirus in it. The following is what he said in full.

(65) So I asked Bill a question some of you are thinking of if you're into that world, which I find to be pretty interesting. So, supposing we hit the body with a tremendous, whether its ultraviolet or just very powerful light, and I think you said, that hasn't been checked but you're gonna test it. And then I said, supposing it brought the light inside the body, which you can either do either through the skin or some other way, and I think you said you're gonna test that too, sounds interesting. And I then I see the disinfectant, where it knocks it out in one minute, and is there a way you can do something like that by injection inside, or almost a cleaning. Because you see it gets in the lungs, and it does a tremendous number on the lungs. So it'd be interesting to check that. So you're going to have to use medical doctors, but it sounds interesting to me, so we'll see. But the whole concept of the light, the way it goes in one minute, that's pretty powerful.[63]

Trump's ideas are no doubt wrong and should be corrected. Two of his administration officials were responsible to do the correction. One is Bill Brian (the "Bill" Trump refers to above), the U.S. Department of Homeland Security undersecretary for science. The other is Deborah Birx, the coronavirus response coordinator for the White House Coronavirus Task Force. Bill Brian is said by Trump to have agreed to test hitting the body with light and injecting it with disinfectant, which he did not. Deborah Birx was sitting by the side of the press room while Trump was speaking. She was astounded (her facial expressions went viral on social media right after) and was agonizing over what to do. Both of them had the obligation and interest to repair the president's statements, as they were the top government officials, responsible for the correctness of public health information that came out of the White House. They, too, knew the consequence of not

---

[63] https://www.businessinsider.com/trump-wants-bring-light-inside-the-body-to-kill-coronavirus-2020-4

correcting: the president had the megaphone and a large following, some of them might try disinfectant themselves (and a few indeed tried).

But both decided to withhold correcting Donald Trump. Bill Brian kept silent until the time of writing (end of May 2021). Birx, after Trump's exit from presidency (January 20, 2021), has been speaking out and, in an interview, said she could have been more outspoken about Trump's behaviors regarding the coronavirus pandemic,[64] implicitly admitting that she should have corrected the President.

Brian's and Birx's withholdings of correction of Trump's unscientific proposal to cure the coronavirus disease with disinfectants and light are due to a complicated calculation of image gains and losses. Professionalism dictates that Brian and Birx point out the errors in the president's suggestion and its danger for public health: after all, what a president says on national TV has far reaching consequences. However, to point out the error will hurt the president's image, as Trump views image as of paramount importance for both his presidency and his personal brand. In addition, these withholdings would also avoid the damage to their own image, as Trump is known to attack anyone who dares to differ with his prolific and ungarnished tweets. In this case, the image of other and of self are aligned. Withholding correction is motivated by the need not to hurt both.

6.4 Discourse markers

In the sections above – Sections 6.2 and 6.3 – I demonstrated how MMP accounts for a host of strands in the general area of discourse studies: information packaging, genre analysis, conversation analysis, identity construction studies, and critical discourse analysis. These discussions can be seen as evidence for one aspect of MMP's utility – that it is capable of subsuming a wide range of research areas and accounting for the findings in them coherently. In the current section, we move to the demonstration of another aspect of MMP's utility, that it can help us with microanalysis and in ways that will lead us to more elegant conclusions. Based on a study by Chunmei Hu and me that is currently in submission, we use the discourse maker *so* (DM *so*) as an illustration.

Discourse markers are defined in the literature as linguistic constructions that signal the relationship between two discourse units. They are key to the interpretation of discourse participants' intentions and the understanding of the

---

[64] https://www.cnn.com/2021/01/26/opinions/deborah-birx-interview-filipovic/index.html

interaction between participants and their attitudes towards the propositional content of what they say (Blakemore 1988; Buysse 2012; Fischer 2006; Fraser 1999b; House and Kasper 1981; Redeker 2006; Schiffrin 1987; Schourup 1999). Discourse makers have at least three distinctive properties. First, their functions are dependent on where precisely they are used in a sentence. Schiffrin (1987: 31), for instance, speaks of discourse markers being "sequentially dependent" (See also Fischer 2006; Schourup 1999). Second, a discourse marker covers a chunk of discourse whose exact nature is difficult to define. Schiffrin (1987: 31–36) discusses the difficulty of such a task and adopts the vague term *units* to refer to the chunk of material "bracketed" by a discourse marker. Fraser (1999b: 931) uses a similarly vague term "segment" for the same notion. Third, discourse markers are relational, indicating connections between parts of the discourse, between the speaker and her intention, and between what is said and the cotext/context (Buysse 2012: 1964; Fraser 1999b: 931; Taboada 2010).

In addition, some discourse markers are interjections which do not have a clear semantic content (Norrick 2009). Others are at the same time members of the lexicon of the language. The discourse marker *well* (e.g., "Well, I kind of like it"), for example, is also an adverb (e.g., "He took it well"). DM *so* belongs to the latter type, as it can be used as a coordinating conjunction (66), a subordinating conjunction (67), an adverb (68), a pro-form (69), or as part of a multi-word conjunction of purpose (70).[65]

(66) We were out of milk, *so I went to the store to buy some.*

(67) Grace is saving money *so she can buy her own horse.*

(68) It was *so* nice!

(69) A: I am very happy about that.
B: *So am I.*

(70) He went there early *so as to/so that he would get a good seat.*

This multiplicity of structural properties of *so* leads to its semantic polysemousness. As a conjunction – either coordinating (66) or subordinating (67) – it denotes result. As an adverb (68), it denotes intensity. As a pro-form (69), it replaces the

---

[65] See Biber et al. (1999) and Greenbaum (1996).

material appearing in the previous context, and, as part of a multi-word conjunction (70), it assists in the denotation of purpose.

What we are concerned with in this section, however, is the pragmatic function of *so* when used as a discourse marker, as is seen in (71).

(71) Ah, a great question. *So the technique that Kepler is using to find planets is called the transit technique. So it's actually very difficult to just go out with a telescope and take a picture of a planet around another star and the reason for that is that stars are really bright and they're very far away from us. . . . So if you try to take a picture of them, they're sort of washed out by the glare of the star. . . .*[66]

(Yagoda 2011)

In the literature on DM *so*, a great number of functions have been proposed for the lexeme. Treating *so* as "a marker of main units" that "functions globally over a wide range of talk", Schiffrin (1987) identifies about fifteen functions for DM *so*, among which are beginning a topic (193), "fact-based result of the just-reported reasons" (Schiffrin 1987: 204), "interpretation warranted by background knowledge" (205), specific events in support of the speaker's conclusions (206), participant and topic transition (219), and support for the interlocutor (224).

Later works on DM *so* continue to propose functions for it. Xu (2007) argues that DM *so* assists the speaker in organizing discourse, aiding interaction between participants, and expressing emotions. Howe (1991) notes the topic-introducing function of DM *so*. Johnson (2002) finds that DM *so* can develop and sequence topic in police interviews. Raymond (2004) shows DM *so* invokes "an upshot that is claimed to be available to a recipient" (211) so that the recipient can make connections between a preceding turn and the current. Local and Walker (2005) propose that DM *so* enables the conversationalist to either trail off or to hold the floor. Lastly, Bolden (2006, 2008, 2009) argues that DM *so* ". . . conveys to the addressee that the upcoming course of action is emerging from incipiency". It instructs the hearer "to understand the current turn by reference to some pending

---

[66] This use of *so* has caused much consternation in the general public in the U.S. A guest of a BBC Radio program (http://news.bbc.co.uk/today/hi/today/newsid_9644000/9644002.stm) believes that *so*, thusly used, is a "cliche", its users "lazy", and its uses annoying. Such distain is shared by many in the mainstream media (Giridharadas 2010; Lewis 1999; Shearer 2014; Sterbenz 2014; and Yagoda 2011).

interactional agenda" (Bolden 2009: 996). Putting all these studies together, one finds that a total of 35 functions have been proposed for DM *so*.

These functions of DM *so* all appear to be valid based on the data presented and in the theoretical framework each scholar adopts. However, a common thread seems to run through the studies that have produced them: there does not appear to be an underlying principle to unify the functions an author identifies. Take the functions proposed by Schiffrin (1987) for example. Among the functions she identifies, "Interpretation" refers to the hearer's understanding of the speaker's intended message; "specific events" refers to what has happened in the speaker's or hearer's life, and "participant and topic transition" moves to the domain of the discourse event itself. They are therefore based on different principles and may cut across each other. Likewise, Local and Walker' (2005) propose that DM *so* function to help the speaker to "trail off" and "hold the floor" in different contexts. Granted, a linguistic construction may function differently in different local contexts such as a turn construction unit, but once that construction is found to have opposing functions in different contexts, one wonders if something more underlying should be sought.

In the following pages, an MMP analysis is provided on DM *so*. The basic argument I will be advancing is that DM *so* is motivated by the clarity consideration of the transactional motivation category. Specially, DM *so* helps the speaker to manage topics of discourse so as to reduce the burden of processing on the part of the hearer.

6.4.1 Topic management

The notion of topic originated in syntax, referring to a noun phrase placed in the initial position of a sentence, which is often – but not always – the subject of that sentence. Thus American structuralists such as Bloomfield (1933) speak of a sentence having a "topic" and "comment", which view was also accepted by generative linguists. Topic, too, finds itself playing a role in Prague School's theory of functional sentence perspective – being the rough equivalent to theme as opposed to rheme (Daneš 1974; Firbas 1962, 1992) – and in functional grammar as espoused by Dik (1989) and Givón (1983). Reviews of this long and diverse line of research are found in Berry, Thompson and Hillier (2014), Downing (1991, 2000), and Gómez González (2001).

Evolved but then departing from sentence topic is the notion of discourse topic, the discussion of which began in the 1970s (Van Dijk 1979) until this day (Charolles 2020). Discourse topic differs from sentence topic in important ways. First, while sentence topic has linguistic presentation, often in the form of a noun phrase, discourse topic does not. Thus Asher (2004: 193) calls discourse topics "summarizers" of stretches of discourse and "providers" for entities in subsequent discourse; van Dijk and Kintsch (1983) deem discourse topics "semantic"; and Reinhart (1981: 74) sees them as "propositional". Second, discourse topic refuses to be defined in a precise way (See Charolles 2020 for a comprehensive summary). As a result, scholars seem to have agreed on a very vague notion of "aboutness", i.e., the topic of a discourse (or a part of it) is what the discourse (or the part of it) is about (Asher 2004; Brown and Yule 1983; Charolles 2020).

In this section, we are dealing solely with discourse topic, not sentence topic. Thus no efforts will be made to identify topics of sentences. The topic of (71), we would say, is "Kepler Space Telescope". While we acknowledge it might be different for another reader (e.g., "how the Kepler Space Telescope works"), the difference between the two is irrelevant for our discussion.

The primary reason for topic to be a prominent notion in discourse studies is that it provides a way for the speaker to organize discourse and for the hearer to better understand the speaker (Asher 2004; Charolles 2020).[67] This explains why topic is present in classical pragmatics theories (Charolles 2020). The maxim of relation of Grice's (1975) cooperative principle, for instance, makes reference to the topic of the conversation at hand: something that is seen as relevant only when it has to do with what is being talked about. The understanding of a speech act is crucially dependent on topic also. An utterance "Peter was seeing a woman" can be construed to be a speech act of accusation of Peter's marriage infidelity if the topic is about Peter's difficult relationship with his wife but as a speech act of expressing relief if the topic is about the difficulty Peter faces finding a date. It, too, lies at the heart of Sperber and Wilson's (1986) theory of relevance (Charolles 2020).

The best illustration of the importance of topic in discourse, however, comes from an experiment done by Brandsford and Johnson (1973: 400, quoted in Brown and Yule 1983: 72). In the experiment, subjects were provided the following text.

---

[67] This function of discourse topic is analogous to the function of sentence topic in some aspects. Functional linguists (e.g., Givón 1983) have demonstrated how "topic continuity" determines the interpretation of anaphoric references.

(72) The procedure is actually quite simple. First you arrange things into different groups. Of course, one pile may be sufficient depending on how much there is to do. If you have to go somewhere else due to lack of facilities that is the next step, otherwise you are pretty well set. It is important not to overdo things. That is, it is better to do too few things at once than too many. In the short run this may not seem important but complications can easily arise. A mistake can be expensive as well. At first the whole procedure will seem complicated. Soon, however, it will become just another facet of life. It is difficult to foresee any end to the necessity for this task in the immediate future, but then one never can tell. After the procedure is completed one arranges the materials into different groups again. Then they can be put into their appropriate places. Eventually they will be used once more and the whole cycle will then have to be repeated. However, that is part of life.

Subjects found it far more difficult to interpret the excerpt without knowing what it is about. But interpretation became a lot easier once the topic of the text, "washing clothes," was provided.

If, as this experiment shows, discourse topic heavily influences the hearer's interpretation of a discourse, it must be just as critical for the speaker to manage topic in such a way that her message is understood as intended, a position taken by almost all scholars on discourse topic thus far cited. Van Dijk and Kintsch (1983), for instance, view this need in terms of memory. Since topics are ever present in the minds of the hearer and change as discourse moves along, their processing incurs a heavy burden on the hearer's working memory. Thus various discursive mechanisms are deployed to reduce that burden, one of which is to establish linkage between different topical units. In the parlance of MMP, this linkage is motivated by the need for clarity, one of the transactional considerations.

Now we move to the case study of DM *so*. In the aforementioned paper by Hu and me, we gathered 623 tokens of DM *so* from the Corpus of Contemporary American English (COCA),[68] the Michigan Corpus of Academic Spoken English (MICASE),[69] and our own collection (referred to as COLECTION below). All of the 623 tokens pertain to the topic of the discourse (or discourse segment) in which they occur, functioning to establish a topic, continue a topic, change a topic, resume a topic, and close a topic, as is presented in Table 6.5.

---

[68] https://www.english-corpora.org/coca/
[69] https://micase.state.mi.us/portalapp/public/login.html?execution=e1s1

Table 6.5: Distribution of DW *so* across subfunctions.

SUBFUNCTION	# OF TOKENS
Topic establishment	53 (9%)
Topic continuation	354 (57%)
Topic change	84 (13%)
Topic resumption	73 (12%)
Topic closure	59 (9%)
TOTAL	623 (100%)

The findings presented in Table 6.5 show that the five subfunctions includes *all* the 623 tokens, giving us confidence that topic management is a plausible macro-function for the lexeme. Below we discuss how DM so helps the speaker to manage topic in these five ways.

6.4.2 DM *so* and topic management

We start with topic establishment. Topic establishment refers to the signaling of an upcoming topic. It is similar to "introducing a topic" in Howe (1991) and "beginning a topic" in Schiffrin (1987: 193). It may also be what Bolden means by the function of *so* "to constitute interactional agenda" (2009: 988).

Unsurprisingly, topic establishment tends to happen at the beginning of discourse. Consider Example (73), whereby S stands for *student* and T, for *tutor*.

(73) T: *so is this Kelvin?* is that right?
    S: um, John,
    T: oh John Munt.
    S: yeah, (xx)
    T: oh wow
    S: *so i have to (xx) yeah, (xx)*
    T: okay mkay

(MICASE: *Astronomy Peer Tutorial*)

This is the beginning of a student peer tutorial. Once all eleven participants are seated, the tutor begins the session with *so*: "so is this Kelvin?", effectively calling the roll, indicating that the tutorial is to begin. After a clarification of his name, the student establishes his own topic with "so I have to (xx)", telling the tutor that he has come to seek help with (xx), a notion that has been introduced in a previous astronomy class.

(74)   A: Sorry I don't remember seeing that email. Missed it.
       B: No problem. I will send it to you again.
       C: Okay. *So, it's 2 now. Let's get to our agenda.*

(COLLECTION)

This example comes from a committee meeting, a face-to-face interaction. Before the meeting time, committee members have been chitchatting. When the scheduled time comes, the committee chair, C, calls the attention of all the members to start official business with "Okay, so it's 2 now. Let's get to our agenda", establishing the agenda as the topic.

Bolden (2009) proposes that DM *so* functions to "to break the ice". The following is from her.

(75)   [A married couple in a restaurant]
       A: This one's good. It's got spinach.
       B: That's the sausage. . ..
            (15.0, eating)
       B: *So the skit was good (from) work?*
       A: Everyone had their own skit.
            (12.5, eating)
       B: *So did anybody say anything about the bar today?*

(Bolden 2009: 989, Excerpt 10)

There are two DM *so*s used in this excerpt. The first use occurs after turns about the food – spinach and sausage – followed by a 15 second delay that is taken up by eating. It enables B to establish the topic of the skit. A replies to the skit topic only briefly and the couple launch into another period of eating (12.5 seconds). Since his skit topic has been abandoned, B picks up the topic of the bar with another DM *so*: "So did anybody say anything about the bar today?"

For Bolden (2006; 2009: 989), the speakers use *so* "as a marker of emergence from recipiency reflexively to indicate that the matter is something they had meant to raise, thus emphasizing their engagement with the addressee". Two points can be made about her analysis. First, there is no evidence that the speaker, B, "had meant" to first talk about the skit and then "the bar". Second, "had meant" and "reflexively" do not seem to go together. There is a bigger point still: once we say that DM *so*, or any other discourse marker for that matter, enables the speakers to bring out something they have meant to say, the function of that marker disappears: speakers can be said to *always* say what they mean to say. Our MMP analysis, on the other hand, subsumes the "break the ice" function under topic establishment so that the lexeme is seen as serving the same purpose as it does in other situations, e.g., Examples (73) and (74), above.

We now move to topic continuation. Topic continuation refers to cases in which DM *so* is used to signal that the upcoming discourse material will be on the same topic. It is analogous to Johnson's (2002) notion of topic sequencing. It might also be the reason for Schiffrin's (1987) observation that DM *so* "functions globally over a wide range of talk".

As is seen in Table 6.5, topic continuation is by far the largest category in which the tokens in the dataset belong (354 out of 623, 57%). This is not surprising, as one can assume staying on topic to be the norm of discourse. In Example (71), above, the interviewee uses four DM *so*s to indicate that he is on the topic. The same holds for Example (76), below.

(76) T: yup, mkay, so what we wanna do we wanna look through okay and say what, this is the (P quadrant) this is where the m- most photons will be emitted, emitted by these stars. and uh, that's gonna tell us something pretty important, okay? *so we say you know,* well let's just look uh, let's look here. alright *so five hundred so, what's, what is it, five hundred and seventeen? so uhh, you know it's*
    S1: i know it's part of the other one
    T: yeah *so let's see there's about f- (xx) ruler or a pen actually if you see, yeah so what would happen here we have uh, okay, so here's the distance, and this is about halfway, you*
    S2: this would be the green
    S1: know it's a little less than half it's yeah, it's right in the green, (xx)
    S2: okay yeah it's probably i mean, (most of the) stuff seems to be, in the book
    S1: (xx)
    T: okay, okay *so you (xx) by satellite, two-way mirror, watch (xx) pairs so alright so you've got, um, so you've gotta do like resolutions here,* [S1: mhm] um, you've got, two millimeter mirror, or two meter mirror [S2: yeah] and you've got, wanna be able to resolve some saying, something that's like, half a meter, or something like [S1: okay] yeah say, say [S2: alright] like half a meter. [S2: yeah] *so, y- you wanna be able to resolve,* (it's like what's it,) it's like five meters, and you've got a two meter mirror, (xx) disorganized, so um. . . *so how far above the earth, does the sunlight need to be? so now, you're gonna do, something like this, um,* let's see, what are we gonna do? we are going to, let's see, (xx)

(MICASE: *Astronomy Peer Tutorial*)

This example comes from the same student peer tutorial as does Example (73). The tutor uses 14 *sos* over three turns, all signaling that he is staying on the same topic.[70]

Topic continuation, as it has turned out, can be done in many ways. Most of the DM *sos* used in Example (76), above, belong to explanation. So does the one in (77), in which A offers a more accessible way – invoking the actual driving experience of his TV audience – to understand the ratio between energy consumption and "the cube of the speed", another notion not immediately clear to an average audience.

(77) A: The amount of energy you use is related to the cube of the speed you're driving...
      B: What's that?
      A: *So if you're driving at 75, that's using a lot more energy than 55*
      B: I can imagine.

(COCA: *NPR Science Friday*)

A topic can be advanced by exemplification, with DM *so* used together with "for example" being a frequent choice,[71] as seen in Example (78).

(78) And that's fascinating because it provides not only Hispanics but any group that's recently mixed, from a biomedical point of view, provides leverage to identify genes or risk factors that may have been population-specific. *So for example, one of the most common genetic risk factors for breast cancer in Mexicans is Ashkenazi mutation for breast cancer.*

(COCA: *NPR Science Friday*)

by clarification:

(79) A: [A long narrative about Facebook's business endeavor into mobile application and
          its motivation behind it]

---

[70] Coincidentally, the tutorial is about the same subject matter as Example (73): astronomy, an area known for its inaccessibility to a lay person. Could there be a correlation between the complexity of a topic and the frequency of deployment of so to manage topic continuation? This observation will surface a few more times in subsequent discussions, although it cannot be fully supported at this point.

[71] There are 11 uses of *so for example* in our database. Most of them appear in lectures dealing with dense subject matters.

B: So, it sounds like a customized version of Android seems like the best thing, the *deepest integration you could do without building your own operating system*.

(COLLECTION)

by description:

(80) But because I have my prosthesis then I just get on with it. They're not as clean as the female toilets, generally speaking. It's a prosthesis and it's actually a device for people with female genitals to piss standing up. *So it's a sort of a funnel and it's called a pisser-packer because it's nice and soft silicon so you can actually put it in your underpants and keep it there for when you need to go.*

(COCA: *Venus Boyz*)

and by confirmation to a previously stated or assumed belief:

(81) She's been a big proponent of Brexit and took actually Boris Johnson on during the referendum campaign directly. *So, yes, this is the kind of thing that is going to really mobilize voters in Scotland to say, here we are, an English prime minister doing what's best for the English Conservative Party, against Scottish interests.* There will also, of course, be a question, if there's a hard Brexit, on what happens in Northern Ireland, where a majority also voted to remain during the referendum in 2016. *So, no, I think you can see where the passion that's been built up outside Downing Street, this has come as a shock.*

(COCA: *PBS News Hour*)

Interpretation appears to be another favorite means for topic continuation. In (82), below, the guest of the interview (A) quotes an excerpt from a book about armed resistance by the Palestinians. The interviewer (B) renders his interpretation of the excerpt by drawing a parallel between Israeli soldiers and Nazis.

(82) A: "Armed resistance was used in the American Revolution, the Afghan resistance against Russia (which the U.S. supported), the French resistance against the Nazis, and even in the Nazi concentration camps, or, more famously, in the Warsaw Ghetto. Palestinian resistance arises out of a similarly oppressive situation".
B: *So this writer is actually comparing Israeli soldiers to Nazis.*

(COCA: *CNN Larry King Live*)

Lastly, a topic may have subtopics. For example, if we are talking about the worldwide coronavirus pandemic, we can talk about the ways to fight against in each country, the rate of increase of cases in December 2020 and then July 2021, the speed of vaccination in different regions of the world, or the human suffering that it causes. Here, too, we find *so* being used to continue a topic by moving among subtopics. Example (83) is from a radio talk show on how U.S. National Park Services managed its work during the 2019 U.S. government shutdown. The radio show host moves to who is paying for various supplies from the previous subtopic via the deployment of DM *so*.

(83) A: Campbell's work is being funded by the nonprofit Florida National Parks Association. Jim Sutton runs the group. He says it's literally paying to keep the lights on. *So, you're paying for the electricity.*
       B: Yes.
       A: Who's paying for the toilet paper?
       B: I am.
       A: Who's paying for the soap?
       B: I am.

(COCA: *PBS News Hour*)

The topic of A's first turn – who is paying for what – has a list of subtopics in the form "A is paying for X", "B is paying for Y", and "C is paying for Z". He indeed moves to the first subtopic, "So, you are paying for the electricity" with *so*, and, with the help of B, covers other subtopics in subsequent turns.

While there is a need to keep topic, there is also a need to change topic – the third subfunction of DM *so* – as discourse is not always structured on one topic. In our data, 18 of the 84 topic-changing uses of DM *so* come from TV talk shows, particularly in segments involving a panel. Often, such a covers the key issues of the day and hence requires the host to move from one issue to another within a preset time frame. Example (84), from a news talk show aired on Sunday in the U.S, is a good illustration. In the first three turns, the two guests (G1 and G2) are talking about presidential candidate Hilary Clinton's bringing up economy during the 2016 Democratic primaries. Then the host (T) changes the topic to John Edwards, another presidential candidate.

(84) G1: And she's the only one who brought up the economy. Did you notice?
        G2: Right.
        G1: Anyone could have said, look, we may go into a recession here, it's hard times. Only Senator Clinton with her experience, if you will, managed to bring it up.

H: *So, Donna, you heard John Edwards just now say that he's in until the convention no matter what.* It seems like he's just praying for a two-person race against Barack Obama...

(COCA: *ABC This Week*)

Also from a TV program, Example (85) occurs at the beginning of the show. A is introducing the different segments of the day, beginning with "We got a big show coming up. We have Venus Williams" and, in the next turn, elaborates on what Williams will be talking about. Then she needs to move to the introduction of the next segment and DM *so* appears: "so yesterday we got a lot of feedback on our...".

(85) A: That's sweet.
 B: It's a very happy song.
 A: Sounds sweet. All right. We got a big show coming up. We have Venus Williams.
 B: Yay.
 A: She's going to tell us what we dress like because the US Open is coming up and she's a big star of that. We'll talk to her right after this. *So yesterday we got a lot of feedback on our...*
 B: Yeah.

(COCA: *NBC Today Show*)

In (86), A and B are talking about B's dating with C for the purpose of career advancement. When C enters, A changes the topic to whether C has been on a plane (which is dovetailed with the metaphor B has been using).

(86) A: What you doing going out with a guy like that?
 B: Well, here's the thing. You don't tell the pilot flying the plane you're on that you don't wanna go out with him.
 A: Got you.
 B: You just keep flirting with him until we land. I got ta make it to the Grammys.
 (C enters)
 A: *So, Max, you've really never been on a plane before?*
 C: Well, technically it's my second time if you count Rock-O-Plane ride at the carnival. Guess I was rockin' that plane too hard, cause halfway through the ride, my mini-747 fell off its gears, and I crashed to the ground.

(COCA: *Broken Girls*)

As alluded to above, Bolden (2009) proposes that DM *so* functions to "implement incipient actions". Example (87) is hers.

(87) [Discussing travel arrangements for B's visit]
    A: Yeah
    B: That sounds good.
    A: Okay I'll do ahead and uh confirm that business then tomorrow.
    B: Great.
    A: *So what else is going down there?*
    B: A:hm just watching Johnny Cochran. Schmooze the jury.
    A: Yes. But he's guilty.
    B: You think...
    A: They're gonna come back with a guilty verdict.
    B: Heh-heh-heh you think so?
    [13 lines later]
    B: but I think that he's done a pretty good job of creating a doubt, you know, which is all that he really has to do.
    A: Yep.
    B: Hmm. Yep. Um. (1.5) hh.
    A: *So what else is going on?*

    B: Oh I thought actually you might meet Mich. I guess Mich is not gonna come up this weekend, but he was thinking about it a bit to come up and watch that game with us.
                        (Adopted from Bolden 2009: 992–993, Excerpt 13)

Example (87) covers three topics, which requires two topic changes. The first topic is the caller's (A) travel plans to visit B, which is closed with B's utterance, "Great". If there is no topic coming up, the phone conversation might end (Bolden 2009: 993). Apparently, A does not want to end the call. So, he invites B to provide another topic with "So what else is going doing down there"?

B collaborates with A to complete the first topic change by introducing the second topic: Johnny Cochran, the defense lawyer for O. J. Simpson.[72] That topic is exhausted in about 20 lines of conversation until A says "Ye" and B says "Hmm. Yep. Um. (1.5) hh". For the second time, the possibility of ending the conversation

---

[72] O. J. Simpson trial was a criminal trial in which U.S. former National Football League star and actor O.J. Simpson was accused of two counts of murder in 1994.

emerges. However, A the caller still does not want to part ways with B. He invites B, for the second time, to supply a new topic with in an almost identical way: "So what else is going on?" B obliges and provides the third topic, about Mich's joining them for the game.

To fit this example into her proposal that DM *so* functions to "implement incipient actions", Bolden (2009: 993) speculates that A, the caller, had intended to get updates from the call recipient. That may be true, although Bolden provides no evidence for her speculation. However, it is equally the case that, by saying "So what else is going on?", A is changing the topic of the phone conversation. Furthermore, one cannot say that phone conversations between close friends are always preplanned. This is clearly seen in (86). Prior to C's entrance into the room, A and B were talking about how C is taken advantage of by B, an exchange that C is not supposed to hear. When he enters the conversation expectedly, therefore, A has no choice but change the topic. Furthermore, the topic she changes to is also situation bound. B has said that her dating of C is like dating a pilot "flying a plane you're on", and A asked C (when he enters) "So, Max, you've really never been on a plane before?" A cannot possibly have planned this "incipient action".

The fourth subfunction of DW *so* in topic management is topic resumption. Topic assumption occurs when the speaker wants to bring back a topic that has been unintentionally digressed from or intentionally suspended. Among the functions of DM *so* that have been proposed in the literature, Bolden's (2009: 999) "reopening closed action trajectories" comes the closest to the topic resumption subfunction of DM *so*: "to return and reopen action trajectories that, for all practical purposes, could have been considered closed".

In Example (88), A assumes that the topic of B's coming to him is "some questions about some of our drilling cites". His casual acknowledgment of B's coming is met by a digression from B. He then uses *so* to bring the conversation back to the topic he has assumed, although it is not what B has in mind.

(88) A: Thank you so much for seeing me on such short notice. I know you're very busy.
B: Heck, I always make time for one of Scully's old students. Guy got me my first job with Weststar back in the day. I owe him everything. *So, you have some questions about some of our drilling sites?*
B: No, I'd like to talk to you about a couple of the fixed oil platforms your company has in the Gulf.

(COCA: *Dallas*)

Example (89), below, is from a live TV show. For the host, the topic is the guest's plans for his future life. But the guest digresses to an appreciation of the TV channel the host works for, which takes up three more turns, until the host steers back the interview, resuming the planned topic via the use of *so*: "So you want to keep doing what you're doing?"

(89) H: What do you want to do the rest of the – you're very young, you're 45 years old.
G: Yes, sir, I want to keep going as I am, helping people, because so many are hurting. Like I said on the program that CNN – by the way, really a big thank you to John Kemp and Graham...
H: *Impact* did that.
G: *Impact* – for doing a very fair, very balanced, very fair piece.
H: So you want to keep doing what you're doing?
G: I am going to, yes, because of hurting humanity.
(COCA: *CNN Larry King Live*)

Example (90) is similar. B comes home and is greeted by his father, A. He greets back and then digresses into a phone call. But the greeting utterance "How are you?" means both a greeting and a question: the father does want to know how B is doing, particularly about the flight he has just gotten off. In other words, the father resumes the topic he has in mind, although that topic may not be shared by B.

(90) A: Hey, how are you?
B: Hey, Daddy. Look who I... Well... when the Greenleafs call... Yes.
A: *So, how was your flight?*
B: Well, like riding a wheelchair down a staircase for two straight hours.
(COCA: *Greenleaf*)

The last subfunction of DM *so* in topic management is topic closure, a function that has not been noted in previous research. In (91), the guest of the radio show is talking about *My Life is Murder,* a TV series that she produces and stars in. Once she finishes her turn about how much she enjoys working on the series – the topic of her first turn – she uses *so* to close the topic, saying "So that's that". The host takes her up on the "offer" and immediately announces the end of the segment.

(91) A: And you're problem-solving in order to make the day, getting it all done on time in as joyful, collegial way as possible. That's a really satisfying day's work. You know – and hopefully, you make something that people like. But even if they don't like it – well you're already paid. And you already had a good time. *So that's that*... (Laughter)

B: Lucy Lawless stars in and is executive producer of *My Life Is Murder*, a new Australian crime drama with comedic touches, of course, on Acorn TV. Thanks so much for being back with us.
A: my life is murder.
B: (Laughter) Thank you so much. Take care.
A: Cheers, Scotty.

(COCA: *NPR Weekend Edition*)

In (92), A does not want to leave the gathering he has been a part of. After a few unsuccessful attempts to stay longer, including trying to give B a toy bear, he gives up: "So, I guess there's nothing left to say, but goodbye...". The topic is hence closed and farewell takes place immediately.

(92) A: ... I wanted to give you something. Oh, Fluffers. Your favorite bear.
B: Are you giving him to me for luck? No. I'm eight years old. What do I need a stinking bear for? (sighs)
B: Are you gonna miss me, Morgan?
A: I already do.
B: *So, I guess there's nothing left to say, but goodbye.* I, um... I love you all very much.

(COCA: *Boy meets World*)

In the next example, the chair of a university faculty senate (A) announces the conclusion of the day's business and utters "sooo" to invite the motion to adjourn. Her colleagues respond by quickly running through the required parliamentary rules – moving and seconding – to reach the official end of the meeting.

(93) A: That concludes our business of the day. *Sooo...* [looks around the room]
B: [Raises her hand]
A: Senator X?
B: I Move to adjourn.
A: Second?
C: Seconded.
A: Today's Senate meeting is adjourned.

(COLLECTION)

In sum, we have seen in this section that DM *so* servers a unitary function of topic management. Further, topic management is seen as being undergirded by clarity, a transactional motivation of MMP. This analysis is drastically different from earlier studies, which have identified several dozens of functions for the lexeme.

6.5 Chapter summary

In this longest chapter of the monograph, on MMP and discourse studies, we discussed a variety of topics. Several important arguments have been advanced. The first is that the structures of many aspects of discourse and the structures of different types of discourse are motivated by the clarity consideration of the transactional motivations. This includes information structure. By representing information in a given-before-new order, information packaging assists the hearer to conceptualize and understand the unknow in terms of the known, which is in keeping with the general cognitive and learning principle that human beings conceptualize and learning new things in terms of the old, a point that will come up again in Chapter 7, on metaphor.

The pressure for clarity, as it has turned out, also motivates the structures of different genres and the structures of different parts of a genre. We have seen, as a result, that the introduction part of research articles achieves clarity for academic writers by providing them a space to establish the territory of their expertise and to interact with their readers about the importance of their work via establishing a niche. We surveyed other genre structures and concluded that they are also clarity-motivated mechanisms for respective discourse communities. We also looked at the turn-taking system and the pre-sequence organization of conversation and found them, too, to be useful tools for clarity. Taken together, these findings lead to something more fundamental – that the pressure for clarity, which translates into the ease of information processing for the hearer, has exerted itself to the architect of language in general and to the structures of more specific uses of language in particular.

In Section 6.3, on interactional motivations, I argued that much of what has been revealed in the literature on identity construction, writer stance, and critical discourse analysis is accounted for by the interactional motivation of establishing, maintaining, and enhancing the public image of either other or self. The literature on identity construction informs us how speakers create all kinds of identity in a variety of discourse contexts. Under this variation, however, is the underlying force to establish, maintain, and enhancing the public image of self. These images, further, draw upon aspects of the identity that are either sanctioned by society or particular discourse communities. Writer stance, too, is a realization of the interactional motivation. By expressing different stances, writers create for themselves the image of living up to the expectations of scholars. These images also help the writers to be effective in argumentation. In this case, the transactional and the interactional motivations coincide. Similarly, the interactional motivation underlies the findings in the critical discourse tradition. In the critical discourse literature, users of language are found to use language for ideological and political ends, which is what MMP would precisely predict: these ends are achieved by creating the needed public image for self as well as for other.

Considerable attention was given also to the organization of adjacency pairs and the system of repair. Based on the vast reservoir of knowledge created by conversation analysts, we know a great deal about the preference and dispreference of the seconds of adjacency pairs. Different from conversation analysts, however, I proposed that the reason for a particular second to be preferred or otherwise is the interactional motivation. A preferred second is often one that benefits the public image of other and a dispreferred second is one that hurts that image. The same holds for the repair system of conversation. Conversation analysts have provided us with convincing evidence that, in a complex system of correction, there is a clear preference for self-correction – in terms of both initiation and repair. That preference is also image-based. We give our fellow conversational interactants the opportunity to self-correct because doing so avoids the damage to their image should we did for them via other-repair.

Section 6.4, a case study of DM *so*, was offered to demonstrate how an MMP approach can offer a more coherent and elegant account for a linguistic unit. DM *so* was selected because of its privileged position in the discourse maker literature. MMP analysis led to the conclusion that the lexeme is a tool for topic management, which in turn is motivated by the clarity need of the transactional considerations.

Looking as a whole, this chapter covers the major areas in discourse analysis. It was intended to be a demonstration that MMP is capable of providing a framework for the analysis of language use across disciplines, discourse types, and discourse contexts. I hope that aim is somehow achieved.

6.6 Notes on "the discursive turn"

This chapter started out referencing the "discursive turn" (Section 6.1) and will end with more discussion on it.

The discursive turn has had far-researching consequences in pragmatics. I have expressed my positive evaluation of this intellectual movement at various places, particularly the vast reservoir of knowledge scholars in this tradition have generated for the field via the set of methodological tools they have devised and the microscopic attention they give to the dynamic unfolding of communication, especially face-to-face interactions among the common folk. I have been part and proponent of the movement both in publication and in my teaching of pragmatics and other related fields in graduate and undergraduate classrooms. I will therefore not repeat this positive assessment but comment on a few unintended consequences that appear to be less than positive.

The first unintended consequence is an overemphasis on empirical methodology. I quote below representative views to illustrate the insistence that only one approach works in the investigation of language use. The first is from Manes and Wolfson (1981).

> It is our conviction that an ethnographic approach is the *only* reliable method for collection data about compliments, or indeed, any other speech act function in everyday interaction.
> (Manes and Wolfson 1981: 115. *Italics* mine)

The second is from De Fina (2007):

> ethnicity cannot be understood if it is abstracted from concrete social practices, and that analyses of this construct need to be based on ethnographic observation and on the study of actual talk in interaction. (De Fina 2007: 371)

While no one would doubt the value of ethnography, it seems a bit overstating to call it the *only* way to investigate language use.

Second, with the emphasis on empiricism comes the distrust in abstraction and generalization. I have discussed the consequence of missing deeper explanations for surface phenomena thus far throughout the book and illustrated it with the case study of DM *so* in Section 6.4. But there is at least one more unintended consequence, i.e., the contradiction between the position against generalization and the researchers' own act of generalization. In all the works cited and reviewed in the ethnographic tradition, for example, every author ends up generalizing. Bolden's (2006, 2008, 200) notion of "incipient actions" with regard to the DM *so* cannot be proposed without her own interpretation and generalization. In one word, researchers' mediation between reality from which data are collected for knowledge making and the knowledge that ends up being made is indispensable and should not be denied. The only difference between an empiricist and a "theorist" (for lack of a better term) is the degree to which one introspects and the level at which one generalizes.

Related to the above is another difficulty facing the empiricist – that a researcher should not approach the findings with preconceived assumptions, particularly theoretical assumptions. However, the structures of turn-taking and adjacency pair, the rules of preferred vs. dispreferred seconds, and the patterns of repair that were revealed by the first-generation conversation analysts have been widely accepted and used to guide research in a vast field until this day. They are theories whether one wants to call them that way; they may result from a "bottom-up" approach but, once used by subsequent researchers, they become "preset" and appear very much "top-down".

Lastly, the issue about the fluidity of meaning and the dynamism in meaning making. I discussed it earlier in Chapters 1 and 2, but I revisit it here one more time. I start with Stuart Hall, one of the most influential scholars in identity studies in particular and culture studies in general.

> Identity is a process, identity is split. Identity is not a fixed point. (Hall 1989: 15)

> [Identities] are ... points of temporary attachments to the subject position which discursive practices construct for us. (Hall 1996a: 19)

> Cultural identity is not a fixed essence at all, lying unchanged outside history and culture. It is not some universal and transcendental spirit inside us on which history has made no fundamental mark. It is not once-and-for-all. It is not a fixed origin to which we can make some final and absolute Return. (Hall 1996b: 213)

Hall's views are shared by many (Blommaet 2005; Bucholtz & Hall 2004, 2008, 2010; Butler 1990; De Fina 2007, 2010; De Fina, Schiffrin and Bamberg 2006; Ho 2010; Locher and Hoffmann 2006; Zimmerman 1988, 1992, 1998). The following is a random collection of quotes by some of them.

> [Identity is an] emergent product rather than the pre-existing source of linguistic and other semiotic practices. (Bucholtz & Hall 2005: 588)

> [Identity depends on] context, occasion, and purpose. (Blommaert 2005: 203).

> Researchers in the field of identity studies have shown that individuals and groups build and project images of themselves that are not independent of and do not preexist the social practices in which they are displayed and negotiated. Participants in social activities "do" identity work and align with or distance themselves from social categories of belonging depending on the local context of interaction and its insertion in the wider social world. Therefore, analysts cannot presuppose a priori that interactants will identify with categories related to their social profile, since identity claims and displays are embedded in social practices and respond to a complex interplay of local and global factors.
> (De Fina 2007: 372)

Very few of us would deny that identity is constructed in social interaction, fewer still would insist that if Speaker A belongs to X, she would be expected to always behave in ways characteristic of the assumed identity of X. However, the statement that identity has no "fixed points" may be a bit too absolute. The way to test it, as it has turn out, is not particularly difficult: one needs only to go back to the very works by those colleagues who make such claims. So, we go back to Bucholtz and Hall (2005) and De Fina (2007) one more time.

As is recalled from Section 6.3.1, Bucholtz and Hall (2005: 589–590) show how a *hijra* (fictitiously named "Sulekha'") uses the feminine case marking to refer to herself. Her estranged family members refer to her in the masculine gender. Based on this, Bucholtz and Hall (2005: 590) conclude that "Under these circumstances, gender marking becomes a powerful tool used by Sulekha to construct herself as feminine in opposition to her family's perception of her gender". But the authors do not comment on the "powerful tool" itself. Specifically, the morphological marking in the language, according to Sapir and Whorf, influences (or determines, as some scholars argue) thought. In the Sulekha case, she is not creating a new, non-preexisting identity of femininity. She is "returning to" the feminine case marking system to *affirm* femininity (Chen 2019). In other words, while we can certainly say that Sulekha's identity of femininity "emerges" from her interactions with others, but the identity that emerges is essentially a point fixed in the very architect of the language.

The second case study in Bucholtz and Hall (2005: 592–593) is even more straightforward. On the one hand, the authors emphasize the emergent nature of the identities created by the use of quotative verbs: the use of *go* and *be like* for the "nerdy" identity and the use of *be all* for the "trendy" identity. On the other hand, they acknowledge the semiotic relationship between the quotative verbs and the identities they index in the relevant speech community. This, possibly unbeknownst to the authors, demonstrates the opposite of what they argue – that identity *has* fixed points. What speakers do in the dynamic discourse context seems to be creating the desired identity that is sanctioned by the speech community or society in general.

De Fina (2007)'s study of code-switching between Italian and English by members of a card playing club, likewise, demonstrates that identity construction can be a process of conformation (Chen 2019). In the study, De Fina starts out by discussing how the club is intent on keeping an identity of exclusivity, marked in part by the speaking of some Italian among its members. Moreover, when Carl, the new member of the club who does not speak Italian, is frustrated with the club's using of Italian cards, Paul (who is teaching Carl how to read Italian cards), tells him that using Italian cards is *tradizionale* "traditional". Clearly, to be "traditional" is part of the fixed identity of the club. The co-construction of Carl's identity as a member of the club, simply put, is a process of enabling him to reach that point or, using Hall's words, "return to" it.

Chapter 7
MMP and metaphor

In this chapter, I discuss metaphors in relation to MMP. The major argument is that metaphors are motivated by both the transactional and the interactional needs depending on where they are used. Transactionally, some metaphors help the metaphorist to be clear, some effective, and others both. Interactionally, metaphors enable the metaphorist to benefit the public image of other as well as self, again, depending on the context in which they occur.

Thematically, this chapter should be part of Chapter 8: MMP and the non-literal, with "non-literal" referring to the type of use of language in which what is said is different from what is meant, including an assortment of things such as irony, parody, and sarcasm. For metaphor is no doubt the best representation of the group. However, due to its privileged status in linguistics, rhetoric, and literary analysis, particularly the attention it has received from cognitive linguists, a full and independent chapter is herein devoted to it.

The outline of this chapter is as follows. In Section 7.1, I provide a background for metaphor research in cognitive linguistics. In Section 7.2, we discuss how metaphors fulfill the transactional motivational needs – both clarity and effectiveness – albeit with more emphasis on how effectiveness is achieved via domain mapping, domain elaboration, and domain elaboration. Also discussed are ways in which the metaphorist takes advantage of context to make the metaphor more effective in getting her meaning across to the audience. In Section 7.3, on interactional motivations, we will see some metaphors are used to enhance the image of other as well as self while others, to enhance the image of self *and* hurting the image of other. In Section 7.4, I will provide a quick look at the motivations of simile and metonymy, which are related to metaphor in some way but are less effective than metaphor.

7.1 Setting the scene

The ubiquity of metaphor in language use hardly needs demonstrating, neither does the attention it has received from a multitude of disciplines: philosophy, sociology, literary criticism, cultural studies. However, metaphor has been met with relative silence in pragmatics. The rare discussions of metaphor in pragmatics include Grice (1975), who treats metaphor as a violation of the Maxim of Quality, due to the fact that a metaphor, by definition, is semantically false, and Davis's (1991) edited volume entitled *Pragmatics,* in which metaphor is grouped together with irony, under "Non-literal use of language".

The papers in Davis (1991, Chapter 7) offer broadly two kinds of account for metaphor from a pragmatic perspective. One kind proposes that metaphor acts in the same way as its literary counterparts (Bergmann 1991; Davidson 1991); the other kind argues that metaphors have to be treated differently from their non-literal counterparts (Martinich 1991; Searle 1991). All agree, however, that metaphor cannot be interpreted without considering its "interpreter". This places metaphor squarely in the sphere of concern for pragmatics.

On the other hand, metaphor has been front and center in cognitive linguistics, an area of linguistics that takes a usage-based approach to the study of language and views language as part of human cognition (Langacker 1987, 1991; Talmy 2000). Lakoff and Johnson's (1980) book, *Metaphors We Live By*, sparked a huge interest in what is now known as the conceptual metaphor theory, which has been further developed and refined by many others (Barcelona 2000, 2003; Lakoff 1993; Kövecses 2010, 2020).

The basic tenets of conceptual metaphor theory are the following two. First, metaphor is a mapping between a source domain and a target domain. In a metaphor such as *Argument is war,* the source domain is WAR and the target domain is ARGUMENT. A domain is defined as an image schema, with accompanying component features in it. The image scheme of the domain of WAR includes the kind of things that the speech community shares about war: battles, weapons, defense, offence, casualty, devastation, blood-shedding. The metaphor *argument is war* thus maps the source domain WAR with the target domain of ARGUMENT for the purpose of understanding the target domain ARGUMENT *in terms of* the source domain WAR. Second, because metaphor facilitates understanding of the target domain in terms of the source domain, the source domain tends to be more concrete, more familiar, and – in a word – more *experiential*. This had led to the embodiment "doctrine", as it were, of language in cognitive linguistics.

These two tenets reflect the most revolutionary aspect of conceptual metaphor theory – that metaphor, instead of being an ornament of language as had been believed since the Greeks – is a way of thought by providing a structure for human cognition. Metaphors based in the source domain of SPACE, for instance, account for why many things in life are seen as containers or conduits. The terms we use in the sphere of computer technology, for example, are almost all spatial: *world wide web, internet, folder, menu, mouse, navigate, cloud, go to a web page, upload*. It may be fair to say that we conceptualize computer technology entirely in spatial terms.

Note that to say A IS B (wherein the linking verb is used to express an equation), which has become a standard formula for a metaphor, is essentially a logical fallacy. For if A and B are different things, A cannot, *a priori*, be B. The formula therefore is a condensed form of *A is conceptualized/understood to be*

B with respect to X, wherein X stands for parts of the source domain. When we say "Argument is war", we are saying that argument can be understood as war with respect to confrontation, to the fact that we attack each other's positions and defend our own, and to the consequence of it, that it can end up being a win, a lose, or a draw. In other words, *mapping of domains in metaphor is always partial*. In the next section, I will offer a more detailed discussion of it.

One of the persistent critiques of conceptual metaphor theory, however, is its purported inability to address the specificity of discourse metaphors. Metaphors used in literature and advertising, for instance, are found to be notoriously unique and sometimes outlandish (Chen 1993b; Gibbs 1994; Kimmel 2011; Steen 2017, 2018; Steen and Gibbs 2004; Tsur 2002). Metaphors used in politics are found to serve the metaphorist's context-dependent needs (Lakoff 2008). According to Eubanks (1999: 193, see also Cai and Deignan 2019), for example, the use of each political metaphor "is shaped by the utterer's individual commitment, by the utterer's willingness to adhere to the standard etiquette, by the utterer's immediate rhetorical goals, and so on". Similarly, allegory is used in Western history texts to "produce unique generic constructs" (Crisp 2001:5). Metaphors used in epitaphs in the Eastern Highgate Cemetery in London serve to "imply a positive value-judgment of human mortality and aim at assisting those left alive in coping with the pain of loss and the fear of dying" (Fernández 2011:198). Metaphors are also used to show sarcasm (Piata 2016), to persuade (Charteris-Black 2005), to express emotion, to assist reasoning, and to be strategic (Schoor 2015). They have been shown also to be a major structuring mechanism for scientific communication (Johnson-Sheehan 1995). These and other critical comments have led to a number of attempts to account for discourse metaphor, e.g., the repeated urging that genre be introduced into the conceptual metaphor theory (Steen 2008, 2011, 2018), the view that conceptual metaphor theory should be combined with the Aristotelian theory of metaphor so as to increase its explanatory power (Eubanks 1999; Schoor 2015); the proposal that literary metaphor be accounted for within the framework of blending theory (Fauconnier and Turner 2002; Richie 2003; Turner 1996); the suggestion that all conceptual metaphors be treated as resulting from spatial metaphors (Vervaeke and Kennedy 2004); and – finally and most recently – the promotion of a multi-level view of analysis (Kövecses 2019, 2020).

It is against this backdrop that the need for the present chapter arises. With its (at least original) aim at accounting for human thought in general, conceptual metaphor theory has not treated metaphor in context as seriously as it has treated conventional metaphors. But to examine how metaphor works in context falls squarely within the realm of pragmatics. In fact – I argue – any theory of pragmatics should offer an account of metaphor, at least at the macro level. This chapter, therefore, is an attempt to show that MMP offers an adequate account of metaphor.

The overall thesis of the chapter is that metaphor is motivated by multiple considerations under both the transactional and the interactional. It should be point out that it is not always the case that one kind of metaphor is matched with one kind of motivation. Quite often, a metaphor is motivated by more than one consideration simultaneously. Therefore, the organization of the rest of the chapter – by motivation – is done only for the ease of argumentation, being no indication that there is a one-to-one relationship between metaphors and motivations.

7.2 Metaphors for the transactional

MMP (Figure 2.2) has two transactional motivations: clarity and effectiveness. Clarity, as discussed in Chapter 2, is a cover term for the need to get the message across in such a way that the hearer gets it with the least possible effort. This will include, among other things, brevity (or succinctness). So, "The traffic accident created a *bottleneck* for the flow of cars" would be clearer than "The traffic accident created the condition in which the closing of lanes caused the cars to move at a much slower speed...".

Metaphors motivated by clarity are the ones that are either built in in the architecture of the language or are accepted by the speech community. Those that are built in the language are the ones that have been codified in all dimensions of grammar: morphology (Janda 2004; Panther and Thornburg 2009), writing system (Chen 2010c), lexicon (Mihatsch 2009), and construction (Baicchi 2011). The most obvious dimension at which we see metaphors at work is the lexicon. In the above, we discussed terms in computer technology. I am using my mouse as I am typing now, and there is no good alternative for me to name *mouse* otherwise: "a gadget that functions to direct the cursor to a desired location on the computer screen"?

The second kind are metaphors for certain concepts. TIME, for instance, is believed to be mapped with SPACE in most if not all languages, albeit in different ways (Evans 2005). In English, TIME is understood with the assistance of two types of metaphors: TIME AS A MOVING OBJECT (e.g., "June is coming soon" and "The week came and went") or TIME AS A POINT to which the ego (speaker) moves toward or away from (e.g., "As we approach Christmas..."). There is no other way, therefore, to describe TIME.[73] Another group of examples would be

---

[73] This has to do with the difficulty of understanding TIME in the first place. In physics, for instance, there does not appear to be a definition of TIME on its own terms. All theories in physics define TIME in terms of space.

metaphors through personification: non-human objects are seen as humans. Examples are the *eye* of a needle, the *legs* of a chair, and the *foot* of a hill.

These entrenched metaphors help us to understand one thing in terms of another; they also help us to be brief, achieving clarity of the message we convey to each other on a day-to-day basis. Since these metaphors are relatively context-independent, I will not dwell further on them until the end of the chapter but move to the second transactional motivation: effectiveness.

The second motivation under the transactional, effectiveness, is more important, as effectiveness is context dependent. Effectiveness as a motivation for metaphor – further – is a new proposal for the study of metaphor, in both cognitive linguistics and pragmatics. It is therefore discussed in detail below, in three aspects: domain mapping, domain elaboration, and contextual interaction.

7.2.1 Effectiveness through domain mapping

Since, as shall be seen below, much of the effectiveness of metaphor comes from domain mapping, we take a short detour to further highlight the partiality of the mapping between the source domain and the target domain.

The image schema of a source domain is made up of a number of components, which we shall call "features". The image schema of BUILDING has features such as foundation, outer shell, roof, rooms, corridors, and staircases. However:

> The part of the concept BUIDING that are used to structure the concept of THEORY are the foundation and the outer shell. The roof, internal rooms, staircases and hallways are parts of a building not used as part of the concept of THEORY. Thus the metaphor THEORIES ARE BUIDLINGS has a "used" part (foundation and outer shell) and an "unused" part.
> (Lakoff and Johnson 1980: 52)

In general, the partiality of the mapping between the domains is assumed rather than stated. Thus, when I say "My mouse needs new battery", I do not specify that the thing I am using to control the movement of the cursor on the computer screen is understood to be a mouse only in terms of shape, not in terms other features such as carrying diseases, chewing on things in the attic, or being nocturnal in behavior.

The MOUSE metaphor belong to what is dubbed *conventional metaphor,* ones that have been entrenched in the speech community. But context-dependent metaphors seem to be different. Take the source domain of EARTHQUAKE for example. EARTHQUAKE undoubtedly has a number of features: the abruptness of its occurrence, the difficulty in bracing it, the possibility of aftershocks, and the challenge it poses for recovery, among others. In a metaphor such as "New York is the epicenter of the coronavirus in the U.S", epicenter is the selected feature. However, that selection does not stop the audience from imagining those other, unselected features. Such mental associations are schematized in Figure 7.1.

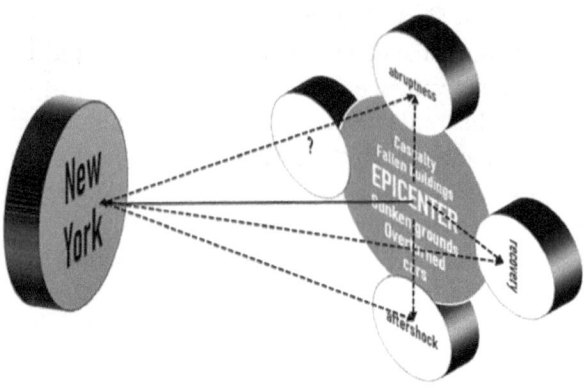

TD: NEW YORK   **SD: EARTHQUAKE**

Figure 7.1: Domain Mapping.

In Figure 7.1, the solid line between the domains connects the selected feature in the source domain – *epicenter* – to the target domain. The dotted arrows represent the possible mental associations between unselected features and the target domain, and such associations can be said to go through two steps. The first is the association between the selected feature and those which are not selected, as the selected feature can conjure up the images of those other features. Second, these unselected features are mapped to the target domain in the mind of the audience. As we shall see below, the potential of these unspoken associations is a source of effectiveness.

Below, most of the tokens of metaphor used for analysis were collected in the U.S. news media during the 2020 U.S. presidential campaigns and subsequent election, as they occurred in real time. The collection of data began on August 15, 2020, right before the Democratic National Convention,[74] and ended on November 7, 2020, when the Democratic nominee Joe Biden was deemed by media outlets (Associated Press, CNN, NBC, ABC, FOX News) to be the President-elect. During these 15 weeks, I set a Google search alert for *US 2020 Presidential Election*. The

---

[74] In the U.S. presidential election, the national convention of a party officially names its nominee for president during what is called the "primary". The end of the primary marks the beginning of the general election.

result was the constant influx of breaking news, opinion articles, social media posts, and video clips from major (and sometimes minor) news outlets. At least 30 entries were read a day, the selection of which was random.

Within a week, it became obvious that it was impossible (and unnecessary) to record every metaphor from what I was reading. The decision was then made to record only those that might be relevant to the present analysis. As a result, of the estimated 3,200 entries that were read, 246 ended up in the database, with a total of 882 metaphor tokens recorded. The examples used below are from this database.

News media was chosen as data source because it includes a wide range of genres, contents, media, and contexts. In terms of genre, what appears in the news media can be hard news, opinions, press conferences, tweets, blogs, and other types of discourse. In terms of content, the search phrase *U.S 2020 Election* generated entries on all kinds of topics: politics, the economy, the coronavirus pandemic, global warming, international relations, and the stock market. In terms of medium, these entries came from cable TV, newspapers, magazines, radio, and various online media such as social media and podcasts. As a result, tokens that ended up in the database appear to be quite representative of the diversity of contexts in which metaphors occur. The tokens used for analysis in the rest of the section is referenced by Roman numerals with DS, standing for Data Source. The sources are seen in Appendix.

In addition, real-time news offers us the opportunity to closely examine contextual factors that are useful for interpreting metaphor. Quite often, news is reported continuously; the same news appears in multiple outlets; actors often appear to explain, to clarify, and sometimes to retract; facts are often checked. These are valuable sources of information in my interpretation of metaphors and in my analysis of them in the framework of MMP.

We start with Examples (1) through (4).

(1) He's grasping at straws. (DS i)

(2) Brennan said he hopes Trump gets soundly spanked by the American electorate on Nov. 3 so he has no room to cry foul. (DS xxv)

(3) I shake my whatever to Mitch McConnell. He really has outdone himself, best comedy writer of our generation... And he's literally about to punch the country in the penis? I mean, I'm sorry. There's no other way of saying it. It's literally a dick punch. (DS ii)

(4) "It's not just challenging the Constitution", Woodward said, "it's putting a dagger in the Constitution". (DS xlvi)

In (1), the speaker talks about Trump's desperation in terms of a "drowning man grasping at straws". The source domain of DROWNING brings the hearer to a specific event, showing rather than telling the state Trump is in, forcing the reader to visualize a person fighting for life in water and the futility of the effort due to what is available to him – straws. It further invites the mental association between other unselected features in the source domain, such as the sight of choking with water and the inevitable death. In (2), the metaphor is LOSING ELECTION IS BEING SOUNDLY SPANKED. The act of spanking invokes the image of a child being punished by a parent. Other features of the SPANKING domain – the anger of the parent, the misdeed of the child, his possible crying, and the hurt he endures – are candidates also for the reader to associate with the target domain: Trump's losing of the election. Example (3) is about the U.S. Senate's decision to fill the Supreme Court seat left by late Justice Ruth Bader Ginsberg against her will and the Senate precedence that such a seat should not be filled during an election year, an act widely condemned by progressives and the media as an act of hypocrisy. To call it an act of "punching the country in the penis", once again, asks the audience to visualize the speaker's point. The audience is not simply told that the relevant act is low and despicable. They are forced to see in their mind's eye what it amounts to and to make mental associations between other features of the DICK PUNCH source domain with the target domain. The same can be said about the metaphors in (4): TO DELEGITIMIZE ELECTION IS PUTTING A DANGER IN THE CONSTITUTION.

These examples show us that metaphors thusly used achieve effectiveness in two ways. The first is the mapping itself of selected features of the source domain with the target domain. The former is typically more concrete, more familiar, and more vivid. In (2), for example, the selected feature of the source domain, SPANKING, creates a more vivid picture for the audience, as spanking is something many have had the experience of. Second, the source domain has its accompanying images, one of which is that SPANKING is applied only to young children; therefore the use of the metaphor also implies that Trump is a child. But that may not be all: the image of a child can also remind the readers of the childish behavior Trump has exhibited: he has been compared to a child since he became the president (Chen 2019b). In addition, there are also the association the metaphor invites the audience to make: the pain and humiliation, among others, as discussed above.

One way to appreciate the effectiveness of a metaphor is to compare it with its non-metaphorical counterpart. The non-metaphorical counterpart of (1) could be "He is desperate", the one for (2) could be "Brennan said he hopes Trump gets voted out of office by the American electorate on Nov. 3". The difference in terms of effects should be easy to discern.

7.2 Metaphors for the transactional — 223

The metaphors in (1) through (4) are primarily visual. Those below invoke other senses.

(5) Swamp Thing: Meet The Man Tracking What Smells Fishy At Trump's D.C. Hotel. (DS xxxiii)

(6) The fish rots from the head, but everyone around Trump stinks (DS xxxii)

(7) On 14 October, the New York Post (owner: Rupert Murdoch) splashed with the screaming headline "Biden Secret Emails". (DS xxxiv)

(8) . . . that he either didn't know associates who'd soured on him or has downplayed his relationship with those people. (DS xl)

(9) Trump's soft touch with China's Xi worries advisers. (DS xxxv)

(10) Democrats wet the bed. (DS xvii)

In the metaphor "smell fishy" in (5), the target domain is SUSPICION, which is mapped to the source domain of FISH. The selected feature of FISH is the smell that betrays staleness. The metaphor in (5) – "stinks" – is also olfactory, but the smell of fish is stronger and more offensive – one that indicates rottenness. In (7), "headlines", something visual, are transported to the auditory – "screaming" – hence highlighting their attention-grabbing effects. In (8), Trump's displeasure of his associates is mapped to "soured on", in the gustatory sense. "Soft touch" in (9) invokes the somatosensory, inviting the readers to feel the way Trump dealt with Xi Jinping, the leader of China. The most interesting metaphor appears to be the one in (10). Democrats' fear is mapped to "wet the bed", which combines, it seems, several senses: the visual, the somatosensory, and the olfactory, if not the auditory. In each of these metaphors, the target domain is abstract, and the source domain is more sensorily accessible, which is accounted for by conceptual metaphor theory's corner-stone belief in experientialism and embodiment. These accessible source domains help the metaphorists to create more direct and vivid imageries in their audience.

The importance of source domains is also seen in the metaphorist's choice of the features from the same source domain. Take the source domain BUBBLE. The features of BUBBLE include the inevitable and often eminent popping, air-tightness, fragility, and lightness. It may also conjure up images of floating in the air as a reminder of childhood.[75] Example (11) is the title of a *New York Times* article about Trump's three-day hospitalization for treating his Covid-19 infection. Example (12) is about Trumps' loss of re-election.

(11) A coronavirus test just burst the Trumpworld bubble. (DS xlv)

(12) When the MAGA Bubble Burst. (DS xliii)

Clearly, the features of BUBBLE selected in these two metaphors is inevitable burst. This is consistent with other BUBBLE metaphors in the new media in the past, such as the "internet bubble" (used for the steep spike in the internet stocks in late 1990s to early 2000s) and the "real estate bubble" (used for the irrational housing market before the global financial crisis in 2009). However, in the following, the BUBBLE metaphor focuses on the state of being completely sealed from the outside world.

(13) My Wild 2 Weeks Inside the Trump Campaign Bubble. (DS xxxvi)

Example (13) is one of the many that invokes the X IS A BUBBLE metaphor. The target domain X in (13) is the Trump campaign and the article is about how the campaign had created a culture that is insulated from the reality of U.S. politics. In other articles, X is Trump's White House, and the BUBBLE metaphor points to the fact that the White House interacts only with its allies and friendly media to create "an echo chamber" (another metaphor) with critics kept out and disloyal aides purged. This has led, the author argues, to a "psychological bubble" for Trump, believing, inaccurately, that he was "popular, winning, and 'loved'". There is the "data bubble", too. The president is presented with only data and information to his liking (DS ix).[76] All these examples are evidence that the choice of features of source domain depends on the metaphorist's purpose in a particular context, which, in turn, is motivated by the need to be effective under the transactional in MMP (Figure 2.2).

---

[75] These features were identified from a Qualtrics survey of 85 American English speakers conducted in October 2020.

[76] In the summer of 2020, American Basket ball Association created an isolation zone in Disney World, in Orlando, Florida, for its playoff games to protect those involved from Covid-19. The zone was known by *the NBA Bubble, Disney Bubble,* and *Orlando Bubble.* Apparently, the selected feature of the source domain, BUBBLE, is the same: complete enclosure and isolation.

7.2.2 Effectiveness through domain elaboration

When a metaphor is deployed, its source domain becomes immediately activated so that the metaphorist oftentimes does not dwell on it. However, there are times when the metaphorist further zeroes in on the source domain. This *domain elaboration* also helps the effectiveness of metaphor, albeit in a different way. Example (14) is about calling Trump's bluff.

(14)   He not only loves to bluff, but he loves to bluff big (DS x).
...
Never back down against Trump. If you want to win, you must call his bluff. (DS x)

Line 1 in Example (14) is the title and Line 3 is the ending one-sentence paragraph of the article. In the article, the author first explains what bluffing is in a game of poker (betting higher and higher with a weak hand with the hope of scaring the opponent into folding), preparing readers with the knowledge of the source domain of POKER. Then the author provides evidence that Trump's strategy in both governing and campaigning is very much one of bluffing. In order to win the election, the Democrats have to keep a "blank face" and "be willing to go all the way". The entire article therefore is about the domain of POKER, both what it is and how Trump's strategy – bluffing – is best mapped to that source domain. As a result, the reader is invited to look at both the source domain and the target domain in great detail.

Example (15) is similar.

(15)   So, he has been throwing political haymakers for weeks. He will likely intensify that strategy during the debates.
In boxing, a haymaker is a wildly thrown punch, delivered in desperation. If it connects, it can immediately and completely change the outcome of a fight. Most often it doesn't.
Trump has been throwing every haymaker he can think of. . . .
Perhaps the only way Trump will win these debates is if he can get someone else to climb into the ring for him. (DS i)

The entire article from which (15) is taken is about the source domain BOXING. The author first explains what a haymaker is, as seen in the second paragraph. Then she describes the kind of campaign tactics deployed by Trump, such as "suggesting that Biden is drugged up, that he's senile, that his administration will be dispatching poor people to terrorize the suburbs, that he is 'against God', that he's a puppet for a Marxist cabal that will destroy America, and so on" in the text omitted in (15). The last paragraph, which ends the article, goes back to BOXING again, invoking its feature "the ring".

The elaboration of the source domain in these two metaphors takes the audience inside the source domain, forcing them to zero in on the details of particular aspects of it. When the audience sees the target domain in terms of the source domain, the image schema that is invoked is one of nuance and minutia. Compared to those metaphors we discussed in Section 6.2.1, whose effectiveness comes from what is not said, metaphors containing domain elaboration achieves its effectiveness through what *is* said.

The metaphorist, too, can take advantage of domain elaboration to be playful, thus increasing the effectiveness of her message, as seen in (16).

(16)   On Friday, President Donald Trump, not much of a reader, tweeted out an article from The Babylon Bee, a satirical news site with a Christian bent, that describes itself as "Fake news you can trust". And at that moment, Trump managed to throw himself a perfectly timed alley-oop, which he leapt to grab midair, double pump, and dunk... on himself... on the wrong basket. (DS xxiv)

The writer of (16) introduces the fact first – that Trump took a satirical article about "fake news", a phrase of his own creation – at its face value. He then delves into the source domain of the metaphor, "a perfectly timed alley-oop", describing expected features of an alley-oop: "he leaped to grab midair, double pump, and dunk", before revealing the unexpected: "... on himself... on the wrong basket". A typical alley-oop is one that dunks on an opponent and on the right basket. The writer of (16), however, literally adds a feature to that source domain, a feature that is atypical but possible. By doing so, the metaphorist ends up scathingly revealing the ironic nature of Trump taking a piece of self-acclaimed "fake news" as real news.

7.2.3 Effectiveness through contextual interaction

In the discussions above, the effectiveness of metaphors comes from context. But the contextual factors lay "hidden", as is the case with most communication. In this section, we look at efforts by the metaphorist to bring such contextual factors to the fore, thus achieving a greater degree of effectiveness. For the sake of convenience, I divide context into epistemic and linguistic. Epistemic context refers to the knowledge of the public, the assumed audience of news media. Linguistic context refers to the surrounding linguistic environment in which a metaphor occurs.

When Jared Kushner, the US president's son-in-law, told journalist Bob Woodward that one of the best ways to understand Donald Trump is to study Lewis Carroll's *Alice's Adventures in Wonderland*. Kushner paraphrased the Cheshire Cat's philosophy: "If you don't know where you're going, any path will get you there" (DS iii). In response to the reporting of Kushner's statement, a commentator wrote:

(17) Donald in Blunderland: Trump won't commit to peaceful power transfer at surreal press briefing.
Wednesday was one of those days when to have a seat in the White House briefing room felt like stepping through the looking-glass into Blunderland, where the mad hatter has an authoritarian streak a mile wide.
Indeed, earlier Trump had claimed, "Our approach is pro-science. Biden's approach is anti-science" – words to remember when he heads to Florida on Thursday for the latest of his packed, nearly mask-free campaign rallies in Wonderland. (DS iii)

Alice's Adventures in Wonderland, a nonsense fiction (1865) that has been made into numerous movies and other shows, is popular in the English-speaking world. It was parodied in 1907 by John Kendrick Bangs in a novel *Alice in Blunderland: An Iridescent Dream*, which gave rise to another parody in 1934 in the form of a cartoon created by Max Feischer, entitled *Betty in Blunderland*. In 2021 came yet another parody, in the form of variety show, by Eri Schmalenberger, which attracted considerable attention. By selecting Blunderland as a source domain for Trump in opposition to Wonderland, the writer of (17) taps into the knowledge of the audience about both Blunderland and Wonderland.

Consider (18).

(18) "I don't know why the press doesn't make more of this, to be very honest with you", added Pelosi. "If he says that people swallow Clorox, we hear about it for the rest of our lives, but he's trying to have the Constitution of the United States swallow Clorox. . ." (DS viii)

The metaphor in (18) is about Trump's refusal to commit to a peaceful transition of power if he loses the election. The metaphor can therefore be stated as NOT TO COMMIT TO PEACEFUL TRANSITION IS TO HAVE THE CONSTITUTION SWALLOW CLOROX. The source domain comes from Trump's suggestion, at a Coronavirus Taskforce press conference, that scientists study the possibility of curing the disease by injecting disinfectants into patients' bodies (See Section 6.3.4 for an earlier discussion). The speaker of (18) sets up that fact as a means to prepare for the source domain before the metaphor occurs. Apparently, this helps her to increase the power of the metaphor: a person can be killed by swallowing Clorox, so can the U.S. constitution if a president refuses to leave office after losing an election.

Also notable is the fact that the speaker of the metaphor in Example (18) "manipulated" the original source domain. Trump's original statement is "injecting disinfectants", but the speaker of (18) changed it into "swallow Clorox" through lexical narrowing: "swallow" can be said – with considerable stretch – to be one type of injecting and Clorox is possibly the most common brand of bleach (a disinfectant) among U.S. households.

The next example is similar. At the Democratic National Convention, Kristin Urquiza, an ordinary citizen whose father had died of the coronavirus, said the following in her speech.

(19) His [the diseased father's] only preexisting condition was trusting Donald Trump.. … The coronavirus has made clear that there are two Americas: the America that Donald Trump lives in and the America that my father died in. (DS xiv)

The source domain, PREEXISTING CONDITION, comes from the national debate about health care. The Affordable Care Act (ACA) – a health law enacted prior to Trump's presidency – mandates that insurance companies not deny people with chronic diseases (preexisting conditions) insurance policies. The Trump administration was trying to repeal ACA, which, if successful, would deny these people access to health insurance. The speaker of (19) draws on this multi-year national debate, using a source domain that is known to most U.S. citizens. The metaphor enables her to map TRUSTING TRUMP with a chronic disease – A PREEXISTING CONDITION. The cleverness and creativity of the metaphor made the speaker into a household name within hours.

There is also the metaphor TRUMP CARD. The term *trump card* is used in poker, referring to a card that is elevated above its usual rank (usually as a card in the entire trump suit). However, during Trump's presidency, TRUMP CARD became a metaphor for Trumpism: his authoritarian bent, his propensity to tell untruth, his refusal to apologize, his vulgarity and abuse (DS xlviii, Chen 2019b). The creativity of this metaphor lies in its redefining of a ready-made source domain, adding new features (characteristics of Trumpism) to its existing features (the status above all others).

Metaphors are also seen to interact with linguistic context to create rhetorical effects. Consider the following.

(20) "The Proud Boys", Mr. Trump said. "Stand back and stand by". (DS xxi)[77].

(21) Biden's plan will crush Florida, my plan will crush the virus. (DS xi).

(22) Trump gave a load and lock order. (DS xxiii)

(23) Dump Trump

(24) Basement Biden

(25) . . . in a row that has been rumbling since the interview was taped on Tuesday. (DS xxxvii)

All of these examples have alliteration (repetition of consonants) and/or assonance (repletion of vowels). Some of them include syntactic parallelism – "stand back and stand by" in (20), "crush Florida. . . crush the virus" in (21), and "load and lock" in (22). According to Leech (1969, 1985; see also Leech and Short 1983), such stylistic devices serve an important rhetorical purpose. Invoking the principle of iconicity, they invite the audience to assume similarity in meaning based on similarity in form. "Dump Trump" links Trump with the act of dumping, a slogan to rally voters to reject the then president. "Basement Biden" links Biden to basement, echoing the accusation that Biden was too frail and too mentally challenged to get out of his basement where he had set up his personal office and studio due to the coronavirus.

In this section, I have discussed how metaphor is motivated by the transactional considerations of both clarity and effectiveness. My focus has been on the latter, as effectiveness has not been highlighted as a motivation (or function) of metaphor. Metaphor, however, is motivated by interactional needs as well, to which we now turn.

---

[77] This is said by Trump at the first presidential debate. Despite what has been said about Trump during his four-year presidency (Chen 2019b), I marvel at his more than occasional display of linguistic creativity.

7.3 Metaphor for the interactional

As is recalled from Chapter 2, there are two motivating considerations under the interactional: establish, maintain, or enhance the public image of other and establish, maintain, or enhance the public image of self. More space will be devoted in this section on the second: the motivation to benefit the image of self, than to the first.

Also recall that the two motivations under the interactional are related on a confictive vs. assistive cline (Figure 2.2): there are times when the two are mutually assistive, whereby an utterance can fulfill both; there are times when they are conflictive with each other, whereby the benefiting of one results in the hurting of the other. This seems to be precisely what happens with metaphor. We find metaphors in our daily life that benefit other, such as:

(26)　You're such a saint!

(27)　You're our queen of curriculum.

These common metaphors of praise and approbation occur when the two interactional motivations are aligned. The benefiting of other-image results in the benefiting of self-image, or at least does not result in the hurting of it.

Sometimes the beneficiary of the metaphor – it should be noted – is not the speaker but a third party.

(28)　My mother always keeps him grounded.

(29)　She rebuilt a broken man.

Example (28) was said by Ashley Biden, speaking of her parents Joe and Jill Biden, the 46th President of the U.S., and his wife. "Keep him grounded" amplifies the role Jill Biden plays in the life of her husband. Example (29) was said by Joe Biden, speaking of how Jill Biden helped him recover from an automobile accident that had killed his first wife and daughter. The two-part metaphor – himself being a "broken man" and the act of his wife being an act of "rebuilding" – enables the speaker to enhance the public image of his wife.

Assuming that such other-image enhancing metaphors are uncontroversial, we move to metaphors for the benefit of self-image only. As we will see, those metaphors take place largely in the context in which other-image and self-image come into conflict (at or toward the conflictive end of the conflictive/assistive continuum in Figure 2.2). Since the data we are using have come primarily from the 2020 U.S. presidential campaigns, the self-image the metaphorist attempts to establish, maintain, or enhance has the most to do with her political views.

In the summer and early fall of 2020, former president Trump was promoting the idea that Covid-19 was disappearing. When responding to a question about how the pandemic could be gone without a vaccine, he said:

(30) "It's gonna go, it's gonna leave, it's gonna be gone, it's gonna be eradicated. It might take longer, it might be in smaller sections. It won't be what we had". "If you have a flare-up in a certain area – I call them burning embers – boom, we put it out. We know how to put it out now". (DS xxvii)

In the beginning of Trump's speech, he repeatedly asserts the imminent disappearance of Covid-19. Then he resorts to the source domain of BURNING EMBERS, as it visualizes the pandemic as something at the end of its life, thus increasing the rhetorical impact of his message.

The media, however, generally disagreed and pushed back by selecting a different source domain – WILDFIRE – for the target domain:

(31) Trump has repeatedly said that the government is prepared to handle the pandemic, ready to put out any embers that emerge (or more rarely, to put out any small fires). The nature of the outbreak is such that anything can be an "ember" if you look at it narrowly enough – and you can say all is well if you are similarly motivated. (DS xxviii)

The entire article from which (31) is taken is a dispute of the EMBERS source domain and argument for the WILDFIRE source domain, presenting evidence that the pandemic was spreading in most states of the country.

At the time, there was a national debate on the severity of the pandemic. The Trump administration held the view that the pandemic was under control so that businesses could remain open, presumably for the purpose of keeping the economy moving. Public health professionals and much of the media believed otherwise – that the pandemic was out of control and drastic measures were needed to protect the health of the American public. This explains why the two opposing sides chose different metaphors for the same issue. Trump used the BURNING AMBER metaphor – with its feature of being close to dying out mapped to the target domain – to argue that he was right. His opposition fought back with the WIDEFIRE metaphor to argue for the opposite.

While the debate about wildfire and embers is one about the spread of the virus, the following debate, about whether the pandemic is a wildfire or a wave, is about the trajectory of its spread. This occurred also during the summer of

2020, when the rate of new cases threatened to go up after a downward trend due to a national lockdown. The surge of cases was widely seen in the media as a second wave. But scientists did not see it that way, as seen in the following three examples.

(32) A wave or a wildfire? Media talking about a second wave, but scientists disagree.

(33) "It's a wildfire, not a wave". (DS vi)

(34) I am not sure that it is that useful to think about the dynamics that we are seeing as waves. There is no reason that we should be seeing the kind of wavelike epidemic dynamics that we have seen for other respiratory pathogens. Instead what we are seeing is a massive epidemic that could burn through the population rapidly unless we do something to slow transmission, which is what we are currently doing with interventions such as social distancing and masks. It is possible that, over time, COVID-19 could start developing cyclical, flulike waves. But that is years away. (DS xlvii)

(35) Like a wildfire, the virus relentlessly seeks out fuel (human hosts), devastating some areas while sparing others. It will continue spreading until we achieve sufficient herd immunity – when 50 to 70% of the population has developed protective antibodies – to significantly slow transmission. We will achieve herd immunity either through widespread infection or an effective and widely available vaccine. No amount of official happy talk will change that course. (DS vii)

All three articles from which (32) through (35) are taken offer scientific arguments for thinking about the pandemic not as a wave but as a wildfire. The central point is that the pandemic is different from "many other respiratory pathogens that cause these wavelike epidemics, where the crests and troughs of the waves are set by the fraction of the population that is susceptible", per the author of (34). Instead, it "spreads by the human contact and mixing that occurs in areas of high population density", per the author of (35).

The reason for the scientists' arguing against the WAVE metaphor seems to reside in the features of the source domain WAVE. Of all the features of the source domain of WAVE, the regular cycle of ebbs and flows could be the most salient. If the public considers the pandemic to be a wave, the pandemic will be thought of as something that comes and goes, something that is determined by forces of nature, something human beings have little control over. Therefore, if the WAVE metaphor is accepted, there would be the risk of the public giving up efforts to control the pandemic.

The scientists – it should be noted – did not just argue against the WAVE metaphor. They attempted to replace it with another: the WILDFIRE metaphor. Unlike a wave, a wildfire is not predictable; it is more difficult to avoid; and it can be (if not always is) controlled by human efforts. Therefore, if the general public accepts the WILDFIRE metaphor, it will be easier to promote behaviors such as mask-wearing, social distancing, and handwashing to alter the trajectory of the pandemic's progression.

To benefit his image, particularly his view that the coronavirus pandemic was disappearing from March to the eve of Election Day (November 3, 2020), Trump also relied on the "rounding the corner" or "rounding the turn" metaphor (in addition to the AMBER metaphor discussed above). The metaphor may have made its first appearance in September and Trump used it dozens of times in different venues (on Twitter, at press conferences, and at campaign rallies). The following three are a sampling.

(36) We are rounding the turn [on coronavirus]. We are rounding the corner. (DS xii)

(37) We are rounding the final turn. (DS xiii)

(38) We're rounding the turn. (DS xxx)

Curiously, it is difficult to ascertain the origin of this metaphor. My survey of native English speakers reveals two possibilities: horse race or car race. In either case, my respondents reported that the phrase could refer to turning the last corner of a (car or horse) racetrack. Once that turn is made, the race participants (either a horse or a car driver) will make the final push towards the finish line (in the "homestretch", in the case of a horse race).

The pushback to the "rounding the turn" metaphor was more sustained and wide-ranging than the pushback against the WAVE metaphor. The first person to argue against the metaphor was Anthony Fauci, National Institute of Allergy and Infectious Diseases Director, who said "I'm sorry but I have to disagree with that". He cautioned Americans not to "underestimate" the pandemic and warned they shouldn't "try and look at the rosy side of things" (DS xiii). Of the 22 entries – including articles, tweets, and video clips – that explicitly argue against the metaphor, Example (39) is the most substantive.

(39)   No, fight against coronavirus isn't rounding the corner, as Donald Trump said.
       "We are rounding the turn" on coronavirus, Trump said in the Oct. 22 debate in Nashville. "We are rounding the corner".
       No one knows the future course of the coronavirus pandemic. But "rounding the corner" suggests that significant and sustained improvements are being made in the fight against the virus, and that's not the case in the U.S., according to the data. (DS xxxi)

The first line is the title of the article published on Oct. 23, 2020, the day after the final presidential debate, followed by the beginning paragraphs of the article. In the rest of the article, the author provides five graphs and detailed analysis to demonstrate that the key metrics used to assess the pandemic were not improving. He concludes that "rounding the corner" is not "happening".

Trump's presidential election opponent, Joe Biden, entered the fray, too, and said the following.

(40)   "He said 'we have turned the corner'", Mr. Biden said. "As my grandfather Finnegan might say if he were here. . . he's gone around the bend. Turned the corner – my Lord. It's not disappearing – in fact, it's on the rise again". (DS xxvi)

"Around the bend" is a metaphor to mean mental confusion. The origin of the source domain BEND is not clear. According to one website,[78] it could be nautical, with *bend* referring to a series of sailors' knots; it could also refer to long, curved driveways leading to a mental hospital. Either way, the effectiveness of fighting a metaphor with metaphor is clear: Biden parodied Trump by partially copying his (Trump's) own metaphor and challenging Trump's accusation of his (Biden's) lack of mental acuity.[79]

The metaphorist can also take advantage of the availability of a feature in the source domain for her own argument.

(41)   He is not rounding the corner. He hasn't gotten into the car and started driving yet. (DS xxxix)

Although there is ambiguity regarding the origin of *rounding the corner* (see above), the speaker of (41) apparently decides on car racing (as opposed to horse

---

[78] https://www.vocabulary.com/dictionary/around%20the%20bend
[79] To portray Biden as mentally unfit for presidency was a major strategy of the Trump campaign.

racing) as the source domain of Trump's metaphor. A racing car has a driver. The driver has to get into the car before the race begins. By asserting that "He hasn't gotten into the car...yet", the speaker picks out the "getting into the car" feature to effectively argue that the fight against the coronavirus has not started, let alone being close to completion.

Such engagement with metaphor can occasionally be a source of comic relief. The first presidential debate between Trump and Biden was characterized by Trump's repeated interruption of his opponent and the moderator, earning the designation of being "the most shameful interaction between two leaders ever" and an "embarrassment for the United States of America" (DS xxii). Example (42) is the title of an article that recounts the debate.

(42) Biden called Trump a clown. Media called the debate a circus. (DS xxii)

In the post-debate coverage on CNN, a commentator said that "people are referring to this as a circus, but my team is getting emails from circus workers saying they are careful and respectful, and that the comparison is wrong". It is not common for real people to protest being used as a source domain for a metaphor, even in jest as is the case here.

Lastly, speakers can explicitly create metaphors as a way to benefit self-image by advancing their own views. During the vice-presidential debate, a fly landed on the top of the Republican vice-presidential nominee (who was also the vice president at the time), Mike Pence's head and stayed there for a few minutes. Many on social media call it a "metaphor" for Pence's vice presidency, apparently treating the fly as the source domain and trying to map it with the target domain of then U.S. vice president. After one of his last campaign rallies in late October 2020 in Nebraska, hundreds of President Trump's supporters were stranded in near-freezing weather while Trump flew away on Air Force One (the aircraft used exclusively by the U.S. president), leaving his supporters out in the cold. Example (43) is the title of an article about the incident.

(43) The perfect metaphor for Trump's treatment of his loyal supporters (DS xlii)

The incident of Trump's indifference to the wellbeing of his supporters is treated as the source domain for the attempted metaphor for Trump's treatment of them. The point of the article is to criticize Trump's notion of loyalty, that he demands loyalty but does not reciprocate.

On November 7, 2020, Trump's personal lawyer and former New York City Mayor Rudy Giuliani was hosting a press conference at the parking lot of Four Seasons Total Landscaping, an unheard-of Philadelphia-based gardening firm while the declaration of Joe Biden being elected president was made. Besides the temporary coincidence of the two events, there is the fact that the parking lot was adjacent to a crematorium and a porn store, and the fact that the person Giuliani had called to the podium to testify for voter fraud was immediately recognized as a sex offender. Within minutes, dozens of posts on the internet began to call Total Landscaping conference a "perfect metaphor" for the end of Trump's presidency (DS xliv).[80] The end of Trump's presidency is thus mapped to the CREMATORIUM source domain, and the porn store evokes Trump's alleged affair with an adult movie star in 2007,[81] an irony that generated endless posts on social media.

7.4 Further notes

In our discussions thus far, we have seen that metaphor can enable the metaphorist to fulfill both transactional needs – clarity and effectiveness – as well as both interactional needs – benefiting the public image of other and self. This may be the reason why metaphor is so ubiquitous.

My analysis has been conducted within the framework of MMP, but it could not have been done without the conceptual metaphor theory in the field of linguistics. It can be therefore seen as an attempt to complement one field with the other, a call that has been made by a few previous scholars (Chen 2019a; Kertész and Rákosi 2005; Panther and Thornburg 1998; Schmid 2012, 2016).

In the rest of the chapter, I discuss what may be called two "loose ends": a comparison between metaphor on the one hand and metonymy and simile on the other and metaphor in specialized genres.

7.4.1 In comparison with simile and metonymy

In the cognitive linguistic literature, metonymy has figured quite prominently after the conceptual metaphor theory was established in the 1980 (Barcelona 2000, 2002, 2003). Two arguments are salient about metonymy vs. metaphor – that metonymy is a mapping inside the same domain (as opposed to metaphor which involves the mapping between domains) and that metonymy is more fundamental than meta-

---

[80] And a Twitter account was created to parody the press conference and Trump's presidency, with tens of thousands of followers.
[81] Trump denies the allegation but the lawsuit against him on his hush money payment to the porn star is still pending at the time of writing.

phor in the architecture of language. As for how it differs from metaphor when used in actual discourse, there has been little literature. Simile, on the other hand, has been treated with silence by cognitive linguists, presumably because it expresses a literal comparison in the formula A IS LIKE B, as seen below:

(44) "I've used this phrase so much that I ought to wear it as a lapel pin". (DS v)

(45) My relationship with Trump is like "women who get married and think they're going to change their spouse". (DS xxxviii)

(46) Like some second-rate comic, Trump is telling the same jokes from 2016: that he's the Washington outsider, his opponent is a swamp creature, it should be the 1950s all over again and the election is rigged. (DS i)

(47) It is as clear as the writing on the wall. (DS xviii)

The key to all these examples of simile is that the aspect in terms of which the comparison is made is explicitly spelled out. In (44), the aspect for comparison is "used this phrase so much". In (45), the aspect for comparison is women getting married "thinking they are going to change their spouse". In (46), Trump is "like a second-rate comic" only because he is "telling the same jokes from 2016". Similarly, the comparison in (47) is about the aspect of clarity: "It is like the writing on the wall" only in the sense that "it" is clear. Based on this, we might modify the A IS LIKE B simile formula into A IS LIKE B WITH RESPECT TO X.

X in the formula functions to specify and clarify. But specification and clarification are limiting in terms of the effects a simile achieves. If we turn the similes in (44) through (47) into metaphors, differences emerge. The metaphorical counterpart of the simile in (45) – a crude approximation at best – could be "My relationship with Trump is a woman in marriage". The source domain of MARRIAGE could have a long list of features, and – as discussed above – the audience would have the liberty to make mental associations between these features and the target domain. But these associations are blocked in a simile.

Granted, there are times when the speaker goes to great lengths to elaborate on X. In (48) below, the speaker warns her audience of the danger of keeping Trump in the White House for four more years before she utters the simile "We have got to vote for Joe Biden like our lives depends on it". In (49), the speaker likens the Republican National Convention to "a cocaine convention" by spelling out only the "being high" part of "a cocaine convention".

(48) "If you think things cannot possibly get worse, trust me, they can; and they will if we don't make a change in this election. . . If we have any hope of ending this chaos, we have got to vote for Joe Biden like our lives depend on it". (DS xix)

(49) Then the hosts take a trip with Mandel down Republican National Convention memory lane: "I've never seen a convention where you thought to yourself as you were watching, 'Boy, a lot of these people seem really high on cocaine'. Like, person after person after person. What convention could you even say that about? I'm not even sure you could say that about a cocaine convention, that this many people [are high]. I think at a cocaine convention, people pull themselves together for their big speech and they'd go, 'I'll do cocaine after my speech'. Not before I address the nation from the White House". (DS ii).

The similes in these two tokens seem to be more rhetorically effective than those in (44) through (47). They are limiting, nonetheless, as the effectiveness does not go beyond X. In this sense, the presence of X in a simile is like a container, keeping everything inside. A metaphor, in contrast, seems like an expanse without a clear boundary, leaving room for the audience's imagination. In the parlance of MMP, simile can thusly be said to be less effective in its ability to help the speaker to fulfill her motivational needs.

Metonymy seems to work in yet a different way. In the U.S., there are the oft-used metonymies such as "the White House", "the (Capitol) Hill", "the Pentagon", "Washington", "the bench", all of which is based on LOCATION STANDS FOR ENTITY. These tokens are clearly motivated by economy and simplicity, which are components of clarity. Once entrenched in the minds of the public, for instance, it seems to be easier to refer to the executive branch of the U.S. federal government as "the White House". There is also the category of PERSON STANDS FOR EVENT. *Kavanaugh* in "another Kavanaugh" (DS xvi) stands for Brett Kavanaugh's Senate hearing, which is known for its contentiousness over sexual assault charges against the now Supreme Court Justice. *Comey* in "another Comey" (DS xxxiv) stands for the former Federal Bureau of Investigation's (FBI) Director James Comey's announcement, eleven days before the 2016 presidential election, that the FBI had launched an investigation into the Democratic presidential nominee Hilary Clinton's emails. These cases are evidence that economy is the underlying motivation for metonymy: it is more succinct to use the name of the major participant in an event to stand for the event itself.

Less predictable metonymies do exist and seem capable of producing a degree of vividness. In the examples below, for instance, "nose" stands for interference (50); "loud mouth" for being outspoken (50); "point fingers" for blame (51), "rubbed elbows" (52) and "hobnobbed" (53) for intimate interaction in a social gathering.

(50) The federal government should keep its *nose* out. (DS xv)

(51) Brian Karem describes himself on Twitter as a *"Loud Mouth"* (DS iii)

(52) Even to this day, Clinton insiders continue to *point fingers over* who should be blamed for Maxwell's addition to the event (DS ii).

(53) Hours earlier, the men *rubbed elbows*. . . .. (DS ii)

(54) Trump also apparently *hobnobbed* with Maxwell. (DS ii)

These examples illustrate the view that metonymy is a process of mapping within the same domain well. Take (52) for instance. Since socializing often involves face-to-face contact in close proximity, which would lead to participants rubbing elbows with one another, *rubbing elbows* has thus become a form of socializing. According to the terminology we are using in this paper, *rubbing elbows* is a feature of the domain of SOCIALIZING. Once again – as is the case with simile – this intradomain mapping appears to be limiting as well. For, the source domain being part of the target domain, the scope of inference does not go beyond the target domain itself. In sum, it seems plausible to say that both metonymy and simile are less effective and less versatile for the speaker to fulfill her various motivations. This may be the reason why they are less prevalent in use and have received less attention in the literature.

But once metaphor, simile, and metonymy are used together, the effectiveness seems to increase.

(55) The attempt at humor hovered awkwardly in the air like a coronavirus particle. (DS vi)

(56) Blue wall, blue wave, red firewall, red mirage[82] (DS xli)

---

82 Referring to the possibility that Trump may have enough votes to declare victory on the election day based on the votes tallied, but he may eventually lose due to mailed-in ballots that would be tallied after that day (DS xl).

In (55), the metaphor "hovered" interacts with the simile "like a coronavirus particles", which, in turn, is anchored in the Covid-19 pandemic that dominated the U.S. and much of the world at the time. Example (56) lists candidates for what might be called "metonymic metaphor". "Red" and "Blue", referring respectively to the conservatives and liberals in the U.S., are metonymies of COLOR STANDS FOR IDEOLOGY.[83] But "wall", "wave", "firewall" are clearly metaphorical, due to the cross-domain mapping they invoke. These juxtapositions appear to help the speaker to achieve a greater degree of effect.

7.4.2 Metaphor in specialized genres

Most of the metaphors used for analysis in this chapter are stock metaphors. The BUBBLE metaphors, the ROUND THE CORNER metaphor, the WILDFIRE metaphor, the BLUNDERLAND metaphor, the TRUMP CARD metaphor, and the WET THE BED metaphor are clear examples. The effectiveness of these metaphors comes, therefore, not from being new but from being ready-made. They are existing tools deployed for new tasks.

At the same time, metaphor is known to be a favorite literary device and has been analyzed by literary critics as much as by scholars in any other discipline (Hawkes 1972; Kimmel 2011; Leech 1969, 1985, Leech and Short 1983; Semino and Steen 2008). One of the widely recognized features of literary metaphors is their creativity, earning the reputation of being "outlandish" and "crazy" (Gibbs, Okonski, and Hatfield 2013). Consider (57), from a poem by Carol Ann Duffy.

(57) Then a butterfly paused on a trembling leaf is your breath.
Then the gauze mist relaxed on the ground is your pose.
Then the fruit from the cheery tree falling on grass is your kiss, your kiss.
Then the day's hours are theatres of air where I watch your entrance.
(Quoted in Steen 2018: 318)

Each of these four lines contains a metaphor. The "outlandishness" of these metaphors results from the domains selected by the poet. The target domains are specific, mundane happenstances – "butterfly paused on trembling leaf, the gauze mist relaxed on the ground", "the fruit from the cheery tree falling on the grass", and "the day's hours" – so that it is difficult to imagine that metaphors are

---

[83] These colors mean different things in different countries.

needed to understand them. The source domains are just as unpredictable, with each having to do with the audience, presumably the lover of the speaker: "*your* breath", "*your* pose", "*your* kiss", "theatres of air where I watch *your* entrance". Upon close examination, however, these metaphors greatly strengthen the message that the poet speaker is conveying: she is so much consumed by love that she sees everything in life *in terms of* the person she loves.

Another genre in which metaphor is used in very creative ways is advertising. In 2010, footwear manufacturer Nike conducted a "My butt is big" campaign for its toning shoes. Example (58), below, is one variation of the text of the ad.

(58) My butt is big
And round like the letter c
And that's just fine
It's a space heater
For my side of the bed
It's my embassador [sic]
To those who walk behind me
...

The rear end of the woman in the accompanying picture (omitted) is metaphorized into "a space heater", an "ambassador", and "a border collie". These are undoubtedly innovative metaphors, as the image schema for each cannot be claimed to be shared by the intended audience of the ad, at least before they encounter it. However, the usefulness of these metaphors is just obvious: they help the ad to portray the size of the woman's buttocks as being advantageous. If society views a "big butt" as negative, the ad fights against that socially constructed narrative, displaying the confidence of the portrayed women and – by definition – those who buy Nike toning shoes.

Two points may be made about these unpredictable metaphors used in predictable contexts. The first is the context of the genre. In stylistics, advertising is seen as sharing a great deal of commonality with literature, as both aim to influence their respective audience. A piece of literature is supposed to have a theme, i.e., a message. But that message is seldomly stated and often hidden (Booth 1981; Leech and Short 1983, among others). The same is true of advertising. Suppose that the message of an ad is "buy X". To tell the audience simply to "buy X" may not be able to generate a lot of sales. So, as far as theme is concerned, the transactional motivation of clarity is its antithesis in genres of this kind. Instead, the effectiveness motivation becomes paramount. Metaphor, with its many unique characteristics, particularly the freedom it allows the metaphorist in the choosing of domains for mapping, seems to be a natural tool for poets and ad writers.

Secondly, it is worthwhile to reiterate that the creativity of metaphors is closely related to the context in which metaphors are deployed. In Sections 7.2 and 7.3 where we discussed how metaphors are motivated by both the transactional and the interactional considerations, we noted that almost all the tokens were stock, ready-made metaphors – those that exist in the mental inventory of conventional metaphor toolbox. This makes sense, as the sources of our examples are primarily from news media, whose major mission it is to inform the public. These metaphors, being entrenched in the speech community, have their built-in image schemas which members in the news media can tap into. But specialized genres such as literature and advertising aim to surprise – even to shock – so that practitioners turn to the creating of novel, "crazy" metaphors.

The primary contribution that pragmatics makes to the study of language is its focus on context and its ability to reveal meaning from actual discourse. The discussions of metaphor within the framework of MMP in this chapter is a demonstration of both.

As alluded to at the outset of the chapter, metaphor is one of the non-literal uses of language. Other such uses are dealt with in Chapter 8, to which we now turn.

Chapter 8
MMP and the non-literal

This chapter is devoted to discussing how MMP can shed light on a group of specific uses of language that can be called *non-literal:* verbal irony, sarcasm, parody, satire, humor, and lies. Metaphor belongs to this group as well, but its privileged position warrants an entire chapter, which we just have had. The gist of my argument is that MMP provides an economical and coherent framework for accounting for the behaviors of the members of this group while, at the same time, explains the specific behaviors of each in specific contexts.

Section 8.1 provides a background for non-literal uses of language, sorting out the relationships among them. Section 8.2 discusses how these uses are motivated to create camaraderie between the speaker and hearer, an important part of the interactional motivations. Section 8.3 focuses on how non-literal uses of language can enhance the public image of both other and self to varying degrees depending on the motivation of the user in specific contexts. After that, we move to three specific non-literal uses: irony in Section 8.4, parody in 8.5, and lies in 8.6. A few further comments are made in Section 8.7.

8.1 Setting the scene

The term *non-literal* refers to the type of language use in which the semantics of what is said is different from what the speaker intends to get across. This would sound like the difference between Grice's natural meaning and non-natural meaning discussed in Chapter 1. But a distinction is assumed. The non-natural meaning, per Grice, needs context. An utterance "The phone is ringing" can mean "Pick up the phone" only in the right contest, as it can easily mean what it says in a different context (e.g., in a narrative, as a background for an event). However, a verbal irony, for example, is *defined* as saying the opposite of what one means, although its interpretation depends crucially on context. The same holds for sarcasm, parody, hyperbole, innuendo, and lie. In other words, the fact that language has given these things names is enough indication that their non-literalness is accepted by its speakers.[84]

---

[84] One may wonder why we are not using the term *figures of speech*. We cannot do that because lying is not a figure of speech. Another reason against that approach is that figures of speech may include things that *are literal*: litotes (emphasis by negation), onomatopoeia, alliteration, and many others.

Of the types of non-literal uses to be discussed in this section – irony, sarcasm, parody, joke, humor, and lies – the first three hang together for their non-literalness and rhetorical effects. The next two – joke and humor – are more encompassing terms whose definition rest on rhetorical effects and the reaction they generate in the audience. As such, each of them can be the result of the deployment of any of the first three and other uses of language not here listed. The last one, lie, is an obvious "odd man out". It may or may not be literal – a "white lie" is non-literal and an intended lie is literal. But since it at least *can be* non-literal and I believe it should be given some attention, it is included in this chapter. For sake of convenience, we will use the acronym NLU (non-literal use [of language]) to label these different uses of language, with acknowledgement of obvious imprecision.[85]

Note should be taken, first, that these NLUs are of very different kinds. Verbal irony[86] has a received definition: saying the opposite of what one means. The non-literalness of it is therefore one of opposition in polarity. Parody is essentially the copying and exaggeration of a previous act, the non-literalness of it is therefore one of pretense and hyperbole. A lie must first of all be an untrue assertion, no matter the nature of the untruth.

Second, about the commonality among these NLUs. Since the speaker does not directly say what she means, what she ends up saying is often ambiguous and has the potential for misinterpretation. An irony could be taken as literal, the pretense in a parody may not be seen through, and a teasing may fail to reach the audience. These things are therefore implicatures per Grice (1975) and require more efforts on the part of the hearer to process per Sperber and Wilson (1986). This loss of clarity – one of the two transactional motivations in MMP – therefore must be offset somehow. That gain – as we shall see – is menifold: the building of commadarie, the opportunity for creativity, and the achieving of effectiveness.

Third – and making explicit what has been implied above – these NLUs overlap and there does not seem to be a way to tease them apart precisely. Irony, for instance, is closely related to sarcasm. In fact, there seems to be strong evidence for treating sarcasm as a subset of irony, as sarcasm is intended to hurt the target while irony can be deployed for jocular or humorous purposes as well as to ridicule. (The near impossibility of making clear distinctions among all these NLUs are either explicitly expressed or implied in most studies on the subject: Attardo 1994, 2000, 2001; Bateson [1955] 1972; Gibbs 2000; Ivanko, Pexman and

---

[85] A careful delineation of these different yet related notions is found in Dynel (2009).
[86] We will not be discussing other types of ironies such as *dramatic irony* or *situational irony* (Booth 1974; Leech and Short 983).

Olineck 2004; Pexman and Zvaigzne 2004; Skalicky and Crossley 2015). Jokes, on the other hand, can be sarcastic on one occasion but humorous on another. Therefore, we will be discussing these NLUs as a group first, in Sections 8.1 and 8.2. After that, we will pick out irony, parody, and lies and discuss them separately.

8.2 NLUs and camaraderie

As discussed in Chapter 2, the relationship between the two interactional motivations – creating, maintaining, and enhancing the image of other and creating, maintaining, and enhancing the image of self – is one of a cline on the dimension of conflictiveness vs. assistiveness. At one end of the cline is the relationship in which the two conflict and, at the other, the two are mutually assistive. We will see that NLUs occupy the entire continuum. Some uses of NLUs occur in cases whereby the image of other and self are in conflict; some in cases whereby the image of other and self are mutually beneficial; while others are situated at different points in between. As a group, however, NLUs appear to share an important feature – that they can be used to benefit the image of both other and self (the *assistive* end of the continuum as seen in Figure 2.2 above) via the creation of camaraderie between the user and her audience.

The ability of NLUs to establish camaraderie rests on their non-literalness. To mean Q while saying P entails a gap in meaning. That gap must be bridged by the hearer: she has to "travel" from P to Q, guided by either Grice's (1975) cooperative principle or Sperber and Wilson's (1986) relevance. In the sense that not every hearer can bridge that gap – jokes do fail; ironies can be taken literally; and parodies are not always seen through – the bridging of the gap becomes notable, although it seems to be the norm than deviation. The following example shows this well.[87]

On January 28, 2021, MSNBC 11th Hour anchor Brian Williams asked his guests on the program to watch an "exclusive" clip of Donald Trump meeting with House Representative Kevin McCarthy, a Republican law maker from California, in Trump's residence Mar-a-Lago and then comment on it. But what was shown on the screen was not the promised Trump and McCarthy tape but a footage of the 1996 romantic comedy *Jerry Maguire* – a close-up of actor Tom Cruise and co-star Renée Zellweger delivering one of the film's more schmaltzy exchanges.

---

[87] https://www.nydailynews.com/snyde/ny-brian-williams-trump-mccarthy-jerry-maguire-20210129-6zjswep7ejhnxnzczdwsmtqyku-story.html (accessed 3 February 3, 2021).

(1)   Maguire: I love you. [Eyes tearing] You complete me.
     Zellweger: Shut up. Just shut up – you had me at hello.[88]

The screen then cuts back to Williams issuing an apology to viewers.

(2)   Obviously we have rolled the wrong clip and we were sold a bill of goods here.

While his guests grinned, Williams repeated that he thought the clip was going to be from the meeting between the former president and the House minority leader and that he would get to the bottom of whatever went wrong.

(3)   Someone is going to be of course in big trouble.

Semantically, the legendary TV anchor makes several false statements: promising to show a video clip of Trump and McCarthy (while knowing that he is not going to), stating that a wrong tape was rolled (while knowing that he planned for it), accusing someone else for deception ("We were sold a bill of goods"), and stating that someone – most likely his support staff – will be held accountable ("in big trouble"). It is worth stressing that while doing all this, Williams does not show any sign that he is "playing" with his TV audience.

Falsehood is not the only thing that works here. There is the situational irony that Williams accurses others to have sold him "a bill of goods" while he was selling it to his audience. There is the apparent comparison of the relationship between the U.S. president and the majority leader of the House of Representatives to the romantic relationship between two people deeply in love, and – in that love relationship – there is the insinuation that the love of the House majority leader has for the president was love at first sight. We will pick up some of these elements later in this this section. What is interesting for us presently is that the layers of "deception" by Williams, delivered in a deadpan manner, requires quite a bit of work from the audience. In order to see through these layers, the audience need to quickly discern the similarity between the video clip that was shown and the one that was supposed to be shown. In order to do that, they need to know the relationship between Trump and McCarthy, particularly the fact that McCarthy had criticized Trump on the House floor for his encouragement of the rioters to breach the Capitol building – which cooled their relationship – but then

---

88 Apparently, *at hello* has since become an accepted phrase to mean "at first sight" (https://www.urbandictionary.com/define.php?term=you%20had%20me%20at%20hello (accessed 3 February 2021).

flew to the former president's residence to patch things up[89]: "to kiss the ring and God knows what else, meeting with a deposed former president in his under-decorated Florida home", Williams was to observe later.[90] Finally, the audience also need to have some sense of Williams' style – the fact that he is witty and can trick his audience once in a while.[91]

Because of all this, Williams' performance generated an overwhelming positive reaction online. Twitter and Facebook posters praised his "smartness" and declared that he "nailed it". There was an apparent sense of community among those who realized that Williams was intentionally showing the *Jerry McGuire* tape, a sense of bondage and superiority that comes from Williams' courage to trust his audience's ability to get his meaning despite the lack of discernible signs. This biding is part of what has been termed "ambient affiliation" (Zappavigna 2011, 2014) and "conviviality" (Varis & Blommaert 2015) that lead to "this fleeting, often momentary, connections" between speakers and hearers (Vásquez 2019).

What if the intended message of an NLU is not realized? Hyon (2018: 169) recounts a well-known parody going undetected: the "Sokal hoax." In 1996, Alan Sokal, a physics professor at New York University and University College London, submitted an article to *Social Text*, an academic journal of postmodern cultural studies. The article, "Transgressing the Boundaries: Towards a Transformative Hermeneutics of Quantum Gravity", proposed that quantum gravity is a social and linguistic construct (Sokal 1996). It was meant "as a critique of the journal's cultural studies bent and of what Sokal perceived as a general decline of academic rigor in the humanities" (Hyon 2018: 169), the editors did not realize it and published it as a real article. When Sokal revealed that the article was fake three weeks later, the editors of the journal was embarrassed and some of the journal's readers were enraged. The hoax developed into a debate between proponents of the cultural studies theoretical orientation, including Derrida (1997) and those who argue for the objectivity of truth and reality, demonstrating how confrontation – the opposite of camaraderie – can result if the non-literalness of an NLU is *not* realized.

The camaraderie-building function of NLUs is widely recognized in the literature. Dynel (2008) examines the functions of teasing and banter and finds that

---

[89] Following the deadly siege on the Capitol by Trump supporters trying to help the former president overturn the results of the 2020 election, McCarthy said Trump "bears responsibility" for the violence.
[90] https://money.yahoo.com/msnbc-brian-williams-invokes-jerry-161607540.html (accessed 3 February 2021).
[91] Also relevant may be the fact that Williams was once caught showing a fake video about himself, which caused a setback in his career. It is possible therefore that he was at the same time making fun of himself.

"teases, even if ostensibly aggressive, i.e., face-threatening, are geared towards solidarity" (Dynel 2008: 241). Analyzing mockery sequences among a group of friends, Robles (2019) shows how nonserious tearing down of each other in a peer group manages the practical problem of in-group difference by reaffirming shared stances and norms around masculinity, revealing how the moral organization of in-group and out-group assessments are built in the mundane world of conversation (Robles 2019: 85). Likewise, Gong and Ran (2020: 64) show how teasing can be a useful tool to get an interviewed guest to disclose information and to achieve "audience involvement" in Chinese entertainment TV programs. Kwon et al. (2020) demonstrate how ironic personae – created via the expression of humorous verbal irony and aggressive conversational humor – can help participants to become a member of the "in-group" (Kwon et al. 2020: 50). Yang and Ren (2020) provide evidence for the use of jocular mockery for the purpose of managing relationship with interactants of different social statuses on a national TV show in China. Chovanec (2012: 139) likewise argues that conversational humor "makes it possible for the audience to get involved in collective humor and even in joint fantasizing" in online newspapers (see also Tsakona 2018).

There is evidence that the camaraderie-creating aspect of the interactional motivation is ritualized in some communities. In the U.S., an organization – e.g., a department in a university or a business – may call a retirement or departure party "Roast and Toast", at which participants are licensed to poke fun at the honoree. An episode about teasing in a village in Southeastern Senegal found in Sweet (2020) is particularly interesting. In the relevant linguaculture, a new-born is named at a *denabo*, a village-wide naming ceremony, and the host will distribute kola nuts to those in attendance as tokens of having born witness to the event. Those who are absent perform a routine parodic teasing to claim participation and inclusion. Sweet describes one such event. After a young infant in the lineage of the village chief has been named at a *denago*, a woman who had been absent puts out such a teasing performance:

(4) The cloaked figure's reliance on a long staff betrayed the stride of an elder. In cascading moments of recognition, cries of shock and laughter rebounded inside the small walled compound as the figure drew near. Shrugging off any hands that attempted to impede its advance, the cloaked figure thrust the staff into the earth, planted two feet beside it, and bellowed: "the name of this child has come, and it is Trash Owl". The compound erupted in a cascade of laughter at this teasing nickname. (Sweet 2020: 86)

The communality of the event is vividly portrayed by Sweet: the woman's attire, manner of walking, and specific actions when declaring the name of the infant;

the reception of her performance by the crowd that has been gathered; and the nickname itself – *Trash Owl* – all create a sense of inclusion, belonging, and camaraderie. The performance won the woman the gifts. Such gifts, however, are highly symbolic, as Sweet informs us:

> However, gifts such as kola, and through them names, persons, and states of witnessing, were susceptible to rerouting and recontextualization as negotiated through routines of verbal creativity such as teasing. While kola often began as commodities and were often purchased based on their uniformity, ritual oration and subsequent performances showed them to be a nexus of value transformations in which they could link together particular people, places, and participation frame-works. (Sweet 2020: 87)

Lastly, the motivation of establishing camaraderie for NLUs is seen in the special frame of discourse it creates. Once such a frame is created by the speaker, the hearer has no choice but stay in it. Take irony for instance.

(5) A: Lovely weather, isn't? (Said about a downpour)
    B1. Lovely indeed.
    B2: Yes. What lousy weather!

In Example (5), A means "what lousy weather". Suppose B agrees with A's intended meaning, she cannot say "Yes. What lousy weather", which responds to what A means. She has to say something along the lines of "Lovely indeed" or "Absolutely", responding to the intended meaning also ironically. In other words, with an NLU, the speaker takes the discourse onto a different plain, that of the non-literal, as if saying to the hearer "We are now in a different frame of experience. I will not mean what I say. As long as you want to participate in the exchange, you will also have to do the same: not *saying* what you mean." Let us illustrate this "staying in the frame" nature of NLUs with one more example.

In a family messaging group, the father told the group that he had made a Covid-19 vaccine appointment. This happened at a time when vaccines were distributed in phases. The father – the oldest of the family – would be the first to be vaccinated, ahead of others in the group. To the news, one of his children responded:

(6) Now dad is going to go on a solo cruise without all of us (followed by an emoji of a crying face).

to which another of his children responded with:

(7) Sh::::. Don't give him ideas!

Saying something for which she has no evidence, the writer of (6) creates a new frame for the exchange, as if indicating that "I am joking and I trust you will see that I am joking". To carry on the joke, the writer of (7) assumes that (6) is serious, further pretending that the father may actually do what is said in (6) and engage in other solo entertainments. (Note the plural on the word *ideas*). Further, he does a verbal whisper with "sh::::", with full knowledge that the father has access to what is supposed to be a private exchange. Throughout this thread, everyone has to operate within the playful frame. Imagine a response to the joking frame with one in the literal frame from the father: "No. You know that I would never do that!" It would be disappointing to all in the group, indicating a breakdown of communication and the inability of the father to be an insider of the joke.

8.3 NLUs for image

In the last section, we discussed the interactionality of NLUs – the fact that NLUs can be used to create a sense of camaraderie, solidarity, and community. In this section, we move to the ways in which NLUs are used to benefit the public image of both other and self, focusing on a review of Dynel (2020).

Dynel (2020) offers a detailed account of the use of humor by the U.S. fast-food chain restaurant Wendy's, involving snappy posts commonly called "roasting". According to Dynel (2020: 2), The Twitter account of Wendy's (Wendy's@Wendy's) registered over 125% follower growth in the span of one year (from just over 1 million in January 2017 to 2.24 million in December 2017) and then reached 3,5 million in January 2020. Dynel shows that the most important reason for the success was its Twitter promotion based on witty jibes, which was "unwittingly started" by the company's social media manager, Amy Brown, on 2nd January, 2017. It started with a few tweets by a user in response to Wendy's advertising tweet couched in a humorous pun (based on the polysemy of *cool*). The user addressed the company's account, casting doubt on its "fresh never frozen" policy. After receiving a polite informative reply, the user asked a rather naïve question, which in turn was met with a response involving Socratic irony in the form of a simple riddle. The user ignored the question and endorsed another fast-food chain, which he may have wished to promote from the outset. This caused the manager to close the interaction with a snarky retort that rhetorically turned the tables on the interlocutor, accusing, in an overtly pretending manner, that the man had forgotten about the existence of fridges and got defensive by mentioning the competing brand. The actual exchange is presented below as Example (8). The last reply went viral, unexpectedly putting the social media manager in the limelight.

The unexpected rise of Wendy's visibility on Twitter is significant. Being snappy and snarky, attempting to win a war of words with a potential customer would be risky, particularly in an environment in which things can get out control in the form of trending and memes. But apparently surprising even to Wendy's management, the accidental episode put Wendy's in a positive spotlight, suggesting the value of humor-creating NLUs.

Wendy's capitalized on the success and received constant media attention – Dynel further recounts – in the next three years. The official Twitter account for Wendy's celebrated the National Roast Day on 4th January for three consecutive years (2017–2019). In order to join in the fun, social media managers for other brands, celebrities, and ordinary users requested to be "roasted" on Wendy's Twitter account not only on the National Roast Day but also on a daily basis, presumably as a badge of honor. While the National Roast Day was no longer officially celebrated after 2019, Wendy's has not ceased to fire witty tweets.

Several conclusions are possible about Wendy's tweets. First, NLUs benefit the self-image of the speaker. In a competitive market, the image of wit and humor helps Wendy's to stand out, which has the potential to increase its sales, although Dynel does not provide evidence for that. Second, the target of NLUs – those who *ask* to be "roasted", including competitors – can also benefit via the visibility that results from the exposure. While this is in part explained by the time we now live in, wherein public attention is very much valued (and craved), is reveals to us the power of NLUs: it can benefit the public image of the victim as well as the "aggressor".

While to benefit the public image of both other and self is an inherent feature of NLUs, the deployment of NLUs requires skill, as aggression, by definition, is meant to hurt the target and it often does. The examples from Dynel (2020) demonstrates how the roasts launched by Wendy's Twitter account achieve this difficult feat. We start with the initial exchange described earlier (Dynel 2020: 3). The original is a screenshot of the Twitter page, with time stamps, so that the different tweets in Example (8) were posted over a period of several days.

(8) Wendy's: Our beef is way too cool to ever be frozen.
 User: your beef is frozen and we all know it. Y'all know we laugh at your slogan "fresh, never frozen" right? Like you are really a joke.
 Wendy's: Sorry you think that! But you are wrong, we've only ever used fresh beef since we were founded in 1969.
 User: so you deliver it raw on a hot truck?
 Wendy's: Where do you store cold things that aren't frozen?
 User: y'all should give up. @McDonalds got you guys beat with the dope ass breakfast

Wendy's: you don't have to bring them into this just because you forgot refrigerators existed for a second there.

The first tweet by Wendy's takes advantage of the pun *cool*. But it is met by an aggressive accusation. Wendy's is firm in reply ("You are wrong"). The user continues his aggression but Wendy's reply is a rhetorical question, pointing out that things can be cold and unfrozen. The aggression of the user intensifies with the mentioning of McDonalds and the using of words that are meant to attack. The last reply by Wendy's is again firm, sarcastic, and understating ("for a second there"). Wendy's tweets are thus biting without being rude, pointing out the folly of the user without being explicitly aggressive.

The skills of Wendy's account with NLUs are also seen in its actual roasts of business (9) and people (10).

(9) Firefox: Fire away
    Wendy's: Sorry it took so long. Firefox encountered a problem with Windows.

(10) User: I set a notification for this moment. DO YOUR WORST! [with a picture of himself sitting on weights]
     Wendy's: Most people lift weights. They don't just sit on them.

and in the way it defends itself and attacking the opponent:

(11) User: McDonald's is better.
     Wendy's: At freezing beef.

(12) McDonald's: Today we're announcing that by mid-2018, all Quarter Pounder burgers at the majority of our restaurants will be cooked with fresh beef.
     Wendy's: So you'll still use frozen beef in MOST of your burgers in ALL of your restaurants? Asking for a friend.

In (9), Firefox, an internet browser, is being "smart" by playing on its brand name ("Fire away"). Wendy's responds with an insincere apology and a falsehood that is clearly intended to be seen through but implies that the browser is unsatisfactory. In (10), the user challenges Wendy's with "DO YOUR WORST", only to be outdone by being mocked for sitting on weights in the picture. In (11), the user provokes Wendy's by stating that its fierce competitor is "better". Wendy's dovetails with the challenging statement: "at freezing beef" (Freezing beef is a perpetual motif

Wendy's uses to disparage its competitors). In (12), McDonalds announces the upcoming use of fresh beef in one of its burgers, but Wendy's points out immediately that the declaration means McDonald's is still using frozen beef in other burgers. It also pretends to be "asking for a friend". In all of these, Wendy's image comes through as witty, perceptive, aggressive yet in good taste, and able to turn the table on the opponent without appearing mean-spirited.

Dynel (2020: 10–11) points out several of aspects of Wendy's tweets. Many of these tweets are "benevolent jocular insults openly solicited by the targets, both brands (companies and public figures) and ordinary users". Its roasting of ordinary persons brings them "popularity if a creative roasting tweet should go viral". For brands, being roasted means "free advertising through building a positive self-image". When teasing Wendy's, users wish to be outwitted or, at least, to test the social manager's wits "with evident intent to cause public amusement". Genuine disparagement of other fast-food companies is "conveniently sneaked into the otherwise humorously playful activity, allowing Wendy's to deny responsibility for any sincere criticism. This enables Wendy's to hit two birds with one stone: to non-humorously point to the competitors' flaws or weaknesses and, simultaneously, to amuse the general public at their expense" (Dynel 2020: 11).

Dynel's (2020) study thus demonstrates an important aspect of NLUs: that of their ability to help establish, maintain, and enhance the public image of both of other and self in a highly specific discourse context, a context that was incidentally created so that both sides – Wendy's and those who interact with it – can take advantage of. Generally, matches – sports games, political campaigns, school yard fights – will lead to winners and losers, with the former's image enhanced and the latter's damaged. Wendy's Twitter account portrays a different picture: a match of wit ending up benefiting the public image of both. There are two discernible reasons. The first is the online mode of communication whereby exposure itself enhances image, which explains the willingness of ordinary people and businesses to ask to be roasted. However, a far more important reason is the NLUs themselves. In the last section we discussed the camaraderie-building aspect of NLUs – that the frame these NLUs create offers an opportunity for both sides of the engagement to show their ability to be its members. This seems to be what is happening here with Wendy's tweets. In this frame, the winner – apparently Wendy's most if not all the time – get its image enhanced by being the "winner". The losers – those who volunteer to be "roasted" – get their image enhanced by being able to appreciate the wit and being courageous to "lose". The first reason – exposure resulting from the mode of communication – is therefore only a contributing factor for NLUs to enhance the public image of both, not a necessary condition for it. The routine "Toast and Roast" retirement or departure party (referred to above) that seems to be popular in the U.S. testifies to this: the honoree of such a party often enjoys it for the limelight, for being the center of attention, and for being able to "take the beating".

There is another aspect in the image-enhancing ability of NLUs seen in Wendy's tweets: creativity (Dynel 2020). Studies on linguistic creativity (Carter 2016; Carter and McCarthy 2004; Jones 2016; Vásquez 2019; Vásquez and Creel 2017) inform the importance of creativity in one's public image, although these authors use different terms for public image. According to Carter and McCarthy (2004: 83), creativity in language use is "not a capacity of special people but a special capacity of all people". It is thus small wonder that "all people" strive to be creative at appropriate times to enhance their public image.

While the establishment, maintenance, or enhancement of public image is an *a priori* motivation for NLUs, it also leads to payoffs: a positive, socially-approved public image can also help "get things done". Wendy's roasting tweets play an important role in the promotion of its business in a fiercely competitive fast-food business in the U.S. In addition, there is evidence in the literature that the enhancement of public image often leads to tangible results. Kwon et al. (2020: 44) show how the ironic personae helps the board of an agency to test new positions on topics in a non-committal way. Demjén (2016) discusses how laughter and humor help cancer patients to cope with the disease. Dynel & Poppi (2018: 382) argue that dark humor is a way for internet users to convey their true beliefs about the sociopolitical situation after the 2016 terrorist attack in Nice, primarily to criticize terrorism-related themes such as "inept security enforcement, radical Islam, political and public reactions and integration policies". In all these instances, NLUs serve a utilitarian purpose – one that benefits either the overall mission of an institution or a transitory objective of an individual.

8.4 Irony (and sarcasm)

Verbal irony, the focus of our discussion in this section, involves an incongruity in the form of opposition: in the discourse context, one expects A to be said but hears its opposite B. This defining feature is widely agreed upon, regardless of whether one views irony as pretense (Clark and Gerrig 1984) or echoic mention (Sperber and Wilson 1981), a spirited debated that has stretched decades (Wilson 2006; Wilson and Sperber 2012; Ibáñez Ruiz de Mendoza and Lozano-Palacio 2019; Popa-Wyatt 2014).

Clark and Gerrig (1984: 122, see also Chen 1990: 6) point out the tendency that the evaluation in an irony is overwhelmingly positive. An ironist is far more likely to say "What a clever idea!" to mean "What a stupid idea!" than "What a stupid idea!" to mean "What a clever idea!" (but see below). However, the intended message of the positive evaluation is negative (Dynel 2013, 2018a, 2018b) most of the time. In a study on readers' Facebook comments on a post of a controversial Israeli politician – Miri Regev – Hirsch (2020) finds that irony was reserved primarily for criticisms of Regiv: out of all the 119 anti-Regiv comments, 27.7% (n = 33) were ironic (Hirsch 2020: 51). The nine instances of irony that were pro-Regiv – Hirsch points out – supports Regev by directing the criticism towards Regev's opponents (50–51). Therefore, all ironies are critical of their target: those against Regev use irony directly to ridicule her; those for Regev use irony to directly ridicule her opponent. If we look at the full range of irony tokens more closely, however, the reality appears to be more nuanced – that there is a gradience of benefitting/hurting other-image, the discussion of which I omit.

In Sections 8.2 and 8.3, above, we discussed how irony, together with other NLUs, can be motivated by the interactional motivations of creating camaraderie and enhancing the self-image of creativity. In this Section, we focus on how irony behaves with regard to what it does for and to other-image, with the assumption that it usually if not always enhances self-image. We start with ironies meant to enhance the image of other and end with those that hurt the image of other.

In the following example, from the film *The Sound of Music*, Maria, the new governess of the Von Trapp family, has found a frog in her pocket after the children surrounded her, telling her how to be a "good governess". Then she comes to the dining room where the Von Trapps have already began to eat. While she was sitting down, she sees what looks like another small animal on her chair. Screaming, she finds that it is a pinecone. She sits herself at the dining table and the following conversation takes place.

(13) Maria: I would like to thank everyone of you for your precious gift you left in my pocket earlier today. [referring to the frog]
    Von Trapp: What gift?
    Maria: [Seeing that the children are staring at her] It's a secret between the children and me, captain.
    Von Trapp: If it is a secret, I suggest that you keep it, and let us eat.
    Maria: [After a period of silence] Knowing how nervous I must have been as a stranger in a new household, knowing how important it was for me to feel accepted, it is so kind and thoughtful of you to make my first moment of her to warm, happy, and present.
                [The children are moved to tears, with one weeping loudly.]
                                                               (Quoted in Chen 1990: 37)

Maria first tells a bald-faced lie, as she knows that most of her audience – the Von Trapp children – know that the frog is not a gift. Then she says that the children are "thoughtful" to make her arrival "warm, happy, and present" while her first encounters with them have been miserable. But there is clearly no intention to hurt the image of the children. In fact, the irony is meant to enhance their image. That message is delivered effectively, as is seen in the reaction of the Von Trapp children (all moved to tears, with one sobbing loudly).

Example (14) is a conversation between a group of college students, which took place outside a campus coffee shop (Gibbs 2000):

(14) Kayla: How are you doing?
Cherie: Um . . . good. We're going to study Latin but the coffee shop is just packed.
David: It's rockin'.
Sarah: . . . study Latin . . . Latin language?
Kayla: It's wet out here.
Sarah: You guys are taking Latin? (laughs).
Cherie: Yeah . . . (laughs).
Kayla: (whiny tone of voice) But that's a dead language (everyone laughs). I'm just kidding. Is that not what everyone tells you?
Cherie: It's true and we don't really know how to pronounce everything.
David: It's really hard.
Cherie: Yeah, but it's only a year-long program.
David: *So, you're fluent in Latin after a year* (everyone laughs).
Kayla: *Right . . . right.*
David: *It's true* (everyone laughs).
Sarah: You read all those ancient texts, that's cool (laughs).
Cherie: Why you guys dissin' on Latin?
David: (mocking tone) What, wo-ah, you're dissin' my Latin.
Kayla: Actually, Latin helps because, doesn't it, it helps with etymology, it helps with words, breaking words down.
David: *Totally . . . yeah, yeah, she got it . . . yeah.*
Cherie: Structure, parts of speech, yeah.
David: *I'm a changed person since the last couple of weeks of Latin.*
(Gibbs 2000: 7–8)

There are at least five ironic utterances in (14) (*italicized*). But, as Gibbs observes, these utterances "enable[s] speakers to bond together through. . . mockful teasing of the addressee" (Gibbs 2000: 7). In other words, the ironies are meant to enhance the image of the victims rather than hurt it.

The following is from Joe Biden, the U.S. present. At one of the 2020 campaign rallies, his wife Jill protected him from a group of protesters by physically positioning herself between him and the protesters, shoving them away. At an interview on TV, he comments on the episode.

(15) I thought I heard on the news on the way over that that the committee in charge of Secret Service decided they have to start providing Secret Service for us. I think that's because they're afraid Jill's going to hurt someone. I tell you what man, I married way above my station.[92]

The purpose of providing secret service to him, Biden says, is to prevent his wife from hurting someone. But he is clearly not portraying his wife as a violence-prone person. Instead, his ironic statement is meant to enhance her image as a loving and protective spouse. To make sure that the audience get his message, he ends his remarks with a metaphor: "I married way above my station".

The U.S. president is not the only one who uses what seems to be a negative evaluation to make a positive point. At a party of teenagers (in Southern California), Speaker A told the group how he had punished a bully with a well-carried out prank. All present greeted the episode with admiration. A young woman said:

(16) That was so mean of you!

When asked whether she meant what she said afterward – "Did you really mean that what A did was mean?" – the speaker of (16) responded: "You are sooo adult! That's the way people in my generation speak. *Bad* means *good*. *Stupid* means *smart*". In other words, in this particular community, commentary that appears negative (at the level of what is said) can be positive (at the level of what is meant). What would seem to be a deviation from the positivity restriction on irony turns out to be an adherence to it. More importantly, it shows irony, possibly surprisingly to some, can be used to enhance the image of the target. The key seems to be the close relationship between the discourse participants and the shared values and camaraderie that are already there.

We now move to the "gray area" of irony, cases in which the image of other seems to be targeted but not particularly attacked. In February 2021 when the former U.S. president Donald Trump was being impeached by the House repre-

---

[92] https://www.insider.com/joe-biden-jill-biden-relationship-timeline-2020-8#march-2020-she-fought-off-protesters-who-stormed-the-stage-on-super-tuesday-leading-joe-to-joke-improbably-the-only-candidate-running-for-president-whose-wife-is-my-secret-service-20

sentatives for inciting insurrection at the Capitol, eleven members of his own party voted for the impeachment article, led by Liz Cheney, the number three leader of the House Republican Conference. The top leader of the conference, Kevin McCarthy, voted against impeachment. The rift between the two leaders was well-known to the public. At a press conference held by the House Republicans at the end of February 2020, the following exchange took place.[93]

(17) Reporter: Former president Donald Trump has been invited to deliver a speech at the CPAC. Do you think he should?
McCarthy: Yes. He should
Reporter: How about you, Congresswoman Cheney?
Cheney: That's up to CPAC. I've been clear on my views about President Trump. I don't believe that he should be playing a role in the future of the party or the country.
McCarthy: On that high note, thank you very much.
[Laugher bursts out. Press conference adjourns.]

Cheney's remarks about Trump directly contradict McCarthy's, causing what the media called later "an awkward moment", as public rifts of this kind are both rare and unhelpful. McCarthy, however, calls that embarrassing display of defiance of him as the leader and disunity of the party he leads a "high note". The intended victims of the irony are not only Cheney but also himself and the party – after all, the party was split on its decision to impeach their own president. But that "bite" is clearly not meant to be deep and hurtful. It sounds more like a fake bite so as to deflect further embarrassment. The irony worked well: the tension was diffused, the reporters present appreciated his quick and self-duplicating wit, and the meeting ended amidst a round of hearty laughter emitted from both the reporters and members of his own party.

In the majority of cases, an irony is meant to be sarcastic: to show contempt, to mock, to ridicule, and – in rare cases – to attack frontally. However, how much sarcasm is meant or received depends on contextual factors of various kinds, the relationship between the ironist and the victim being the most determinative. The following is an assortment of instances from Dynel (2009).

(18) I know you have an open mind. I can feel the draught from where I'm sitting.
(Dynel 2009: 1289)

---

[93] https://www.nbcnews.com/politics/congress/mccarthy-cheney-clash-over-whether-trump-should-speak-cpac-n1258743 (accessed 25 February 2021).

(19) A: Do you mind if I smoke?
    B: Do you mind if I throw up on your trousers?

(Dynel 2009: 1293)

(20) A: Fashion today goes toward tiny...
    B: So you've got the most fashionable brain.

(Dynel 2009: 1292)

All the ironies in these examples are sarcastic and can be hurtful, although in different ways and to different degrees. However, we can imagine situations in which they be taken as "friendly", if the requisite close relationship exists. Even the insult on the hearer's intelligence expressed in B's utterance in (20) can be a sign of extreme ingroupness.

It seems that ironies whose targets are not present tend to be sarcastic. In (22), what the mother says does feel to be a scathing ridicule, although the irony is delivered as an indirect understatement.

(21) Daughter: Dylan took a tampon from Gabby's backpack, stuck it in his mouth and it got real big from his spit.
    Mother: I've been seriously underestimating him.

(Dynel 2009: 1292)

In (22), the mockery of the husband, who is also absent, is inescapable.

(22) A: How is your husband?
    B: He's OK. He's been sober several times in the past few months.

(Chen and Houlette 1990)

The following conversation between two college students, which occurred in their apartment and focused on some visitors who were staying with them at the invitation of another roommate, is also from Gibbs (2000):

(23) Anne: By the way, were our wonderful guests still here when you came out and ate lunch?
    Dana: I had a sandwich and...
    Anne: Isn't it so nice to have guests here?
    Dana: Totally! Anne: I just love it, you know, our housemates. They bring in the most wonderful guests in the world and they can totally relate to us.
    Dana: Yes, they do.

Anne: (laughs) Like I would just love to have them here more often (laughs) so I can cook for them, I can prepare (laughs) . . .
Dana: to make them feel welcome?
Anne: Yeah, isn't this great, Dana? Like today I was feeling all depressed and I came out and I saw the guests and they totally lightened up my mood. I was like the happiest person on earth.
Dana: Uh huh. Anne: I just welcome them so much, you know, ask them if they want anything to drink or eat (laughs).

(Gibbs 2000: 6)

Of the nine turns in this conversation among two friends, all but one ("I had a sandwich and. . .") are ironic. Gibbs is certainly right that irony is used to establish camaraderie between Anne and Dana. But to their roommate who had invited the guests and the guests themselves, these ironic utterances are brutally sarcastic and mean-spirited. One wonders if Anne and Dana would ever want their roommate to know this exchange and what she – their roommate – would do if she did.

The most mean-spirited example of irony in this section, however, is credited to Donald Trump. On October 31, 2020, trucks with Trump signs and flags surrounded a Biden campaign bus on a Texas highway and attempted to slow it down and run it off the road before the campaign staff called 911, the emergency phone number in the U.S. At his own campaign rally the following day, Trump said:

(24) It is something. Did you see the way our people, they . . . you know, they were protecting his bus yesterday, because they're nice.[94]

Attempting to push a campaign bus off a freeway is physically dangerous and morally deplorable. But to Trump, that is "something", an understatement made with apparent approbation. Then he uses the word "protecting" to characterize the caravan of his supporters surrounding the bus in trucks and sport utility vehicles.

Trump is known for his crassness in speech, among others, and was the antithesis of presidentiality (Chen 2019b). But (24) shows another aspect of him: his cruel sarcasm. Note that he is not addressing the rival campaign but his sup-

---

[94] https://www.irishpost.com/news/donald-trump-defends-supporters-accused-of-trying-to-run-joe-biden-campaign-bus-off-road-196708

porters. The propositional content of what he says are positive, but it is not easy to believe that he really thinks what his supporters did "is "nice".

We end this section with one more example from American politics. During the Senate trial of Trump's second impeachment (referenced above), Senators Lindsay Graham, Ted Cruz, and Mike Lee met with Trump's defense team to strategize. On Twitter, Michael Steele, a republican who had turned into a fierce Trump critic, posted the following.[95]

Figure 8.1: Tweet by Steele.

Steele's words, as seen in Figure 8.1, are:

(25) Objective. Impartial. Swore an oath. What a joke.

The first three phrases refer to the oath the senators take each day of the trial that they will act as objective and impartial jurors. More importantly, all three senators have been trial lawyers. When they met the Trump defense team, they were essentially colluding with them to violate their oath of objectivity and impartiality. The tweet sets up the contrast between what they have sworn to do and what they have done. It is scathing.

In sum, irony, an NLU that has stayed in the attention of pragmaticists, rhetoricians, and literary critics for decades, is seen as being motivated primarily by the interactional needs of the language user. Besides creating camaraderie with and the perception of creativity in the eyes of the hearer to enhance self-image, it

---

[95] https://twitter.com/MichaelSteele/status/1360119315622731776

is also a tool to benefit other-image in some contexts and to hurt other-image in others. In the latter case, it becomes sarcasm.

8.5 Parody (and satire)

The term *parody* comes from the Greek word παρῳδία 'parodia', which is made up of two components παρά 'papa', meaning "beside", "counter", or "against"; and ᾠδή 'oide', meaning "song". The genre has existed since the Greeks and seems to be more popular currently, with the flourishing of late-night talk shows in the past four decades and video-sharing internet platforms such as YouTube and Tiktok and social media platforms such as Twitter and Facebook.

Like irony, parody is well defined. A parody has two features. The first is imitation: a parody has to simulate some aspects of the original (Bateson 1972; Bex 1996; Chen and X. Hu 2020; Dynel 2017, 2018b, 2021; Highfield 2016; Hyland 2004; Hyon 2018; Rossen-Knill and Henry 1997; Skalicky and Crossley 2015). As for how much such imitation is appropriate, the answer seems to be "enough for the audience to realize the connection between the parody and its target". Second, a parody amplifies elements of the original in content and/or form (Chen and X. Hu 2020).

In this section, we explore the motivation of parody. My major argument is that parody stems from interactional motivations. As is recalled in Chapter 2, the relationship between the two interactional motivations – to benefit other-image and to benefit self-image – is one of a continuum on the dimension of conflictiveness vs. assistiveness (Figure 2.2). So, we categorize parody accordingly, into three types: those in which that relationship is assistive, resulting in parody for amusement; those in which the relationship is conflictive; resulting in parody for satire; and those in which the relationship is both conflictive and assistive, leading to parody for amusement and satire.[96] I will provide two examples for each of the three types.

---

[96] Given the nature of parody, more precise statements than these are not possible. It is therefore acknowledged here that even the most "amusing" parody will have some element of satire and the most satirical parody will contain some element of amusement.

8.5.1 Parody for amusement

The first example of parody for amusement is a parody of Shakespeare's Sonnet 18.

(26)   *William Shakespeare - Sonnet 18*
Shall I compare thee to a summer's day?
Thou art more lovely and more temperate:
Rough winds do shake the darling buds of May,
And summer's lease hath all too short a date:
Sometime too hot the eye of heaven shines,
And often is his gold complexion dimm'd;
And every fair from fair sometime declines,
By chance, or nature's changing course untrimm'd;
But thy eternal summer shall not fade,
Nor lose possession of that fair thou ow'st;
Nor shall Death brag thou wander'st in his shade,
When in eternal lines to time thou grow'st:
So long as men can breathe, or eyes can see,
So long lives this, and this gives life to thee.

Possibly the best known of Shakespeare's 154 sonnets, Sonnet 18 has had numerous parodic reincarnations. The following is by Howard Moss, the poetry editor of the *New Yorker* from 1950 to 1987.[97]

(27)   Who says you're like one of the dog days?
You're nicer. And better.
Even in May, the weather can be gray,
And a summer sub-let doesn't last forever.
Sometimes the sun's too hot;
Sometimes it is not.
Who can stay young forever?
People break their necks or just drop dead!
But you? Never!
If there's just one condensed reader left
Who can figure out the abridged alphabet,

---

[97] https://www.poetryfoundation.org/poets/howard-moss (accessed 6 February 6, 2021).

After you're dead and gone,
In this poem you'll live on.[98]

Moss imitates the original by writing about love (and addressed to the lover) and by mimicking the structures of some lines (e.g., the interrogative in Line 1), barely enough to be recognized for its connection to Shakespeare's original. But the parody departs from the original in most other aspects. Thematically, Moss's love is more blunt. Stylistically, Moss's version is more colloquial ("People break their necks or just drop dead"!). Structurally, Moss' version departs from the Shakespearean Sonnet in major ways: instead of having fourteen lines, his has thirteen. Instead of having ten syllables in each line, Moss's includes much shorter lines. The shortest – "But you? Never!" – has only four syllables. Instead of using the iambic meter (an unstressed/stressed pattern), Moss does not seem to care about what kind of meter he is deploying – there is hardly any regularity in the metrical scheme of his version. The parodist could be poking fun at Shakespeare, but the amusing effect it generates is undeniable.

To amuse is serious business: the line between amusing others and embarrassing oneself is a thin one. This explains why an internet user by the name of Christos Rigakos, for instance, posts her own parody of Shakespeare's Sonnet 18 entitled "shall i compare you to a pia pie"? with a confession of unsureness: "It's just a joke, just written for laughs, while eating a slice of pia and thinking of love. An example of really bad poetry. It's terrible, I know"![99]

The second parody-for-amusement example is rooted in the coronavirus pandemic that started in 2020. Dynel (2021) provides a number of internet memes about masking.

Figure 8.2: Parodies of masking (Dynel 2021: 184).

---

[98] http://www.online-literature.com/forums/showthread.php?33102-Howard-Moss-quot-Shall-I-Compare-Thee-to-a-Summer-s-Day-quot-Analysis (accessed 6 February 2021).
[99] https://hellopoetry.com/poem/198436/shall-i-compare-you-to-a-pia-pie-parody-of-shakespeares-sonnet-18/ (accessed 6 February 2021).

According to Dynel (2021:184), the three subjects in Figure 8.2 are selfies. The woman on the left has a panty liner glued to her mouth and two tampons stuck in her nostrils. The man in the middle is wearing a complicated structure of three plastic bottles and some filtering material. The subject on the right is wearing a saucepan lid by tightening her hoodies around it. "Given the context (private, closed spaces, where masks are otiose), the close shots and the evident absurdity", Dynel explains, the three persons are not endorsing their respective "homemade safety measures". The pictures are "humor-oriented parodies of masks" "through parodic imitation done for fun by individuals stranded at home". These parodies, Dynel observes (2021: 175), do not need "to involve any serious criticism or meanness towards the parodied voice or principles (e.g., the need to wear masks)..." but are "humorous play for its own sake".

It seems, further, that there is a relationship between the kind of parody and the assumed identity of the subjects which Dynel does not comment.[100] In the first picture, the use of a panty liner and two tampons apparently has to do with the gender of the subject. In the second, the complication of the structure of what the man is wearing could be targeting the stereotypical image of American men being proud of engaging in do-it-yourself projects. In the third, the subject appears to be a middle-aged woman who, again stereotypically, is supposed to be the main cook in the house, hence the utilization of a saucepan lid. At least three points can be made about this observation. First, the self-image these subjects end up enhancing is not random. It is rooted in their identity. Second, if these selfies have a "target" to poke fun of, the target in each case is directed at the self. As demonstrated in humor research, self-targeted humors are often more appreciated. Third – which is the corollary of the second point – to target at others would be risky. It is not a sure thing, for instance, if the first picture features a man, as a man wearing panty liner and tampons has the potential of leading to a wide range of interpretations, not all of which would be positive.

8.5.2 Parody for satire

Satirical parodies,[101] as we have alluded earlier, are motivated by the interactional need to hurt the image of the victim. As a result, they help the satirist to be effective in the conveying of the intended message. Again, this is a well-recognized category that has been studied widely through the centuries. Our first of the two examples is Jonathan Swift's "A Modest Proposal" (Swift [1792] 1995),

---

100 No criticism is implied; Dynel uses the example for a different purpose than mine.
101 A sizeable collection of satirical parodies is found in MacDonald (1960).

touted as the best satire ever written in the English language.[102] In it, Swift pretends to be a concerned government official writing a formal proposal to solve Irelands' problem of poverty resulting from the exploitation of Irish farmers by English land owners. He starts by describing the problem: women beggars on streets with young children trotting behind. Since this is a "a deplorable state of the kingdom, a very great additional grievance", "whoever could find out a fair, cheap and easy method of making these children sound and useful members of the commonwealth, would deserve so well of the public, as to have his statue set up for a preserver of the nation".

Then comes the grandiose mask of the proposer. First, his plan is ambitious, covering children in poverty of the entire kingdom:

(28) But my intention is very far from being confined to provide only for the children of professed beggars: it is of a much greater extent, and shall take in the whole number of infants at a certain age, who are born of parents in effect as little able to support them, as those who demand our charity in the streets.

Second, the proposer refutes other alternatives:

(29) As to my own part, having turned my thoughts for many years, upon this important subject, and maturely weighed the several schemes of our projectors, I have always found them grossly mistaken in their computation.

After critiquing a few such possibilities, the proposer offers his own solution:

(30) I do therefore humbly offer it to public consideration, that of the hundred and twenty thousand children, already computed, twenty thousand may be reserved for breed, whereof only one fourth part to be males; which is more than we allow to sheep, black cattle, or swine, and my reason is, that these children are seldom the fruits of marriage, a circumstance not much regarded by our savages, therefore, one male will be sufficient to serve four females. That the remaining hundred thousand may, at a year old, be offered in sale to the persons of quality and fortune, through the kingdom, always advising the mother to let them suck plentifully in the last month, so as to render them plump, and fat for a good table. A child will make two dishes at an entertainment for friends, and when the family dines alone, the fore or

---

[102] Jennifer Andersen and Peter Schroeder, personal communication.

hind quarter will make a reasonable dish, and seasoned with a little pepper or salt, will be very good boiled on the fourth day, especially in winter.

The biting effect of the piece, thus, lies in Swift's ability to create the persona for the proposer. His concern for the wellbeing of the kingdom, his willingness to make a proposal, his carefulness to defend his position, the pains he takes to lay out the proposed scheme in great detail, and the writing style that bespeaks formality and dignity (not in what he proposes), all lure the readers – in the beginning of the proposal – into thinking that what they are reading is truly a proposal presented to a government. In other words, stylistically, Swift imitates an official document closely. But not too long into the proposal, the real intention is revealed. For the readers realize that what is in front of them can only come from someone completely devoid of humanity, a truly evil and grotesque murderer. Therefore, the power of the piece comes from the features of parody alluded to earlier: imitation and exaggeration. Swift imitates as closely as he can, it seems, and amplifies what the English landowners were doing to the point of absurdity and inhumanity. "A Modest Proposal" thus demonstrates well how the motivation to hurt the public image of the targeted victim motivates parodies of its kind.

The satire by Swift targeting the English landowners in Ireland in the 18th Century is believed to be scathing for the victim. But the "proposal" was a publication and there is no record on how the victims reacted. Our second example documents a feud between the *Times* and the *New Yorker* editors over the style of writing, and the parody produced tangible results. For background information, I use an article by Hendrik Hertzberg, published in *The New Yorker* (2/21 and 28, 2000: 232), which is short enough to cite in its entirety and is a piece of parody in its own right.

(31) Today almost forgotten is *Time*style, overheated method of newswriting by which, in Roaring Twenties, Turbulent Thirties, Time sought to put mark on language of Shakespeare, Milton. Featured in adjective-studded *Time*style were inverted syntax (verbs first, nouns later), capitalized compound epithets (Cinemactor Clark Gable, Radiator H. V. Kaltenborn), astounding neologisms (rescued from Asiatic obscurity were Tycoon, Pundit & Mogul, oft-used still by newshawks, newshens), sometime omission of definite, indefinite articles, ditto final "and"s in series except when replaced by ampersands. Utterly unlike *Time*style was *New Yorker* style. Relied latter heavily then, relies it still on grammatical fanaticism, abhorrence of indirection, insistence on comma before final "and" in series. Short, snappy were *Time*'s paragraphs. Long, languid were *The New Yorker*'s.

> Inevitable, then that feud would develop between pompous, Yaleducated *Time* Co-Founder Henry Robinson Luce and profane, brush-haired, Aspen-born *New Yorker* Founding Editor Harold Wallace Ross. Fired in 1934 was feud's first shot: long, catty piece on Ross, *New Yorker* in Lucenterprise *Fortune*. Came Ross's riposte two years later, via devastating Wolcott Gibbs profile of Luce. Weapon of choice: *Time*style itself. Read Profiler Gibbs's choicest jibe: "Backward ran sentences until reeled the mind". Concluded piece: "Where it all will end, knows God!" (Recognized by cognoscenti: inversion of favorite Rossexpletive: "God knows".) Wounded went Luce to Ross's apartment for long, boozy evening of complaint & mollification. Thus was hatchet buried, albeit in jut-jawed, beetle-browed skull of Tycoon Luce and latter's A.O.L-destined magazinempire. (Hertzberg 2000)

In other words, due to the differences in style, the cross-town rival magazines – two of the most influential and long-lasting magazines in the U.S. – developed a feud, particularly between the co-founder of one and the co-founding editor of the other. *Time* fired the first shot. *The New York*'s Wolcott Gibbs fired back two years later with a parody profile of Ross. The "weapon of choice" is the inverted construction in English, a defining feature of *Time* style. According to Chen (2003: 248), In the 4,500-word long text, there are 51 full verb inversions (e.g., "In came the unicorn"), 12 quotation inversions (e.g., "said he"), three subject-auxiliary inversions (e.g., "Never have I seen a unicorn"), two inversions without fronting ("protested Tycoon Baruch that..."), and three structures in which the predicate comes before the subject without a verb ("most brilliant he", "handicapped he").

The overkill is also qualitative, as seen below.

(32) Twenty months after commencement, in the city room of Paper-killer Frank Munsey's *Baltimore News*, met again Luce, Hadden.

(33) Published *Time* in first six months of 1936, 1,590 pages.

(34) Strongly contrasted from the outset of their venture were Hadden, Luce.

(35) In 1952, when *Time* moved its offices to Cleveland, bored, rebellious was Editor Hadden.

(36) Although in 1935 Fortune made a net profit of $500,000, vaguely dissatisfied was Editor Luce.

(Quoted in Chen 2003: 259–264)

And – imagine being the butt of the following parodied inversions:

(37) "Great word! Great word!", would crow Hadden, coming upon "snaggle-toothed", "pig-faced". Appearing already were such maddening coagulations as "cinemaddict", "radiorator". Appearing also were first gratuitous invasions of privacy. Always mentioned as William Randolph Hearst's "great & good friend" was Cinemactress Marion Davies, stressed was the bastardy of Ramsay MacDonald, the "cozy hospitality" of Mae West. Backward ran sentences until reeled the mind.

The reasons why some of these inversions are "odd" English while others are plainly ungrammatical do not concern us here. What is relevant is the effects of the parody: by absurdly overusing inversion and inventing ones which lie outside the boundaries of language's acceptability (hence producing a prose that is obtuse and difficult to understand), the parody turned out to be devastating, as Hertzberg recounts above, for the target – a magazine that prided itself for its clear style. MacDonald (1960: 338) documented the consequence: the profile "made Luce so furious he meditated some terrible journalistic revenge, such as a 'take-out' piece in *Time* about Harold Ross", then editor of *The New Yorker*. Hertzberg seems to know more about what actually happened: the wounded Luce went to Ross' apartment "for [a] long, boozy evening of complaint and mollification".

8.5.3 Parody for amusement and satire

The first of our parody for amusement and satire example is closer to home. In 1982, Michael Swan and Catherine Walter published an article in *ELT Journal* entitled "The use of sensory deprivation in foreign language teaching".
In the abstract, the authors write:

> This article gives a detailed account of a methodology of language teaching which, though as yet not fully developed, has already aroused a lot of interest. The authors take the reader through the various stages of the method, and end with suggestions for those who wish to try it out informally in classroom settings before investing in the expensive hardware.
> (Swan and Walters 1982: 183)

In terms of structure, the publication resembles a real research article, with expected headings and rhetorical moves per Swales' CARS model of academic writing as we discussed in detail in Section 6.2.2. But in the Methodology section, one reads that language students

> [. . .] are taken to their individual SD [sensory deprivation] chambers . . . each containing a bath in which the water is kept at a constant temperature of 37° C – blood heat.
>
> (Swan and Walter 1982: 184)

After about three to five hours of sensory deprivation in the chamber, the students begin to hallucinate in the second language (L2) input they heard before entering the chamber. However, they find it difficult to communicate because "each subject has attached his own private hallucination-generated meanings ("H-meanings") to the L2 elements that he has internalized" (Swan and Walter 1982: 184). The critiquing intention of the authors is obvious. Bex (1996), for instance, argues that the parody is meant to be satirical, poking fun at the "the dangerous faddishness" (Bex 1996: 235) where eccentric and trendy methods often come and go (Hyon 2018: 168). Those who were familiar with the state of affairs of the time would likely agree with Swan and Walters: the 1970s does seem to be a time in which the field was in a flux, with teaching methods frequently promoted and soon forgotten.

On the other hand, the satirical intent of the parody is delivered in a way that is "more collegial fun than bite", as observed by Hyon (2018: 168). Granted, the "article" imitates elements of a research article expected of a publication in the journal, with English language teaching practitioners as its targeted audience in both structure and diction (e.g., "input", "communicate", "L2", "meanings", and "internalized"). But the authors warn their audience from the start (Note ". . .before investing in the expensive hardware") and display their parodic intention explicitly early on the second page. This is very different from Jokal Hoax discussed in Section 8.2 and Jonathan Swift's "A Modest Proposal" discussed above. The authors seem to be telling their readers to have fun while at the same time be aware of the absurdity the trend in the profession might lead to.

The second set of examples of parody for amusement and satire come from the late-night talk shows in the U.S. Such shows are generally structured around humorous monologues about the day's news, guest interviews, comedy sketches' and music performances. The competition in the genre is fierce: there are at least thirteen shows in the country[103] at the time of writing trying to keep the audience from grabbing the remote control. So, the image of self has existential significance for both the host and the media outlet they represents. Further, one key element of these shows is to poke fun at others: it could be guests or anyone else who happens to be headlined in the day's news. This gives late-night shows the second motivation: to mock the target of its parodic act. For a detailed analysis

---

103 The most popular, at the time of writing, are The Late Show with Stephen Colbert (CBS), Jimmy Kimmel Live! (ABC), The Tonight Show Starring Jimmy Fallon (NBC), and Conan (CBS).

of the many aspects of these shows, I refer the reader to Fonseca, Pascual, and Oakley (2020): *The Daily Show with Jon Stewart* (1999–2015, Comedy Central).

Below, we analyze instances of late-night shows taken from Saturday Night Live, a show that includes television sketches. Example (38) is a parody of a press conference given by Sean Spicer (cast Melissa McCarthy) in the early days of Donald Trump's presidency.[104]

(38) *Sean Spicer:* Good afternoon. [yelling] Settle down! Settle down! Settle down! Before we begin, I know that myself and the press have gotten off to a rocky start. [cheers and applause] Alright! Alright! alright! alright! In a sense, when I say rocky start, I mean it in the sense of "Rocky" the movie because I came out here to punch you in the face. And also, I don't talk so good. So, I'd like to begin today by apologizing on behalf of you, to me for how you have treated me in the last two weeks. And that apology is not accepted. Coz I'm not here to be your buddy. I'm here to swallow gum, and I'm here to take names.

The White House press secretary is portrayed as a crass, rough-talking, and rude individual. He complains about how he has been treated while ignoring the fact that he has created an antagonistic environment for the journalists himself. He declares he is there to swallow the journalists and to backlist them. But these are not street-fight jibes or sports trach talks. They are exaggerations of the past behavior of the press secretary. Although Sean Spicer had been on the job for only about a couple of weeks by the time this show was aired, he had already shown his penchant to lie about the most verifiable facts (e.g., Trump's 2017 inauguration crowd was the "biggest ever" while it was much smaller than Obama's[105]), his unwillingness to acknowledge his mishaps, and his caustic style that deviates from norms expected of a spokesperson of the highest office in the U.S. Also should be noted is the fact that, by then, the person he worked for – Donald Trump – had already declared that press was "the enemy of the people", which is the reason why his character on stage says "Coz I'm not here to be your buddy. I'm here to swallow gum, and I'm here to take names". In a word, the cold open presented above parodies Spicer not by inventing facts but by stretching facts to the point of absurdity and ideocracy.

---

104 https://snltranscripts.jt.org/17/sean-spicer-press-conference-melissa-mccarthy.phtml (accessed 6 February 2021).
105 https://time.com/5088900/sean-spicer-screwed-up-inauguration-hitler/ (accessed 7 February 2021).

The sketch continues:

(39) Sean Spicer: Okay, we'll do a couple of questions. Go, Glen Flush, New York Times.
Boo, go ahead.
Glen Flush: Yeah, I wanted to ask about the travel ban on Muslims?
Sean Spicer: It's not a ban.
Glen Flush: I'm sorry?
Sean Spicer: It's not a ban. The travel ban is not a ban which makes it not a ban.
Glen Flush: But you just called it a ban.
Sean Spicer: Because I'm using your words. You said ban. You said ban, now I'm saying ban.
Glen Flush: The president tweeted and I quote, "If the ban were announced with a one-week notice–"
Sean Spicer: [interrupting] Yeah, exactly. You just said that. He's quoting you. It's your words. He's using your words when you used the words and he uses them back, it's circular using of the word and that's from you. Seriously, Glen, are you going to start with me right out of the gate? I mean, what do you want? Me to take my nuts out so you can get a better kick at them?
Glen Flush: Okay. You had to have known that I would ask that question.

The exchange between the press secretary and a reporter about the travel ban that Trump had put in place on January 31, 2017 has factual basis. In the days after the first executive order was issued, Sean Spicer objected to the characterization of the executive order as a "travel ban": "It's not a Muslim ban. It's not a travel ban", Spicer told reporters. "It's a vetting system to keep America safe".[106] However, Trump himself referred to the executive order as a "travel ban". One of his tweets, for example, says "People, the lawyers and the courts can call it whatever they want, but I am calling it what we need and what it is, a TRAVEL BAN"![107] The performance of the actors in Example (39), therefore, only amplifies the reality, not invent it. The biting effects result.

The next Saturday Night Live example came on December 2020. By then, Donald Trump had lost the 2020 election, but he and his allies continued to

---

[106] https://thehill.com/homenews/administration/317144-spicer-trump-executive-order-not-a-travel-ban
[107] https://www.newsweek.com/sean-spicer-no-travel-ban-trump-insists-ban-tweets-620848

argue, both in the media and in court, that the election had been stolen from him. Featured prominently in Trump's effort to overturn the election was Rudy Giuliani, his personal lawyer.

(40) Colin Jost: Hi. Yeah. I get it. Hi, Rudy. Thanks so much for being here.
Rudy Giuliani: Yeah. Good times. Did you see my press conference today? It was at the Four Seasons. Fancy.
Colin Jost: Yeah. It sounds fancy but it was at a landscaping company called Four Seasons. Was that a mistake?
Rudy Giuliani: What? No. Anyway, I'm glad I made it to the show on time because first I went to 30 rocks. That's a granite quarry in new Rochelle. What a night.
Colin Jost: Okay. Rudy. So, the president said he will be mounting some legal challenges to a lot of the votes out there. What is your strategy to do that?
Rudy Giuliani: Okay. Listen, man. I got tons of strategies, okay? First, we're going to throw out bogus mail in ballots. Colin, these ballots, they could be coming from Mars.
Colin Jost: Right. Yes. That is a real thing that you really did say.
Rudy Giuliani: That's right. So, we're going to demand that we look at all the names. If the name is Meatthorpe Zandar and the address is Mars, we're gonna get those ballots thrown out. Plus, we got no idea if they really are ballots. They might be tortillas. We're going to eat them and see if they're tortillas. If my butt blows after I eat it, you know that's a tortillas.
Colin Jost: That sounds like a great process. Now, your team, they want to get more poll watchers in there to make sure they're counting is happening correctly.
Rudy Giuliani: Exactly. We're going to go in there. We're going to get our poll watchers so close, we're going to get this close. [Rudy Giuliani climbs on Colin Jost's chair] See? This is legally close. Nuts on back, that's where a poll watcher au to be.[108]

Once again, we observe the amplification of facts. In Section 7.3, we alluded to the Four Seasons Landscape Company where Giuliani had just had his press conference, a dreary locale with a porn shop in its vicinity but was mistaken to be the

---

[108] https://snltranscripts.jt.org/2020/weekend-update-rudy-giuliani-on-trumps-election-lawsuits.phtml (accessed 6 February 2021).

hotel that bears the same name. When the supposed interviewer, Colin Jost, asks him, the former New York major denies the mistake but instead calls the place "fancy". Further exaggeration of Giuliani's outlandish claims about election ballots is seen in his assertion that some of the ballots "might be tortillas". How to know they are tortillas? Giuliani has an answer: "We're going to eat them and see if they're tortillas. If my butt blows after I eat it, you know that's a tortillas". When the "interview" moves to allow the poll watchers to be close to the ballot counting officials, Giuliani climbs onto the chair of the interviewer to demonstrate how close he wants the poll watchers to be and declares that "This is legally close", poking fun at his lawyer status.

In this section on parody, we have looked at parody in terms of MMP. Parodies for amusement are demonstrated to be motivated by the interactional need to enhance the public image of both other and self. Parody for satire is motivated by the interactional need to hurt the image of other (the victim) and to enhance the image of self, which may be further motivated by the transactional need for effectiveness. Parody for amusement and satire is an in-between category via which the parodist aims at "hitting two birds with one-stone", taking advantage of the NLU to deliver a biting message as well as to entertain the audience.

8.6 Lies

Lying has been a topic of investigation for scholars in a variety of disciplines. Social scientists, particular sociologists and psychologists, for example, inform us that, in terms of prevalence, while Americans self-report telling an average of close to two lies a day, sixty percent of subjects reported telling no lies at all, and almost half of all lies are told by only 5% of subjects. In other words, if self-reporting is a reliable source of data, "most lies are told by a few prolific liars" (Serota, Levine, and Boster 2009: 21). We, too, have evidence that the general public has a "truth-bias", meaning that the default position we take when judging the truthfulness of what others say is truth, not falsity (Street and Richardson 2014). Developmentally, there is evidence that lying is acquired by children in early childhood and the ability to lie is correlated with the acquisition of perspective-taking, theory of mind, and communication skills (Vasek 1986; see Knapp 2008: 91–116 for a summary discussion of lying and development). As the child reaches adolescence, lying skills are perfected, but the acceptance of lying declines in early adulthood (Jensen et al. 2004).

Lying at the heart of lies is the issue of definition. In the above cited studies, for example, not having an agreed upon definition have negatively affected the validity of the empirical findings. Serota, Levine, and Boster's (2009) study, for instance, is based on data asking more than 1,000 Americans to self-report whether they had lied in the previous twenty-four hours without telling them what lie means. The truth-lie judgement study by Street and Richardson (2014) did not offer a definition either. The question, then, is: "What, exactly, constitutes the concept of lying"? as asked by Arico and Fallis (2013: 790).

The most accepted definition of lies is the one that specifies two conditions: falsehood and intention. A lie is a statement that is false but made with the intention to deceive (i.e., to lead to the belief in the hearer that it is true), as seen in many studies in the literature (Augustine 1952; Bok 1999; Coleman and Kay 1983; Ford, King, and Hollender 1988; Simpson 1992; Sweetser 1987; cf, Meibauer 2014, 2016).[109] However, debates have continued. Carlson (2006: 290), for instance, provides an example of a student who, despite having openly bragged about cheating, knows that the dean (out of fear of a lawsuit) will only punish the student if he confesses. Although everyone, including the dean, knows that the student cheated – and the student knows that everyone knows that he had cheated – the student denies any wrongdoing when questioned by the dean. This would, according to the falsehood-and-deception definition, not be an act of lying. But Carson and many others (Fallis 2009; Sorensen 2007) argue it is, based on a new definition: that "you lie if and only if you warrant the truth of something that you believe to be false, and you warrant the truth if you implicitly promise, or offer a guarantee, that what you assert is true" (Carson 2006).

If we move out of the realm of language philosophy – the area in which the debate about the definition of lies has been primarily carried out – and into the realm of pragmatics, we find that the falsehood-and-deception criterion would qualify a large number of things as lies. First, some such "lies" would seem to be institutionalized. In the legal system of much of the world, a defendant can plead not guilty while being fully aware that he is. In the world of intelligence, spies say false things, with the full intention to deceive, but are these untruths the same kind of "lies" as those about dissing school by a pupil? Second, we might find ourselves saying that a dinner a colleague has cooked for us in her home is "fantastic", but we actually think otherwise (Levine, Kim, and Hamel 2010). Third, in some society (also in some communities in the U.S.), the relatives of a person with an uncurable disease are expected to not tell the sick of the truth (Coleman and Kay 1981: 37). Are they lying? Lastly, there is the Santa Claus story in many parts of the world – that Santa Claus comes through the chimney on Christmas Eve to deliver presents to children. Those who tell their children so no doubt have

---

109 But Danziger (2010) reports an interesting case whereby intentionality does not seem to be a factor in the speakers' judgment of lying. In the relevant culture – the Mopan Maya of Eastern Central America – untruth is judged solely by how the statement matches to reality.

the intention to "deceive". Is the Sant Claus story a lie? (See Turner, Edgley, and Olmstead 1975 for similar observations).

Societies and communities seem to be aware of these and other socially sanctioned intentional untruths. The term *white lies* in English appears to be designed for some of these intentional untruths (Camden, Motley, and Wilson 1984). The same have been observed about speakers in languages other than English. Zhang (2008), for instance, discusses *shanyi huangyan* 'well-meant lies' in Chinese. Brown (2002) relates untruth with the need to be indirect in the Tzeltal of Mexico, arguing that in a given culture there may be different attitudes to individual responsibility for the untruth of statements. Hardin (2010: 3200–3201) speaks of "justifiable lies" and reviews the literature to show that untruth is allowed in many cultures and religions. In addition, there is a sizeable literature on "deception" in close relationships such as with parents and romantic partners (Cole 2001; Metts1989), adding to the complexity of lying.

What would MMP say about lies, then? More accurately, what motivates a lie, given that lying is considered to be a morally reprehensible act? Morality is closely related to public image. To be viewed as a liar is a loss to the public image. But what if one is put in a position in which to tell the truth will incur greater cost to the self-image? It seems that in such a situation, a choice has to be made, and it would not be surprising for one to choose the lesser of the two evils: lying.

This view, which will be expanded later in the section, is in fact consonant with some of the theories in the literature. Bok's (1999) principle of veracity is a case in point. According to Bok, the moral culpability associated with deception creates an initial imbalance in the assessment of truth vs. untruth, as the latter requires justification whereas the former does not. As a result, untruth is generally employed as a tactical or strategic option of last resort or path of least resistance (McCornack 1997). Similarly, Hample (1980) and Metts (1989) categorize motives for deception in terms of benefit. Hample proposes that deception motives can be categorized by whether it primarily benefits the self, other, or the relationship between the self and other.

There is also empirical evidence for the MMP account of lies. Two studies will be discussed below in this respect: one by Chen, Hu, and He (2013) and the other by Levine, Kim, and Hamel (2010)

In Chen, Hu, and He (2013), my colleagues and I asked American and Chinese college students to rate the lie-likeness of nine scenarios that belonged to four groups. The first group includes untruths that are meant to be seen through: a metaphor (S1. *Doll:* telling a three-year old girl "You are such a doll") and a joke (S6. *Spelling:* A professor saying "I was just checking your spelling" after misspelling a word on board). It is important to point out that, in cases like these, the untruth teller has a vested interest in the hearer's seeing through the untruth of the assertion, as metaphor or joke would fail if taken literally.

The second group of scenarios – S2, S3, and S4 – involve untruth for politeness. Both S2 (*Dinner:* Telling the host that the dinner is "very good" but thinking otherwise) and S3 (*Movie:* A young woman ejecting invitation to a movie by falsely claiming that she has a paper due) contain untruth for the sake of others' positive politeness, as to say falsely that a dinner is nice (S2) and to decline an invitation with a false excuse are both done for the purpose of saving the hearer's positive face – the want to be liked, respected, and appreciated (Brown and Levinson 1987). In S4 (*Business*), the speaker blames his business failure on external circumstances while he is fully aware that the failure is due to his own doing. It thus represents self-politeness, that the speaker tells an untruth in order to save his own face (Chen 2001).

Thirdly, we selected two scenarios that involve untruth with the intent to benefit the hearer. The first is the aforementioned Santa Claus scenario (S8, *Santa*) and the second is about a parent falsely telling a young child, "Doughnuts make people sick" (S9, *Doughnuts*) as a reason not to allow the child to eat doughnuts.

The last group of scenarios are the ones in which false assertions are made for the purpose of benefiting self (and hurting others). S5 (*Fraud*) uses the real-life Wall Street Bernie Madoff story that he took money from investors, telling them that their funds would be invested in the market. But in reality, he kept the money in his own accounts and paid these investors high interests with money he got from new investors, to whom he would tell the same story. S7 (*Funeral*) is about a homeless person getting money via a false assertion about a non-existent funeral.

For all these scenarios, we asked our survey respondents to rate the lie-likeness of the assertion in each scenario on a 0-to-5 scale and their moral objection to that untruth, also on a 0-to-5 scale. Once the English version was decided upon, we translated it into Chinese. The translation is not the exact semantic equivalent of the English version: we altered a few things so that the scenarios would be more accessible and familiar to the Chinese group. First, all the original (Anglo-) names were rendered into Chinese names, including Bernie Madoff. Second, we slightly altered the episode of a couple of scenarios. In S7, the English version is about a homeless person coming to the door, asking for money to pay for his daughter's funeral.[110] The Chinese version, instead, is about a woman on the street, begging for money to pay her husband's funeral.

The results of these two surveys (N=70 in both group) on lie-likeness is presented in Figure 8.3. While we see that the two groups – Americans and Chinese –

---

[110] An anonymous reviewer comments that this scenario "might be considered particularly invasive" for Americans, as "a person's home is his/her property". We agree. We doubt, however, that the offensiveness of the homeless in the scenario would cause our American correspondents to rate his untrue statement any differently.

exhibit differences in their rating of the lie-likeness of the nine scenarios, the overall pattern is similar. That is, both groups view untruth for self-benefit as the most lie-like. Untruth for other-politeness (S3 and S2) follows. The second similarity is that the two groups converge on the least lie-like scenario: S1, indicating that the untruth that is intended to be seen through is the least lie-like.

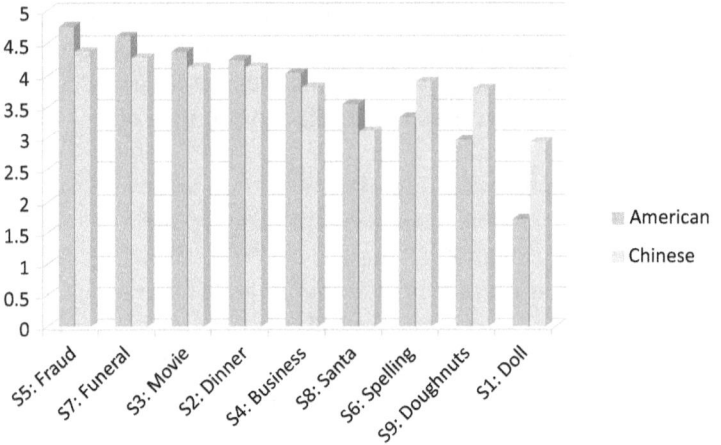

Figure 8.3: Lie-likeness.

Regarding the second question of the survey, the two groups again converge on the overall patterns in the rating of objectionability of the nine scenarios. That is, the more the untruth benefit the self, the more objectionable it is rated. The less the untruth is meant to be concealed, the less objectionable it is rated.

Based on these findings, we proposed the following definition of lying:

(41) Lying is a speech act that
    a. presupposes the semantic untruth of an assertion, p, and
    b. displays various degrees of lie-likeness depending on
        i. the extent to which the speaker intends to conceal the untruth of p from the hearer (Other things being equal, the more the speaker intends to conceal the untruth of p, the more lie-like p is);
        ii. the extent to which p benefits self and/or hurts other (Other things being equal, the more p benefits self, the more lie-like it is); or
        iii. the extent to which p benefits other (Other things being equal, the more p benefits other, the less lie-like it is).

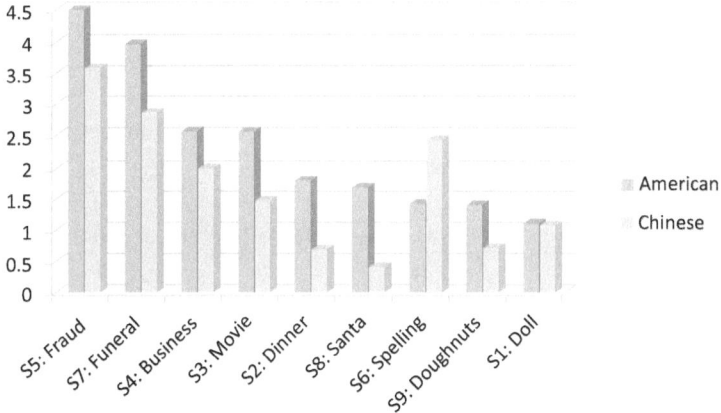

Figure 8.4: Objectionability.

The parts of this definition that lend support to MMP is b.i. and b.ii. both of which rest on the distinction between self and other. The interactional motivation of MMP, as is recalled from Chapter 2, Figure 2.2, includes two lower-level motivations: to establish, maintain, and/or enhance the public image of other and to establish, maintain, and enhance the public image of self. The fact that raters in the study are found to use benefiting self as one of the most important criteria for their judgement of lie-likeness indicates that the motivation for telling a lie is the need to protect self-image.

It is also interesting to see objectionability of lies being closely aligned with the notions of self and other. Comparing Figure 8.3 and Figure 8.4, we find that, at the macro-level, the more lie-like the untruth, the more objectionable it is to both group of raters. In other words, both Americans and Chinese base their moral judgement on whether an act is performed with self's or other's image/interest in mind, i.e., untruths that benefit other are more acceptable than untruths that benefit self.

We move to Levine, Kim, and Hamel (2010), who report three experiments to test Bok's principle of voracity that people lie for a reason. In the first experiment, the authors provided subjects (university students) two versions of each of six situations. We use the situation involving the quality of a friend's cooking by way of example. In one version, there is no motive to deceive (42); in the other, there is (43).

(42) You're having dinner at a friend's house. You hate the food. They say, "I hope you like the food. I spent all afternoon cooking. How do you like it?"

(43) You're having dinner at a friend's house. You love the food. They say, "I hope you like the food. I spent all afternoon cooking. How do you like it?"

The researchers then asked the subjects to choose between two options to respond to each of the versions. For the dinner situation, the options are:

(44) It was kind of you to invite me over and put so much effort into preparing the food, but it is not one of my favorites.

(45) I think the dinner is fantastic. This is one of the best home-cooked meals I have ever had.

If one were to be truthful – saying what one feels about the food – one would choose (44) for (42) and (45) for (43). However, while all subjects chose (45) for (43), saying the food is good while they indeed love it, only 12.5% of them chose (44) for (42); the rest, 87.5% chose (45) instead. The pattern holds for the rest of the six situations (Levine, Kim, and Hamel 2010: 275) and for the second experiment, which we omit.

The authors' third experiment was designed to determine whether cheaters would be more likely to lie than non-cheaters. The subjects were provided the opportunity to win cash awards. Some of them cheated for that purpose while others did not. The "interrogation" phase of the study asked the subjects to tell if they had cheated. The result is that "60% of the cheaters lied, whereas no non-cheaters did so" (Levine, Kim, and Hamel 2010: 281). The following is the authors' conclusion of all three experiments.

> It is proposed here that there exists a set of motives that guide most human behavior. People want to self-enhance and feel good about themselves. People self-present and want to be seen in a favorable light by others. People do not want to needlessly hurt others, and are disinclined to threaten others' face. . ... However, situations are sometimes such that the truth thwarts goal attainment. In these situations, people tacitly or actively consider deceit, and deceit is more or less probable depending on the importance of the goal, the difficulty of goal attainment absent deceit, and the probability of avoiding detection.
> (Levine, Kim, and Hamel 2010: 284)

Although the expressed purpose of Levine, Kim, and Hamel's (2010) experiments is to test Bok's (1999) principle of voracity, the findings and conclusions of the study provide concrete support for MMP. In other words, since truth is assumed in communication and valued in society, we default to truth-telling for clarity – one of the two transactional motivations – and for the maintenance of self-image, as being a truth teller is both easier (no need to justify or remember) and is awarded (truth-telling can be picked out as a positive trait). However, there are times when we are put in a position to make a choice – where the default of truth-telling comes into conflict with other motivations – we would make our decisions on an estimate of cost and benefit to other- or self-image. In cases where an untruth is estimated to be beneficial to other-image and incur no cost to or benefit self-image, we would readily tell "white lies", such as telling a terminally-ill loved one that he is going to recover, saying that a colleague has had a nice haircut while the haircut is less than desirable, or declare that we are at fault for a mishap so as to free a friend from trouble. In cases where the untruth will benefit self-image and not hurt other-image, we may feel justified to tell untruth, and whether we do that or not depends on our level of tolerance and specifics of the situation we are in. If we fail to show up at a meeting, some of us may simply acknowledge the negligence: "Sorry, my bad!" while others may invent a reason, such as the stock excuse of having had a flat tire. The kind of meeting seems to be relevant as well. It is plausible to assume that the same person might make different choices depending on whether the meeting is a casual chat over a brown-bag lunch, a job interview, or a date with a potential romantic partner. If – lastly – the concealed untruth will benefit self *and* hurt other, most of us will surely opt to truth-telling. But there are always a few among us to do the opposite. They are real liars and will be judged as such, as Chen, Hu, and He's (2013) investigation demonstrates.

8.7 Further notes

In this section, I aimed to show how MMP can provide a coherent account of a group of non-literal language uses. First, these NLUs, as a group, were seen as being capable of meeting multiple motivation needs. They can help the speaker to establish camaraderie with the hearer as well as establish, maintain, and/or enhance the image of the speaker herself by appearing creative and considerate. They can also be utilized to hurt the image of the hearer or a third party when demanded by other transactional and/or interactional needs. Then we zeroed in on three types of NLUs: irony, parody, and lie and discussed the different uses of them in different discourse contexts. In this concluding section, I make two additional notes.

First, while we did not discuss other types of NLUs, it seems that MMP is capable of accounting for them in the same vein. Hyperbole, for instance, seems to fulfill both the transactional and the interactional needs. When we say "Everyone knows that", the hyperbole helps us to strengthen our point that the validity of *that* is beyond dispute (cf, Colston, and Keller 1998; Norrick 2004). Interactionally, in certain groups of teenagers in the U.S., hyperbole is a routine form of verbal taunting. *Yo mama* jokes, for example, inflict insult on the hearer's mother (e.g., "Yo mama's so fat, when she fell I didn't laugh, but the sidewalk cracked up") by frontally attacking her weight, appearance, or intelligence. However, these hyperboles are not meant to hurt but to establish camaraderie and show creativity. Innuendo (Fraser 2001), on the other hand, seems to be motivated by the need to protect the image of self via implication. Since what is conveyed by an innuendo is often negative, not saying it but allow it to get to the hearer through understating, implying, insinuating, or otherwise suggesting offers the benefit of appearing polite and, if needed, the benefit of plausible deniability.

The second note is about the relationship between NLUs and genre. The non-literalness of NLUs entails that these uses are necessarily ambiguous and/or vague. This obscurity of meaning will lead to greater processing efforts (Sperber and Wilson 1986) and misunderstanding, which might be the reason for the limited appearance of NLUs in genres which value clarity. For instance, there does not seem to be a lot of irony in business letters, nor parody in official documents such as memos, financial reports, or peace treaties. Instead, NLUs are found to be heavily concentrated in genres that value effectiveness of the transactional motivations and both of the interactional motivations (Figure 2.2). In the genres of literature – particularly poetry – advertisements, and religious sermons, for instance, clarity is not the major consideration. We do not go to poetry to get a clear message; we know that an advertisement wants us to buy the product it promotes and, if we are regular church goers, we would be quite clear about the central message our pasters have for us week after week. In these genres, therefore, the transactional motivation of the speaker/writer is effectiveness: whether and how much she can make herself "heard".

To make oneself "heard" can be achieved through a variety of means. NLUs, as we saw in the beginning of the chapter, have the capability of aiding the speaker to build camaraderie with the audience and to enhance her public image. They, too, can be "weaponized" to attack the audience if necessary. These are interactional motivations in MMP, ones that exist for their own right; they also assist the effectiveness of the transactional.

To say that NLUs favor some genres more than others does not mean that they are absent in everyday interactions among the common folk. On the contrary, they can be as prevalent in these "ordinary" contexts. However, a moment's reflection would tell us that ordinary speakers are not "equal" in their uses of NLUs: some of us are better at NLUs than others and we use them more in some contexts than others. I know no research linking the use of NLUs with personality or social context, but suspect that the eventual findings of such future studies would lend further support for MMP.

Afterword

Advancing a theoretical model for as diverse a field as pragmatics is no doubt a risky exercise. To appear over-ambitious is not the worry. The anticipated criticism of MMP is more likely to come from the philosophical assumption upon which the proposal is made. The Afterword is therefore the "last defense": that such a model is needed in the first place.

As can be gleaned from the brief history of pragmatics in Chapter 1, there are two major stages in the life of pragmatics. The first stage was theory building. Pioneered by Oxford ordinary language philosophers, researchers joined what can be truly called a "movement" to bring factors outside language into the study of it. By the end of the 1980s, most of theories that have guided the field till this day had been constructed, including theories of speech acts by Austin and Searle, of conversational implicature by Grice, of politeness by Brown and Levinson and by Leech, and of relevance by Sperber and Wilson. These are classics. They led the way and gave rise to other theories.

The second stage in the development of pragmatics commenced a few years later and has lasted till this day. This stage is the stage of diversification, of zeroing in, and of branching out. Diversification took place on several dimensions. In terms of the coverage of languages and cultures, we have reason to take pride in the fact that a great many languages have been brought into our attention than was the case only a few decades ago. In terms of the kind of discourse we investigate as a field, one is encouraged to find research on virtually anything one wishes to look into. The zeroing in part of this stage is seen in the way researchers examine language use, that is, we are far better today than yesterday to demonstrate the granular details of a linguistic reality. Much of this development should be credited to conversation analysts. Coming from the ethnographic tradition, these trailblazers offered pragmatics a breath of fresh air (in the late 1970s) and then set the field on fire. Their works provided practitioners a set of tools to analyze how meaning is made (by both the speaker and hearer) and how social interactions are conducted via the slight rising of the intonation, an almost unnoticeable deepening of the voice, a twitch on the face, or the movement of the body – things that had long been unjustifiably ignored. Finally, the branching out of the field is seen in both the influence pragmatics has been exerting and in its interaction with other, sister disciplines not only inside linguistics but also outside: social sciences, anthropology, communication, media studies, cultural studies, literary studies – you name it.

This second stage of pragmatics seem to have led to an undercurrent – in some cases, an open cry – against the search for deeper explanations of surface linguistic realities. Classical theories have been dubbed EuroAmerican-centric; rationality has been blacklisted; meaning is said to be always fluid; values are believed to be relative; top-down is bad, bottom up is good. Avery one of these beliefs makes sense in some way, but few can withstand scrutiny. A moment's reflection would make us realize the unintended consequences of some of these beliefs. It is true that rationality, as a mode of human thought, has been "discovered" by scholars in Europe, but that does not necessarily mean that rationality is a feature of *only* Western thought. In other words, to argue against rationality just because it was first proposed by the Europeans – "a bunch of dead white men", as remarked by a colleague during a lunch at a conference – is not much different from arguing against the solar calendar just because it was first developed by the Egyptians.

The belief that there is no stability in meaning may be just as a tad too sweeping. If we believe that meaning is entirely fluid, there would be little need for much of linguistics. It is true that a linguistic unit can be used to mean a multitude of things in different discursive contexts, it is equally true that there is always a core semantic element in that unit that *enables* speakers to mean different things in different contexts. The same is observed in specific areas of investigation. In identity studies, it is vogue to demonstrate how identity emerges from the dynamic unfolding of discourse, but often the identity that ends up being constructed is found to be related to – and sometimes simply *is* – the category identity the constructor desires to achieve or break away from.

The trend I am discussing here has emerged against a larger intellectual backdrop of postmodernism, a school of thought that seems to have made its way into many strands of pragmatics. Postmodernism and its sister schools of thought – multiculturalism and social constructionism – came into being as a reaction to hegemony and power, with the good intention to champion for the underrepresented and to promote social justice, the sort of belief that most if not all of us (me surely included) are oriented toward. But I am beginning to feel that we have not given enough examination to our beliefs. In Chapter 4, for instance, I demonstrated the prevalence of the Different Position – that East and West do not have the same politeness – in the East-West debate. To emphasize difference is popular; to hint at the possibility of universalism is a sign of intellectual naivety (and may be treated as an ideological and intellectual outcast).[111] But is it wise to have the undoubtedly valid dictum "Every culture is different" to always be the driver of our research? Cultures *are* different from each other, and it would be

---

[111] There is anecdotal evidence that a submission to a journal written in the universalist orientation is met with more rejection than one in the opposite approach.

foolish to think otherwise. But so are Californians vs. their neighbors in Nevada; so are the cities in California; so are the different ethnic groups in one city; so are the different families in one ethnicity; so are the different members of a family, and – finally – so are identical twins, as not any two human beings are exactly alike, nor the same human being in all situations. We should study differences and we have. But could it be possible that our emphasis on differences have led us a bit too far away from the other equally valid pursuit: to look for commonality. There must be something we all share, something that transcends the boundaries among us either as groups or as individuals.

The emphasis on fluidity, on specificity, and on difference has given rise to a distrust – and complete rejection by a few of us – of theories that seek to account for fluidity with stable notions, to generalize from specifics, and to seek commonality from differences. There are theories galore in recent decades, but most of them are anti-theories: arguing against theories that attempt to seek deeper principles. This suspicion is not helpful, I argue. For without theories that seek generality, commonality, and deeper reasons for surface phenomena, we may stand to miss things. What we have accumulated in the literature will continue to look like an ever-growing list of unrelated items. The prospect of gaining the sight of the forest will be delayed because we are too busy spending time *inside* it, examining each tree with a magnifying glass. As long as we keep talking about how different we all are, we are dimming the prospect of discovering what binds us. There appears to be an irony here. On the one hand, we know that disagreeing is less preferred than agreeing. On the other, we seem to be relentless in pursuing differences – the very source of disagreement.

About theorists. There seems to be the assumption that those who propose theories do so via introspection in an armchair (call it *a*). Therefore, what they end up saying may be detached from reality (call it *b*). However, *a* does not necessarily lead to *b*. The validity of a theory should depend on the testing of it. The speech act theory could be said to be the result of introspection by Austin and his student Searle; the conversational implicature theory, the product of introspection by Grice; and the universal theory of politeness, by Brown and Levison. But they have been repeatedly shown to be among the most useful despite decades' worth of critique (and frontal attack by a few of us). So, to cast aide a theory purely because it is a result of introspection may not be the wisest we can do for – and *to* – ourselves.

Furthermore, even *a* may not always be true, i.e., a theory that seems to be proposed based on introspection may be more apparent than real. MMP, a theory advanced in this monograph, for instance, is not proposed merely (or even chiefly) through introspection. It is the result of research conducted by colleagues in the past four decades, an abstraction of concrete findings by scholars who are cited as well as many more who are not. It is now proposed in part because there is sufficient literature for the proposer to summarize, to generalize, and eventually to theorize. Introspection has no doubt played a part, but possibly no greater a part than in other, more empirical studies.

References

Abbamonte, Lucia. 2008. Scientific communication and authorial identities in cognitive neuroscience handbooks. *Linguistica e Filologia* 27. 59–76.
Ahmad, Ummul K. 1997. Research article introductions in Malay: Rhetoric in an emerging research community. In Anna Duszak (ed.), *Culture and styles of academic discourse*, 273–303. Berlin: Mouton de Gruyter.
Aisulu, Kulbayeva. 2020. Balancing power and solidarity through indirectness: A case study of Russian and Kazakh meeting chairs. *Journal of Politeness Research* 16(2). 159–191.
Alderfer, Clayton. 1989. Theories reflecting my personal experience and life dent. *The Journal of Applied Behavioral Science* 25(4). 351–365.
Allen, Rachel. 2018. Dialogues in diachrony: Celebrating historical corpora of speech-related texts. *Journal of Historical Pragmatics* 19(2). 167–185.
Amos, H. Will. 2020. English in French commercial advertising: Simultaneity, bivalency, and language boundaries. *Journal of Sociolinguistics* 24(1). 55–74.
Arico, Adam J. & Don Fallis. 2013. Lies, damned lies, and statistics: An empirical investigation of the concept of lying. *Philosophical Psychology* 26(6). 790–816.
Arnovick, Leslie K. 1999. *Diachronic pragmatics: Seven case studies in English illocutionary development*. Amsterdam & Philadelphia: John Benjamins.
Arundale, Robert. 2013. Face as a research focus in interpersonal pragmatics: Relational and emic perspectives. *Journal of Pragmatics* 58. 108–120.
Arvay, Anett & Gyula Tanko. 2004. A contrastive analysis of English and Hungarian theoretical research article introductions. *Iral* 42(1). 71–100.
Asfaha, Yonas Mesfun. 2020. Multilingual language policy discourses and superdiversity at the peripheries: exploring language policy and practice in Eritrea. *Journal of Multicultural Discourses* 15(4). 404–421. DOI: 10.1080/17447143.2020.1771346
Asher, Nicholas. 2004. Discourse Topic. *Theoretical Linguistics* 30(2–3). https://doi.org/info:doi/
Atkinson, J. Maxwell & Paul Drew. 1979. *Order in court*. London: Macmillan.
Attardo, Salvatore. 1994. *Linguistic theories of humor*. New York: Mouton de Gruyter.
Attardo, Salvatore. 2000. Irony as relevant inappropriateness. *Journal of Pragmatics* 32. 793–826.
Attardo, Salvatore. 2001. *Humorous texts: A semantic and pragmatic analysis*. New York: Mouton de Gruyter.
Augustine. 1952. Lying (M. Muldowney, Trans.). In Roy Deferrari (ed.), *Treatises on various subjects*, 53–120. New York: Catholic University of America.
Austin, John L. 1962. *How to do things with words*. Cambridge, MA: Harvard University Press.
Baicchi, Annalisa. 2011. The caused-motion construction from the perspective of the lexical-constructional model. In Klaus-Uwe Panther and Günter Radden (eds.), *Motivation in grammar and the lexicon*, 149–169. Amsterdam: John Benjamins.
Barcelona, Antonio. 2000. On the plausibility of claiming a metonymic motivation for conceptual metaphor. In Antonio Barcelona (ed.), *Metaphor and metonymy at the crossroads*, 31–58. Berlin & New York: Mouton de Guyter.
Barcelona, Antonio. 2002. Clarifying and applying the notions of metaphor and metonymy within cognitive linguistics. In Rene Dirven and Ralph Pörings (eds.), *Metaphor and metonymy in comparison and contrast*, 207–278. Berlin & New York: De Gruyter.
Barcelona, Antonio. 2003. *Metaphor and metonymy at the crossroads: A cognitive perspective*. Berlin: De Gruyter.

Bardovi-Harlig, Kathleen. 2010. Exploring the pragmatics of interlanguage pragmatics: Definition by design. In Anna Trosborg (ed.), *Pragmatics across languages and cultures*, 219–260. Berlin: De Gruyter Mouton.

Bardovi-Harling, K., K. B. Hartford, R, Mahan-Taylor, M. J. Morgan & D. W. Reynolds. 1991. Developing pragmatic awareness: Closing the conversation. *ELT journal* 45(1). 4–15.

Barron, Anne & Klaus Schneider. 2005. Irish English: A focus on language in action. In Anne Barron and Klaus Schneider (eds.), *The pragmatics of Irish English*, 3–15. Berlin: De Gruyter Mouton.

Barron, Ann, Yueguo Gu & Gerard Steen (eds.). 2018. *The Routledge handbook of pragmatics*. New York: Routledge.

Bateson, Gregory. 1972 [1955]. A theory of play and fantasy. In: Gregory Bateson (ed.), *Steps to an ecology of mind*, 177–193. San Francisco: Chandler.

Bazerman, Charles. 1994. Systems of genres and the enactment of social intentions. In Freeman Aviva and Peter Medway (eds.), *Genre and the new rhetoric*, 79–101. London: Taylor and Francis.

Beebe, Leslie. 1995. Politeness fictions: Instrumental rudeness as pragmatic competence. In James E. Alatis, Carolyn A. Straehle, Brent Gallenberger, & Maggie Ronkin (eds.), *Linguistics and the education of language teachers: Ethnolinguistic, psycholinguistics, and sociolinguistics aspects*, 154–168. [Georgetown University Round Table on Language and Linguistics]. Washington, DC: Georgetown University Press.

Bella, Spyridoula & Amalia Moser. 2018. What's in a first? The link between impromptu invitations and their responses. *Journal of Pragmatics* 125(02). 96–110.

Bella, Spyridoula & Eva Ogiermann. 2019. An intergenerational perspective on (im)politeness. *Journal of Politeness Research* 15(2). 163–193.

Bergmann, Merrie. 1991. Metaphorical assertion. In Steven Davis (ed.), *Pragmatics*, 485–494. Oxford: Oxford University Press.

Berry, Margaret, Geoff Thompson, and Hilary Hillier. 2014. Theme and variations. In María de los Ángeles Gómez González, Francisco José Ruiz de Mendoza Ibáñez, and Francisco Gonzálvez-García (eds.), *Theory and practice in functional-cognitive space*, 107–126. Amsterdam: John Benjamins.

Bess, Fed H. & Larry E. Humes. 2008. *Audiology: The fundamentals*. Philadelphia: Lippincott Williams & Wilkins.

Bex, Tony. 1996. Parody, genre and literary meaning. *Journal of Literary Semantics* 25. 225–244.

Bhatia, Tej K. 2019. Emotions and language in advertising. *World Englishes* 38(3). 435–449.

Bhatia, Vijay & Aditi Bhatia. 2011. Legal discourse across cultures and socio-pragmatic contexts. *World Englishes* 30(4). 481–495.

Bhatia, Vijay & Paola Evangelisti Allori (eds.). 2011. Discourse and identity in the professions: Legal, corporate, and institutional citizenship. Bern: Peter Lang.

Biber, Douglas, Stig Johansson, Geoffrey Leech, Susan Conrad & Edward Finegan. 1999. *Grammar of spoken and written English*. London: Longman.

Blakemore, Diane, 1988. "So" as a constraint on relevance. In Ruth Kempson (ed.), *Mental representations: The interface between language and reality*, 183–195. Cambridge: Cambridge University Press.

Blitvich, Pilar Garcés-Conejos & Maria Sifianou. 2019. (Im)politeness and discursive pragmatics. *Journal of Pragmatics* 145. 91–101.

Blommaet, Jan. 2005. *Discourse: A critical approach*. Cambridge: Cambridge University Press.

Bloomfield, Leonard. 1933. *Language*. New York: Holt, Rinehart and Winston.

Blum-Kulka, Shoshana & Elite Olshtain. 1984. Requests and apologies: A cross-cultural study of speech act realization patterns (CCSARP). *Applied Linguistics* 5(3). 196–213.

Blum-Kulka, Shoshana, Juliane House & Gabriele Kasper (eds.). 1989. *Cross-cultural pragmatics: Requests and apologies*. Norwood, NJ: Ablex Publishing Corporation.

Bok, Sissela. 1999. *Lying: Moral choice in public and private life*. New York: Vintage.

Bolden, Galina B. 2006. Little words that matter: Discourse markers "so" and "oh" and the doing of other-attentiveness in social interaction. *Journal of Communication* 56(4). 661–688.

Bolden, Galina B. 2008. "So what's up?": Using the discourse marker "so" to launch conversational business. *Research on Language & Social Interaction* 41(3). 302–327.

Bolden, Galina B. 2009. Implementing incipient actions: The discourse marker "so". *Journal of Pragmatics* 41(5). 974–998.

Booth, Wayne C. 1974. *A rhetoric of irony*. Chicago: Chicago University Press.

Booth, Wayne C. 1983. *The rhetoric of fiction*. 2nd edn. Chicago: Chicago University Press.

Bou-Franch, Patricia & Pilar Garcés-Conejos Blitvich (eds.). 2019. *Analyzing digital discourse: new insights and future directions*. Cham, Switzerland: Palgrave Macmillan.

Bousfield, Derek. 2008. *Impoliteness in Interaction*. Amsterdam: Benjamins.

Bousfield, Derek. 2010. Researching impoliteness and rudeness: issues and definitions. In Miriam Locher & Sage Lambert Graham (eds.), *Interpersonal pragmatics*, 101–134. Berlin: De Gruyter.

Bousfield, Derek & Mariam Locher. 2008. Impoliteness in language: Studies on its interplay with power in theory and practice. Berlin: Mouton de Gruyter.

Brandsford, John D. & Marcia K. Johnson 1973. Considerations of some problems of comprehension. In William G. Chase (ed.), *Visual information processing*, 383–438. New York: Academic Press.

Brinton, Laurel J. 1998 "The flowers are lovely; only, they have no scent": The evolution of a pragmatic marker in English. In Raimund Borgmeier, Herbert Grabes & Andreas H. Jucker (eds.), *Historical pragmatics: Anglistentag 1997 Gießen Proceedings*, 9–33. Trier: Wissenshaftlicher Verlag Trier.

Brinton, Laurel J. 2001. Historical discourse analysis. In Deborah Schiffrin, Deborah Tannen & Heidi E. Hamilton (eds.), *The Handbook of discourse analysis*, 138–160. Oxford: Blackwell.

Brinton, Laurel J. 2006. Pathways in the development of pragmatic markers in English. In Ans van Kemenade & Bettelou Los (eds.), *The handbook of the history of English*, 307–334. New Jersey: Wiley-Blackwell.

Brinton, Laurel J. 2008. The comment clause in English: Syntactic origins and pragmatic developments. Cambridge: Cambridge University Press.

Broadbent D. E. 1958. *Perception and communication*. Oxford, England: Pergamon

Brockway, Diane. 1981. Semantic constraints on relevance. In Herman Parret, Marina Sbisa & Jef Verschueren (eds.), *Possibilities and limitations of pragmatics: Proceedings of the Conference on Pragmatics, Urbino July 8–14, 1979*, 57–78. Amsterdam: John Benjamins.

Brown, Gillian & George Yule. 1983. *Discourse analysis*. Cambridge: Cambridge University Press.

Brown, Penelope. 2002. Everyone has to lie in Tzeltal. In Shoshana Blum-Kulka & Catherine E. Snow (eds.), *Talking to adults: The contribution of multiparty discourse to language acquisition*, 241–275. Mahwah, NJ: Lawrence Erlbaum Associates.

Brown, Penelope & Stephen Levinson. 1978. Politeness: Politeness phenomena. Some universals in language usage. In Esther Goody (ed.), *Questions and answers: Strategies in social interaction*, 56–311. Cambridge: Cambridge University Press.

Brown, Penelope & Stephen Levinson 1987. *Politeness: Some universals in language usage*. Cambridge: Cambridge University Press.

Brown, Roger & Albert Gilman. 1989. Politeness theory and Shakespeare's four major tragedies. *Language in Society* 18(2). 159–212.

Bucholtz, Mary. 2009. From stance to style. In Alexandra Jaffe (ed.), *Stance: Sociolinguistic perspectives*, 146–170. Oxford: Oxford University Press. DOI: 10.1093/acprof:oso/9780195331646.001.0001

Bucholtz, Mary & Kira Hall. 2004. Language and identity. In Alessandro Duranti (ed.), *A companion to linguistic anthropology*, 369–394. Oxford: Blackwell.

Bucholtz, Mary & Kira Hall. 2005. Identity and interaction: A sociocultural linguistic approach. *Discourse Studies* 7(4&5). 585–614.

Bucholtz, Mary & Kira Hall. 2008. Finding identity: Theory and data. *Multilingua* 27(1&2). 151–163.

Bucholtz, Mary & Kira Hall. 2010. Locating identity in language. In Carmen Llamas and Dominic Watt (eds.), *Language and identities*, 18–28. Edinburgh: Edinburgh University Press.

Burton, Noel. 1989. *The limits to debate: A revised theory of semantic presupposition*. (Cambridge studies in linguistics 51). Cambridge: Cambridge University Press.

Butler, Judith. 1990. *Gender Trouble: Feminism and the subversion of identity*. New York: Routledge.

Buysse, Lieven. 2012. So as a multifunctional discourse marker in native and learner speech. *Journal of Pragmatics* 44. 1764–1782.

Cai, Dongman & Alice Deignan. 2019. Metaphors and evaluation in popular economic discourse on trade. In Ignasi Navarro i. Ferrando (ed.), *Current approaches to metaphor analysis in discourse*, 57–78. Berlin: De Gruyter.

Camden, Carl, Michael T. Motley & Ann Wilson. 1984. White lies in interpersonal communication. *Western Journal of Speech Communication* 48. 309–325.

Carson, Thomas L. 2006. The definition of lying. *Nous* 40. 284–306.

Carson, Thomas L. 2010. *Lying and deception*. New York, NY: Oxford University Press.

Carter, Ronald. 2016. *Language and creativity: The art of common talk*. 2nd edn. London: Routledge.

Carter, Ronald & Michael McCarthy. 2004. Talking, creating: Interactional language, creativity and context. *Applied Linguistics* 25(1). 62–88.

Cedar, Payung. 2006. Thai and American responses to compliments in English. *The Linguistics Journal* 1. 6–28.

Chang, Peichin & Mary Schleppegrell. 2011. Taking an effective authorial stance in academic writing: Making the linguistic resources explicit for L2 writers in the social sciences. *Journal of English for Academic Purposes* 10(3). 140–151.

Chang, Wei-Lin Melody and Michael Haugh. 2011. Evaluations of (im)politeness of an intercultural apology. *Intercultural Pragmatics* 8(3). DOI: 10.1515/iprg.2011.019

Charolles, Michel. 2020. Discourse topics and digressive markers. *Journal of Pragmatics* 161. 57–77. https://doi.org/10.1016/j.pragma.2020.01.005.

Charteris-Black, Jonathan. 2005. *Politicians and rhetoric: The persuasive power of metaphor*. Houndmills: Palgrave MacMillan.

Chen, Rong. 1990. *Verbal irony as conversational implicature*. Muncie, IN: Ball State University dissertation.

Chen, Rong. 1991. Book notice on *The limits to debate: A revised theory of semantic presupposition* (Noel Burdon, Cambridge University Press). *Language* 67(1). 170–171.

Chen, Rong. 1993a. Responding to compliments: A contrastive study of politeness strategies between American and Chinese speakers. *Journal of Pragmatics* 20. 49–75.

Chen, Rong. 1993b. Conversational implicature and poetic metaphor. *Language and Literature* (Trinity University, Texas) 1993. 53–74.
Chen, Rong. 1995. Communitive Dynamism and word order in Mandarin Chinese. *Language Sciences* 17(2). 201–222.
Chen, Rong. 1996a. Food-plying and Chinese politeness. *Journal of Asian and Pacific Communication* 7(3 & 4). 143–155.
Chen, Rong. 1996b. Conversational implicature and characterization in Reginald Rose's *Twelve Angry Men*. *Language and Literature* (Poetics and Linguistics Association) 5(1). 31–47.
Chen, Rong. 2001. Self-politeness: A proposal. *Journal of Pragmatics* 33. 87–106.
Chen, Rong. 2003. English inversion: A Ground-before-Figure construction. [Cognitive Linguistics Research 25]. Berlin & New York: Mouton de Gruyter.
Chen, Rong. 2005. Universalism vs. particularism: whither pragmatics? *Foreign Languages Studies* 28(2). 122–128.
Chen, Rong. 2010a. Compliment and compliment response research: A cross-cultural survey. In Anna Trosborg (ed.), *Pragmatics across languages and cultures*, 79–101. Berlin & New York: Mouton de Gruyter.
Chen, Rong. 2010b. Pragmatics between East and West: Similar or different? In Anna Trosborg (ed.), *Pragmatics across Languages and Cultures*, 167–188. Berlin & New York: Mouton de Gruyter.
Chen, Rong. 2010c. WATER networks, the Chinese radical, and beyond. *International Journal of Cognitive Linguistics* 1(2). 91–115.
Chen, Rong. 2019a. Complementing cognitive linguistics with pragmatics and vice versa: Two illustrations from Chinese. In Dingfang Shu, Hui Zhang & Lifei Zhang (eds.), *Cognitive linguistics and the study of Chinese*, 207–223. Amsterdam: John Benjamins.
Chen, Rong. 2019b. Identity studies and identity construction: Insights from Donald J. Trump's (un)presidentiality. *Pragmatics and Cognition* 26(2&3). 386–413.
Chen, Rong. 2020. Single-author self-reference: Identity construction and pragmatic competence. *Journal of English for Academic Purposes* 45. 1–14.
Chen, Rong. 2022. Figure and Ground: A linguistic universal. In Thomas Fuyin Li (ed.), *Handbook of cognitive semantics*. Leidon: Netherlands: Brill.
Chen, Rong. 2023. Why impolite? *East Asian Pragmatics* (forthcoming).
Chen, Rong & Chunmei Hu. 2020. End-of-dinner food offering: A three-way contrastive study. *Contrastive Pragmatics* 1. 242–269.
Chen, Rong & Dafu Yang. 2010. Responding to compliment in Chinese: Has it changed? *Journal of Pragmatics* 42. 1951–1963.
Chen, Rong & Dafu Yang. 2022. The identity of modesty in Chinese academic writing. *Pragmatics and Society* (forthcoming).
Chen, Rong & Forest Houlette. 1990. Towards a pragmatic account of irony. *Language and Style* 23(1). 29–37.
Chen, Rong & Sunny Hyon. 2007. Faculty evaluation as a genre system: Negotiating intertextuality and interpersonality. *Journal of Applied Linguistics* 2(2). 153–184.
Chen, Rong & Xiaoxia Hu. 2020. "Be suicided": The innovative *bei* construction in Chinese. *Cognitive Semantics* 5. 248–271.
Chen, Rong & Xinren Chen (eds.). 2020. Identity under Construction: Evidence from Chinese. *East Asian Pragmatics*. [Special Issue].
Chen, Rong, Chunmei Hu & Lin He. 2013. Lying between English and Chinese: An intercultural study. *Journal of Intercultural Pragmatics* 10(3). 375–401.

Chen, Rong, Lin He & Chunmei Hu. 2013. Chinese requests: In comparison with American English and Japanese and with reference to the "East-West divide". *Journal of Pragmatics* 55. 140–161.

Chomsky, Noam. 1957. *Syntactic structure*. Berlin & New York: Mouton de Gruyter.

Chovanec, Jan. 2012. Conversational humor and joint fantasizing in online journalism. In Jan Chovanec & Isabel Ermida (eds.), *Language and humour in the media*, 139–61. Newcastle: Cambridge Scholars.

Clark, Herbert H. & Adrian Bangerter. 2004. Changing ideas about reference. In Ira Noveck and Dan Sperber (eds.), *Experimental pragmatics*, 25–49. New York: Palgrave Macmillan.

Clark, Herbert H. & Susan Haviland. 1975. *Comprehension and the given-new contract*. School of Social Sciences, University of California, Irvine.

Clark, Herbert H. & Richard J. Gerrig. 1984. On the pretense theory of irony. *Journal of Experimental Psychology, Gernal* 113. 121–126.

Cole, Tim. 2001. Lying to the one you love: The use of deception in romantic relationships. *Journal of Social and Personal Relationships* 18(1). 107–129.

Coleman, Linda & Paul Kay. 1981. Prototype semantics: The English word *lie*. *Language* 57. 26–44.

Colston, Herbert L. & Shauna B. Keller. 1998. "You'll never believe this": Irony and hyperbole in expressing surprise. *Journal of Psycholinguistic Research* 27(4). 499–513.

Conboy, Martin. 2014. Exploring the language of the popular in American and British newspapers 1833–1988: Introduction. *Journal of Historical Pragmatics* 15(2). 159–164.

Cook, Guy. 1988. Stylistics with a dash of advertising. *Language and Style* 21(2). 151–161.

Cook, Guy. 1989. *Discourse*. Oxford: Oxford University Press.

Cordella, Marisa, Heather Large & Veronica Pardo. 1995. Complimenting behavior in Australian English and Spanish speech. *Multilingua* 14(3). 235–252.

Côté, James. 2006. Identity Studies: How close are we to develop a social science of identity – an appraisal of the field. *Identity: An International Journal of Theory and Research* 6(1). 3–25.

Coulmas, Florian. 1992. Linguistic etiquette in Japanese society. In Richard Watts, Sachiko Ide & Konrad Ehlich (eds.), *Politeness in Language: Studies in Its History, Theory, and Practice*, 299–323. Berlin: Mouton de Gruyter.

Coulthard, Malcolm. 1985. *An introduction to discourse analysis*. 2nd edn. Harlow: Longman.

Crisp, Peter. 2001. Allegory: Conceptual Metaphor in History. *Language and Literature* 10. 5–19.

Culpeper, Jonathan. 1996. Towards an anatomy of impoliteness. *Journal of Pragmatics* 25(3). 349–367

Culpeper, Jonathan. 2011. *Impoliteness: Using language to cause offence*. Cambridge: Cambridge University Press.

Culpeper, Jonathan. 2012. (Im)politeness: Three issues. *Journal of Pragmatics* 44. 1128–1133.

Culpeper, Jonathan & Jane Demmen. 2011. Nineteenth-century English politeness: Negative politeness, conventional indirect requests and the rise of the individual self. *Journal of Historical Pragmatics* 12(1–2). 49–81.

Culpeper, Jonathan, Jim O'Driscoll & Claire Hardaker. 2019. Notions of politeness in Britain and North America. In Eva Ogiermann & Pilar Garcés-Conejos Blitvich (eds.), *From speech acts to lay understandings of politeness: Multilingual and multicultural perspectives*, 177–200. Cambridge: Cambridge University Press.

Cummings, Michael. 2003. The role of Theme and Rheme in contrasting methods of organization of texts. In Christopher S. Butler, María de los Ángeles Gómez González & Susana M. Doval-Suárez (eds.), *Dynamics of language use: Functional and contrastive perspectives*, 129–154. Amsterdam & Philadelphia: John Benjamins.

Dahl, Roald. 1964. *Charlie and the chocolate factory*. New York: Alfred A. Knopf.
Daikuhara, Midori. 1986. A study of compliments from a cross-cultural perspective: Japanese vs. American English. *Penn Working Papers in Educational Linguistics* 2. 23–41.
D'Andrade, Roy G. & Claudia Strauss (eds.). 1992. *Human motives and cultural models* Vol. 1. Cambridge: Cambridge University Press.
Daneš, Frantisek. 1974. Functional sentence perspective and the organization of the text. e77906168e3025b7198c5000bb22114d6998.pdf (accessed 28 December 2020)
Danziger, Eve. 2010. On trying and lying: Cultural configurations of Grice's Maxim of Quality. *Intercultural Pragmatics* 7. 199–219.
Danziger, Roni. 2018. Compliments and compliment responses in Israeli Hebrew: Hebrew university in Jerusalem students in interaction. *Journal of Pragmatics* 124. 73–87.
Davidson, Donald. 1991. What metaphors mean. In Steven Davis (ed.), *Pragmatics*, 495–506. Oxford: Oxford University Press.
Davies, Bethan. 2018. Evaluating evaluations: what different types of metapragmatic behavior can tell us about participants' understandings of the moral order. *Journal of Politeness Research* 14. 121–151.
Davis, Joseph. 2008. Moral order. *Culture* 2(1). 17.
Davis, Steven. 1991. Introduction. In Steven Davis (ed.), *Pragmatics: A reader*. Oxford: Oxford University Press.
De Fina, Anna. 2007. Code switching and the construction of ethnic identity in a community of practice. *Language in Society* 36. 371–392.
De Fina, Anna. 2010. The negotiation of identities. In Miriam A. Locher & Sage L. Graham (eds.), *Interpersonal pragmatics*, 205–224. Berlin: Mouton de Gruyter.
De Fina, Anna, Deborah Schiffrin & M. Bamberg. 2006. *Discourse and identity*. Cambridge: Cambridge University Press.
Demjén, Zsofia. 2016. Laughing at cancer: Humor, empowerment, solidarity and coping online. *Journal of Pragmatics* 101. 18–30.
Derrida, Jacques. 1997. *Sokal et Bricmont ne sont pas sérieux* [Sokal and Bricmont are not serious]. *Le Monde*, 17 November, 1997.
Dik, Simon. 1989. The theory of functional grammar. Part I: The structure of the clause. Dordrecht: Foris Publications.
Docherty, Thomas. 2019. Political English: Language and decay of politics. Boomsbury.
Dongil, Shin & Eunhae Cho. 2020. Discursive conflicts in news media and the suspension of a government-led test of English in Korea. *Language Testing in Asia* 10(1). doi:http://dx.doi.org.libproxy.lib.csusb.edu/10.1186/s40468-020-00100-7.
Donnellan, Keith. 1966. Reference and definite descriptions. *Philosophical Review* 15(3). 281–304.
Downing, Angela. 1991. An alternative approach to theme: A systemic-functional perspective. *Word* 42(2). 119–143.
Downing, Angela. 2000. Talking Topically. In Angela Downing, A. Jesús Moya Guiljarro & J. I. Albentosa Hernandez (eds.), *Talk and text: Studies in written and spoken discourse*, 31–50. Cuenca: Universidad de Castilla-La Mancha.
Du Bois, John W. 2007. The stance triangle. In Robert Englebretson (ed.), *Stance taking in discourse: subjectivity, evaluation, interaction*, 139–182. Amsterdam: John Benjamins.
Dueñas, P. 2007. "I/we focus on. . .": A cross-cultural analysis of self-mentions in business management research articles. *Journal of English for Academic Purposes* 6(2). 143–162.
Dynel, Marta. 2008. No aggression, only teasing: The pragmatics of teasing and banter. *Lodz Papers in Pragmatics* 4(2). 241–261.

Dynel, Marta. 2009. beyond a joke: Types of conversational humour. *Language and Linguistics Compass* 3(5). 1284–1299. https://doi.org/10.1111/j.1749-818X.2009.00152.x
Dynel, Marta. 2013. When does irony tickle the hearer? Towards capturing the characteristics of humorous irony. In Marta Dynel (ed.), *Developments in linguistic humor theory*, 298–320. Amsterdam: John Benjamins.
Dynel, Marta. 2017. But seriously: On conversational humour and (un)truthfulness. *Lingua* 197. 83–102.
Dynel, Marta. 2018a. Deconstructing the myth of positively evaluative irony. In Manuel Jobert & Sandrine Sorlin (eds.), *The pragmatics of irony and banter [Linguistic Approaches to Literature 30]*, 41–57. Berlin: John Benjamins.
Dynel, Marta. 2018b. *Irony, deception and humour: Seeking the truth about overt and covert untruthfulness*. Berlin: Mouton de Gruyter.
Dynel, Marta. 2020. On being roasted, toasted and burned: (meta)pragmatics of Wendy's twitter humor. *Journal of Pragmatics* 166(09). 1–14.
Dynel, Marta. 2021. COVID-19 memes going viral: On the multiple multimodal voices behind face masks. *Discourse & Society* 32(2). 175–195.
Dynel, Marta & Fabio I. M. Poppi. 2018. In tragoedia risus: Analysis of dark humor in post-terrorist attack discourse. *Discourse & Communication* 12(4). 382–400.
Eelen, Gino. 2001. *A critique of politeness theories*. Manchester: St. Jerome Publishing.
Er, Ibrahim. 2020. The Voiceless in *the Voice*: A Multimodal critical discourse analysis. *Text & Talk* 40(6). 705–732.
Erikson, Eric H. 1968. *Identity: Youth and crisis*. New York: Norton.
Ervin-Tripp, S. 1979. Children's verbal turn-taking. In E. Ochs and B. B. Schieffelin (eds.), *Developmental pragmatics*, 391–414. New York: Academic Press.
Escandell-Vidal, Victoria, 1996. Towards a cognitive approach to Politeness. *Language Sciences* 180(4). 629–650.
Eslami, Zohreh R. 2005. Invitations in Persian and English: Ostensible or genuine? *Intercultural Pragmatics* 2(4). 453–480.
Eslami, Zohreh R., Nasser Jabbari & Li-Jen Kuo. 2015. Compliment response behavior on Facebook: A study with Iranian Facebook users. *International Review of Pragmatics* 7(2). 244–277.
Eubanks, Philip. 1999. Conceptual metaphor as rhetorical response: A reconsideration of metaphor. *Written Communication* 16(2). 171–199.
Evans, Vyvyan. 2005. *The structure of time*. Amsterdam: John Benjamins.
Fairclough, Norman. 1989. *Language and power*. London: Longman
Fairclough, Norman. 1992. *Discourse and social change*. Cambridge: Polity Press
Fairclough, Norman. 1995. *Critical discourse analysis*. London: Longman
Fallis, Don. 2009. What is lying? *Journal of Philosophy* 106. 29–56.
Farghal, Mohammed & Madeline Haggan. 2006. Compliment behavior in bilingual Kuwaiti college students. *International Journal of Bilingual Education and Bilingualism* 9(1). 94–118.
Farghal, Mohammed & Mahmoud A. Al-Khatib. 2001. Jordanian college students' responses to compliments: A pilot study. *Journal of Pragmatics* 33(9). 1485–1502.
Fauconnier, Gilles and Mark Turner. 2002. *The way we think*. New York: Basic Books.
Fernández, Eliecer Crespo. 2011. Euphemistic conceptual metaphors in epitaphs from Highgate Cemetery. *Review of Cognitive Linguistics* 9(1). 198–225.
Firbas, Jan. 1962. The function of the sentences in the act of communication. *SPFFBU* 11A. 133–148.

Firbas, Jan. 1974. Some aspects of the Czechoslovak approach to the problems of functional sentence perspective. In Frantisek Daneš (ed.), *Papers on functional sentence perspective*, 106–128. Prague: Academia.
Firbas, Jan. 1992. *Functional sentence perspective in written and spoken communication.* Cambridge: Cambridge University Press.
Fischer, Kerstin (ed.). 2006. *Approaches to discourse particles.* Amsterdam: Elsevier.
Fong, Mary. 1998. Chinese immigrants' perceptions of semantic dimensions of direct/indirect communication in intercultural compliment interactions with North Americans. *The Howard Journal of Communications* 9(3). 245–262.
Fonseca, Paula, Esther Pascual & Todd Oakley. 2020. "Hi, Mr. president!": Fictive interaction blends as a unifying rhetorical strategy in satire. *Review of Cognitive Linguistics* 18(1). 180–212.
Ford, Charles V., Bryan H. King & Marc H. Hollender. 1988. Lies and liars: Psychiatric aspects of prevarication. *American Journal of Psychiatry* 145. 554–562.
Foucault, Michel. 1976/1984. *History of sexuality* [3 vols]. New York: Pantheon Books.
Fowler, Roger, Bob Hodge, Gunther Kress & Tony Trew. 1979. *Language and Control.* New York: Routledge.
Fraser, Bruce. 1990. Perspectives on politeness. *Journal of Pragmatics* 14(2). 219–236.
Fraser, Bruce. 1999. What are discourse markers? *Journal of Pragmatics* 31(7). 931–952.
Fraser, Bruce. 2001. An account of innuendo. In István Kenesei & Robert M. Harnish (eds.), *Perspectives on Semantics, Pragmatics, and Discourse: A Festschrift for Ferenc Kiefer.* [*Pragmatics & Beyond New Series 90*], 321–336. Amsterdam: John Benjamins.
Frege, Gottlob. 1990 [1892]. On sense and nominatum. In A.P. Martinich (ed.), *The philosophy of language*, 2nd edn., 190–202. Oxford: Oxford University Press.
Fukada, Atsushi & Noriko Asato. 2004. Universal politeness theory: Application to the use of Japanese honorifics. *Journal of Pragmatics* 36(11). 1991–2002
Fukushima, Saeko. 2000. *Requests and culture: Politeness in British English and Japanese.* Bern: Peter Lang.
Fukushima, Saeko. 2011. A cross-generational and cross-cultural study on demonstration of attentiveness. *Pragmatics* 21(4). 549–571.
Fukushima, Saeko. 2019. A metapragmatic aspect of politeness with a special emphasis on attentiveness in Japanese. In Eva Ogiermann & Pilar Garcés-Conejos Blitvich (eds.), *From speech acts to lay understandings of politeness: Multilingual and multicultural perspectives*, 226–249. Cambridge: Cambridge University Press.
Fukushima, Saeko & Sifianou, Maria. 2017. Conceptualizing politeness in Japanese and Greek. *Intercultural Pragmatics* 14(4). 525–555.
Gachigua, Sammy Gakero. 2016. Conceptual metaphor of the nation-state in newly-independent Africa: Kenyatta's regime state-as-a-family metaphor in Kenyan parliamentary discourse. *Linguistics & the Human Sciences* 12(2&3). 223–242.
Gajaseni, Chansongklod. 1995. *A contrastive study of compliment responses in American English and Thai including the effect of gender and social status.* Urbana-Champaign: University of Illinois dissertation.
Gao, Hong. 1999. Features of request strategies in Chinese. *Working Papers* 47. 73–86. Lund University.
Garver, Eugene. 2009. Aristotle on the Kinds of Rhetoric. *Rhetorica: A Journal of the History of Rhetoric* 27(1). 1–18. doi:10.1525/rh.2009.27.1.1.

Gee, James Paul. 2005. *An introduction to discourse analysis*, 2nd edn. New York & London: Routledge.
Ghaleb, Rabab'ah & Fowler Al-Hawamdeh Rose. 2020. Apologies in Arabic and English: A cross-cultural Study. *Journal of Psycholinguistic Research*. 49(6). 993–1009. DOI:10.1007/s10936-020-09723-6
Gibbs, Raymond W. 1994. *The poetics of mind: Figurative thought, language, and understanding*. Cambridge: Cambridge University Press.
Gibbs, Reymond W. 2000. Irony in talk among friends. *Metaphor & Symbol* 15(1 & 2). 5–27.
Gibbs, Raymond W., Lacey Okonski & Miles Hatfield. 2013. Crazy creative metaphors: Crazy metaphorical minds? *Metaphor and the Social World* 3(2). 141–159.
Gibbs, Wolcott. 2000 [1936]. Backward ran sentences until reeled the mind. In David Remnick (ed.), *Life stories: Profiles from The New Yorker*, 339–252. New York: Random House.
Giridharadas, Anand. 2010. "Follow my logic? A connective word takes the lead". *The New York Times*, 30 May, 2010.
Givón, Talmy (ed.). 1983. *Topic continuity in discourse: A quantitative cross-language study*. Amsterdam & Philadelphia: John Benjamins.
Goffman, Erving. 1967 [1955]. On face-work. In Erving Goffman (ed.), *Interaction ritual: Essays on face-to-face behavior*, 5–45. Harmondsworth: Penguin. (Originally in *Psychiatry: Journal for the Study of Interpersonal Processes*, 18(3). 213–231).
Goffman, Erving. 1974. Frame analysis: An essay on the organization of experience. New York: Free Press.
Goffman, Erving. 1979. Footing. *Semiotica* 25(1&2) 1–30.
Golato, Andrea. 2002. German compliment responses. *Journal of Pragmatics* 34(5). 547–571.
Golato, Andrea. 2005. Compliments and Compliment Responses: Grammatical structure and sequential organization. Amsterdam: John Benjamins.
Gómez González, María de los Ángeles. 2001. *The theme-topic interface: Evidence from English*. Amsterdam: Benjamins.
Gong, Lili & Yongping Ran. 2020. Discursive constraints of teasing: Constructing professionality via teasing in Chinese entertainment interviews. *Chinese Journal of Applied Linguistics* 43(1). 64–82.
Gotti, Maurizio & Françoise Salager-Meyer. 2006. *Advances in medical discourse analysis: Oral and written*. Bern: Peter Lang.
Grainger, Karen & Sara Mills. 2016. *Directness and indirectness across cultures*. Basingstoke: Palgrave Macmillan.
Grainger, Karen, Kerkam Z. Mansor & Sara Mills. 2015. Offering and hospitality in Arabic and English. *Journal of Politeness Research* 11(1). 41–70.
Grandy, Richard E. & Richard Warner. 1986. *Philosophical grounds of rationality: Intentions, categories, ends*. Oxford: Oxford University Press.
Green, Georgia. 1989. *Pragmatics and natural language understanding*. Hillsdale, NJ: Lawrence Erlbaum.
Greenbaum, Sidney. 1996. *The Oxford English grammar*. Oxford: Oxford University Press.
Grice, H. Paul. 1957. Meaning. *The Philosophical Review* 66(3). 377–388.
Grice, H. Paul. 1969. Utterer's meaning and intention. *The Philosophical Review* 78(2). 147–177. https://doi.org/10.2307/2184179.
Grice, H. Paul. 1975. Logic and conversation. In Peter Cole & Jerry Morgan (eds.), *Syntax and Semantics 3: Speech acts*, 41–58. New York: Academic Press.

Grice, H. Paul. 1978. Further notes on Logic and Conversation. In Peter Cole (ed.), *Syntax and Semantics volume 9: Pragmatics*, 183–197. New York: Academic Press. (Reprinted in Grice 1989).
Grice, H. Paul. 1989. *Studies in the way of words*. Harvard: Harvard University Press.
Gu, Yueguo. 1990. Politeness phenomena in modern Chinese. *Journal of Pragmatics* 14. 237–257.
Hacker, P. M. S. 2004. Austin, John Langshaw (1911–1960). In *Oxford Dictionary of National Biography*. Oxford: Oxford University Press.
Hall, Stuart. 1989. Ethnicity: Identity and difference. *Radical America* 23. 9–20.
Hall, Stuart. 1996a. Introduction: who needs identity? In Stuart Hall & Paul Du Gay (eds.), *Questions of cultural identity*, 1–17. London: Sage.
Hall, Stuart. 1996b. Cultural identity and cinematic representation. In Houston A. Baker Jr., Manthia Diawara & Ruth H. Lindeborg (eds.), *Black British cultural studies: A Reader*, 210–220. Chicago: Chicago University Press.
Halliday, M. A. K. 1967. Notes on transitivity and theme in English. *Journal of Linguistics* 3. 199–244.
Halliday, M. A. K. 2003. On the "architecture" of human language. In *On language and linguistics* [Volume 3 in the Collected Works of M.A.K. Halliday]. London & New York: Equinox.
Halliday, M. A. K. 2014 [1985]. *Halliday's introduction to functional grammar*, 4th edn. London & New York: Routledge.
Halliday, M. A. K. and Ruqaiya Hasan. 1976. *Cohesion in English*. New York: Routledge.
Hample, Dale. 1980. Purpose and effects of lying. *Southern Speech Communication Journal* 46. 33–47.
Han, Chung-hye. 1992. A comparative study of compliment responses: Korean females in Korean interactions and in English interactions. *Working Papers in Educational Linguistics* 8(2). 17–31.
Hardin, Karol J. 2010. The Spanish notion of *lie*: Revisiting Coleman and Kay. *Journal of Pragmatics* 42. 3199–3213.
Harris, Sandra. 2001. Being politically impolite: extending politeness theory to adversarial political discourse. *Discourse & Society* 12(4). 451–472.
Harwood, Nigel. 2005. "Nowhere has anyone attempted... In this article I aim to do just that": A corpus-based study of self-promotional I and we in academic writing across four disciplines. *Journal of Pragmatics* 37(8). 1207–1231.
Haugh, Michael. 2005. The importance of "place" in Japanese politeness: Implications for cross-cultural and intercultural analysis. *Intercultural Pragmatics* 2(1). 41–68.
Haugh, Michael. 2007. Emic conceptualisations of (im)politeness and face in Japanese: Implications for the discursive negotiation of second language learner identities. *Journal of Pragmatics* 39(4). 657–680.
Haugh, Michael. 2013. (Im)politeness, social practice and the participation order. *Journal of Pragmatics* 58. 52–72.
Haugh, Michael. 2015. *(Im)politeness implicatures*. Berlin: De Gruyter Mouton.
Haugh, Michael. 2018. Offence, public denunciation and the blurring of public and private life. Keynote presented at the 1st International Symposium on Internet Pragmatics, Fuzhou, China, September.
Haugh, Michael & Derek Bousfield. 2012. Mock impoliteness, jocular mockery and jocular abuse in Australian and British English. *Journal of Pragmatics* 44(9). 1099–1114. https://doi.org/10.1016/j.pragma.2012.02.003

Haugh, Michael & Klaus Schneider. 2012. (Im)politeness across Englishes. *Journal of Pragmatics* [special issue] 44(9). 1017–1021.
Haugh, Michael & Wei-Lin Melody Chang. 2019. "The apology seemed (in)sincere": Variability in perceptions of (im)politeness. *Journal of Pragmatics* 142. 207–222. https://doi.org/10.1016/j.pragma.2018.11.022
Haviland, Susan E. & Herbert H. Clark. 1974. What's new? Acquiring new information as a process in comprehension. *Journal of Verbal Learning and Verbal Behavior* 13(5). 512–521.
Hawkes, Terence. 1972. *Metaphor*. London: Methuen & Co.
Hempel, Carl G. 1950. Empiricist criteria of cognitive significance: problems and changes. *Revue Internationale de Philosophie* 11. 41–63.
Herbert, Robert K. 1986. Say "thank you" – Or something. *American Speech* 61. 76–88.
Herbert, Robert K. 1989. The ethnography of English compliment responses: A contrastive sketch. In Wieslaw Oleksy (ed.), *Contrastive pragmatics*, 3–35. Amsterdam: Benjamins.
Herbert, Robert K. 1990. Sex-based differences in compliment behavior. *Language in Society* 19. 201–224.
Herbert, Robert K. 1991. The sociology of compliment work: An ethnocontrastive study of Polish and English Compliments. *Multilingua* 10(4). 381–402.
Herbert, Robert K. & Stephen Straight. 1989. Compliment-rejection versus compliment-avoidance: Listener-based versus speaker-based pragmatic strategies. *Language and Communication* 9(1). 35–47.
Heritage, John. 2003. Conversation analysis. *Annual Review of Anthropology* 19(1). 283–307.
Heritage, John. 2013. Turn-initial position and some of its occupants. *Journal of Pragmatics* 57. 331–337.
Heritage, John & Chase Wesley Raymond. 2016. Are explicit apologies proportional to the offenses they address? *Discourse Processes* 53. 5–25. DOI:10.1080/0163853X.2015.105669
Heritage, John & Geoffrey Raymond. 2012. Navigating epistemic landscapes: Acquiescence, agency and resistance in responses to polar questions. In J. P. De Ruiter (ed.), *Questions: Formal, functional and interactional perspectives*, 179–192. Cambridge: Cambridge University Press.
Heritage, John & Steven E. Clayman. 2010. *Talk in action: Interactions, identities and institutions*. Oxford: Blackwell-Wiley.
Heritage, John, Chase Wesley Raymond & Paul Drew. 2019. Constructing apologies: Reflexive relationships between apologies and offenses. *Journal of Pragmatics* 142. 185–200.
Hertzberg, Hendrik. 2000. Luce vs. Ross. *The New Yorker* 2(21) & 2(28). 232.
Highfield, Tim. 2016. News via Voldemort: Parody accounts in topical discussions on Twitter. *New Media & Society* 18(9). 2028–45.
Hill, Beverly, Sachiko Ide, Shako Ikuta, Akiko Kawasaki and Tsunao Ogino. 1986. Universals of linguistic politeness: Quantitative evidence from Japanese and American English. *Journal of Pragmatics* 10(3). 347–371.
Hindriks, Frank. 2007. The status of the knowledge account of assertion. *Linguistics and Philosophy* 30(3). 393–406.
Hirsch, Galia. 2020. Humorous and ironic readers' comments to a politician's post on Facebook: The case of Miri Regev. *Journal of Pragmatics* 164. 40–53.
Ho, Victor. 2010. Constructing identities through request e-mail discourse. *Journal of Pragmatics* 42. 2253–2261.
Hoey, Michael. 2005. *Lexical priming: A new theory of words and language*. New York: Routledge.
Holmes, Janet. 1988. Compliments and compliment responses in New Zealand English. *Anthropological Linguistics* 28. 485–508.

Hori, Motoko. 1986. A sociolinguistic analysis of the Japanese honorifics. *Journal of Pragmatics* 10(3). 373–386.

Horn, Lawrence. 1984. Toward a new taxonomy for pragmatic inference: Q-based and R-based implicature. In Deborah Schiffrin (ed.), *Meaning, form and use in context*, 11–42. Washington: Georgetown University Press.

Horn, Lawrence. 2004. Implicature. In Lawrence Horn and Gregory Ward (eds.), *Handbook of pragmatics*, 3–28. Oxford: Blackwell.

Horowitz, Donald L. 1985. *Ethnic groups in conflict*. Berkeley, CA: University of California Press.

House, Juliane. 2013. Developing pragmatic competence in English as a lingua franca: Using discourse markers to express (inter) subjectivity and connectivity. *Journal of Pragmatics* 59. 57–67.

House, Juliane & Gabriele Kasper. 1981. Politeness markers in English and German. In Florian Coulmas (ed.), *Conversational Routine*, 157–186. The Hague: Mouton.

Howe, Mary L. 1991. *Topic change in conversation*. Lawrence: University of Kansas dissertation.

Hu, Chunmei & Rong Chen. 2017. Backchannelling for positive politeness. In Xinren Chen (ed.), *Politeness Phenomena across Chinese Genres*, 229–252. Bristol, UK: Equinox.

Huang, Mei-Chen. 1996. Achieving cross-cultural equivalence in a study of American and Taiwanese requests. Urbana-Champaign: University of Illinois dissertation.

Hugly, Philip & Charles Sayward. 1979. A problem about conversational implicature. *Linguistics and Philosophy* 3. 19–25.

Huth, Thorsten. 2006. Negotiating structure and culture: L2 learners' realization of L2 compliment-response sequences in talk-in-action. *Journal of Pragmatics* 38. 2025–2050.

Hyland, Ken. 1999. Disciplinary discourses: Writer stance in research articles. In Chris Candlin and Ken Hyland (eds.), *Writing: Texts, Processes and Practices*, 99–121. London & New York: Longman.

Hyland, Ken. 2001. Humble servants of the discipline? Self-mention in research articles. *English for Specific Purposes* 20. 207–226.

Hyland, Ken. 2002. Authority and invisibility: Authorial identity in academic writing. *Journal of Pragmatics* 34. 1091–1112.

Hyland, Ken. 2004. *Genre and second language writing*. Ann Arbor: University of Michigan Press.

Hyland, Ken. 2005. Stance and engagement: A model of interaction in academic discourse. *Discourse Studies* 7(2). 173–192.

Hyland, Ken. 2008. Disciplinary voices: Interactions in research writing. *English Text Construction* 1(1). 5–22.

Hyland, Ken & Polly Tse. 2005a. Hooking the reader: A corpus study of evaluative *that* in abstracts. *English for Specific Purposes* 24(2). 123–139.

Hyland, Ken & Polly Tse. 2005b. Evaluative *that* constructions: Signaling stance in research abstracts. *Functions of Language* 12(1). 39–63.

Hyon, Sunny. 1996. Genre in three traditions: Implications for ESL. *TESOL Quarterly* 30(4). 693–722.

Hyon, Sunny. 2008. Convention and inventiveness in an occluded academic genre: A case study of retention–promotion–tenure reports. *English for Specific Purposes* 27(2). 175–192. DOI: 10.1016/j.esp.2007.07.003.

Hyon, Sunny. 2018. *Introducing genre and English for specific purposes*. London & New York: Routledge.

Hyon, Sunny & Rong Chen. 2004. Beyond graduate school, beyond the research paper. *English for Specific Purposes* 23. 233–263.

Ibáñez Ruiz de Mendoza, Francisco José & Inés Lozano-Palacio. 2019. A cognitive-linguistic approach to complexity in irony: Dissecting the ironic echo. *Metaphor and Symbol* 34(2). 127–138.

Ide, Risako. 1998. "Sorry for your kindness": Japanese interactional ritual in public discourse. *Journal of Pragmatics* 29(5). 509–529.

Ide, Sachiko. 1982. Japanese sociolinguistics: Politeness and women's language. *Lingua* 57(2–4). 357–385.

Ide, Sachiko. 1989. Formal forms and discernment: Two neglected aspects of linguistic politeness. *Multilingua* 8. 223–248.

Ide, Sachiko. 1992. On the notion of "wakimae": Toward an integrated framework of linguistic politeness. In Michiko Takeuchi (ed.), *Kotoba no mozaiku. Collection of Papers in Honor of Professor Natsuko Okuda*, 298–305. Tokyo: Mejiro Linguistic Society.

Ide, Sachiko. 2012. Roots of the *wakimae* aspect of linguistic politeness: Modal expressions and Japanese sense of self. In Michael Meeuwis & Jan-Ola Östman (ed.), *Pragmaticizing understanding*, 121–138. Amsterdam: John Benjamins.

Idemaru, Kaori, Bodo Wintre & Lucien Brown. 2019. Cross-cultural multimodal politeness: The phonetics of Japanese deferential speech in comparison to Korean. *Intercultural Pragmatics* 16(5). 517–555.

Ivanić, Rosalind. 1994. I is for interpersonal: Discoursal construction of writer identities and the teaching of writing. *Linguistics and Education* 6(1). 3–15.

Ivanić, Rosalind. 1995. Writer identity. *Prospect* 10(1). 8–31.

Ivanić, Rosalind. 1998. Writing and identity: The discoursal construction of identity in academic writing. Amsterdam: John Benjamins.

Ivanko, Stacey L., Penny M. Pexman & Kara Olineck. 2004. How sarcastic are you? Individual differences and verbal irony. *Journal of Language and Social Psychology* 23(3). 244–271.

Jacobs, Andreas & Andreas H. Jucker. 1995. The historical perspective in pragmatics. In Andreas H. Jucker (ed.), *Historical pragmatics: Pragmatic developments in the history of English*, 3–33. Amsterdam & Philadelphia: John Benjamins.

Jakobson, Roman. 1971 [1957]. *Selected Writings II: Word and Language*. The Hague: Mouton.

Janda, Laura. 2004. A metaphor in search of a source domain: The category of Slavic aspects. *Cognitive Linguistics* 15(4). 471–527.

Janney, Richard W. & Horst Arndt. 1993. Universality and relativity in cross-cultural politeness research: A historical perspective. *Multilingua* 12. 13–50.

Jaworski, Adam. 1995. "This is not an empty compliment!": Polish compliments and the expression of solidarity. *International Journal of Applied Linguistics* 5(1). 63–94.

Jensen, Lene Arnett, Jeffrey Jensen Arnett, Shirley Feldman & Elizabeth Cauffman. 2004. The right to do wrong: Lying to parents among adolescents and emerging adults. *Journal of Youth and Adolescence* 33(2). 101–112.

Johansson, Ingvar. 2003. Performatives and antiperformatives. *Linguistics and Philosophy* 26(6). 661–702.

Johnson, Alison. 2002. So. . .?: pragmatic implications of *so*-prefaced questions in formal police interviews. In Janet Cotterill (ed.), *Language in the Legal Process*, 91–110. New York: Palgrave Macmillan.

Johnson-Sheehan, Richard D. 1995. Scientific communication and metaphors: An analysis of Einstein's 1905 Special Relativity paper. *Journal of Technical Writing* 25(1). 71–83.

Jones, Rodney H. (ed.). 2016. *The Routledge handbook of language and creativity*. London: Routledge.

Jucker, Andreas H. 2008. Historical Pragmatics. *Language and Linguistics Compass* 2(5). 894–906.
Jucker, Andreas H. 2009. Speech act research between armchair, field and laboratory: The case of compliments. *Journal of Pragmatics* 41(8). 1611–1635
Jucker, Andreas H. 2012. Pragmatics in the history of linguistic thought. In Keith Allan & Kasia Jaszczolt (ed.), *The Cambridge Handbook of Pragmatics*, 495–512. Cambridge: Cambridge University Press.
Jucker, Andreas H. (ed.). 1995. *Historical pragmatics. Pragmatic developments in the history of English*. Amsterdam & Philadelphia: John Benjamins.
Jucker, Andreas H. & Irma Taavitsainen. 2008a. Apologies in the history of English: Routinized and lexicalized expressions of responsibility and regret. In Andreas H. Jucker & Irma Taavitsainen (eds.), *Speech Acts in the history of English*, 229–244. Amsterdam & Philadelphia: John Benjamins.
Jucker, Andreas H. & Irma Taavitsainen (eds.). 2008b. *Speech Acts in the History of English*. Amsterdam & Philadelphia: John Benjamins.
Jucker, Andreas H. & Irma Taavitsainen. 2010. Trends and development in historical pragmatics. In Andreas H. Jucker & Irma Taavitsainen (eds.), *Historical Pragmatics*, 3–30. Berlin & New York: De Gruyter Mouton.
Jucker, Andreas H. & Irma Taavitsainen. 2012. Pragmatic Variables. In Juan M. Hernández Campoy & J. Camilo Conde-Silvestre (ed.), *The handbook of historical sociolinguistics*, 303–317. Oxford: Blackwell.
Jucker, Andreas H. & Irma Taavitsainen. 2013. *English historical pragmatics* [Edinburgh Textbooks on the English Language]. Edinburgh: Edinburgh University Press.
Kádár, Daniel Z. 2008. Terms of (im)politeness: A study of communication properties of traditional Chinese (im)polite terms of address. *Journal of Politeness Research* 4(2). 327–330.
Kádár, Dániel Z. 2013. *Relational rituals and communication: Ritual interaction in groups*. Basingstoke: Palgrave Macmillan.
Kadar, Daniel Z. & Ling Zhou. 2020. Self-Denigration in 21st Century Chinese. *Journal of Politeness Research: Language, Behaviour, Culture*. https://doi.org/10.1515/pr-2018-0043
Kádár, Daniel Z. & Juliane House. 2020a. Revisiting the duality of convention and ritual: A contrastive pragmatic inquiry. *Poznan Studies in Contemporary Linguistics* 56(1). 83–111.
Kádár, Daniel Z. & Juliane House. 2020b. The pragmatics of ritual: An introduction. [Special issue]. *Pragmatics* 30(1). 1–14.
Kádár, Dániel Z. & Melvin de la Cruz. 2015. Rituals of outspokenness and verbal conflict. *Pragmatics & Society* 7(2). 265–290. https://pdfs.semanticscholar.org/09c9/1deb368223 20b1532d1765db0605508d91a5.pdf
Kádár, Dániel Z. & Michael Haugh. 2013. *Understanding politeness*. Cambridge: Cambridge University Press.
Kádár, Dániel Z. & Rosina Márquez-Reiter. 2015. (Im)politeness and (im)morality: Insights from intervention. *Journal of Politeness Research* 11(2). 239–260.
Kádár, Dániel Z. Vahid Parvaresh & Puyu Ning. 2019. Morality, moral order, and language conflict and aggression: A position paper. In Dániel Z. Kádár & Vahid Parvaresh (eds.), *Morality and language aggression*. [Special issue]. *Journal of Language Aggression and Conflict* 7(1). 6–31.
Kanoksilapatham, Budsaba. 2005. Rhetorical structure of biochemistry research articles. *English for Specific Purposes* 24(3). 269–292.

Karns Christina M., Elif Isbell, Ryan J. Giuliano & Helen J. Neville. 2015. Auditory attention in childhood and adolescence: An event-related potential study of spatial selective attention to one of two simultaneous stories. *Developmental Cognitive Neuroscience* 13. 53–67.

Kasper, Gabriele. 1990. Linguistic politeness: Current research issues. *Journal of Pragmatics* 14(2). 193–218.

Kasper, Gabriele & Ken Rose. 2001. *Pragmatic development in a second Language*. Oxford: Blackwell.

Kasper, Gabriele & Shonna Blum-Kulka (eds.). 1993. *Interlanguage Pragmatics*. Oxford: Oxford University Press.

Kau de Marlangeon, Silva. 2008. Impoliteness in institutional and non-institutional contexts. *Pragmatics* 18(4). 735–749.

Kecskes, Istvan. 2015. Intercultural impoliteness. *Journal of Pragmatics* 85. 43–47.

Kecskes, Istvan & Jacob Mey. 2008. *Intention, common ground, and the egocentric speaker-hearer*. Berlin: Mouton de Gruyter.

Kempton, Ruth M. 1975. *Presupposition and the delimitation of semantics*. Cambridge: Cambridge University Press.

Kertész, András & Csilla Rákosi. 2005. Remarks on the cognitive base of pragmatic principles. *Acta Linguistica Hungarica* 52(1). DOI: https://doi.org/10.1556/aling.52.2005.1.2.

Kiesling, Scott F. 2004. Dude. *American Speech* 79(3). 281–305.

Kim, Alan Hyun-Oak. 2010. 일본어 공손법 <desu/masu>의 한국어 기원에 대하여: 새로운 은유화이론의 사각에서" 이정민/ 정성여(편) 한국어 연구의 새지평. 서울:태학사. [On the Evolution of Japanese politeness marker desu/masu from old Korean sources]. In C. Lee and S-Y Chung (eds.), *New horizons of Korean language studies*, 227–283. Seoul: Thaehaksa.

Kim, Alan Hyun-Oak. 2014. アラン・ヒョンオク・キム. (2014)『メタファー体系としての敬語: 日本語におけるその支配原理』[*Grammatical encoding of politeness: A systemic metaphorization in Japanese honorifics*]. Tokyo: Akashi Shoten.

Kim, Alan Hyun-Oak. Unpublished Paper. Grammaticalization in sentence final politeness marking in Korean and Japanese. https://www.academia.edu/7657520/Grammaticalization_in_Sentence_Final_Politeness_Marking_in_Korean_and_Japanese

Kimmel, Michael. 2011. Metaphor sets in *The Turn of the Screw*: What conceptual metaphors reveal about narrative Functions. In M. Fludernik (ed.), *Beyond cognitive metaphor theory: Perspectives on literary metaphor*, 197–223. New York: Routledge.

Kitagawa, Chisato. 1980. Saying "yes" in Japanese. *Journal of Pragmatics* 4(2). 105–120.

Knapp, Mark L. 2008. *Lying and deception in human interaction*. Boston: Pearson Education.

Knoblock, Natilia. 2020. Negotiating dominance on Facebook: Positioning of self and others in pro- and anti-trump comments on immigration. *Discourse & Society* 31(5). 520–539.

Kohnen, Thomas. 2008. Linguistic politeness in Anglo-Saxon England? A study of Old English address terms. *Journal of Historical Pragmatics* 9(1). 140–158.

Kopykto, Roman. 1995a. Against rationalistic pragmatics. *Journal of Pragmatics* 23. 475–491.

Kopykto, Roman. 1995b. Linguistic politeness strategies in Shakespeare's plays. In Andreas H. Jucker (ed.), *Historical Pragmatics: Pragmatic developments in the history of English*, 515–540. Amsterdam: John Benjamins.

Koutsantoni, Dimitra. 2004. Attitude, certainty and allusions to common knowledge in scientific research articles. *Journal of English for Academic Purposes* 3(2). 163–182.

Kövecses, Zoltán. 2010. *Metaphor: A practical introduction*, 2nd edn. Oxford: Oxford University Press.

Kövecses, Zoltán. 2019. Some Consequences of a multi-level view of metaphor. In Ignasi Navarro i. Ferrando (ed.), 2019. *Current approaches to metaphor analysis in discourse*, 19–33. Berlin: De Gruyter.

Kövecses, Zoltán. 2020. A multi-level view of metaphor and some of its advantages. In Annalisa Baicchi (ed.), *Figurative meaning and construction in thought and language*, 72–88. Amsterdam: John Benjamins.

Koyama, Wataru. 2003. Discussion note: How to do historic pragmatics with Japanese honorifics. *Journal of Pragmatics* 35. 1507–1514.

Kumatoridani, Tetsuo. 1999. Alternation and co-occurrence in Japanese thanks. *Journal of Pragmatics* 31(5). 623–642.

Kuo, Chih-Hua. 1999. The use of personal pronouns: Role relationships in scientific journal articles. *English for Specific Purposes* 18(2). 121–138.

Kurzon, Dennis. 1994. Linguistics and legal discourse: An introduction. *Revue internationale de semiotique juridique* 7. 5–12.

Kwon, Winston, Rowan Mackay, Ian Clarke, Ruth Wodak & Eero Vaara. 2020. Testing, stretching, and aligning: Using "ironic personae" to make sense of complicated issues. *Journal of Pragmatics* 166. 44–58.

Labov, William. 2006 [1966]. *The social stratification of English in New York City*, 2nd edn. Cambridge: Cambridge U. Press.

Labov, William. 1969. *The study of nonstandard English*. Washington, DC: National Council of Teachers of English.

Labov, William. 1970. *Sociolinguistic patterns*. Philadelphia: University of Pennsylvania Press.

Labov, William. 2001. *Linguistic diversity in America: The politics of language change*. Charlottesville: University of Virginia Press.

Labov, William. 2012. *The Language of life and death*. Cambridge: Cambridge University Press.

Lakoff, George. 1993. The contemporary theory of metaphor. In Andrew Ortony (ed.), *Metaphor and thought*, 201–251. Cambridge: Cambridge University Press.

Lakoff, George. 2008. *The political mind*. New York: Penguin.

Lakoff, George & Mark Johnson. 1980. *Metaphors we live by*. Chicago: University of Chicago Press.

Lakoff, Robin. 1973. The logic of politeness, or minding your p's and q's. In Claudia Corum, T. & Cedric Smith-Stark (eds.), *Papers from the Ninth Regional Meeting of the Chicago Linguistic Society*, 292–305. Chicago: CLS.

Lakoff, Robin. 1977. What you can do with words: Politeness, pragmatics, and performatives. In Andy Rogers & Bob Ball (eds.), *Proceedings of the Texas Conference on Performatives, Presuppositions, and Implicature*, 79–106. Austin, TX: Center for Applied Linguistics.

Langacker, Ronald W. 1987. *Foundations of cognitive grammar, vol. 1: Theoretical prerequisites*. Stanford: Stanford University Press.

Langacker, Ronald W. 1991. *Foundations of Cognitive Grammar, Vol. 2: Descriptive application*. Stanford: Stanford University Press.

Larina, Tatiana & Douglas Mark Ponton. 2020. Tact or frankness in English and Russian blind peer reviews. *Intercultural Pragmatics* 17(4). 471–496.

Lee, Sun. 2001. *A contrastive rhetoric study of Korean and English research paper introductions*. Urbana-Champaign: University of Illinois dissertation.

Leech, Geoffrey. 1969. *A linguistic guide to English poetry*. London: Longman.

Leech, Geoffrey. 1974. *Semantics: The study of meaning*. Middlesex, UK: Penguin Books.

Leech, Geoffrey. 1983. *Principles of pragmatics*. London: Longman.

Leech, Geoffrey. 1985. Stylistics. In Teun A. van Dijk (ed.), *Discourse and literature: New approaches to the analysis of literary genres*, 39–57. Amsterdam: John Benjamins.

Leech, Geoffrey. 1992. Pragmatic principles in Shaw's *You Never Can Tell*. In Michael Toolan (ed.), *Language, text, and context*, 259–278. London: Routledge.

Leech, Geoffrey. 2007. Politeness: Is there an East-West divide? *Journal of Politeness Research* 3(2). 167–206.

Leech, Geoffrey & Mick Short. 1983. *Style in fiction*. London: Longman.

Lee-Wong, Song Mei. 1994. *Qing/please* – a polite or request marker? Observations from Chinese. *Multilingua* 13(4). 343–360.

Levine, Timothy R., Rachel K. Kim & Lauren M. Hamel. 2010. People lie for a reason: Three experiments documenting the principle of veracity. *Communication Research Reports* 27(4). 271–285. DOI: 10.1080/08824096.2010.496334.

Levinson, Steven. 1983. *Pragmatics*. Cambridge: Cambridge University Press.

Lewis, Michael. 1999. *The new new thing: A silicon valley story*. New York: W. W. Norton & Company.

Li, Wei & Li Yue. 1996. "My stupid wife and ugly daughter": The use of pejorative references as politeness strategy by Chinese speakers. *Asian Pacific Communication* 7(3&4). 129–142.

Li, Yue'e & Jianghong Feng. 2000. Compliments and compliment responses in Mandarin. *Foreign Languages and Their Teaching* 9. 28–32.

Local, J. K. & Gareth Walker. 2005. Methodological imperatives for investigating the phonetic organization and phonological structures of spontaneous speech. *Phonetica* 62. 120–130.

Locher, Miriam. 2004. *Power and politeness in action: Disagreement in communication*. Berlin & New York: Mouton de Gruyter.

Locher, Miriam & Richard Watts. 2008. Relational work and impoliteness. Negotiating norms of linguistic behavior. In Derek Bousfield & Miriam Locher (eds.), *Impoliteness in language*, 77–99. Berlin: De Guyter Mouton.

Locher, Miriam & Sebastian Hoffmann. 2006. The emergence of the identity of a fictional expert advice-giver in an American Internet advice column. *Text and Talk* 26(1). 67–104.

Loh, W. C. T. 1993. Reponses to compliments across languages and cultures: A comparative study of British and Hong Kong Chinese. *Department of English, Research Report Series* 30. 1–89. City University of Hong Kong.

Loi, Chek Kim & Moyra Sweetnam Evans. 2010. Cultural differences in the organization of research article introductions from the field of educational psychology: English and Chinese. *Journal of Pragmatics* 42(10). 2814–2825,

Lorenzo-Dus, N. 2001. Compliment responses among British and Spanish university students: A contrastive study. *Journal of Pragmatics* 33(1). 107–127.

Loveday, Leo John. 2018. The sarcastic implicatures of an ambivalent villain: Dahl's Willy Wonka. *Language and Literature* 27(2). 86–102.

Luyckx, Koen, Luc Goossens & Bart Soenens. 2006. A developmental contextual perspective on identity construction in emerging adulthood: Change dynamics in commitment formation and commitment evaluation. *Developmental Psychology* 42(2). 366.

Ly, Annelise. 2016. Internal e-mail communication in the workplace: Is there an "East-West divide"? *Intercultural Pragmatics* 13(1). 37–70.

Lyons, John. 1977. *Semantics* (2 vols). Cambridge: Cambridge University Press.

MacDonald, Dwight. 1960. *Parodies: An anthropology from Chaucer to Beerhohm – and after*. New York: Random House.

Maiz-Arevalo, Carmen. 2013. "Just click 'like'": Computer-mediated responses to Spanish compliments. *Journal of Pragmatics* 51. 47–67.

Manes, Joan. 1983. Compliments: A mirror of cultural values. In Nessa Wolfson & Elliot Judd (eds.), *Sociolinguistics and language acquisition*, 96–102. Rowley, MA: Newbury House.
Manes, Joan & Nessa Wolfson. 1981. The compliment formula. In Florian Coulmas (ed.), *Conversational routines*, 115–132. The Hague: Mouton.
Mao, Robert LuMing, 1992. Invitational discourse and Chinese identity. *Journal of Asian Pacific Communication* 3(1). 79–96.
Mao, Robert LuMing. 1994. Beyond politeness theory: "Face" revisited and renewed. *Journal of Pragmatics* 21(5). 451–486.
Marcia, James E. 1980. Identity in adolescence. In Joseph Adelson (ed.), *Handbook of adolescent psychology*, 159–187. New York: Wiley.
Marques-Aguado, Teresa. 2009. Lexical expressions of possibility in specialized discourse: A corpus-based analysis. *Linguistica e Filologia* 29. 99–122.
Marsh, Jessica. 2019. Why say it that way? Evasive answers and politeness theory. *Journal of Politeness Research* 15(1). 55–75.
Martinich, A. P. 1990. Truth and meaning. In A.P. Martinich (ed.), *The philosophy of language*, 2nd ed., 11–12. Oxford: Oxford University Press.
Martinich, A. P. 1991. A theory of metaphor. In Steven Davis (ed.), *Pragmatics*, 507–518. Oxford: Oxford University Press.
Maslow, Abraham H. 1943. A theory of human motivation. *Psychological Review* 50. 370–396.
Matsumoto, Yoshiko. 1988. Reexamination of the universality of face: Politeness phenomena in Japanese. *Journal of Pragmatics* 2(4). 403–426.
Matsumoto, Yoshiko. 1989. Politeness and conversational universals: Observations from Japanese. *Multilingua* 8. 207–221.
Matsumoto, Yoshiko. 2003. Discussion note: Reply to Pizziconi. *Journal of Pragmatics* 35. 1515–1521.
McCornack, Steven A. 1997. The generation of deceptive messages: Laying the groundwork for a viable theory of interpersonal deception. In John O. Greene (ed.), *Message production: Advances in communication theory*, 91–126. Mahwah, NJ: Lawrence Erlbaum Associates, Inc.
McNamee, Gregory. 2015. Shame vs. guilt. *Virginia Quarterly Review* (University of Virginia) 91(1). 197.
Meibauer, Jörg. 2011. On lying: intentionality, implicature, and imprecision. *Intercultural Pragmatics* 8(2). 277–292.
Meibauer, Jörg. 2014. *Lying at the semantics-pragmatics interface*. Berlin & New York: De Gruyter.
Meibauer, Jörg. 2016. Topics in the linguistics of lying: A reply to Marta Dynel. *Intercultural Pragmatics* 13(1). 107–123.
Merritt, M. 1976. On questions following questions (in service encounters). *Language in Society* 5(3). 315–357.
Metts, S. 1989. An exploratory investigation of deception in close relationships. *Journal of Social and Personal Relationships* 6. 159–179.
Mey, Jacob L. 1993. *Pragmatics: An introduction*. Oxford: Blackwell.
Migdadi, Fathi Hassan. 2003. Complimenting in Jordanian Arabic: A socio-pragmatic analysis. Muncie, Indiana: Ball State University dissertation.
Mihatsch, Miltrud. 2009. Nouns are THINGS: Evidence for a grammatical metaphor? In Klaus-Uwe Panther, Linda L. Thornburg, and Antonio Barcelona (eds.), *Metonymy and metaphor in grammar*, 75–98. Amsterdam: John Benjamins.
Mills, Sara. 2003. *Gender and politeness*. Cambridge: Cambridge University Press.
Mir, Montserrat & Joseph Maria Cots. 2017. Beyond saying thanks: Compliment responses in American English and peninsular Spanish. *Languages in Contrast* 17(1). 1–20.

Miyahara, Arika, Min-Sun Kim, Ho-Chang Shin & Kak Yoon. 1998. Conflict resolution styles among collectivist cultures: A comparison between Japanese and Koreans. *International Journal of Intercultural Relations* 22(4). 505–525.
Mohammad, Yahya Alrousan, Mat Awal Norsimah & Binti Salehuddin Khazriyati. 2016. Compliment responses among male and female Jordanian university students. *Gema Online Journal of Language Studies* 16(1). 19–34.
Moratti, Arthur F. & Chanita Goodblatt. 2013. *Religious diversity and early modern English texts: Catholic, Judaic, feminist, and secular dimensions*. Detroit, MI: Wayne State University Press.
Morgan, Jerry. 1978. Two types of convention in indirect speech acts. In Peter Cole (ed.), *Syntax and Semantics 9: Pragmatics*, 261–280. New York: Academic Press.
Morris, Charles W. 1938. Foundations of theories of signs. In Otto Neurath, Rufolf Carnap & Charles Morris W. (eds.), *International encyclopedia of unified science*, 77–138. Chicago: Chicago University Press.
Morpurgo-Tagliabue, Guido. 1981. Grammar, Logic, and rhetoric in a pragmatic perspective. In Herman Parret, Marina Sbisa, and Jef Verschueren (eds.), *Possibilities and limitations of pragmatics: Proceedings of the Conference on Pragmatics, Urbino July 8–14, 1979*, 493–508. Amsterdam: John Benjamins
Morsy, E. 1992. Sex differences in complimenting behavior: A contrastive analyses between Egyptian Arabic and American English. Cairo: The American University MA thesis.
Murray, Amy Jo & Kevin Durrheim (eds.). 2019. *Qualitative studies of silence: The unsaid as social action*. Cambridge: Cambridge University Press,
Mursy, Ahmad Aly & John Wilson. 2001. Towards a definition of Egyptian complimenting. *Multilingua* 20(2). 133–154.
Nelson, Gayle L., Mahmoud Al-Batal & Erin Echols. 1996. Arabic and English compliment responses: Potential for pragmatic failure. *Applied Linguistics* 17(4). 411–432.
Nelson, Gayle L., Joan Carson, Mahmoud Al Batal & Waguida El Bakary. 2002. Cross-cultural pragmatics: Strategy use in Egyptian Arabic and American English refusals. *Applied Linguistics* 23(2). 163–189.
Nelson, Gayle L., Waguida El Bakary and Mahmoud Al-Batal. 1993. Egyptian and American compliments: A contrastive study. *International Journal of Intercultural Relations* 17. 293–313.
Ning, Puyu, Dániel Kádár & Rong Chen. 2020. Evaluation of explanation in interaction. *Modern Foreign Languages* 43(2). 161–173.
Norrick, Neal R. 2009. Interjections as pragmatic markers. *Journal of Pragmatics* 41(5). 866–889.
Ochs, Elinor. 1990. Indexicality and socialization. In James W. Stigler, Richard A. Shweder & Gilbert Herdt (eds.), *Cultural psychology: Essays on comparative human development*, 287–308. Cambridge: Cambridge University Press.
Ochs, Elinor. 1992. Indexing gender. In Alessandro Duranti & Charles Goodwin (eds.), *Rethinking Context: Language as an interactive phenomenon*, 335–58. Cambridge: Cambridge University Press.
Ochs, Elinor. 1993. Constructing social identity. *Research on Language and Interaction* 26(3). 287–306.
Ochs, Elinor. 2012. Experiencing language. *Anthropological theory* 12(2). 142–160.
Ogiermann, Eva & Pilar Blitvich (eds.). 2019. *From speech acts to lay understandings of politeness: Multilingual and multicultural perspectives*. Cambridge: Cambridge University Press.
Ogiermann, Eva & Vasiliki Saloustrou. 2020. Conceptualising politeness in Greece and Great Britain. *Γλωσσολογία* [Glossologia] 28. 1–25.

Ohashi, Jun. 2003. Japanese culture specific face and politeness orientation: A pragmatic investigation of *yoroshiku onegaishmasu*. *Multilingua* 22. 257–274.
Ohashi, Jun. 2008. Linguistic rituals for thanking in Japanese: Balancing obligations. *Journal of Pragmatics* 40(12). 2150–2174.
Oreström, Bengt. 1983. *Turn-taking in English conversation*. Lund: CWK Gleerup.
Ouellette, M. A. 2008. Weaving strands of writer identity: Self as author and the NNES "plagiarist". *Journal of Second Language Writing* 17(4). 255–273.
Pan, Yuling & Daniel Kádár Z. 2011. *Politeness in Historical and Contemporary Chinese*. London: Continuum.
Panther, Klaus-Uwe & Linda L. Thornburg. 1998. A cognitive approach to inferencing in conversation. *Journal of Pragmatics* 30. 755–769.
Panther, Klaus-Uwe & Linda L. Thornburg. 2009. Introduction: On Figuration in grammar. In Klaus-Uwe Panther, Linda L. Thornburg & Antonio Barcelona (eds.), *Metonymy and metaphor in grammar*, 1–44. Amsterdam: John Benjamins.
Panther, Klaus-Uwe & Gunter Radden (eds.). 2011. *Motivation in grammar and the lexicon*. Amsterdam & Philadelphia: John Benjamins.
Parvaresh, Vahid & Tahmineh Tayebi. 2018. Impoliteness, aggression, and the moral order. *Journal of Pragmatics* 132. 91–107.
Peters, R. 1960. *The Concept of Motivation*. London: Routledge. https://doi.org/10.4324/9781315712833
Pexman, Penny M. & Meghan Zvaigzne. 2004. Does irony go better with friends? *Metaphor and Symbol* 19(2). 143–163.
Piata, Anna. 2016. When metaphor becomes a joke: Metaphor journeys from political ads to internet memes. *Journal of Pragmatics* 106. 39–56. https://doi.org/10.1016/j.pragma.2016.10.003
Pirsig, Robert M. 1976. *Zen and the art of motor-cycle maintenance*. London: Corgi Books.
Pizziconi, Barbara. 2003. Re-examining politeness, face and the Japanese language. *Journal of Pragmatics* 35(10&11). 1471–1506.
Pizziconi, Barbara. 2012. The regulation of normative interpersonal behavior and public morality in Japanese public service encounters. http://www.liar3.illinois.edu/revabs/LIAR3Pizziconi.pdf
Placencia, María Elena, Amanda Lower & Hebe Powell. 2016. Complimenting behaviour on Facebook: Responding to compliments in American English. *Pragmatics and Society* 7(3) 339–365. DOI: https://doi.org/10.1075/ps.7.3.01pla
Pomerantz, Anita. 1975. *Second assessment: A study of some features of agreements/disagreements*. Irvine: University of California, Irvine dissertation.
Pomerantz, Anita. 1978. Compliment responses: Notes on the cooperation of multiple constraints. In Jim Schenkein (ed.), *Studies in the organization of conversational interaction*, 79–112. New York: Academic Press.
Pomerantz, Anita. 1984. Agreeing and disagreeing with assessments: Some features of preferred dispreferred turn shapes. In J. Maxwell Atkinson & John Heritage (eds.), *Structures of social action*, 57–101. Cambridge: Cambridge University Press.
Popa-Wyatt, Mihaela. 2014. Pretense and echo: Towards an integrated account of verbal irony. *International Review of Pragmatics* 6(1). 127–168.
Posner, Michael (ed.). 2011. *Cognitive neuroscience of attention*. New York and London: The Guilford Press.

Potter, Lorena. 2016. Ideological representations and Theme-Rheme analysis in English and Arabic news reports: a systemic functional approach. *Functional Linguistics* 3(10). 1186/s40554-016-0028-y.

Prince, Ellen. 1981. Toward a taxonomy of given/new information. In Peter Cole (ed.), *Radical pragmatics*, 223–254. New York: Academic Press.

Prince, Ellen. 1992. ZPG letter: Subjects, definiteness, and information status. In Sandra Thompson & W. Wann (eds.), *Discourse description: Diverse analyses of a fundraising Text*, 399–416. Amsterdam & Philadelphia: John Benjamins.

Putnam, Hilary. 1973. Meaning and reference. *The Journal of Philosophy* 70. 699–711.

Qin, Kongji. 2020. Curriculum as a discursive and performative space for subjectivity and learning: understanding immigrant adolescents: Language use in Classroom Discourse. *The Modern Language Journal* 104(4). 842–859. doi:http://dx.doi.org.libproxy.lib.csusb.edu/10.1111/modl.12675.

Ran, Yongping & Linsen Zhao. 2019. Impoliteness revisited: Evidence from *qingmian* threats in Chinese interpersonal conflicts. *Journal of Politeness Research* 15(2). 257–291. https://doi.org/10.1515/pr-2017-0027

Ran, Yongping, Linsen Zhao & Dániel Kádár. 2020. The rite of reintegrative shaming in Chinese public dispute mediation. *Pragmatics* 30(1). 10.1075/prag.19019.ran.

Raymond, Geoffrey. 2004. Prompting action: the stand-alone "so" in ordinary conversation. *Research on Language and Social Interaction* 37(2). 185–218.

Redeker, Gisele, 2006. Discourse markers as attentional cues at discourse transitions. In Kerstin Fischer (ed.), *Approaches to discourse particles*, 339–358. Amsterdam: Elsevier.

Reinhart, Tania. 1981. Pragmatics and linguistics: an analysis of sentence topics. *Philosophica* 27. 53–94.

Ren, Wei. 2019. Emancipating (im)politeness research and increasing its impact. *Acta Linguistica Academica* 66(2). 289–298. DOI: 10.1556/2062.2019.66.2.8

Ritchie, David. 2003. "Argument is war" – Or is it a game of chess? Multiple meanings in the analysis of implicit metaphors. *Metaphor and Symbol* 18(2). 125–146.

Robles, Jessica S. 2019. Building up by tearing down. *Journal of Language and Social Psychology* 38(1). 85–105.

Rodriguez, Gonzalez & Milton Fernando. 2020. Compliment responses in Icelandic. *Language and Dialogue* 10(2). 194–214.

Rorty, Amelie (ed.). 1976. *The identities of persons*. Berkeley: University of California Press.

Rose, Kenneth R. & Kwai-Fong Connie Ng. 1999. Inductive and deductive approaches to teaching compliments and compliment responses. *Perspectives* 11(2). 124–169.

Ross, Andrew S. & Damian J. Rivers. 2020. Donald Trump, legitimization and a new political rhetoric. *World Englishes*. 39(4). 623–637

Rossen-Knill, Deborah & Richard Henry. 1997. The pragmatics of verbal parody. *Journal of Pragmatics* 27. 719–759.

Rue, Yong-Ju and Grace Qiao Zhang. 2008. Request Strategies: A comparative study in Mandarin Chinese and Korean. Amsterdam: John Benjamins.

Ruhi, Sukriye. 2006. Politeness in compliment responses: A perspective from naturally occurring exchanges in Turkish. *Pragmatics* 16(6). 43–101.

Ruhi, Sukriye. 2007. Higher–order intentions and self-politeness in evaluations of (im)politeness: The relevance of compliment responses. *Australian Journal of Linguistics* 27(2). 107–145.

Ruhi, Sukriye & Daniel Kádár Z. 2010. "Face" across historical cultures: A comparative study of Turkish and Chinese. *Journal of Historical Pragmatics* 12(1&2). 25–48.

Russell, Bertrand. 1905. On Denoting. *Mind, New Series* 14(56). 479–493. https://www.jstor.org/stable/2248381

Russell, Bertrand. 1919. Descriptions. In *Introduction to Mathematical Philosophy*, 167–180. London: George Allen and Unwin.

Sacks, Harvey. 1992 [1964–1972]. *Lectures on conversation* [1964–72], vol. 2. Oxford: Blackwell.

Sacks, Harvey, Emanual A. Schegloff & Gail Jefferson. 1974. A simplest systematics for the organization of turn-taking for conversation. *Language* 50. 696–735.

Sacks, Harvey, Emanual A. Schegloff & Gail Jefferson. 1978. A simplest systematics for the organization of turn-taking in conversation. In J. Schenkein (ed.), *Studies in the organization of conversational interaction*, 7–55. New York: Academic Press.

Saito, Hidetoshi & Masako Beecken. 1997. An approach to instruction of pragmatic aspects: Implications of pragmatic transfer by American learners of Japanese. *The Modern Language Journal* 81. 363–377.

Sala, Michele. 2008. Argumentative styles as cultural identity traits in legal studies. *Linguistica e Filologia* 27. 93–113.

Sampson, Geoffrey. 1982. The economics of conversation: Comments on Hoshi's paper. In Neilson Smith (ed.), *Mutual knowledge*, 200–210. London: Academic Press.

Samraj, B. 2002. Introductions in research articles: Variations across disciplines. *English for Specific Purposes* 21(1). 1–17.

Schegloff, Emanual A. 2002. Beginnings in the telephone. In James E. Katz & Mark Aakhus (eds.), *Perpetual contact: Mobile communication, private talk, public performance*, 284–300. Cambridge: Cambridge University Press.

Schegloff, Emanuel A. 2007. *Sequence organization in interaction: A primer in conversation analysis*, vol. 1. Cambridge: Cambridge University Press.

Schegloff, Emanual A., Gail Jefferson & Harvey Sacks. 1977. The preference for self-correction in the organization of repair in conversation. *Language* 53. 361–382.

Schiffer, Steven. 1990. *Meaning*. Oxford: Clarendon Press.

Schiffrin, Deborah. 1987. *Discourse markers*. New York: Cambridge University Press.

Schmid, Hans-Jörg (ed.). 2012. *Cognitive pragmatics*. Berlin: De Gruyter Mouton.

Schmid, Hans-Jörg. 2016. Why cognitive linguistics must embrace the social and pragmatic dimensions of language and how it could do so more seriously. *Cognitive Linguistics* 27(4). 543.

Schneider, Klaus P. 2012. Appropriate behavior across varieties of English. *Journal of Pragmatics* 44(9). 1022–1037.

Schneider, Klaus P. & Anne Barron. 2008. *Variational pragmatics: A focus on regional varieties in pluricentric languages*. Amsterdam: John Benjamins.

Schneider, Klaus P. & Iris Schneider. 2000. *Bescheidenheit in vier Kulturen: Komplimenterwiderungen in den USA, Irland, Deutschland und China* [Modesty in four cultures: Reciprocals of compliments in the US, Ireland, Germany and China]. In Mariann Skog-Södersved (ed.), *Ethische Konzepte und mentale Kulturen 2: Sprachwissenschaftliche Studien zu Höflichkeit und Respektverhalten* [Ethical Concepts and Mental Cultures 2: Linguistic studies on politeness and respectful behavior], 65–80. Vaasa: Vaasan Yliopisto.

Schoor, Carola. 2015. Political metaphor, a matter of purposeful style. *Metaphor and the Social World* 5(1). 82–101.

Schourup, Lawrence, 1999. Discourse markers: Tutorial overview. *Lingua* 107. 227–265.

Searle, John, 1965. What is a speech act? In Black Max (ed.), *Philosophy in America*, 221–239. Ithaca, NY: Cornell University Press.
Searle, John. 1969. *Speech Acts*. Cambridge: Cambridge University Press.
Searle, John. 1991. Metaphor. In Steven Davis (ed.), *Pragmatics*, 519–549. Oxford: Oxford University Press.
Searle, John. 1991 [1975]. Indirect speech acts. In Steven Davis (ed.), *Pragmatics: A reader*, 265–277. Oxford: Oxford University Press.
Semino, Elena & Gerard Steen. 2008. Metaphor in literature. *The Cambridge handbook of metaphor and thought*, 232–246. Cambridge: Cambridge University Press.
Serota, Kim B., Timothy Levine & Franklin J. Boster. 2009. The prevalence of lying in America: Three studies of self-reported lies. *Human Communication Research* 36(1). 2–25. DOI: 10.1111/j.1468-2958.2009.01366.x
Sharifian, Farzad. 2005. The Persian cultural schema of *shekasteh-nafsi*: A study of compliment responses in Persian and Anglo-Australian speakers. *Pragmatics and Cognition* 13(2). 337–361.
Sharifian, Farzad. 2008. Cultural schemas in L1 and L2 compliment responses: A study of Persian-speaking learners of English. *Journal of Politeness Research* 4(1). 55–80.
Shearer, Harry. 2014. *So*'s of the week. *Le Show*. Public Radio. http://harryshearer.com/le-shows/august-10-2014/, 2014.
Shi-Xu. 2005. *A cultural approach to discourse*. Houndmills & Basingstoke, UK: Palgrave Press.
Sifianou, Maria. 1992. *Politeness phenomena in England and Greece: A cross-cultural perspective*. Oxford: Oxford University Press.
Sifianou, Maria. 2001. "Oh, how appropriate!" Compliments and politeness. In Arin Bayraktaroglu & Maria Sifianou (eds.), *Linguistic politeness across boundaries*, 391–430. Amsterdam: John Benjamins.
Sifianou, Maria. 2015. Conceptualizing politeness in Greek: Evidence from Twitter corpora. *Journal of Pragmatics* 86. 25–30.
Sifianou, Maria. 2019. (Im)politeness and in/civility: A neglected relationship? *Journal of Pragmatics* 147. 49–64. https://doi.org/10.1016/j.pragma.2019.05.008
Sifianou, Maria & Angeliki Tzanne. 2010. Conceptualizations of politeness and impoliteness in Greek. *Intercultural Pragmatics* 7(4). 661–687.
Simpson, David. 1992. Lying, liars and language. *Philosophy and Phenomenological Research* 52(3). 623–639.
Skalicky, Stephen & Scott Crossley. 2015. A statistical analysis of satirical Amazon.com product reviews. *European Journal of Humor Research* 2. 66–85.
Skewis, Malcolm. 2003. Mitigated directness in *Hongloumeng*: Directive speech acts and politeness in eighteenth century Chinese. *Journal of Pragmatics* 35(2). 161–189.
Sokal, Alan D. 1996. Transgressing the boundaries: toward a transformative hermeneutics of quantum gravity. *Social Text* 46 & 47. 217–252.
Sorensen, Roy. 2010. Knowledge-lies. *Analysis* 70. 608–615.
Spencer-Oatey, Helen. 2007. Theories of identity and the analysis of face. *Journal of Pragmatics* 29(4). 639–656.
Spencer-Oatey, Helen. 2008. *Culturally speaking: Culture, communication and politeness*. London: Continuum.
Spencer-Oatey, Helen & Patrick Ng. 2001. Reconsidering Chinese modesty: Hong Kong and Mainland Chinese evaluative judgments of compliment response. *Journal of Asian Pacific Communication* 11(2). 181–201.

Sperber, Dan & Deirdre Wilson. 1981. Irony and the use-mention distinction. In Peter Cole (ed.), *Radical pragmatics*, 295–328. New York: Academic Press.
Sperber, Dan & Deirdre Wilson. 1986. *Relevance: Communication and cognition*. Oxford: Blackwell.
Steele, Godfrey A. 2020. Visibility and meaningful recognition for first peoples: A critical discourse studies approach to communication, culture and conflict intersections in seeking social justice. *Discourse & Communication* 14(5). 489–511.
Steen, Gerard. 2008. The paradox of metaphor: Why we need a three-dimensional model of metaphor. *Metaphor and Symbol* 23. 213–241.
Steen, Gerard. 2011. Genre between the humanities and the sciences. In Marcus Callies, Wolfram R. Keller & Astrid Lohöfer (eds.), *Bi-directionality in the cognitive sciences: Examining the interdisciplinary potential of cognitive approaches in linguistics and literary studies*, 21–42. Amsterdam: John Benjamins.
Steen, Gerard. 2017. Deliberate metaphor theory: Basic assumptions, main tenets, urgent issues. *Intercultural Pragmatics* 14(1). 1–24. DOI: 10.1515/ip-2017-0001
Steen, Gerard. 2018. Metaphor: Metaphor and style through genre, with illustrations from Carol Ann Duffy's "Rapture". In Violeta Sotirova (ed.), *The Bloomsbury companion to stylistics*, 308–324. London & New York: Bloomsbury.
Steen, Gerard & Raymond Gibbs. 2004. Questions about metaphor in literature. *European Journal of English Studies* 8(3). 337–354.
Sterbenz, Christina. 2014. So here's why everyone is starting sentences with the word "*so*". http://www.businessinsider.com/heres-why-everyone-is-starting-sentences-with-the-word-*so*-2014-5.
Strauss, Susan & Parastou Feiz. 2014. *Discourse analysis*. New York & London: Routledge.
Strawson, Peter Frederick. 1956. On referring. In Anthony Few (ed.), *Essays in conceptual analysis*, 21–52. London: Macmillan.
Street, Chris N. & Daniel C. Richardson. 2014. Lies, damn lies, and expectations: How base rates inform lie–truth judgments. *Applied Cognitive Psychology* 29. 149–155. https://doi-org.libproxy.lib.csusb.edu/10.1002/acp.3085
Stryker, Sheldon. 1987. Identity theory: Developments and extensions. In Yardley, Krysia & Honess, Terry (eds.), *Self and identity: Psychosocial perspectives*, 89–104. Chichester: Wiley.
Suau-Jiménez, Francisca. 2020. Closeness and distance through the agentive authorial voice: Construing credibility in promotional discourse. *International Journal of English Studies* 20(1). 73–92.
Swales, John. 1981. *Aspects of article introductions*. Birmingham: University of Aston.
Swales, John. 1990. *Genre analysis: English in academic and research settings*. Cambridge: Cambridge University Press.
Swales, John. 2011. The concept of discourse community. In Elizabeth Wardle & Doug Downs (eds.), *Writing about writing: A college reader*, 215–227. Boston, MA: Bedford & St. Martin's.
Swan, Michael & Catherine Walter. 1982. The use of sensory deprivation in foreign language teaching. *ELT Journal* 36(3). 183–185. https://doi.org/10.1093/elt/36.3.183
Sweet, Nikolas. 2020. Ritual contingency: Teasing and the politics of participation. *Journal of Linguistic Anthropology* 30(1). 86–102.
Sweetser, Eve E. 1987. The definition of lie: An examination of the folk models underlying a semantic prototype. In Dorothy Holland & Maomi Quinn (eds.), *Cultural models in language and thought*, 3–66. Cambridge: Cambridge University Press.

Swift, Jonathan. 1995 [1729]. *A modest proposal*. London: Penguin Books.
Taavitsainen, Irma & Andreas H. Jucker (eds.). 2003. *Diachronic perspectives on address term systems*. Amsterdam & Philadelphia: John Benjamins.
Taavitsainen, Irma & Andreas H. Jucker. 2008. "Methinks you seem more beautiful than ever": Compliments and gender in the history of English. In Andreas H. Jucker & Irma Taavitsainen (eds.), *Speech acts in the history of English*, 195–228. Amsterdam: John Benjamins.
Taavitsainen, Irma and Andreas Jucker. 2015. Twenty years of historical pragmatics: Origins, developments and changing thought styles. *Journal of Historical Pragmatics* 16(1). 1–24.
Taboada, Maite. 2010. Discourse markers and coherence relations: Comparison across markers, languages and modalities. *Linguistics and the Human Sciences* 6(1–3). 17–41.
Tajfel, Henri. 1974. Social identity and intergroup behavior. *Social Science Information* 13. 65–93.
Tajfel, Henri. 1981. *Human groups and social categories*. Cambridge: Cambridge University Press.
Tajfel, Henri (ed.). 1982. *Social identity and intergroup relations*. Cambridge, UK: Cambridge University Press.
Talmy, Leonard. 2000. *Towards a cognitive semantics* (2 Vols). Cambridge, MA: MIT Press.
Tang, Ramona & John Suganthi. 1999. The "I" in identity: Exploring writer identity in student academic writing through the first person pronoun. *English for Specific Purposes* 18. S23–S39.
Tang, Chen-Hsin & Grace Qiao Zhang. 2009. A contrastive study of compliment responses among Australian English and Mandarin Chinese speakers. *Journal of Pragmatics* 41(2). 325–345.
Tannen, Deborah. 1986. *That's not what I meant: How conversational styles makes or breaks relationships*. New York: Ballantine Books.
Tayebi, Tahmineh. 2016. Why do people take offence? Exploring the underlying expectations. *Journal of Pragmatics* 101. 1–17.
Tedeschi, James T. & Richard B. Felson. 1994. *Violence, aggression, and coercive actions*. Washington DC: American Psychological Association.
Terkourafi, Marina & Michael Haugh. 2019. "Quo Vadis, Pragmatics?" *Journal of Pragmatics* 145. 1–3. https://doi.org/10.1016/j.pragma.2019.04.005
Tracy, Karen. 2002. *Everyday talk: Building and reflecting identities*. New York: Guilford.
Traugott, Elizabeth Closs. 2008. The State of English language studies: A Linguistic Perspective. In Marianne Thormählen (ed.), *English Now: Selected Papers from the 20th IAUPE Conference in Lund 2007*, 199–225. Lund: Lund Studies in English.
Traugott, Elizabeth Closs & Graham Trousdale. 2010. *Gradience, gradualness and grammaticalization*. Amsterdam & Philadelphia: John Benjamins.
Trier, Jost. 1931. *Der deutsche Wortschatz im Sinnbezirk des Verstandes. Die Geschichte eines sprachlichen Feldes* [The German vocabulary in the sense of the mind: The story of a linguistic field]. Heidelberg: Winter.
Tsakona, Villy. 2018. Online joint fictionalization. In Villy Tsakona & Jan Chovanec (eds.), *The dynamics of interactional humor: Creating and negotiating humor in everyday encounters*, 229–255. Amsterdam: John Benjamins.
Tseng, Miao-Fen. 1996. An examination of Chinese invitational discourse: How Chinese accept an invitation. *Studies in the Linguistics Sciences* 26. 341–356.

Tsur, Reuven. 2002. Aspects of cognitive poetics. In Elena Semino & Jonathan Culpepper (eds.), *Cognitive stylistics: language and cognition in text analysis*, 279–318. Amsterdam: Benjamins.

Turner, Mark. 1996. *The literary mind*. New York: Oxford University Press.

Turner, Ronny E., Charles Edgley & Glen Olmstead. 1975. Information control in conversations: Honesty is not always the best policy. *Kansas Journal of Sociology* 11. 69–89.

Upadhyay, Shiv R. 2003. Nepali requestive acts: Linguistic indirectness and politeness reconsidered. *Journal of Pragmatics* 35. 1651–1677.

Usami, Mayumi. 2002. Discourse politeness in Japanese conversation: Some implications for a universal theory of politeness. Tokyo: Hituzi Syobo.

Van Dijk, Teun A. 1979. Pragmatic connectives. *Journal of Pragmatics* 3. 447–456.

Van Dijk, Teun A. 1998. *Ideology: A multidisciplinary approach*. London: Sage Publications.

Van Dijk, Teun A. & Walter Kintsch. 1983. *Strategies of discourse comprehension*. New York: Academic Press.

Varis, Piia & Jan Blommaert. 2015. Conviviality and collectives on social media: Virality, memes, and new social structures. *Multilingual Margins: A journal of Multilingualism from the Periphery*. DOI: 10.14426/mm.v2i1.55 (accessed 30 January 2021).

Vasek, M. E. 1986. Lying as a skill: The development of deception in children. In Robert W. Mitchell & Nicholas S. Thompson. (eds.), *Deception perspectives on human and nonhuman deceit*, 271–292. Albany: State University of New York Press.

Vásquez, Camillia. 2019. *Language, creativity and humor online*. Cambridge: Cambridge University Press.

Vásquez, Camilla & Samantha Creel. 2017. Conviviality through creativity: Appealing to the reblog in Tumblr Chat posts. *Discourse, Context & Media* 20. 59–69.

Verschueren, Jef. 1999. *Understanding pragmatics*. New York: Routledge.

Vervaeke, John & John Kennedy. 2004. Conceptual metaphor and abstract thought. *Metaphor & Symbol* 19(3). 213–231.

Vygotsky, Lev. S. 1987. *The collected works of L. S. Vygotsky*. New York: Springer.

Wardhaugh, R. 1998. *An introduction to sociolinguistics*, 3rd edn. Oxford: Blackwell Publishers.

Watts, Richard J. 1991. *Power in family discourse*. Berlin & New York: Mouton de Gruyter.

Watts, Richard J. 1992 Linguistic politeness and politic verbal behavior: Reconsidering claims for universality. In Richard Watts, Sachiko Ide & Konrad Ehlich (eds.), *Politeness in Language: Studies in Its History, Theory, and Practice*, 43–69. Berlin: Mouton de Gruyter.

Watts, Richard J. 2003. *Politeness*. Cambridge: Cambridge University Press.

Watts, Richard J., Sachiko Ide & Konrad Ehlich. 1992. Introduction. In Richard J. Watts, Sachiko Ide & Konrad Ehlich (eds.), *Politeness in language: Studies in its history, theory and practice*, 1–17. Berlin: Mouton de Gruyter.

Weiner, Bernard. 2012. *Human motivation*. New York: Springer and Business Media.

Westberg, Gustav. 2021. Affective rebirth: Discursive gateways to contemporary national socialism". *Discourse and Society* 32(2). 214–230. doi:http://dx.doi.org.libproxy.lib.csusb.edu/10.1177/0957926520970380.

Wieland, Molly. 1995. Complimenting behavior in French/American cross-cultural dinner Conversations. *The French Review* 68(5). 796–812.

Wierzbicka, Anna. 1985. Different cultures, different languages, different speech acts. *Journal of Pragmatics* 9. 145–178.

Wierzbicka, Anna. 1992. *Semantics, culture, and cognition: Universal human concepts in cultural-specific configurations*. Oxford: Oxford University Press.

Wierzbicka, Anna. 2003. *Cross-cultural pragmatics: The semantics of human interaction*, 2nd edn. Berlin & New York: Mouton de Gruyter.

Wierzbicka, Anna. 2010. Intercultural scripts in international communication. In Anna Trosborg (ed.), *Pragmatics across languages and cultures*, 43–78. Berlin: Mouton de Gruyter.

Wierzbicka, Anna and Cliff Goddard (eds.). 2004. *Cultural scripts*. [Special Issue]. *Intercultural Pragmatics* 1(2).

Wilson, Dan. 2006. The pragmatics of verbal irony: Echo or pretense? *Lingua* 116. 1722–1743. doi:10.1016/j.lingua.2006.05.001

Wilson, Deirdre & Dan Sperber. 1980. On Grice's theory of conversation. In Paul Werth (ed.), *Conversation and discourse*, 155–178. Kent, UK: Croom Helm.

Wilson, Deirdre & Dan Sperber. 2012. Explaining irony. In Dan Wilson & Deidre Sperber (eds.), *Meaning and relevance*, 123–145. Cambridge: Cambridge University Press.

Wodak, Ruth. 2001. What CDA is about. In Ruth Wodak & Michael Meyer (eds.), *Methods of Critical Discourse Analysis*. London: Sage.

Wolfson, Nessa. 1981. Compliments in cross-cultural perspective. *TESOL Quarterly* 15. 117–124.

Wolfson, Nessa. 1983. An empirically based analysis of complimenting in English. In Nessa Wolfson & Elliot Judd (eds.), *Sociolinguistics and language acquisition*, 82–95. Rowley, MA: Newbury House.

Wolfson, Nessa. 1989. *Perspectives: Sociolinguistics and TESOL*. New York: Newbury House.

Xia, Dengshan & Chun Lan. 2019. (Im)politeness at a Chinese dinner table: A discursive approach to (im)politeness in multi-party communication. *Journal of Politeness Research* 15(2). 223–256.

Xu, Honger. 2007. The discourse making and pragmatic functions of *so*. *Journals of the Hangshi College of Science and Technology* 1. 100–103.

Yabuuchi, Akio. 2006. Hierarchy politeness: What Brown and Levinson refused to see. *Intercultural Pragmatics* 3(3). 323–351.

Yagoda, Ben. 2011. "So it turns out that everyone's starting sentences with 'so'". *Lingua Franca*. The Chronicle of Higher Education. http://chronicle.com/blogs/linguafranca/2011/12/02/so-it-turns-out-that-everyones-starting-sentences-with-so/.

Yang, Na & Wei Ren. 2020. Jocular mockery in the context of a localized playful frame: Unpacking humour in a Chinese reality TV show. *Journal of Pragmatics* 162(06). 32–44.

Yates, Linda. 2010. Pragmatic challenges for second language learners. In Anna Trosborg (ed.), *Pragmatics across languages and cultures*, 287–308. Berlin: De Gruyter Mouton.

Ye, Lei. 1995. Complimenting in Mandarin Chinese. In Gabriel Kasper (ed.), *Pragmatics of Chinese as native and target language*, 207–302. Honolulu: Second Language Teaching and Curriculum Center, University of Hawai'i at Manoa.

Ye, Ning, Le Cheng & Yun Zhao. 2019. Identity construction of suspects in telecom and internet fraud discourse: From a sociosemiotic perspective. *Social Semiotics* 3. 319–335.

Ye, Zhengdao. 2004. Chinese categorization of interpersonal relationships and the cultural logic of Chinese social interaction: An indigenous perspective. *Intercultural Pragmatics* 1(2). 211–230.

Ye, Zhengdao. 2019. The politeness bias and the society of strangers. *Language Sciences* 76. 1–11.

Yokota, A. 1986. Homerareta toki no hentoo ni okeru bokokugo kara no shakai gengogakuteki ten'i [Sociolinguistic transfer from the native language in the response to compliments]. *Journal of Japanese Language Teaching* 58. 203–223.

Yoon, Kyung-Joo. 2004. Not just words: Korean social models and the use of honorifics. *Intercultural Pragmatics* 1(2). 189–210.

Yu, Ming-Chung. 2003. On the universality of face: Evidence from Chinese compliment response behavior. *Journal of Pragmatics* 35(10&11). 1679–1710.

Yu, Ming-Chung. 2004. Interlinguistic variation and similarity in second language speech act behavior. *The Modern Language Journal* 88(1). 102–119.

Yuan, Chuanyou. 2019. A battlefield or a lecture hall? A contrastive multimodal discourse analysis of courtroom trials. *Social Semiotics* 29(5). 645–669. DOI:10.1080/10350330.2018.1504653

Yuan, Li. 2002. Compliments and compliment responses in Kunming Chinese. *Pragmatics* 12(2). 183–226.

Yuan, Zhoumin. 2020. Identity rhetoric in Chinese radio-mediated consultation. *East Asian Pragmatics* 5(1). 41–65.

Zappavigna, Michele. 2011. Ambient affiliation: A linguistic perspective on Twitter. *New Media and Society* 13(5). 788–806. DOI: 10.1177/1461444810385097.

Zappavigna, Michele. 2014. Enacting identity in microblogging through ambient affiliation. *Discourse and Communication* 8(2). 209–228.

Zhang, Guofu. 2008. Pragmatic analysis of white lie and its perlocutionary act. *Journal of Zhaotong Teachers College* 30(4). 27–30.

Zhong, Xiyun & Yantao Zeng. 2020. "Guess who I am": Construction false identity for fraudulent purposes. *East Asian Pragmatics* 5(1). 99–122.

Zhou, Ling & Shao-Jie Zhang. 2018. Reconstructing the Politeness Principle in Chinese: A response to Gu's approach. *Intercultural Pragmatics* 15(5). 693–721.

Zhu, Hua, Wei Li, & Yuan Qian. 2000. The sequential organization of gift offering and acceptance in Chinese. *Journal of Pragmatics* 32. 81–103.

Zimmerman, Don H. 1988. On conversation: The conversation analytic perspective. In International Communication Association (ed.), *Communication Yearbook* 11, 406–432. Newbury Park: Sage.

Zimmerman, Don H. 1992. Achieving context: Openings in emergency calls. In Watson, Graham and Sieler, Robert M. (eds.), *Text in context*: Contributions to ethnomethodology, 35–51. Newbury Park: Sage.

Zimmerman, Don H. 1998. Identity, context and interaction. In Charles Antaki and Susan Widdicombe (eds.), *Identities in Talk*, 87–106. London: Sage.

Appendix

i. https://www.cnn.com/2020/09/24/opinions/trumps-amateurish-mistake-ahead-of-debatesi-bden-silva-mcgowan/index.html, accessed 2020/09/24.
ii. https://www.thedailybeast.com/mitch-mcconnell-is-about-to-punch-america-in-the-penis, accessed 2020/09/22.
iii. https://www.theguardian.com/us-news/2020/sep/23/donald-trump-press-conference-us-elections-breonna-taylor, accessed 2020/09/23.
iv. https://www.kten.com/story/42668913/ruth-bader-ginsburgs-army-of-clerks-to-stand-guard-at-the-supreme-court, accessed 2020/09/24.
v. https://www.cnn.com/2020/09/23/opinions/debate-advice-for-biden-graham/index.html, accessed 2020/09/23.
vi. https://www.medscape.com/viewarticle/933458, accessed 2020/08/18.
vii. https://www.theguardian.com/commentisfree/2020/aug/04/coronavirus-pandemic-wave-wildfire, accessed 2020/08/28.
viii. https://news.yahoo.com/trumps-refusal-to-commit-to-peaceful-transfer-of-power-draws-dem-outrage-implicit-condemnation-from-the-gop-152217617.html, accessed 2020/09/28.
ix. https://www.washingtonpost.com/, Sept. 24, 2020, accessed 2020/09/24.
x. https://www.politico.com/news/magazine/2020/09/24/time-for-democrats-to-call-trumps-bluff-421381, accessed 2020/09/24.
xi. https://www.independent.co.uk/news/world/americas/us-politics/trump-news-live-us-coronavirus-update-election-2020-cases-deaths-b592779.html, accessed 2020/09/25.
xii. https://www.oann.com/president-trump-were-rounding-the-corner-on-the-pandemic/, accessed 2020/10/01.
xiii. https://www.cnn.com/2020/09/23/politics/coronavirus-donald-trump-election-2020/index.html, accessed 2020/09/23.
xiv. https://www.cnn.com/2020/08/17/politics/kristin-urquiza-democratic-national-convention-coronavirus-father-trump/index.html, accessed 2020/08/18.
xv. https://www.theguardian.com/us-news/2020/sep/25/bill-barr-donald-trump-election-steal-fears, accessed 2020/09/25.
xvi. https://www.bloomberg.com/news/articles/2020-09-26/trump-supreme-court-pick-seen-unlikely-to-jump-start-campaign, accessed 2020/09/26.
xvii. https://www.politico.com/news/2020/09/25/biden-campaign-lid-trump-421824, accessed 2020/09/25.
xviii. https://www.bing.com/videos/search?q=it+is+time+for+you+to+resign&docid=13986310469127&mid=F8F47FF4CEC30161925FF8F47FF4CEC30161925F&view=detail&FORM=VIRE accessed 2020/10/02.
xix. https://www.rt.com/usa/498273-michelle-obama-biden-trump/, accessed 2020/09/20.
xx. https:/www.washingtonpost.com/opinions/2020/09/29, accessed 2020/09/29.
xxi. https://www.cbsnews.com/news/proud-boys-stand-back-and-stand-by-trump-refuses-to-condemn-white-supremacists/, accessed 2020/10/03.
xxii. https://www.cbsnews.com/news/proud-boys-stand-back-and-stand-by-trump-refuses-to-condemn-white-supremacists/, accessed 2020/10/02.
xxiii. https://www.msnbc.com/the-reidout/watch/steve-schmidt-says-trump-gave-a-lock-and-load-order-to-white-supremacist-groups-during-debate-92893253770, accessed 2020/10/05.

xxiv. https://slate.com/news-and-politics/2020/10/trump-tweets-twitter-story-satirical-site-the-babylon-bee.html, accessed 2020/10/06.
xxv. https://www.usatoday.com/story/news/politics/elections/2020/10/18/john-brennan-ex-cia-director-fears-trump-havoc-after-election/3676392001/, accessed 2020/10/18.
xxvi. https://www.washingtontimes.com/news/2020/oct/16/joe-biden-trump-has-gone-around-bend-coronavirus-c/, accessed 2020/10/16.
xxvii. https://www.motherjones.com/coronavirus-updates/2020/04/trump-coronavirus-campfire-embers-phew/, accessed 2020/10/03.
xxviii. https://www.washingtonpost.com/politics/2020/07/24/trump-white-house-every-coronavirus-wildfire-is-an-ember/, accessed 2020/10/05.
xxix. https://www.cnn.com/videos/politics/2020/10/23/daniel-dale-supercut-fact-check-final-presidential-debate-sot-vpx.cnn, accessed 2020/10/23.
xxx. https://www.cnn.com/videos/politics/2020/10/22/coronavirus-response-trump-biden-reaction-dbx-2020-vpx.cnn/video/playlists/final-2020-presidential-debate/, accessed 2020/10/22.
xxxi. https://www.politifact.com/factchecks/2020/oct/23/donald-trump/no-fight-against-coronavirus-isnt-rounding-corner-/, accessed 2020/10/23.
xxxii. https://www.metrotimes.com/detroit/the-fish-rots-from-the-head-but-everyone-around-trump-stinks/Content?oid=22861522. accessed 2020/10/25.
xxxiii. https://citigold.citi.com/?cmp=bac|acquire|2010|cons|retailbank|gold|forb|hi&dclid=CjkKEQjwxNT8BRC0-4WyzuGUi5IBEiQATD3LWdoOHW8Ms87f2pbkdvka3XiCEyvpapkevJiJFqBpPw_wcB, accessed 2020/10/25.
xxxiv. https://www.theguardian.com/us-news/2020/oct/24/trump-biden-dirty-tricks-presidential-election, accessed 2020/10/24.
xxxv. https://www.facebook.com/washingtonpostpolitics/posts/trumps-soft-touch-with-chinas-xi-worries-advisers-who-say-more-is-needed-to-comb/10158143335454729/. accessed 2020/10/31.
xxxvi. https://www.politico.com/news/magazine/2020/10/22/two-weeks-inside-trump-campaign-431134, accessed 2020/10/22.
xxxvii. https://www.theguardian.com/us-news/2020/oct/26/cbs-releases-footage-trump-walking-out-60-minutes-interview, accessed 2020/10/26.
xxxviii. https://thehill.com/homenews/senate/521609-cornyn-relationships-with-trump-like-women-who-get-married-and-think-theyre, accessed 2020/10/20.
xxxix. https://www.msnbc.com/deadline-white-house, accessed 2020/10/09.
xl. https://www.nydailynews.com/news/politics/us-elections-government/ny-trump-anonymous-miles-taylor-does-not-know-him-does-20201029-v4lfnvutbje67ffgo5l72ew6l4-story.html, accessed 2020/10/29.
xli. https://amp.theguardian.com/us-news/2020/oct/31/red-mirage-trump-election-scenario-victory#aoh=16041407201819&referrer=https%3A%2F%2Fwww.google.com&amp_tf=From%20%251%24s, accessed 2020/10/31.
xlii. https://www.cnn.com/2020/10/28/opinions/trump-rallygoers-stranded-in-cold-in-omaha-lockhart/index.html, accessed 2020/10/28.
xliii. https://www.theatlantic.com/politics/archive/2020/11/trump-bannon-election-party/617020/, accessed 2020/11/07.
xliv. https://www.boredpanda.com/someone-made-four-seasons-total-landscaping-spoof-twitter-account/?utm_source=google&utm_medium=organic&utm_campaign=organic, accessed 2020/11/08.

xlv.	https://economictimes.indiatimes.com/news/international/world-news/a-coronavirus-test-just-burst-the-trumpworld-bubble/articleshow/78479469.cms, accessed 2020/10/04.
xlvi.	https://www.huffingtonpost.ca/entry/bob-woodward-trump-election-comments_n_5f6d2126c5b6cdc24c167227?utm_hp_ref=ca-us-politics, accessed 2020/09/24.
xlvii.	https://www.scientificamerican.com/article/misplaced-analogies-covid-19-is-more-like-a-wildfire-than-a-wave/, accessed 2020/08/19.
xlviii.	https://www.stjameshydepark.org/index_files/TrumpCard.pdf, accessed 2020/08/20.

Subject index

adjacency pair. *See also conversation analysis*
– definition of 60
– dispreferred second 132, 183–184, 190, 211–212
– preferred second 132, 183–185, 211
advertisement 282. *See also NLUs*
amusement 253, 262–264, 269–270
Anglo-Saxon 119
Arabic
– Egyptian 86
– Jordanian 86, 92
– Syrian 86, 92
Asia 80, 87
Australia 69, 78, 81–82, 85, 127, 209

backchanneling 46
Bell curve 70
Biden, Joe 114, 220, 230, 234, 236–238, 257
bottom up 284
British 46, 62–63, 97, 119, 129, 136, 148
bystander 61

camaraderie 19, 66–67, 167–168, 245, 247–250, 255, 260–261
Canadian 111
CBS 55, 270
Chinese. *See also compliment responding (responses); East-West divide*
– benefit offering 99, 102
– Cantonese 82
– face 98–99, 109
– food-offering (plying) 99–100, 102, 128–144
– Gift-giving 100, 102
– invitation 162–165
– politeness 16–17, 42, 80, 98, 101
– Xi'an 80–82, 124–130, 136–137, 140–144
clarity 22, 26, 29–32, 39, 41, 147, 153–165, 182, 184, 197, 209–211, 215, 218–219, 229, 237–238, 241, 249, 280, 282
CNN 55, 193, 203, 208, 220, 235

code-switching 169–170, 214
cognitive linguistics 117, 215–216, 219
coherence 21, 30, 150
cohesion 29, 149, 153, 156
cohesive ties 149, 156
collectivist 102, 116
complaining 65–66, 93
compliment responding (responses) 40, 74–77, 80–83, 86–92, 99, 123, 126–127, 143, 145
– acceptance 84
– deflect(ing) 76, 80, 82–86, 90–91, 123–125, 127, 258
– deflection(ing)/evasion(ing) 76, 83, 89–91, 123, 127
– evading 76, 79–80, 83–84, 123–124, 127
– functions of 124–127
– gender difference 78, 88
– object of compliment 87, 90
– rejection 75–76, 83–84
– returning of the object of compliment 87
conceptual metaphor theory 41, 157, 216–217, 223, 236. *See also cognitive linguistics*
– domain features 224
– domain mapping 215, 219–220
– partiality of 219
– source domain 219–220
– spatial metaphor 217
– target domain 219–220
– TIME metaphor 218
conflict 28, 34–37, 40, 53, 56–57, 61, 176, 184–185
conflictive-assistive 29, 32
– assistive(ness) 22, 26, 28–29, 31–32
– conflictive(ness) 22, 26, 28–32, 230, 245, 262
confrontation 37, 53, 167, 180, 217, 247
context
– epistemic 23
– physical 23
– sociocultural 23

contextual interaction 219, 226
conversation analysis 17, 19, 37–38, 153, 165, 181, 185, 193. *See also adjacency pair; repair*
conversational implicature 7–8, 10–12, 14. *See also cooperative principle*
– cancellability 9, 11
– implicature 7–14
– non-detachability 9
– violation of maxims 8
cooperative principle 7, 10–11, 16, 28, 37, 39, 88, 197, 245. *See also conversational implicature*
– adherence to maxims 8
– maxim of manner 8, 30
– maxim of quality 8, 215
– maxim of quantity 8, 30
– maxim of relation 10
– violation of maxims 8
Covid-19 224, 231, 240, 249
creativity 66, 90, 228–229, 254–255, 261, 282
credit and debt 96
cross-/intercultural 46, 73–74, 82, 84, 88, 98, 102, 108, 123
cross-generation study 120–121
cultural logic 17
cultural studies 17, 73, 117, 215, 247, 283
culture 117. *See also society of intimates; society of strangers*
– guilt culture 117
– high context 117
– horizontal culture 117
– individualist 117
– low context 117
– shame culture 117
– vertical culture 117

deixis 3
denigration 16, 98–99, 132, 145–146, 184
diachronic changes 143
diachronic pragmatics 118–120
discernment 15, 42, 94–96, 103–108, 110
discourse
– analysis 17–18, 40, 117, 147, 151–153, 176, 178, 193, 210–211

– critical discourse analysis 17, 147, 151–153, 193, 210
– displaced 36
– marker 41, 119, 193–197, 199–201, 209
– metaphor 217
– of the profession 151
– structure 167
– topic 196–198
– types 30, 32, 148, 211
discourse analysis 17–18, 40, 117, 147, 151–153, 176–181, 193, 210–211
discourse completion test (DCT) 78, 80–82, 84, 90–91, 124
discursive turn 68, 117–118, 147, 211, 213
DM so 193–202, 204–209. *See also discourse analysis*
– topic change 199, 206
– topic closure 199, 208
– topic continuation 199, 201–203
– topic establishment 199, 201
– topic management 196, 199, 207–209
– topic resumption 199, 207
domain elaboration 215, 219, 225–226
domain selection 231
Dreams of the Red Chamber 99
dude 69, 166–168, 170

East-West divide 40, 73, 92–93, 101–117
– different position 93–99
– similar position 93
effectiveness 22, 218–222, 225–226, 229, 234–241
embodiment 216, 223. *See also cognitive linguistics; conceptual metaphor theory; metaphor*
emergency 33, 44, 260
end-of-dinner food offering 40, 123, 128–144
– American 133
– Chinese 133, 140, 143
– structure of 130
English for Specific Purposes 151
English spoken in 76
– America 76
– Britain 63, 82
– Hong Kong 81–82
– Ireland 76

– New Zealand 76–77
– South Africa 74
ethnography 212
Euro-centrism 5, 14
experiential 2, 216. *See also embodiment*

face. *See also politeness by Brown and Levinson*
– identity 16
– needs 52, 95
– negative 13, 43–44, 47–48, 102, 140, 142
– other-face 50, 52–53, 66–67
– positive 43–44, 47–48, 54, 64, 85, 98–99
– self-face 49–58, 62–67
– threat 44, 67, 94
Facebook 59–60, 75, 148, 178–180, 262
fake news 54–55, 226
family 85, 101, 104, 108, 111–112
felicity condition 5–7, 11, 164
fiction 32, 120, 148, 157, 227
freedom of action 43, 100, 107, 115, 143. *See also politeness by Brown and Levinson*
French 76, 78, 91, 203
Functional Sentence Perspective 148, 196. *See also discourse analysis*
– rheme 149, 155, 196
– theme 196

genre analysis 17, 40, 151, 153, 157, 159–160
– academic writing 158
– CARS, 157–159
– moves 158–160
– research article 157–160
German 76–78, 90–91
grammaticalization 107
Greek 70–71, 76–80, 92, 121–122, 143–144, 216, 262
Güey 167–168

harmony 74, 99, 101–102, 110
historical pragmatics 18, 20, 118–119
Honorifics 93–94, 97, 107, 119
– Japanese 93
– Korean 93

humor 243–244
hurricane Dorian 54–55
hurting image 89
hyperbole 243–244, 281–282

Icelandic 76, 78–79, 91
identity
– category 284
– collective 169
– ethnic 116, 168, 170
– feminine 214
– group 170
– individual 96
– masculine 166
– social 59
identity construction 19, 37, 41, 147, 160, 165–166, 171–172, 193, 210, 214
– co-construction 37, 170, 214
– dynamic process 68
– indexing 168
ideology 17, 21, 152, 178–179, 240
impoliteness 13, 16, 34, 37, 40, 42, 46–58, 61–68, 84–85, 115, 121
– bald on record 46
– entertaining 47, 53, 62–63, 65
– institutional 53, 62–63
– mock politeness 53, 65–67
– negative 47
– positive 47
individualism 43, 109–110. *See also culture; politeness by Brown and Levinson*
information structure 147, 149, 153, 156, 210. *See also discourse analysis*
– given information 149, 155
– new information 149–150, 153–155, 157
ingroup 122
innuendo 243, 282
intention 27, 29
interactional motivation 28, 40, 43, 51, 66, 87–89, 127, 143, 165–166, 170–171, 175, 184, 248, 279, 282
internet pragmatics 20–21
inversion 155, 268–269
irony 8, 19, 41, 65, 215, 243–250, 254–262
Israeli Hebrew 84, 86
Italian 169–170, 214

January 6 capital riot 63
Japanese 42, 91–98, 102–103, 107–108, 120–121, 143
Jerry Maguire 245
jocular mockery 65, 248. *See also impoliteness; politeness*
joking 65–66, 77, 90, 140, 237, 245, 250, 281

Kazakhstan 46
Korean 83, 91–93, 107–108, 180

language contact 20, 159
late-night talk show 63, 262, 270
logical positivism 1–3, 5, 7, 9, 11
longitudinal 100, 127–129, 133, 143–145
lying 62, 276–282

Meaning. *See also conversational implicature; logical positivism; Oxford ordinary language philosophers; Speech acts*
– natural meaning 3, 10, 243
– non-natural meaning 3, 10, 243
Metaphor in news media 221
Metonymy 215, 236, 238–240
modal auxiliaries 178, 180
– deontic 178–179
– epistemic 178–179
A modest proposal 265, 267, 270
modesty 85
moral alignment 61
moral order 47, 53, 58–59, 61
morality 33, 53, 58, 61–62, 276
motivation. *See also interactional motivation; transactional motivation*
– belongingness and love 24–25, 28
– definition of MMP 22, 26
– physiological need 24
– safety and security 24, 28
– self-actualization 25, 33
– self-esteem-status 24, 33, 35
MSNBC 55, 190–191, 245, 247
multiculturalism 17, 284
multimodality 160

NBC 55, 205, 220, 270
Nepali 92

New York Times 55, 224, 272
NLUs 215, 244–245, 247, 249–255, 281–282
notion of place 42, 95, 107–108. *See also East-West divide; Japanese*

offense 49, 67, 69
offering 86–87
Oxford ordinary language philosophers 1, 3, 5, 7, 9–11, 283

parody 19, 215, 227, 236, 243–245, 262–265, 267–271. *See also camaraderie; creativity; effectiveness; NLUs*
Persian 59, 84–86, 90–92
persuasion 32
poetry 120, 148, 157, 263–264, 282
Polish 43, 76–77, 79
politeness by Brown and Levinson
– criticisms of 15, 17, 100
– FTA 14, 46, 48–49
– imposition 14, 24, 44–46, 48, 56, 67, 95, 107, 110–115, 150
– negative politeness 14, 48, 123, 142
– positive politeness 14, 96, 102, 119, 121, 124, 135, 140, 142–143, 277
– power 14, 16, 23, 32, 43, 45, 47–48, 56–58, 98, 108, 147, 151, 175, 181
– ranking of imposition 14, 23, 44, 48
– social distance 14, 45, 97, 115, 117
– $Wx = D(S,H) + P(H,S) + Rx$ 14, 44
politeness by Watts
– emic 15
– etic 15
– first-order 15
– politic 15
– second-order 15
politeness evaluation 15, 42, 71–72
politeness principle 13
– agreement maxim 13, 76–78, 80, 83, 85, 124
– approbation maxim 13
– generosity maxim 13
– modesty maxim 13, 52, 76, 80, 84–85, 124
– sympathy maxim 13
– tact maxim 13

pre-sequence 161–163, 210. *See also adjacency pair; conversation analysis*
– pre-announcement 164
– pre-invitation 163
– pre-request 164
press 93, 221, 227, 236
presupposition 9, 183
promise 5, 119, 176–177, 181, 275

Qingmian relational face 41, 109

rapport management 15–16, 19, 35, 40, 42
rationality 12, 14, 16–17, 177, 284. *See also politeness by Brown and Levinson*
repair. *See also adjacency pair; conversation analysis*
– error 50, 151, 185
– other-initiation 186
– other-repair 186–188
– self-correction 187–190
– self-initiation 186–187
– self-repair 186–187
request 5–7, 11, 73, 96–97, 183–184
ritual 23, 40, 47, 140, 142, 249
Russian 31, 46

sarcasm 19, 34, 47, 243–244, 254–262. *See also humor; NLUs; parody*
satire 243, 265–271. *See also NLUs*
self-denigration 16, 98–99, 145–146, 184
self-politeness 16, 46, 48–53, 57–65
semantics 1–2, 7, 27, 174, 189, 243
Senegal 248
senses 223
sensitivity 107
sentence type
– declarative 4, 98
– imperative 4, 43–44
– interrogative 4, 264
sermon 282. *See also NLUs; persuasion*
simile 215, 236–240. *See also conceptual metaphor theory*
single-author self-reference 174–175. *See also discourse analysis; genre analysis*
– 1st-person plural 172
– 1st-person singular 172–174

– 3rd-person NPs 172–174
– inanimate NPs 172–174
slang 166–168
social constructionism 17, 284
social justice 152, 176, 284
society of intimates 101, 110
society of strangers 101, 109–110
Sokal hoax 247. *See also parody*
solidarity 65, 76–77, 83, 114–115, 167–168. *See also NLUs; politeness by Brown and Levinson; positive politeness*
Sound of Music 255
Spanish 76, 78–79, 90–91, 167–168, 172–173
specialized genres 236, 240, 242
Speech acts
– direct speech acts 6
– illocutionary 10–11
– indirect speech acts 5–6, 10–11
– locutionary 10
– perlocutionary 10
syntax 2, 7, 27, 116, 149, 154, 189, 196, 267

Tautology 8
TCU 164, 181. *See also discourse analysis; Turn-taking*
teasing 34, 244, 247–249, 253, 256. *See also joking; NLUs; solidarity*
Thai 83–84, 91–92
Thematic progression 18, 30, 40, 149–150, 153, 156. *See also discourse analysis*
theory of relevance 31
– cognitive effect 31
– cognitive environment 31
– contextual implication 31
top down 17, 38–39, 213
transactional motivation 26–32, 42, 147, 153–159, 161, 163, 165, 171, 184, 196, 210, 218–219, 241, 244, 280, 282. *See also clarity; effectiveness; motivation*
Trump, Donald 7, 28, 31–32, 48, 53–56, 63–64, 111, 176–180, 191–193, 221–240, 245–247, 257–261, 271–273
truth 2–5, 10, 62, 79, 274–276, 280–281. *See also lying*

truth condition 2–3, 88
Turkish 84–85, 91–92, 119, 128, 181
Turn-taking 30, 151, 161, 163, 181–182, 212
Twitter 36, 54–55, 236, 250–253, 261–262

untrue 244, 277
untruth 228, 244, 275–279, 281. *See also lying*

Vagueness 34–35

Wall street Journal 277
Wendy's tweets 251–254

White lie 106, 244, 276, 281
Writer stance 171. *See also discourse analysis; genre analysis; identity construction*
– author identity 175
– authority 175
– hard fields 172, 174–175
– humbleness 172–173
– objectivity 172, 175
– soft fields 172, 174–175

yo momma jokes 66
YouTube 55, 63–64, 262

Author index

Abbamonte, Lucia 171, 287
Ahmad, Ummul K. 159, 287, 306
Aisulu, Kulbayeva 46, 287
Al-Batal, Mahmoud 86, 92, 306
Al-Khatib, Mahmoud A. 86, 92, 294
Alderfer, Clayton 24–25, 27–28, 33, 287
Allen, Rachel 119, 287, 309
Allori, Paola Evangelisti 288
Amos, H. Will 287
Arico, Adam J. 275, 287
Arndt, Horst 300
Arnett, Jeffrey Jensen 300
Arnovick, Leslie K. 119, 287
Arundale, Robert 33, 42–43, 287
Arvay, Anett 159, 287
Asato, Noriko 295
Asher, Nicholas 197, 287
Atkinson, J. Maxwell 163, 182–184, 287, 307
Attardo, Salvatore 244, 287
Augustine 275, 287
Austin, John L VII, 3, 5, 10–11, 14, 18, 25, 283, 285, 287, 297, 303

Baicchi, Annalisa 218, 287, 303
Bamberg, M. 293
Bangerter, Adrian 292
Bangs, John Kendrick 227
Barcelona, Antonio 11, 216, 236, 287, 305, 307
Bardovi-Harling, K. 288
Barron, Anne 20, 76, 116, 128, 288, 309
Bateson, Gregory 244, 262, 288
Bazerman, Charles 151, 288
Beebe, Leslie 56, 288
Beecken, Masako 309
Bella, Spyridoula 71, 92, 121–123, 143–144, 288
Bergmann, Merrie 216, 288
Bess, Fed H. 161, 288
Bex, Tony 262, 270, 288
Bhatia, Aditi 288
Bhatia, Tej K. 31, 160, 170, 288
Bhatia, Vijay 31, 160, 170, 288
Biber, Douglas 194, 288

Biden, Joe 114, 220, 230, 234, 236–238, 257
Blakemore, Diane 194, 288
Blitvich, Pilar Garcés-Conejos 288–289, 292, 295, 306
Blommaert, Jan 17, 35, 165, 213, 288, 313
Bloomfield, Leonard 1, 149, 196, 288
Blum-Kulka, Shoshana 18, 43, 73, 99, 289, 302
Bok, Sissela 275–276, 279–280, 289
Bolden, Galina B. 195–196, 199–200, 206–207, 212, 289
Booth, Wayne C. 32, 241, 244, 289
Boster, Franklin J. 310
Bou-Franch, Patricia 160, 289
Bousfield, Derek 43, 47, 65–67, 289, 297, 304
Brandsford, John D. 197, 289
Brinton, Laurel J. 118–119, 289
Brockway, Diane 11, 289
Brown, Gillian 289
Brown, Lucien 300
Brown, Penelope VII, 11, 13–16, 23, 33–37, 42–45, 48–52, 60, 67, 76, 81, 84–85, 93–102, 105–110, 122, 134–135, 142, 189, 278, 283, 289
Brown, Roger 290
Bucholtz, Mary 165–168, 213–214, 290
Burton, Noel 2, 290
Butler, Judith 165, 213, 290, 292
Buysse, Lieven 194, 290

Cai, Dongman 217, 290
Camden, Carl 276, 290
Carroll, Lewis 227
Carson, Joan 306
Carson, Thomas L. 275, 290, 306
Carter, Ronald 19, 254, 290
Cauffman, Elizabeth 300
Cedar, Payung 83, 290
Chang, Peichin 290
Chang, Wei-Lin Melody 290, 298
Charolles, Michel 196–197, 290
Charteris-Black 217, 290

https://doi.org/10.1515/9783110787702-013

Chen, Rong I, III, 2, 23, 50–54, 80–85, 123–124, 127–131, 155–156, 171–175, 290–292
Cho, Eunhae 293
Chomsky, Noam 1, 149, 292
Chovanec, Jan 248, 292, 312
Clark, Herbert H 17, 90, 149, 154, 156, 254, 267, 292, 298
Clarke, Ian 303
Clayman, Steven E. 298
Colbert, Stephen 63, 270
Cole, Tim 276, 292, 296–297, 306, 308, 311
Coleman, Linda 275, 292, 297
Colston, Herbert L. 281, 292
Conboy, Martin 120, 292
Conrad , Susan 288
Cook, Guy 25, 31, 85, 134, 137, 146, 163, 260, 265, 292
Cordella, Marisa 78, 292
Côté, James 165, 292
Cots, Joseph Maria 305
Coulmas, Florian 93, 292, 299, 305
Coulthard, Malcolm 163, 182, 292
Creel, Samantha 313
Crisp, Peter 217, 292
Crossley, Scott 310
Culpeper, Jonathan 16, 37, 40, 42, 46–47, 53, 56–57, 62–71, 119, 292
Cummings, Michael 149, 292

Dahl, Roald 293, 304
Daikuhara, Midori 83, 293
D'Andrade, Roy G. 24, 27, 293
Daneš, Frantisek 293, 295
Danziger, Eve 275, 293
Danziger, Roni 73, 86, 293
Davidson, Donald 216, 293
Davies, Bethan 68, 269, 293
Davis, Joseph 293
Davis, Steven 288, 293, 305, 310
De Fina, Anna 165, 168, 170, 212–214, 293
de la Cruz, Melvin 301
de Marlangeon, Kau 302
de Mendoza, Ibáñez Ruiz 254, 300
Deignan, Alice 290
Demjén 293
Derrida, Jacques 247, 293

Dik, Simon 196, 293
Docherty, Thomas 32, 293
Dongil, Shin 176, 180, 293
Donnellan, Keith 2, 293
Downing, Angela 196, 203, 293
Drew, Paul 287, 298
Du Bois, John W. 171, 293
Dueñas, P. 293
Durrheim, Kevin 306
Dynel, Marta 19, 244, 247–255, 258–259, 262–265, 293–294, 305

Echols, Erin 306
Edgley, Charles 313
Eelen, Gino 294
El Bakary, Waguida 306
Er, Ibrahim 294
Erikson, Eric H. 294
Ervin-Tripp, S. 294
Escandell-Vidal, Victoria 294
Eslami, Zohreh R 86, 90, 92, 294
Eubanks, Philip 217, 294
Evans, Moyra Sweetnam 304
Evans, Vyvyan 159, 218, 294, 304

Fairclough, Norman VII, 17, 32, 151–152, 294
Fallis, Don 287, 294
Farghal, Mohammed 86–87, 92, 294
Fauconnier, Gilles 217, 294
Feiz, Parastou 311
Feldman , Shirley 300
Felson, Richard B. 312
Feng, Jianghong 304
Fernández, Eliecer Crespo 217, 294
Fernando, Milton 308
Finegan, Edward 288
Firbas, Jan 149, 196, 294–295
Fischer, Kerstin 194, 295, 308
Fonseca, Paula 271, 295
Ford, Charles V. 275, 295
Foucault, Michel 17, 295
Fowler, Roger 151, 295–296
Fraser, Bruce 15, 37, 42, 51, 194, 282, 295
Frege, Gottlob 2, 295
Fukada, Atsushi 295
Fukushima, Saeko 71, 93, 97, 120–121, 143–144, 295

Gachigua, Sammy Gakero 295
Gajaseni, Chansongklod 83–84, 92, 295
Gao, Hong 295
Garver, Eugene 29, 295
Gee, James Paul 117, 296
Gerrig, Richard J. 292
Ghaleb, Rabab'ah 296
Gibbs, Raymond W 296, 311
Gibbs, Wolcott 268, 296
Gilman, Albert 290
Giridharadas, Anand 195, 296
Giuliano, Ryan J. 302
Givón, Talmy 196–197, 296
Goffman, Erving 33, 43, 48, 296
Golato, Andrea 77–78, 90, 296
Gong, Lili 296
González, Gómez 196, 288, 292, 296
Goodblatt, Chanita 32, 306
Goossens, Luc 304
Gotti, Maurizio 160, 296
Grainger, Karen 71, 128–129, 132, 136, 296
Grandy, Richard E. 109, 296
Green, Georgia 22, 141, 201, 296
Greenbaum, Sidney 194, 296
Grice, H. Paul VII, 3–14, 25, 28, 30, 37, 39, 51, 88, 109, 197, 215, 243–245, 283, 285, 293, 296–297, 314
Gu, Yueguo 288, 297

Hacker, P. M 297
Haggan, Madeline 294
Hall, Kira 290
Hall, Stuart 17, 165–166, 213–214, 290, 297, 315
Halliday, M. A. K 28, 149, 154, 156, 297
Hamel, Lauren M. 304
Hample, Dale 276, 297
Hardin, Karol 276, 297
Harris, Sandra 297
Harwood, Nigel 171, 297
Haugh, Michael 21, 33, 42, 47, 58–59, 65–71, 93–96, 290, 297–298, 301, 312
Haviland, Susan E. 149, 154, 156, 292, 298
Hawkes, Terence 240, 298
Hearst, William Randolph 269
Hempel, Carl G. 298

Herbert, Robert K 74–78, 80, 89, 289, 292, 298
Heritage, John 19, 23, 48–49, 298, 307
Hertzberg, Hendrik 267–269, 298
Highfield, Tim 262, 298
Hill, Beverly VIII, 15, 42, 92–96, 102–105, 219, 238, 298
Hillier, Hilary 288
Hindriks, Frank 11, 298
Hirsch, Galia 255, 298
Ho, Victor 165, 213, 298, 306
Hodge, Bob 28, 68, 227, 295, 303, 319
Hoey, Michael 149, 298
Hoffmann, Sebastian 304
Hollender, Marc H. 295
Holmes, Janet 74, 76–77, 80, 89, 123, 298
Hori, Motoko 299
Horn, Lawrence II, 11, 299
Horowitz, Donald L. 165, 299
House, Juliane 289, 299, 301
Howe, Mary L. 195, 199, 299
Huang, Mei-Chen 99, 299
Hugly, Philip 11, 299 Humes, Larry E. 288
Huth, Thorsten 299
Hyland, Ken 35, 171–173, 175, 262, 299
Hyon, Sunny IX, 151, 171, 247, 262, 270, 291, 299

Ide, Risako 300
Ide, Sachiko 292, 298, 300, 313
Idemaru, Kaori 92, 97, 300
Ikuta, Shako 298
Isbell, Elif 302
Ivanič, Rosalind 175, 300
Ivanko, Stacey L. 244, 300

Jabbari, Nasser 294
Jabbari, Eslami 86
Jacobs, Andreas 119, 300
Jakobson, Roman 68, 300
James, William 5, 7
Janda, Laura 300
Janney, Richard W. 43, 95, 300
Jaworski, Adam 77, 300
Jefferson, Gail 309
Jensen, Lene Arnett 274, 300
Johansson, Ingvar 11, 288, 300

Johansson, Stig 288
Johnson, Alison 300
Johnson, Marcia K. 289
Johnson, Mark 303
Johnson-Sheehan, Richard 217, 300
Jones, Rodney H. 254, 300
José, Francisco 288, 300
Jucker, Andreas 17–18, 20, 76, 78, 81, 90, 118–120, 145, 289, 300–302, 312

Kádár, Dániel 23, 33–34, 40, 47, 50, 58–59, 61, 68, 93, 119, 132, 140, 301, 306–308
Kanoksilapatham, Budsaba 159–160, 301
Kasper, Gabriele 18, 43, 62, 73, 95, 194, 289, 299, 302, 314
Kawasaki, Akiko 298
Kay, Paul 292
Kecskes, Istvan II, IX, 25, 58, 302
Keller, Shauna B. 292
Kempton, Ruth M. 11, 302
Kennedy, John 313
Kertész, András 236, 302
Khazriyati, Binti Salehuddin 306
Kiesling, Scott F 166–168, 302
Kim, Alan Hyun-Oak 107, 275–276, 279–280, 302, 304, 306, 310
Kim, Min-Sun 306
Kim, Rachel K. 304
Kimmel, Michael 217, 240, 270, 302
King, Bryan H. 295
Kinzinger, Adam 111
Kitagawa, Chisato 92, 302
Knapp, Mark L. 274, 302
Knoblock, Natilia 176, 178–180, 302
Kohnen, Thomas 119, 302
Koutsantoni, Dimitra 171, 302
Kövecses, Zoltán 216–217, 302–303
Koyama, Wataru 117, 303
Kress, Gunther 295
Kumatoridani, Tetsuo 303
Kuo, Chih-Hua 86, 90, 171, 294, 303
Kurzon, Dennis 160, 303
Kwon, Winston 19, 248, 254, 303

Labov, William 152, 303
Lakoff, George 303
Lakoff, Robin 303

Lan, Chun 314
Langacker, Ronald W. 2, 216, 303
Larina, Tatiana 46, 303
Lee, Sun 159, 261, 303
Lee-Wong 95, 99, 304
Leech, Geoffrey VII, 288, 303–304
Levine, Timothy R. 274–276, 279–280, 304, 310
Levinson, Stephen VII, 9, 11, 13–16, 19, 22–23, 30, 35–37, 42–51, 60, 67, 81, 84–86, 93–100, 105–110, 122, 134–135, 142, 150, 155, 183–186, 189, 278, 284
Lewis, Michael 304
Li, Wei IX, 36, 100, 128–129, 132, 139, 145, 291, 294, 304, 315
He, Lin 48, 102, 276
Local, J. K. 28, 126, 134–135, 168, 188–189, 195–196, 213, 304
Locher, Mariam 289
Locher, Miriam 43, 47, 56, 68, 165, 213, 289, 293, 304
Loh, W. C. T. 81–82, 304
Loi, Chek Kim 159, 304
Lorenzo-Dus, N. 304
Loveday, Leo John 304
Lower, Amanda 307
Lozano-Palacio, Inés 300
Luyckx, Koen 165, 304
Ly, Annelise 93, 102, 105–107, 304
Lyons, John 2, 304

M., Karns Christina 302
MacDonald, Dwight 265, 269, 304
Mackay, Rowan 303
Maiz-Arevalo, Carmen 79, 86, 90, 304
Manes, Joan 74–75, 78, 83, 124, 212, 305
Mansor, Kerkam Z. 296
Mao, Robert LuMing 43, 93, 95, 98–101, 110, 112, 126, 305
Marcia, James E. 165, 168, 289, 305
María de los Ángeles 288, 292, 296
Marques-Aguado, Teresa 171, 305
Márquez-Reiter, Rosina 301
Marsh, Jessica 46, 305
Martinich, A. P. 216, 295, 305
Maslow, Abraham H. 305

Matsumoto, Yoshiko 92, 94–97, 99, 101, 305
McCarthy, Michael 290
McCornack, Steven A. 276, 305
McNamee, Gregory 117, 305
Mei, Song 304
Meibauer, Jörg 275, 305
Merritt, M 164, 305
Metts, S 276, 305
Mey, Jacob L. 19, 22, 25, 302, 305
Migdadi, Fathi Hassan 92, 305
Mihatsch, Miltrud 218, 305
Mills, Sara 68, 71, 128–129, 132, 136, 296, 305
Mir, Montserrat 79, 305
Miyahara, Arika 92, 116, 306
Mohammad, Yahya Alrousan 86, 306
Moratti, Arthur F. 32, 306
Morgan, Jerry 7, 40, 119, 209, 288, 296, 306
Morpurgo-Tagliabue, Guido 11, 306
Morris, Charles W. VII–VIII, 1, 10, 20, 306
Morsy, E. 86, 306
Moser, Amalia 288 Motley, Michael T. 290
Murray, Amy Jo 26, 306
Mursy, Ahmad Aly 86, 306

Nelson, Gayle L. 306
Neville, Helen J. 302
Ng, Kwai-Fong Connie 308
Ning, Puyu 33, 68, 301, 306, 314
Norrick, Neal R. 194, 281, 306
Norsimah, Mat Awal 306

Oakley, Todd 295
Ochs, Elinor 35, 166, 294, 306
Ogiermann, Eva 68–71, 121–123, 143–144, 288, 292, 295, 306
Ogino, Tsunao 298
Ohashi, Jun 93–94, 96–97, 307
Olineck, Kara 300
Olmstead, Glen 313
Olshtain, Elite 289
Oreström, Bengt 161, 307
Ouellette, M. A. 172, 307

Pan, Yuling 119, 140, 307
Panther, Klaus-Uwe 287, 305, 307

Parvaresh, Vahid 33, 59–61, 301, 307
Pascual, Esther 295
Peters, R. 24, 27, 307
Pexman, Penny M. 244–245, 300, 307
Piata, Anna 217, 307
Pirsig, Robert M. 27, 307
Pizziconi, Barbara 61, 95, 97–98, 305, 307
Placencia, María Elena 75, 90, 307
Pomerantz, Anita 73–75, 77, 83, 87, 89, 123, 183–185, 307
Ponton, Douglas Mark 303
Popa-Wyatt, Mihaela 254, 307
Posner, Michael 162, 307
Potter, Lorena 149, 308
Powell, Hebe 307
Prince, Ellen XV, 149–150, 154, 308
Putnam, Hilary 2, 308

Qin, Kongji 176, 181, 308

Radden, Gunter 307
Rákosi, Csilla 302
Ran, Yongping 296, 308
Raymond, Chase Wesley 298
Raymond, Geoffrey 298, 308
Redeker, Gisele 194, 308
Reinhart, Tania 197, 308
Ren, Wei 101, 248, 308, 314
Richardson, Daniel C. 311
Ritchie, David 308
Rivers, Damian J. 308
Robles, Jessica S. 248, 308
Rodriguez, Gonzalez 73, 79, 308
Rorty, Amelie 308
Rose, Fowler Al-Hawamdeh 296
Rose, Kenneth 18, 46, 82, 291, 296, 302, 308
Ross, Andrew S. 176–177, 268–269, 298, 308
Ross, Harold Wallace 268
Rue, Yong-Ju 308
Ruhi, Sukriye 308
Russell, Bertrand 309

Sacks, Harvey 19, 114, 150, 161–163, 185–191, 309
Saito, Hidetoshi 309

Sala, Michele 171, 309
Salager-Meyer, Françoise 296
Saloustrou, Vasiliki 306
Sampson, Geoffrey 11, 309
Samraj, B 159, 309
Sayward, Charles 299
Schegloff, Emanual A. 19, 150, 161–163, 185–191, 309
Schiffer, Steven 23, 309
Schiffrin, Deborah 165, 194–196, 199, 201, 213, 289, 293, 299, 309
Schleppegrell, Mary 172, 290
Schmalenberger, Eri 227
Schmid, Hans-Jörg 236, 309
Schneider, Iris 309
Schneider, Klaus 20, 43, 47, 51, 74, 76, 78, 81–82, 116, 288, 298, 309
Schoor, Carola 217, 309
Schourup, Lawrence 194, 309
Searle, John II, VII, 3, 5, 7, 10–11, 14, 134, 164, 216, 283, 285, 310
Semino, Elena 240, 310, 313
Serota, Kim B 274, 310
Shakespeare 263–264, 267, 290, 302
Sharifian, Farzad 85–86, 92, 310
Shearer, Harry 195, 310
Shi-Xu 110, 310
Shin, Ho-Chang 306
Shweder, Richard A. 306
Sifianou, Maria 288, 295, 310
Simpson, David 310
Skalicky, Stephen 245, 262, 310
Soenens, Bart 304
Sokal, Alan D. 310
Spencer-Oatey, Helen 15–16, 19, 33, 35, 37, 40, 42, 51, 81–82, 93, 310
Sperber, Dan 12, 31, 37, 109, 197, 244–245, 254, 282–283, 292, 311, 314
Steele, Godfrey A. XV, 176, 261, 311
Steen, Gerard 20, 217, 240, 288, 310–311
Stigler, James W. 306
Strauss, Claudia 293
Strauss, Susan 18, 24–25, 27, 153, 171, 311
Strawson, Peter Frederick 2, 311
Street, Chris N 104, 123, 141, 203, 266, 271, 274–275, 277, 311

Stryker, Sheldon 165, 168, 311
Suau-Jiménez, Francisca 46, 311
Swales, John 151, 157–159, 269, 311
Swan, Michael 269–270, 311
Sweet, Nikolas 184, 205, 248–249, 311
Sweetser, Eve E 275, 311
Swift, Jonathan 265–267, 270, 312

Taavitsainen, Irma 18, 118–120, 145, 301, 312
Taboada, Maite 194, 312
Tajfel, Henri 312
Talmy, Leonard 2, 162, 216, 296, 312
Tang, Chen-Hsin 81–82, 123, 127–128, 175, 312
Tanko, Gyula 287
Tannen, Deborah 112, 114, 289, 312
Tayebi, Tahmineh 59–61, 307, 312
Tedeschi, James T. 56, 312
Terkourafi, Marina 21, 312
Thompson, Geoff 288
Thornburg, Linda L. 305, 307
Traugott, Elizabeth Closs 118, 312
Trew, Tony 295
Trier, Jost 68, 289, 312
Trousdale, Graham 312
Trump, Donald J. 48, 53, 64, 176, 291
Tsakona, Villy 248, 312
Tse, Polly 299
Tseng, Miao-Fen 100, 312
Tsur, Reuven 217, 313
Turner, Mark 217, 276, 294, 313
Turner, Ronny E. 313
Tzanne, Angeliki 310

Upadhyay, Shiv R. 92, 313
Urquiza, Kristin 228
Usami, Mayumi 97, 313

Vaara, Eero 303
Van Dijk, Teun A. 151–152, 196–198, 304, 313
Varis, Piia 19, 247, 313
Vasek, M. E. 274, 313
Vásquez, Camillia 247, 254, 313
Verschueren, Jef 37, 289, 306, 313
Vervaeke, John 217, 313
Vygotsky, Lev. S. 17, 313

Walker, Gareth 304
Walter, Catherine 269, 311
Wardhaugh, R. 163, 313
Warner, Richard 296
Watts, Richard 15–16, 35, 37, 43, 51, 56, 68, 186, 292, 304, 313
Weiner, Bernard 24, 27, 313
Westberg, Gustav 176, 180, 313
Wieland, Molly 78, 91, 313
Wierzbicka, Anna 17, 43, 68, 313–314
Wilmore, Larry 63
Wilson, Ann 290
Wilson, Dan II, 12, 25, 31, 37, 86, 109, 197, 244–245, 254, 276, 282–283, 290, 306, 311, 314
Wilson, Deirdre II, 311, 314
Wilson, John 306
Wintre, Bodo 300
Wodak, Ruth 151–152, 303, 314
Wolfson, Nessa 74–75, 77–78, 81, 83, 212, 305, 314

Xia, Dengshan 43, 314
Xu, Honger 110, 195, 310, 314

Yabuuchi, Akio 95, 117, 314
Yagoda, Ben 195, 314

Yang, Dafu 34, 82, 89, 123, 127–128, 172–174
Yang, Na 34, 81–82, 89, 123, 127–128, 172–175, 248, 291, 314
Yates, Linda 314
Ye, Lei 81, 314
Ye, Ning 33, 314
Ye, Zhengdao 17, 93–94, 101, 314
Yokota, A. 314
Yoon, Kak 306
Yoon, Kyung-Joo 92, 306, 315
Yu, Ming-Chung 81–82, 102, 315
Yuan, Chuanyou 36, 81–82, 127
Yuan, Li 53, 128–129
Yuan, Zhoumin 171
Yue, Li 304
Yule, George 289

Zappavigna, Michele 19, 247, 315
Zeng, Yantao 315
Zhang, Grace Qiao 308, 312
Zhang, Guofu 81–82, 93, 99, 101, 123, 127–128, 276, 291, 308, 312, 315
Zhang, Shao-Jie 315
Zhao, Linsen 308
Zhong, Xiyun 315
Zhou, Ling 34, 50, 93, 101, 128, 146, 301, 315
Zimmerman, Don H. 35, 165, 213, 315

www.ingramcontent.com/pod-product-compliance
Lightning Source LLC
Chambersburg PA
CBHW020220170426
43201CB00007B/269